Legacies of British Slave-Ownership

This book re-examines the relationship between Britain and colonial slavery in a crucial period in the birth of modern Britain. Drawing on a comprehensive analysis of British slave-owners and mortgagees who received compensation from the state for the end of slavery, and tracing their trajectories in British life, the volume explores the commercial, political, cultural, social, intellectual, physical and imperial legacies of slave-ownership. It transcends conventional divisions in history-writing to provide an integrated account of one powerful way in which the Empire came home to Victorian Britain, and to reassess narratives of West Indian 'decline'. It will be of value to scholars not only of British economic and social history, but also of the histories of the Atlantic world, of the Caribbean and of slavery, as well as to those concerned with the evolution of ideas of race and difference and with the relationship between past and present.

CATHERINE HALL is Professor of History at University College London.

NICHOLAS DRAPER is Co-director of the Structure and Significance of British Caribbean Slave-Ownership 1763–1833 project in the Department of History at University College London.

KEITH MCCLELLAND is Co-director of the Structure and Significance of British Caribbean Slave-Ownership 1763–1833 project in the Department of History at University College London.

KATIE DONINGTON is a Research Fellow in the Department of History at University College London.

RACHEL LANG is an Administrator in the Department of History at University College London.

Legacies of British Slave-Ownership

Colonial Slavery and the Formation of Victorian Britain

Catherine Hall, Nicholas Draper, Keith McClelland, Katie Donington and Rachel Lang

CAMBRIDGE
UNIVERSITY PRESS

CAMBRIDGE
UNIVERSITY PRESS

University Printing House, Cambridge CB2 8BS, United Kingdom

Cambridge University Press is part of the University of Cambridge.

It furthers the University's mission by disseminating knowledge in the pursuit of education, learning and research at the highest international levels of excellence.

www.cambridge.org
Information on this title: www.cambridge.org/9781107040052

First published 2014

Printed in the United Kingdom by Clays, St Ives plc

A catalogue record for this publication is available from the British Library

Library of Congress Cataloguing in Publication data
Hall, Catherine, 1946–
Legacies of British slave-ownership : colonial slavery and the formation of Victorian Britain / Catherine Hall, Nicholas Draper, Keith McClelland, Katie Donington and Rachel Lang.
    pages   cm
Includes bibliographical references and index.
ISBN 978-1-107-04005-2 (hard back)
1. Slaveholders–Great Britain–History–19th century.
2. Slavery–Great Britain–History–19th century.   3. Slavery–Great Britain–Colonies–History–19th century.   4. Great Britain–Colonies–History–19th century.   5. Great Britain–History–19th century.   I. Title.
HT1161.H35 2014
306.3´620941090034–dc23
2014012761

ISBN 978-1-107-04005-2 Hardback

Contents

Illustrations

Acknowledgements

This book is one of the fruits of the Legacies of British Slave-ownership project at University College London, and we wish to acknowledge both the funding provided by the Economic and Social Research Council and the support of the Department of History at UCL in hosting the project over its three-year life.

By its nature, the project has been a collaborative venture. Several hundred local, regional and family historians have contributed information and material to us. We cannot thank each of them individually here, but have sought to acknowledge each contributor in the relevant entry or entries in the database (www.ucl.ac.uk/lbs), which captures the raw material of the project. Here we would simply like to record our respect for the rigour of their work and our gratitude for the generosity of so many independent researchers in sharing their findings so freely with us.

Many scholars have helped to shape our work, and as always singling out individuals risks omitting many who contributed to the intellectual formation of the project or to its execution. Nevertheless, we would like to pay tribute especially to Mark Harvey of the University of Essex for the intensity and consistency of his intellectual engagement with us, to Bill Rubinstein (formerly of the University of Aberystwyth) for sharing his unpublished data on the wealth of those dying in the nineteenth century with us, to Verene Shepherd (University of the West Indies, Mona) for her commitment to connecting the project with initiatives in the Caribbean and through UNESCO, and to Margot Finn (University College London) for her reading of, and response to, this volume in manuscript.

One of the features of the project has been the extent to which we have sought to make our work available outside the academe, and in these efforts we have been greatly assisted by a number of independent historians and community representatives. Among many others, we have in particular benefited from the sustained interest in and support of our work in England by Sean Creighton and Arthur Torrington.

We would also like to thank the members of our advisory panel for their individual and collective support: Dr Caroline Bressey (Department of Geography, University College London); Professor P. J. Cain (Research Professor in History, University of Sheffield); Dr Madge Dresser (Associate Professor in History, University of the West of England, Bristol); Professor Mark Harvey (Professor of Sociology and Director of the Centre for Research in Economic Sociology and Innovation, University of Essex); Professor Julian Hoppit (Astor Professor of British History, University College London); Professor R. J. Morris (Professor of Economic and Social History, University of Edinburgh); and Professor David Richardson (Director of the Wilberforce Institute for the study of Slavery and Emancipation and Professor of Economic History, University of Hull).

A number of very able young scholars and researchers were involved in the work of the project in temporary positions, and in this context we would like especially to thank Ben Mechen and John Stevens.

Chapter 6 has been enriched by access to diaries and private papers of the Hibbert family kindly made available by Mr Nick Hibbert Steele.

Michael Watson of Cambridge University Press has been a valued partner to us in bringing our work forward, both in this volume and elsewhere. Dr Susan Forsyth met the challenge of compiling the index for the – at times – densely empirical text.

The book has been published with the help of a grant from the late Miss Isobel Thornley's bequest to the University of London.

1 Introduction

*Catherine Hall, Nicholas Draper and
Keith McClelland*

Slave-ownership is virtually invisible in British history. It has been elided by strategies of euphemism and evasion originally adopted by the slave-owners themselves and subsequently reproduced widely in British culture. The *Oxford Dictionary of National Biography* (*ODNB*), a national Valhalla, the pantheon of not only a handful of heroes but also (unlike, for example, Westminster Abbey) a much wider swathe of the people who are held to have made modern Britain, includes hundreds of Britons who themselves owned enslaved people or whose families owned enslaved people; almost none is identified as a slave-owner. The vast bulk of relevant entries continue to reflect (consciously or otherwise) the strategies of the slave-owners of the early nineteenth century, who evaded the very term 'slave-owner'.[1]

For example, the *ODNB* says of the lawyer Fortunatus Dwarris that he 'inherited considerable property' in Jamaica, where he was born in 1786; that such property of course included men and women remains unsaid.[2] Again, Thomson Hankey, the political economist and governor of the Bank of England, is said by the *ODNB* to have joined his father's firm Thomson Hankey & Co., 'plantation owners and West Indies merchants'; the firm, again, owned men and women as well as plantations.[3] At the same time as eliding slave-ownership, the *ODNB* sustains a discourse that sees the 'West Indian proprietor' as the victim of the slave-system and of abolition. In the 1770s, for example, Anthony Morris Storer's 'Jamaican source of income all but dried up with the economic distress caused by a hurricane compounded by the government's American policies';[4] in 1812, the destruction by volcano of the estate on St Vincent belonging to Frederick Thesiger (later lord chancellor, who had left the navy on becoming heir to his father's estates around 1807 on the death of his brother George) 'considerably impoverished his family';[5] in the early 1800s, the novelist Ellen Pickering's 'family owned property in the West Indies, but losses and relative impoverishment after the abolition of the slave trade compelled their retirement for some years to Hampshire [from Bath]';[6] and, in the early 1830s, the pioneering woman journalist

Frances de Peyronnet and her French husband the Vicomte Jules de Peyronnet 'thanks to the income from the Whitfield sugar plantations [in St Vincent] ... were able to tour Europe in style', but then later in the decade, with gradual abolition, 'this source of revenue began to dry up.'[7]

Such entries in the *ODNB* thus refuse to acknowledge slavery, even by name. There is no difference between pre- and post-Emancipation descriptions of 'West Indian property',[8] and the words 'slave-owner' and even 'slave' do not appear. Moreover, the *ODNB* portrays those who owned enslaved people as vulnerable, the real victims. Elsewhere in the writing of British history, the slave-owners, to the extent they are present at all, have been represented collectively as an outworn and reactionary fragment, the losers of history, irrelevant to an understanding of the formation of modern Britain.[9]

Against this background, our project is to reinscribe slave-ownership onto modern British history. Slave-ownership, *pace* the *ODNB*, permeated the British elites of the early nineteenth century and helped form the elites of the twentieth century. Graham Greene and George Orwell, two of the greatest British writers of the past century, were both descended from slave-owning families. Slave-ownership was and remains hidden in plain sight: the names of slave-owners were preserved in families as diverse as those of the architect Sir George Gilbert Scott, the two Lord Chancellors Douglas McGarel Hogg and Quintin McGarel Hogg (Viscounts Hailsham), the political and diplomatic Akers-Douglas family (Viscounts Chilston), the descendants of George Hibbert (the Holland-Hibberts of Broadclyst House in Devon and Munden in Hertfordshire, Viscounts Knutsford) and the millionaire banker and predecessor of the modern Barclays bank, Robert Cooper Lee Bevan. Such names signal the continuities of slave-ownership in the mainstream of British life.

This book presents some of the fruits of our effort to capture those continuities. In it we draw on the data included in the online Legacies of British Slave-ownership database (www.ucl.ac.uk/lbs) published in parallel with this volume, and in which readers of this volume will find the material and sources underpinning our arguments and conclusions presented here. The database digitises all the awards in the slave-compensation records of the 1830s and develops more detailed entries for the absentee planters living in Britain at the time of Emancipation or moving or returning there after Emancipation. In this volume, we have sought to use this underlying prosopography in order to build a totalising picture of the slave-owners by reintegrating various forms of history rewriting – economic, political, cultural, social – that are increasingly separate as the profession polarises between specialist work and 'global' histories that operate at such high levels of abstraction as to risk losing their moorings in the evidence. We are thus attempting to reintegrate cultural, political and social history into material history, without becoming reductive. We do not believe that material interests determine positions, even on slavery itself (although we have found very few men and women who gave up slave-ownership or compensation[10]) but we do argue that we cannot fully understand such positions without knowing the material interests that were involved.[11]

We believe that the context provided by the database offers a chance to escape the questions of representativeness that haunt, for example, the pioneering work of Eric Williams on the slave-owners in Britain, which presented a powerful litany of examples but no capacity to gauge their significance.[12] We have tried consistently to respond to that question of significance. Our aim is to answer not only 'what happened to the slave-owners in Britain after Emancipation?' but also 'how important were the slave-owners in the period after Emancipation?' In this volume, we have focused on major areas that, as discussed below, appear to us to be central. But we believe that our work here is only a fragment of the work that the database can potentially support. We have in no way exhausted its possibilities, but have tried to highlight key findings and to analyse the types of issues raised by the search for the 'legacies of slave-ownership'. The content of the database is itself fluid, not final: we claim it to be comprehensive in its coverage of the awardees of slave compensation, but, as a database of 47,000 individuals of whom biographical details have been developed for some 3,000, it will always be subject to expansion in the breadth and depth of the knowledge it captures. This book and the online database therefore represent a baseline from which any further work will point to a broader and deeper penetration of British metropolitan life by slave-ownership and its legacies.

We are using the term 'legacies' in three, inter-related, senses. The first refers to a direct, causal relationship between slave-ownership or other financial ties with slavery and the subsequent activities of those who were recipients of slave compensation, including but not confined to the disposal of the money that they gained. Second, we use the term in a looser sense to refer to a less direct connection where we can say that slave-ownership shaped, but did not determine or cause in any strong sense, the activities and bearings of people who were constitutive of nineteenth-century Britain. Finally, we believe that the activities of those descendants of slave-owners in the twentieth and indeed twenty-first centuries who continued to shape Britain were themselves in part legacies of slave-ownership. For example, embedded in George Orwell's description of his family as 'lower-upper middle class' – that is, 'upper-middle class without money' – is the continuing imprint of slave-ownership: while the money derived from slavery had gone by the time of Orwell's father, the social and cultural capital acquired through slave-wealth remained, propelling the family from obscurity in Scotland and sustaining its members within the ranks of a British imperial administrative class.[13]

At the same time, there is a broader context, and we recognise that our definition of legacies is limited. Clearly the social and economic structures of the former slave-colonies themselves are one of the most immediate legacies (perhaps *the* most immediate legacy) of slavery and of slave-ownership, but we do not seek to address here the complex and distinctive paths that led from slave-colony to modern nationhood. These paths have been the subject of much exploration, driven for understandable reasons in large part by the effort to recover the histories of the enslaved people and their descendants. Recent work to (re)integrate the slave-owner into these histories has to date focused on the period of slavery rather than the period after Emancipation.[14] Our sense – and it is no more than that – from our work is that the impact of the former slave-owners in the former slave-colonies themselves was wildly uneven. Many followed the example of the former slave-owner and West India merchant Nathaniel Snell Chauncy, whose will, made in 1848, specified that his property in the Caribbean should be disposed of and that all the money raised should be invested in railway or other companies 'in England, Wales, Scotland or Ireland or any of the British colonies'.[15] That such withdrawal to Britain and disinvestment from the former slave-economies was a material part of the behaviour of absentee slave-owners, who joined the British state and eventually the British people in abandoning their respective previous commitments to the slave-colonies, is one of the refrains in this book. At the same time, however, absentee former slave-owners also remained invested and flourished, especially in the newer slave-colonies. The movement of indentured people into British Guiana and Trinidad was driven by absentee former slave-owners in Britain. A handful of such slave-owners, including Booker Brothers, who went on to dominate the Guyanese sugar industry until its nationalisation, used the disruption of the Emancipation period to transform their position from agents and managers who were at most small-scale slave-owners to large-scale proprietorship in the aftermath of Emancipation. At present, all we can do is point to the possibilities of further work on the role of the slave-owners, both resident and absentee, in the remaking of the slave-colonies in the period after Emancipation.

Equally, and as crucially, this volume is not about another very direct legacy of slave-ownership, the people of colour born of white slave-owners and women of African origin or descent, both enslaved and free. The records do not support systematic identification of them, but such children are interwoven in our stories of absentee slave-ownership, appearing in Britain as slave-owners themselves, as autonomous actors and as dependents. They both were legacies of slave-ownership and in turn left legacies themselves, only a handful of which we have reflected here. Again, the absence of discussion of free people of colour in Britain (or indeed the colonies) as a distinct legacy of slave-ownership does not reflect a failure to register them on our part, but rather a recognition that our best contribution is to make our data available and to work with historians dedicated to this subject.[16]

We do not claim that the legacies of slave-ownership are the same as the legacies of slavery. We have used slave-ownership as a lens through which to re-examine the formation of Britain in the critical decades after Emancipation. But slave-ownership was only one form in which slavery came home to Britain, and the slave-owners were only one means of transmission. The persistence of the language of slavery as the antithesis of English freedom was one of those legacies, used by varied groups of Britons across the nineteenth century, its meanings shifting according to the context, as it was also linked to debates over labour, race, gender and civilisation. The *systemic* effects of slavery on the British economy through the flow of tropical commodities into British metropolitan consumption are not captured in our work. We are also focused on the universe of slave-owners at the end of slavery, at a specific point in the mid-1830s. Such slave-owners were *in situ* on 1 August 1834 (the record date for the compensation records) as a result of processes of transfer and transmission of 'slave-property' unfolding prior to that, often over a century or more, and so there are often long continuities of ownership of estates and the enslaved populations working on them. There are also, however, discontinuities and our work does not capture slave-owning families of the seventeenth and eighteenth centuries who had moved out of the slavery business by the 1830s, such as the Huguenot financier family the Thellussons.[17]

In focusing on slave-owners, we are inevitably privileging their histories over the histories of the enslaved. We have committed resources to retrieving the histories of the slave-owners – resources that might in theory have been deployed in reconstructing the fragments that remain of the lives of enslaved people, lives often truly lost to history. This decision on our part is not because we regard the histories of the enslaved people as less important than those of the slave-owners, but because we approached the project primarily as historians of the British metropole of the mid-nineteenth century. In the course of the project, we have come to see more clearly not only the importance but also the practical possibilities of linking our work on slave-owners to the enslaved populations on whom the system rested, and in a new phase of research we intend to integrate the two histories as fully as possible. It should also be clear that we are not seeking to rehabilitate or to celebrate the slave-owners, but to underscore through the histories of the slave-owners and their families the continuing presence and significance of slavery in British metropolitan society in the mid-nineteenth century and to illuminate the afterlife of slavery following Emancipation. Because of the importance, in our judgement, of stripping away the layers of insulation between modern Britain and its historical involvement in slavery, and because of the investment by the original 'planters' and 'proprietors' in resisting the term 'slave-owner', we are seeking to reinstate that term in British history-writing, including in the titles of our book, of our project and of our online Legacies of British Slave-ownership database, but we are aware that in so doing we are running counter to the emerging preference for the use of 'enslaver' as the logical counterpoint to 'enslaved person' or 'enslaved people'.

The slave-owners, we are suggesting, played an important part in the shaping of modern British society as agents, but also subjects, of that new world. Our investigation of slave-ownership has enabled us to rethink the notion of decline, to measure the impact West Indian proprietors were able to have economically, politically and culturally in the period after Emancipation, and to trace the continuities in the physical and cultural fabric of Britain. Far from surviving as an archaic fragment, with their political power demolished and their wealth undermined by Emancipation, they were able to mobilise sufficient influence to secure major concessions in return for their acceptance of abolition. In addition to the sum of £20 million that they received in compensation for the loss of their 'property' in enslaved men and women they also benefited substantially from the system of 'apprenticeship', which meant that, although formally free, those previously enslaved were compelled to work on the estates of their masters for a further period of four to six years.[18] Since compensation marked the acceptance of the view that the institution of slavery had been legally and politically sanctioned by the state and that 'the nation' (in this case, British taxpayers) ought to bear the cost of the losses to slave-owners, those erstwhile slave-owners saw no reason to assume individual guilt for the part they had played in maintaining the institution. Once abolition was enacted they joined the chorus celebrating Britain's moral superiority and castigating other, less progressive, slave-owning nations.

Former slave-owners were active in multiple ways in the reconfiguration of economy, state and society that took place in the 1830s and 1840s and in which the abolition of slavery was a significant act. In abolishing chattel slavery in 1833, Parliament was intervening in the rights of property owners on a much greater scale than previously.[19] The organisation of compensation was in itself a remarkable bureaucratic achievement, one of the hallmarks of the rapidly expanding state. The shift from the use of enslaved labour to diverse forms of unfree and 'free' labour was one of the key changes in this period and one in which the state played a critical part. Despite the widespread assumption that slavery was the antithesis of freedom and that Emancipation had effected an epochal change, slavery was only abolished in the British Caribbean, Mauritius and the Cape, and it persisted elsewhere. Slavery was still being legislated against in India in 1976.[20] Illegal slave-trading continued in the nineteenth century alongside variegated forms of unfree and bonded labour that persisted well into the twentieth century and beyond.[21] The regulation of labour at home, through the New Poor Law and the Factory Acts, and of labour across the empire through indenture were some of the innovative practices of governments that could combine a commitment to laissez-faire in some areas with a belief in the need to organise labour not just on a national but also an imperial scale. While Eric Williams argued that 1833 marked a critical moment in the demise of mercantilism, the shift from protection to free trade was by no means linear. The freedom of labour was restricted in many ways both at home and in the empire, not least in the regulation of masters and servants,[22] and the West Indians fought a long rearguard action against free trade in sugar, as Keith McClelland documents.[23]

Some of the slave-owners, most notably John Gladstone, had seen the writing on the wall and had started to reorganise their estates before 1833. Gladstone's efforts to inaugurate the use of Indian indentured labour on his Guyanese estates had limited success in the 1820s but were to provide one of the bases for the large-scale adoption of the system by the 1840s.[24] Some slave-owners tried to adapt to the new conditions of labour on their plantations, as did Lord Holland and Matthew James Higgins, for example.[25] Others abandoned their engagement with the sugar economy and moved their investments elsewhere, using the compensation money to move into a variety of other enterprises from railway construction to maritime insurance and banking, as Nicholas Draper shows.[26] The decline of British proprietorship in the West Indies was thus a neglected aspect of the shift from land to commerce and industry that was a feature of this period. Few slave-owners moved directly into manufacture for their interests had long been in land and commerce.

After 1833 the West Indians abandoned the identity of slave-owner and sought to ensure their place in the reconfiguration of the ruling elite that was part and parcel of the 'Age of Reform'. Determinedly not part of a residual formation in a time of realignment when emergent groupings were claiming dominance, they declared themselves as modern men, part of the new 'free' world. Between 1828 and 1833, new rights for dissenters, Catholic Emancipation, parliamentary reform, a Coercion Act for Ireland, the abolition of slavery and new forms of government for India together marked a historic settlement across nation and empire. A new hegemony was established, dependent on an alliance between the landed aristocracy and sections of the middle class, committed to an expansion of laissez-faire and a reforming state. Government was to be by consent, if possible, at home but reliant on force and dominion in the empire, including Ireland. In the metropole, public opinion had an increased weight as the power of the press increased rapidly and more meritocratic systems of appointment began to slowly displace the patronage that had operated for generations. Slave-owners and their descendants were more likely to be Tories than Whigs but they belonged to the elite that effected these changes and (sometimes) benefited from them. William Gladstone and Henry Goulburn in the House of Commons, Charles Trevelyan in the expanding colonial and civil service, Cardinal Manning in the resurgent Catholic Church, and Captain Frederick Marryat and Charles Kingsley, authors who were among the first generation to be able to make a substantial income from writing, were just some of the many former slave-owners or their descendants who established themselves as influential men in the reconfigured public world.

The abolition of slavery meant a shift in the balance of empire. The British West Indies, especially Jamaica, once the jewel in the crown, became increasingly defined as problematic and unproductive. Attention shifted to India and the East and to the new colonies of white settlement. Younger sons who had headed for the Caribbean now found their opportunities in Australia, New Zealand, Canada and South Africa. Henry Kingsley abandoned his family's long-term interest in Barbados and chose New South Wales for his (unsuccessful) colonial careering. Compensation money, or people connected with compensation, moved into new ventures such as the Australian Agricultural Company and the development of South Australia and British Columbia. The Caribbean was no longer seen as a place to make a fortune and was neglected, side-lined in favour of more wealth-producing economies. Slavery was something to be regretted and forgotten, best expunged in so far as was possible from public memory.

Slave-owners and their descendants were active agents in the remaking of race as a hierarchical category. Once slavery no longer fixed the African as inferior, other legitimations for his/her subordination had to be found. Historians, novelists and travel writers with West Indian origins played a significant part in the debates over race in the mid-nineteenth century and the shift from the ascendancy of abolitionist humanitarian discourse to a harsher version of stadial theory, envisioning the civilisational process as glacially slow. They used their eye-witness experience, as Catherine Hall argues, to make claims as to the veracity of their characterisations of racial difference.[27] In the process they also rewrote the history of British involvement in colonial slavery, successfully constituting themselves as the victims of Emancipation.

* * *

In undertaking our research on slave-ownership, five definable though overlapping sets of literature have shaped our thinking or contributed to the intellectual context within which we have undertaken the work: the series of controversies around the work of Eric Williams; the reflections on the social and political formations of nineteenth-century Britain of Cain and Hopkins and William D. Rubinstein; the 'new imperial history'; an emerging literature on the nineteenth-century colonial state; and work on history, family and gender.

Eric Williams' *Capitalism and Slavery* included four connected arguments that are critical for us: slavery was key to the Industrial Revolution; slave-wealth was important to the social, cultural and political fabric of eighteenth-century Britain; the West Indian slave-economy was in decline after 1783 and possibly after 1763; and the West Indian slave-owners were at first a progressive force within mercantilism and then became a reactionary faction in the face of the rise of industrial capitalism.[28] Each of these has a bearing on our work and is in turn illuminated by that work. Each, but especially the first and the third, has attracted sustained controversy and remains too often the subject of an unhelpful polarisation between Anglo-American and Caribbean scholars. Our data might offer the possibility of a commonly accepted basis of evidence for rediscussion of some, although not all, aspects of these sometimes bitter controversies over Williams.

At no stage did Williams argue that slavery 'caused' the Industrial Revolution. 'It must not be inferred', he said, 'that the triangular trade was solely and entirely responsible for the economic development. The growth of the internal market in England, the ploughing-in of the profits from industry to generate still further capital and achieve a still greater expansion, played a large part.'[29] Furthermore, what Williams argued was not simply that the profits of the triangular trade were reinvested in British industry 'where they supplied part of the huge outlay for the construction of the vast plants to meet the needs of the new productive process and the new markets.'[30] In a frequently quoted line he wrote that 'the profits obtained provided one of the main streams of that accumulation of capital which financed the Industrial Revolution.'[31] But he also made the wider argument that the triangular trade gave a triple stimulus to British industry: 'The Negroes were purchased with British manufactures; they produced sugar, cotton, indigo, molasses, and other tropical products, the processing of which created new industries in England [sic]; while the maintenance of the Negroes and their owners on the plantations provided another market for British industry, New England agriculture and the Newfoundland fisheries.'[32] These arguments have been attacked on two grounds, first by a mainstream consensus that capital was not scarce in eighteenth-century England and second by the argument that the slave-trade (and, less consistently argued, implicitly the slave-economy itself) was not large enough to move the needle of British growth.[33] This second argument is embedded in a historical tradition that emphasises the significance of domestic factors over overseas trade as a whole in British economic development.[34]

It appears to us that there is now movement, by no means linear but perceptible, towards a modified version of Williams' position among economic historians. Williams focused on British colonial slavery, rather than the wider nexus including American, Brazilian, French and Spanish slavery. Recent scholarship, with a renewed focus on integrating overseas trade into the context of the domestic drivers of growth, and on a broader conception of the slave-economy, has tended to support Williams. Pomeranz's *Great Divergence* sees the Atlantic slave-economy, with its capacity to add 'phantom land' and coal as the two permissive factors allowing Britain to explode from a base comparable to regions of China from about 1800 onwards.[35] Inikori in 2002 reasserted the Williams thesis in a history of British economic development that begins in the fifteenth century and combines Atlantic slavery with the commercialisation of agriculture as the keys to industrialisation.[36] Despite opposition to Inikori's use of import substitution models, concerns about his conflation of 'the Atlantic world' and 'the slave-economy', and a residual sense that the mechanisms translating 'commercial success ... into long-term self-sustained growth remain to be revealed', Pat Hudson, Maxine Berg and Nuala Zahedieh (among others) broadly accepted Inikori's central thesis about the importance of overseas trade and within that the importance of the slave-economy.[37] Opposition expressed to Inikori over the role and nature of technological change has potentially been qualified recently by recognition of the importance of colonial wealth in determining relatively high wage levels in Britain.[38] Pat Hudson has recently reiterated support for the importance of the slave-trade and slavery in fostering institutional change in Britain's credit markets.[39] Above all, at the micro- rather than macro-economic level, local and regional studies consistently point to the flow of slave-wealth into new institutions and new industries, many concentrated in the centres of commercial and financial power so crucial to financing trade and industrialisation.[40] It might be that such investment could theoretically have been financed from other sources; it is incontrovertible that a significant part of it *was* in fact funded by slavery.

Our material cannot resolve these controversies over Williams' first thesis. By definition, we are concerned with *British* slave-owners of the nineteenth century: Williams' supporters and critics are concerned primarily with the late seventeenth and eighteenth centuries, and his supporters at least increasingly with the Atlantic slave-economy as a whole within these periods. What our material does suggest at the micro-economic level is that the flow of human and financial capital from the British colonial slave-economy was a significant contributor to the remaking of Britain's commercial and to a lesser extent industrial fabric all the way through the first half of the nineteenth century. To this extent, our work confirms the importance of slavery to Britain, but at the same time complicates Williams by qualifying his 'decline' thesis, as we discuss further below.

Williams' second thesis, his insistence on the flow of wealth into British society, culture and politics in the eighteenth century, is distinct from his first thesis on industrialisation because the second is about private wealth rather than national wealth, and about consumption and cultural accumulation outside the commercial and industrial spheres. His pioneering work in this sphere has attracted little controversy (or even interest) compared to the extended disputes over many of his other arguments. In his Chapter 4, 'The West India Interest', Williams sketched the political and social impact of absentee slave-owners on Britain. His method is anecdotal: he presents a series of case studies of individuals and families.[41] The incantatory rhythm of his prose helps the accumulation of examples swell into a rising wall of evidence sweeping the reader along. His examples have subsequently been picked up and repeated: they have become shorthand for illustrating the relationship between Britain and slavery for those who are concerned by it.

What Williams was missing was a context: how representative were his examples? It demands extraordinary effort and resources of course to provide an adequate empirical context. That work is now being done, piecemeal for the eighteenth century: English Heritage, for example, has commissioned systematic work on its properties. Simon Gikandi has recently restated and deepened Williams' themes.[42] Our research now extends Williams' work into the nineteenth century and argues that this process of transfer did not stop in the eighteenth century: instead, all the way through to the 1830s and indeed beyond we can see wealth derived from slave-ownership being redeployed into country-house building, connoisseurship and philanthropy in Britain. Williams used some of the same sources as us, especially the lists of recipients of slave compensation, but a full analysis of those lists would have been beyond any reasonable lifetime's work given the technological era in which Williams worked. Only the advent of the computer and the pooling of knowledge online have made this analysis remotely possible in the Legacies of British Slave-ownership project. And our findings are entirely supportive of Williams in the context of this second thesis: wealth from slave-ownership was among the significant forces reshaping British society and culture in the nineteenth century.

The third Williams thesis, the 'decline' of the West Indies, is linked to but distinct from the fourth thesis, of the 'West Indian' slave-owners as a regressive class fraction confronting rising capitalist hostility. Williams put the peak of the West Indian system variously at 1763 or the eve of the American Revolution. He was heavily influenced by Ragatz, but also by the dominance of Jamaica in both the contemporary eighteenth- and nineteenth-century British mind and in subsequent historiography.[43] Drescher's assault in *Econocide* (1977) has largely been accepted outside the Caribbean as having fatally undermined Williams.[44] Drescher's main case was that the West Indies were as important a part of England's trade in the 1800s as in the 1760s. Drescher did not point out that these were war years. J. R. Ward's work on the profitability of estates shows a fluctuating pattern: it is clear that estates did recover from the American Revolution, but generally at a lower level of profitability than previously.[45] There was a boom in the 1790s, especially in Jamaica. And in some areas (notably British Guiana), as has been argued, it is clear that there was expansion and profitability, even after 1807. But, as Christopher Leslie Brown says, 'decline' is as much an ideological as a technical concept.[46] The argument here is in large part about the salience of the West Indies in the 'official mind'. Measuring that and putting a chronology on it is hard. But it is clear that, during the American Revolution, British strategy sometimes subordinated the defeat of the American colonists to preserving the security of the West Indies, especially Jamaica; that in the early 1780s the idea of abolition of the slave-trade was axiomatically rejected; and that in the 1790s the importance attached to St Domingue by Pitt emphasised the continuing resonance of the West Indies. It is not credible to say that by 1807 the West Indies had ceased to matter; but that is not what Williams argued. He saw a shift in the balance of forces: it was a relative decline, relative to an industrialising metropole. He saw the 1832 Great Reform Act in starker terms than most modern scholars, but it did surely reflect the accommodation of new social forces by the state. Equally clearly, the West Indies were less central to the British economy by the 1830s than not only in the 1760s but also in the 1800s. Williams and his critics were united on this, at least. But to argue that slavery was less important to Britain by the time of Emancipation than at the time of abolition of the slave-trade a quarter of a century earlier is not to argue that it had ceased to matter. Our work suggests that, first, slavery, and specifically slave-ownership, had a cumulative weight, in the sense that wealth, status and privilege derived from slave-ownership in the older colonies where 'decline' by the 1830s is irrefutable did not in fact evaporate but in many cases was sustained for decades beyond Emancipation; and, second, new wealth, status and privilege were being created in newer slave-colonies, above all British Guiana, in the decades after the abolition of the slave-trade.[47]

Decline, and especially decline of political power, is also relevant to the final question to which we have consciously navigated in relation to Eric Williams, the nature of the West Indian interest as regressive or progressive. The place of the slave-owners as a class or class fraction has long troubled Marxists. While Williams' departures in *Capitalism and Slavery* had been strongly influenced by the work of C. L. R. James, which placed slavery centrally within transatlantic history, it also coincided with new accounts within British and American Marxism of capitalist development, notably Paul Sweezy's *The Theory of Capitalist Development* (1942) and Maurice Dobb's *Studies in the Development of Capitalism* (1946), neither of which discussed slavery.[48] Williams' solution was, first, to emphasise the uniqueness of Atlantic slavery, to stress this was not just a continuation of the institution of slavery that had always been embedded in Western European civilisation (as David Brion Davis unhelpfully formulated it[49]) but a historically specific system constructed at what turned out to be a critical moment. Second, he posited that the dialectical relationship of slavery under mercantile capitalism helped to give birth to the industrial capitalism that in turn destroyed it. Slave-owning was first progressive then reactionary. Williams thus transcends the 'Janus-face' characterisation of mercantile capital more generally, and his conceptualisation is infinitely preferable to the Genoveses' increasingly romantic conceptualisation of slave-owners.[50] But Williams relied on treating slave-owners as a whole, and, despite his own background, Williams as noted above was perhaps over-influenced by the dominance of Jamaica. British Guiana in particular provides many examples of the reproduction and repatriation of recognisably modern metropolitan capital in the slave-economy on the part of recognisably modern metropolitan capitalists. We have also found that many West Indians were highly adaptive: they certainly contributed to the formation of new commercial and industrial institutions, and then flourished within these. Slave-owners (who then became former slave-owners) played an important role not only in the birth of the Victorian economy but also in its success, especially in finance and commerce: linkages between slave-ownership and the industrial sectors also exist but appear overall less strong than in finance and commerce.

This approach has some resonances with the influential work of Cain and Hopkins on the economic history of British imperial expansion.[51] Though shaped by (among others) Weber and Schumpeter and by Hobson and Veblen rather than *marxisant* approaches, two aspects of their argument are important for our purposes. The first is the insistence that the specific features of British imperialism are to be found essentially in the inter-relation between economic and social change in the metropole and the imperial sites, both formal and informal, that Britain constructed. More specifically, they argued that what was at the core of imperial expansion was 'gentlemanly capitalism', a phenomenon defined as both an economic and a cultural formation. Capitalism was defined as 'profit-seeking, individualism, specialisation, a market economy, rational calculation and the postponement of present consumption for the sake of future returns'.[52] But what drove capitalist growth and imperial expansion was not, in their view, the development of industrial capitalism and industrialisation so much as financial and commercial services and that the City of London played a crucial and continuing role in determining the forms of imperialism. This is an economic argument; but it is also pivoted on a cultural one, namely the formation and importance of the 'gentleman'. Gentility among men was formed by a Christian sense of duty above self-advancement and the maintenance of a distance from and disdain for production and work. Socially and politically, the dominant classes after 1688 came to be a fusion of the financial and commercial elites with the landed gentry and aristocracy, whose wealth derived from rentier capitalism based on commercial agriculture. But the trick was that the prestige, power and authority of the aristocracy appeared to stem from pre-capitalist sources while embracing the values of commercial society. Finance, commerce and land, distanced from the world of manufacturing, became the prime vehicles of wealth creation; imperial expansion was shaped by the export of gentlemanly capitalism.

Though adopting different arguments, the Cain and Hopkins thesis chimes with the work of William D. Rubinstein on wealth-holding and on the social structure of nineteenth-century Britain.[53] Like Cain and Hopkins, Rubinstein placed great stress on the 'service sector', arguing that there were in effect two middle classes, 'by far the larger and wealthier based on commerce and London, the other on manufacturing and the North of England'.[54] At the same time, the traditional aristocracy, while maintaining its political and cultural domination until at least 1880, was resistant to the absorption of new wealth; the commercial and financial bourgeoisie of the City of London became wealthy on a scale equivalent to, and sometimes surpassing, the aristocratic elites while also outdoing the generation of personal wealth among the industrial middle classes. With the decline of 'Old Corruption' by 1832 and the consequent decay of those whose incomes had been dependent to a considerable extent on the aristocratic state through sinecures and government finance and contracts, there were three predominant segments of the ruling classes: the landed aristocracy and gentry; the financial and commercial middle class; and the industrial middle class. If they were not hermetically sealed off from each other, there was, nonetheless, considerable distance between them. As with Cain and Hopkins, rentier capitalism was crucial for the landed classes, their wealth deriving from not only farming but also mining and urban property; the industrial middle class was based on manufacturing; the commercial and financial middle class turned increasingly to investment in empire and overseas trade.

There has been much debate about the theses of Cain and Hopkins and also of Rubinstein.[55] The role of south-eastern English elites in driving imperialism has been questioned; the degree to which there was a flow of capital between land and industry has been, it is claimed, radically underestimated by Rubinstein. The networks connecting finance and industrial capital have also, it is argued, been underestimated and the nature of supposed hostility or, at the least, distancing from bourgeois culture and values held by the landed elites and the ethos of 'gentlemanly capitalism' have been sharply interrogated. Importantly in the context of this project, neither Cain and Hopkins nor Rubinstein paid any serious attention to the nature and consequences of Britain's involvement in the slavery business and the place of compensation as a source of wealth in Victorian Britain. Rubinstein clearly underestimated the significance of wealth derived from slavery and compensation in the accumulation of personal wealth, as this project shows, although he has revisited this question in his ongoing work and in the light of collaborating with us. Cain and Hopkins have scant reference to slavery or to the British Caribbean, while their definition of capitalism itself excludes a crucial defining feature – a key aspect of both Marxist and Weberian definitions as well of many others – namely the forms of labour underpinning different modes of production and social formations. The empire as a whole rested on the mobilisation of diverse forms of labour extraction and exploitation: the enslaved, apprentices, indentured workers, convict labour, free wage labour, unpaid but 'free' labour, peasantries and hybrid mixes of free, coerced and peasant labour are all to be found at any particular moment in particular settings.[56] Yet, whatever the criticisms, what remains important is the range of questions that have been raised about core problems in understanding the shape of nineteenth-century British society.

Another key debate has concerned the question of the relative positions of the bourgeoisie and the aristocracy. Perry Anderson, for instance, has written of the 'agrarian and aristocratic stamp of English rulers in the era of the Pax Britannica, the subordination of bourgeois manufacturers and mill-owners to them, with all the consequences – economic, political and cultural – that followed from the cadet role of industrial capital in the Victorian age'.[57] Such a view reflects the liberal, middle-class critics of aristocratic power of the period after 1832. Bernard Cracroft, for example, wrote of the landed aristocracy that

So vast is their traditional power, so broadly does it sit over the land, so deep and ancient are its roots, so multiplied and ramified everywhere are its tendrils, and creepers, and feelers, that the danger is never lest they should have too little, but always lest they should have too much power.

Politically, their power had 'the strength of a giant and the compactness of a dwarf'.[58]

On the other hand, there are those who insist that for all the appearances and for all the persistence of aristocratic, gentry and financial elites in the personnel staffing the centres of power, this was a society reshaped by industrial capitalism, the dominance of the urban industrial middle classes and the ascendancy of bourgeois values.[59]

Our work on slave-owners has also been situated in relation to debates over the significance of race and empire in metropolitan life. C. L. R. James was one of the first to insist on the necessary connections between metropole and colony in his classic text *The Black Jacobins* (1938), but his insights were neglected for decades by white historians. A group of scholars variously influenced by post-colonial theory, by Subaltern Studies and by feminism have been in the forefront of arguing for the constitutive place of empire in the making of modern Britain.[60] Efforts to reconnect the histories of Britain and empire and to challenge the myopia of nationalist histories have provided a powerful imperative. A substantive body of work has emerged detailing the impact of empire on metropolitan society, culture and politics in modern Britain.[61] Empire was central, it is argued, to the construction of identities that were and are historically shaped by the production of differences, whether of class, gender, race or ethnicity. National identities, albeit unstable and heterogeneous, were shaped externally as well as internally and empire played a significant role in defining the aspirations, visions and practices of a range of social groups: both planters and abolitionists, for example, saw in the

colonies an opportunity to change the world and themselves. Britons'
self-conception as modern, as Kathleen Wilson has argued, hinged on a
developing historical consciousness that was produced by contact and
exchange.[62]

It was the presence of erstwhile colonised peoples in Britain from the
Caribbean and South Asia that provided one of the inspirations for this
new historical writing. Commonwealth immigration from the late 1940s
marked the beginning of the multicultural present that we now inhabit.
As second- and third-generation children have grown up in Britain, they
have been in search of an inclusive national story, one that makes sense
of the imperial experience and of contemporary racisms. Among people
of African-Caribbean descent the question of slavery has been central.
Why had this figured so marginally in British history-writing and in the
ways in which this history had been taught? Debates around slavery were
given great momentum by the bicentenary of the abolition of the slave-
trade in 2007, when the issue was aired in the press, radio and television;
galleries and museums focused efforts on new exhibitions; innovative
teaching materials were prepared; and community groups organised a
huge range of events and commemorations. One of the sources of controversy at that time concerned the extent to which the forms of remembering were dominated by self-congratulation as to Britain's role in being
the first major power to abolish the slave-trade and whether this effectively displaced a sense of national responsibility for Britain's involvement
in colonial slavery. This mirrored the way in which the abolition of slavery in 1833 was celebrated as a triumphant example of Britain's moral
superiority, effectively erasing the long history of the gains secured for
the metropole by the enslavement and exploitation of African men and
women.[63]

Not surprisingly, most recent scholarly activity has focused on enslaved
men and women in an effort to recover those histories that had been
erased – whether because they were too painful and difficult to remember and so hard to trace archivally or were associated with forms of denial
and disavowal. In Britain the work of forgetting slavery has been aided
by processes of distantiation. The distance from the Caribbean and other
colonial slave-societies has allowed Britons both in the era of slavery and
abolition and since to disassociate themselves from the realities of their
place in that system. In tracing the legacies of slave-ownership using the
compensation records as our starting point, we are deliberately returning
to Britain's/Britons' collusion, both national and individual, and rein-
scribing slavery into the national/imperial narrative.

One of the notions underpinning the work undertaken in this project
has been the concept of an 'imperial social formation'. The phrase has

been particularly associated with the work of Mrinalini Sinha, though it is an approach that informs much recent work in the social, cultural and political history of empire, including that which does not make any particular use of the concept in the way in which Sinha has used it.[64] The concept of an imperial social formation focuses on the ways in which the economic, social, cultural and political dimensions of a whole social formation are inter-related and articulated together. Imperialism is understood as a key constitutive element of the processes of social formation.

Metropole and the imperial are not only mutually 'interacting' or 'influencing' but are also, more strongly, constitutive of each other. It is not, however, a process of equal exchange. The relations between them are determined by relations of power – economic, social and cultural and political – through which relations of dominance and subordination are made and remade. How those relations are played out in any particular historical instance are not, it is generally argued, simply consequent upon a single or overwhelmingly dominant source of causation or determination. For example, it is not possible to assign to economic structures and circumstances the sole, originating cause of domination and subordination between, say, Britain and the Caribbean colonies. Similarly, as Sinha has argued in her work on colonial masculinities, the creation and reworking of the relations between 'the manly Englishman' and the 'effeminate Bengali' was not a process in which either cultural identity was fixed before coming into relation with the other: the construction of each was a consequence of the mutually shaping dialectic between them.

Such an approach has been extremely powerful and influential over the past couple of decades in raising new questions and enabling new histories, not least in reshaping the study of British history. Relations between Britain and its empire were not only formed through political policies and circuits of capital accumulation and investment, it is argued, but also lived and shaped through cultural and political processes such as the ways in which the discourses of 'race' came to shape the 'civilising subjects' of Catherine Hall's study.[65] Furthermore, the cultural and the political had effects, but within contingent circumstances in which no single element predominated. For instance, dominant conceptions of the capacities of the formerly enslaved populations to work in the conditions of 'free labour' were central to the ways in which 'the labour problem' was named, defined and given shape in the Caribbean following abolition and apprenticeship. The problem was determined, in part, by the setting of limits and the exertion of pressures by economic developments: with abolition, the central economic question became what kind of labour regime could replace slavery. But, in turn, how this was played out was shaped by both conceptions of the capacities of labour and particular political circumstances. The push to bring in migrant, indentured labour was contingent upon building an effective political alliance that made possible a reconfiguration of the economy in at least some parts of the Caribbean.[66]

Much work in political history remains resolutely focused on metropolitan Britain to the effective exclusion of imperial dimensions. Within this perspective the defining features of the state between *c*. 1832 and *c*. 1880 are its relative smallness, the commitment to laissez-faire and to free trade from the 1840s and a studied neutrality in relation to social disputes. At the same time as emphasising the laissez-faire character of the state, such views also recognise the extent to which the state intervened as an agent of social discipline in policing, prison regulation and moral reform, most notably in the Contagious Diseases Acts of the 1860s. The state also acted to institutionalise capitalist market relations in a highly punitive, and highly gendered, form through the imposition of the New Poor Law of 1834 while also acting in a 'positive' manner through the Public Health Act of 1848 and in factory acts and the regulation of the hours of labour of working women (1833–53).[67]

However, as Zoë Laidlaw and Kathleen Wilson have shown, if one broadens the horizon of an understanding of the state to see it as an imperial political formation, then a very different picture emerges.[68] As Laidlaw argues, while the British state is often characterised as weak on coercion and strong on consent, colonial states within the empire were frequently prepared to use violence against subject populations. One may see this in the treatment of indigenous groups such as Aborigines in Australia. Slavery itself had been, of course, a system of institutionalised violence; coercion in Ireland was a constant feature of British domination; the suppression of the Indian rebellion of 1857 or the violence meted out in Jamaica by Governor Eyre were not incidental features of imperial rule but structural to it.

Furthermore, as Laidlaw also argues, a consideration of the 'Victorian state' within an imperial context 'reveals the obvious: there was no such thing as "the Victorian state", but rather a series of very different polities across the Empire.'[69] And, while the British state may be characterised as 'liberal', what constituted 'liberalism', seen in an imperial context, has to be severely qualified.[70] The liberal state may have appeared to rest on consent but coercion remains critical to its operations; it may have been laissez-faire but interventionism was a central and persistent strategy; it may have stressed the enlargement of liberties and constitutional freedoms but it required the suppression of indigenous peoples and the cultural re-formation of subject peoples; it may have been shaped by a belief in the rule of 'free markets' but it also depended on state-driven economic policies in relation to Indian cotton or Irish agriculture.

If the colonial state needs rethinking so too do the networks of family and kin. As Davidoff and Hall argued in *Family Fortunes*, the family, with its wide definition including aunts, uncles and cousins not to speak of the in-laws, provided the bedrock of economic organisation in the late eighteenth and early to mid-nineteenth centuries.[71] This was as true for the West Indian networks as for any other, as exemplified by Katie Donington's analysis of the Hibberts.[72] Marriage structured the meaning of property for men as well as women, and marriage, the system of couverture and inheritance strategies were critical to the intergenerational transmission of plantation wealth. John Rock Grossett, for example, Tory MP for Chippenham (1820–6) and active pro-slaver in the 1820s, was able to accumulate his three Jamaican properties through a judicious marriage with his first cousin Mary Spencer Shirley. As David Sabean has demonstrated, over many generations in Western Europe, repeated marriages were contracted among a circle of families who 'circulated god-parents, took over guardianship, tutelage and legal representation creating tight bonds of reciprocity' and extensive overlapping kindreds.[73] These patterns were integral to the transatlantic families of the merchants and planters, and the Legacies of British Slave-ownership database will be an important resource facilitating the linking of these networks.

One great advantage of such alliances, as Leonore Davidoff notes, was that they could act as instruments of trust for those whose capital was spread over long distances, while marriage unions countered the centrifugal effects of partible inheritance.[74] The trust device was widely used as a way of providing for dependents – both women and children – and trustees are an important grouping in the compensation records. The trust was based in equity and had been created to preserve landed property intact while ensuring protection for daughters after marriage. To act as a trustee signified a close relationship to the deceased and involved the taking of responsibility for those widows and minors who could not care effectively for themselves and would not be in a position to actively 'husband' property. The trustees could act on the property, sell or rent and make contracts, and as long as the beneficiary continued to receive the proceeds much was left to the trustees' discretion. Trustees are prominent in the database, as are guardians and executors, undoubtedly underscoring the place of kin, as in the case of the lawyer and historian Archibald Alison, who acted as trustee for his brother-in-law.

Under the laws of equity, married women could own their 'sole and separate estates' in the form of a trust. These were primarily used by upper-class families attempting to protect familial interests and rarely gave women effective power. Married women in common law did not possess an independent persona; they were 'covered' by their husbands. In practice this certainly extensively limited but did not preclude the economic activity of some married women. While Amy Erickson has insisted on the significance of the legal restraints on married women, R. J. Morris has shown that, while imposing the wishes and control of the deceased, the trust could also provide women with some economic independence and proprietorship.[75] Widows and single women, however, could own property and one of the most striking aspects of our findings has been their small-scale ownership of enslaved men and women, particularly in the Caribbean. Women slave-owners are currently beginning to attract attention after the long-sustained assumption that all slave-ownership was a masculine prerogative. Some absentees were able to exercise considerable autonomy, as Hannah Young has explored in her study of Anna Eliza Elletson.[76]

Informed by our hypotheses about what constituted the reconfiguration of Britain after Emancipation and by the issues embedded in the historiography, our re-examination of the formation of modern Britain through the lens of slave-ownership is driven by the prosopographical database of some 2,900 absentee slave-owners. Our primary unit of analysis is thus the individual slave-owner and by extension his or her family.

Such focus on the individual is justified in part by the legal structure of the slave compensation process, which mandated that only individuals could claim and be awarded slave compensation. No firms or other collective bodies were entitled to claim compensation. Moreover, there were no collective investment vehicles for the slave-economy: no West Indian equivalent of the East India Company existed, either administratively or commercially.[77] Finally, the individual is appropriate in tracing commercial legacies in particular because in general the individual was still the fundamental unit among business actors and remained so for the bulk of the nineteenth century, though, of course, individuals were always embedded in wider circuits of family and kin.

Moving from a collection of atomised life stories to general arguments and ultimately to conclusions has raised methodological questions for our work. At the simplest level, our data lend themselves to aggregation, and we have in many cases measured significance by counting and expressing the results as a fraction of a larger whole. The database also allows us to make claims about how representative individual cases are. We can place well-known figures such as John Gladstone in context and determine that he was, for example, one of several dozen merchants to move money into Asia from the Caribbean slave-economy, and one of hundreds to invest in railways. We have used our results to cross-refer to other prosopographical works, for example the *History of Parliament* and William D. Rubinstein's work on the nineteenth-century rich.

There are limitations, too, in our methods that we must acknowledge. Given the scale of the universe of slave-owners with whom we are dealing, we know relatively little about many of them. We have neither the time nor the resources to undertake forensic investigation for individuals with multiple forms of property or multiple business activities to ascertain precisely how much of their wealth flowed from slave-ownership, from other forms of participation in the slave-economy and from non-slavery-related sources. All we can do is to flag up the existence of such other property or activities and be explicit about the basis on which we have reached judgements as to the materiality of slave-ownership for specific individuals.

* * *

The bulk of this volume is organised thematically, bookended by two chapters and an Appendix that bring together our approaches, themes and material. Chapter 2 provides an overview of the universe of British slave-owners and locates them within the British elites of the period. It has been known since Draper's *The Price of Emancipation* (2010) that between five and ten per cent of the British elites (measured by a variety of criteria, social and political) appeared in the slave compensation records in the 1830s as owners, mortgagees, legatees, trustees and executors, and this chapter extends the analysis of this section of the elites over the forty or fifty years following the end of slavery.[78] Our new work also redenominates British slave-owning as fundamentally English and, especially, Scottish as opposed to Irish and Welsh. Ireland had dramatically different patterns of emigration to the sojourning that characterises Scottish slave-owners, and Scotland was wildly over-represented among absentee slave-owners in Britain. Within England, there were local concentrations, as previously known, around Bristol and Liverpool, but slave-ownership was disproportionately concentrated in the south-east and south-west of England. Our new work shows that slave-owners continued to represent the same proportion of wealthy individuals in Britain from the 1810s until the late 1860s, even as the base of wealthy individuals expanded with the diversification of the British economy and the advent of manufacturing wealth. This points to an unexpected resilience of slave-derived wealth for two-thirds of the nineteenth century. The chapter also summarises some of the cultural, physical and imperial legacies of the slave-owners, pointing in the latter case to a perceptible 'swing east' by former slave-owners and their families after Emancipation as in many cases they turned away from the post-slavery Caribbean.

In seeking to summarise the 'commercial legacies' of British colonial slave-ownership in the period after Emancipation, Chapter 3 focuses on what are conceived to be the big changes in Britain's economy and its financial and commercial structure in the period following Emancipation (especially in the decades from the 1830s through to the 1870s), which reflected its emergence as the world's first industrial nation: the explosion of British overseas trade; the reorientation of British long-distance commerce towards Asia, Latin America and the settler colonies; the consolidation of the City of London as the centre of global capital flows with its concomitant growth in financial services, in the professions supporting the City and in merchant banking; the emergence of the joint-stock company; the increased integration of Britain through the railway and of the world through the steamship and telegraph; and the birth of the free-trade nation. All these changes were apparently diametrically opposed to the closed agrarian world of colonial preference in which the slave-owners were embedded. Yet the chapter argues that, while many slave-owners were indeed swept away by these changes, many more not only adapted to the new world order but also were among the most active agents of change, transferring financial and human capital generated in slavery to the new industrial and commercial economy. Such commercial and industrial legacies of slave-ownership were uneven, highly material in some areas but marginal or absent in others. Slave-ownership was one component of many in the consolidation of Britain, and specifically the City, as the centre of global capital in the mid- and late nineteenth century.

Together, Chapters 2 and 3 present a modification to Williams' 'decline' thesis. They argue that, while evidence of financial pressures on the slave-economy and on the post-Emancipation Caribbean are indisputable, wealth was still being created for some individual slave-owners and former slave-owners, especially but not exclusively in the newer slave-frontiers colonies, above all in British Guiana. The overwhelming dominance of Jamaica within metropolitan conceptions of the slave-economy, both for contemporaries and in the subsequent historiography, has tended to conceal the vibrancy of the slave-economy in some areas of the British Caribbean. The contribution from British colonial slave-ownership as a whole to British industrialisation did not cease in 1807 or even in the 1830s, but there is still room for acknowledging its decline relative to the manufacturing capacity it was (as Williams argued) helping to create.

Chapter 4 examines some of the political connections and relationships of men who appear in the compensation records in relation to the institutions and practices of political power between 1833 and the 1860s. Central to this is a consideration of whether we should see them as simply the West India interest in decline, as Eric Williams argued. Having analysed the composition, political affiliations and social bearings of MPs, the chapter then discusses three issues central to the attempted defence of former slave-owners' interests – the debates around apprenticeship in the 1830s, the sugar duties controversies in the 1840s and the introduction of schemes for indentured labour beginning in the 1830s. While the interest was certainly defeated over apprenticeship and sugar, there was no unqualified victory of liberal market capitalism and a culture of anti-slavery. Rather, the abolition of slavery was followed by new forms of coerced labour, facilitated by the mid-Victorian 'liberal' state, and, at the same time, as notions of the anti-slavery nation became dominant, there was also a generalised acceptance both that former slave-owners were victims of abolition and that it was the problem of labour that lay at the core of Caribbean economic and social problems following Emancipation.

Chapter 5 concerns the writings of those slave-owners and their descendants who were concerned to tell their versions of the history of slavery and the plantation and who in the process contributed to the reconfiguration of racial thinking in the aftermath of Emancipation. In a period when literacy was increasing and the reading public rapidly expanding, print culture was assuming ever greater significance in the formation of that important new body – public opinion. Once Britain had defined itself as an anti-slavery nation, these authors speedily aligned themselves with that position, rewrote and disavowed their own histories and were actively involved in the remaking of racial hierarchies. Enthusiasm for the ending of 'the stain' upon the nation could provide a way of screening disturbing associations, partially forgetting and rewriting a long history of British involvement in the slavery business, and at the same time reconfiguring race now that enslavement could no longer be the defining mark of the African. In histories of the nation or the family such as those of William Mackinnon or George Webbe Dasent, in novels such as those of Captain Marryat or the relatively obscure lady author Theodora Lynch, in travel writing such as that by Charles Kingsley and in the poetry of those of greater or lesser fame, authors worked on their own memories and imaginatively reconstructed their relationships to their West Indian connections. Their personal memories and family histories were interwoven with more public forms of remembering and forgetting. Their collective works, discussed in this chapter, provide a formidable case for the weight of the intervention made by erstwhile slave-owners in narrating British history.

Chapter 6 presents a case study of the Hibbert family. It explores some of the ways in which the Hibbert family used the profits of slavery to make an impact on the social, cultural, political and economic landscape over the course of several generations. At the centre of the Hibbert family story is the relationship between colonial labour, transatlantic wealth-generation and metropolitan consumption. Moving between Manchester, Jamaica and London, it outlines the foundation, expansion and consolidation of their wealth and status. The chapter highlights the significance of networks formed through religious identity, marriage, kinship and commerce. It discusses George Hibbert's role in the slavery compensation debates and gives a detailed breakdown of which family members received awards. Both before and after the compensation process, the Hibbert family invested in various forms of acquisition: from town and country houses to cultural consumption, from philanthropic and charitable works to the purchase of political position and finally the reinvestment of funds in new commercial opportunities. In highlighting the imprint that the Hibberts have left behind, this chapter seeks to reconnect the disturbing origins of the wealth that enabled their activities with their tangible legacies. In doing so this chapter demonstrates the potential of the wider data gathered within the database to rethink the ways in which the profits from slavery infiltrated the wider British economy, affecting people and places that remained at a distance from slave-ownership.

Finally, the Appendix, which we regard as an integral part of the volume, describes the structure of the Legacies of British Slave-ownership database, its uses and its limitations. We analyse individuals' 'degree of proximity' to slavery and the capacity in which they were awarded compensation – for example, as owner-in-fee, trustee, executor or mortgagee. We show the interconnections of slave-owners and outline the importance of family networks in the universe of slave-owners. The diachronic nature of the database is explained, showing the geographical movement of slave-owners over time and the development of each of the legacy strands (we have categorised the legacy strands as commercial, political, historical, imperial, cultural and physical). We also outline the main sources we have used, the scope of information we have been able to include and the ways in which these sources bring their own distortions and their own limitations. Central to this is a discussion of the prosopographical approach we have taken and the ways in which we can move from a mass of individual and family biographies to a greater understanding of the significance of the universe of slave-owners as a whole.

Conclusion

In choosing to make the database publicly available online as the Legacies of British Slave-ownership database, we are working in the tradition of recent collaborative projects, notably the Trans-Atlantic Slave Trade Database.[79] However, our data goes beyond the remarkable data assembled by that project because of our development of the biographical data in our prosopography. We are therefore combining a digitisation project (of the Parliamentary Papers list of awards made by the Slave Compensation Commissioners, supplemented by the Register of Claims[80]) with research that has the intention of capturing the imprints of individuals on British life in the mid-nineteenth century and the effect in some cases of linking those individuals to firms, families and institutions that are still identifiable today. We recognise the potential sensitivity of such links. The Legacies of British Slave-ownership project has no position on reparations and restitution, but equally we understand that there are potential implications of our work for the debates around these issues. Against this background, as historians we see our responsibilities to the descendants of the enslaved people, to the descendants of the slave-owners and to other academic and non-academic constituencies to be, first, clarity in presenting our data, so that users can understand, for example, the different contexts in which names can appear among lists of recipients of slave compensation; and, second, appropriate contextualisation of the results. In the Structure and Significance of British Caribbean Slave-ownership 1763–1833 project now underway at UCL, we are committed to achieving a greater degree of integration of the available records and data concerning the enslaved people with those of the slave-owners.

We began this Introduction by pointing to the distortions of the *ODNB*. The *ODNB* is not static, of course. By its nature, it reflects editorial decisions made in the nineteenth century as well as more recently: it is a big ship to turn. It now represents neither the way the world looked to the original compilers in the late nineteenth century nor the way it looks from today's perspective. But, at any given point, it reproduces some essential version of the place of a given thing in British life, and how the *ODNB* represents that thing is a powerful cultural force. We have argued that it cumulatively has the effect of suppressing the memory of slave-ownership in the national consciousness. The recent inclusion in the *ODNB* of Edward Huggins alongside Arthur Hodge as notorious exemplars of the cruelty of slavery indicates a recognition of the need to acknowledge slavery, and not just abolition (although neither man is described as a slave-owner).[81] But the task of adjusting the national narrative cannot wait on the process of adding slave-owners one at a time or revising the 'park' of existing entries that elide slave-ownership. We do not maintain that the slave-owners created modern Britain, but we do not think the making of Victorian Britain can be understood without reference to those slave-owners. This volume is our attempt to accelerate that process of (re)writing slave-ownership back into British history.

NOTES

1 *Oxford Dictionary of National Biography*, online edn., at www.oxforddnb.com (hereafter, *ODNB*). A full text search for the term 'slave owner' in the *ODNB* returns nineteen entries (of which one is Olaudah Equiano, another is John Marrant, five are American slave-owners and one is an incidental reference in the entry for Baron Denman), and 'slave-owner' returns a further two (of which one is an American and one is Francis Williams). In contrast, the combination of 'planter' and 'West Indies' generates seventy-four entries ('planter' and 'West Indian' generate thirty, and 'planter' and 'West India' eighteen), 'planter' and 'Jamaica' return sixty-six, 'proprietor' and 'Jamaica' return forty-one, 'planter' and 'Barbados' return twenty-nine, while 'merchant' and 'West India' and 'merchant' and 'West Indian' return ninety-one and 117 respectively. For a discussion of the inclusiveness and limitations of the *ODNB* as whole, see Stefan Collini, 'National lives: *The Oxford Dictionary of National Biography*', in *Common Reading: Critics, Historians, Publics* (Oxford, 2008), pp. 299–316.

2 W. P. Courtney, rev. Jonathan Harris, 'Dwarris, Sir Fortunatus William Lilley (1786–1860), lawyer and writer', *ODNB*. The entry further states that he 'was an opponent of slavery'; in fact, in common with many slave-owners by the 1820s and 1830s, he professed regret that slavery existed but opposed 'immediate' abolition, by which he meant abolition on any meaningful timescale, and was attacked by the *Antislavery Monthly Reporter* for this.

3 W. P. Courtney, rev. A. C. Howe, 'Hankey, Thomson (1805–1893), politician and political economist', *ODNB*.

4 Ian K. R. Archer 'Storer, Anthony Morris (1746–1799), politician and collector', *ODNB*.

5 J. A. Hamilton, rev. Sinead Agnew, 'Thesiger, Frederick, first Baron Chelmsford (1794–1878), lord chancellor', *ODNB*. Charles Thesiger, who died in 1831, had been comptroller of customs at St Vincent.

6 G. F. R. Barker, rev. David Eastwood, 'Goulburn, Henry (1784–1856), politician', *ODNB*.

7 Martin Russell, 'Peyronnet, (Georgina) Frances de [née Georgina Frances Whitfield], Viscountess de Peyronnet in the French nobility (1815–95), journalist', *ODNB*. Frances de Peyronnet was the daughter of George Whitfield, 'a lawyer and West Indian sugar plantation proprietor' and Georgina Pauline, née Ross, and the mother-in-law of the MP Arthur Russell.

8 See e.g. the *ODNB* entries for Alexander Cray Grant, who in 1841 claimed that he had been 'cultivating his [West Indian] property at a great loss'; Frederick Marryat, who in the 1840s, 'notwithstanding a patrimony in excess

of half a million pounds ... seems to have been permanently short of money, owing partly to the ruin of his West India property'; Robert Wallace, who in 1846 'became embarrassed financially by the depreciation in the value of some of his West Indian estates, and deemed it prudent to resign his seat in parliament'; and Sir Alexander Grant, principal of Edinburgh University 1868–84, whose family 'in 1848–9, by the unexpected emancipation of all the slaves in the Island of Santa Cruz, without any compensation ... was impoverished'.

9 This tradition extends back to Eric Williams' account of the West Indians of the nineteenth century as 'an outworn interest, whose bankruptcy smells to high heaven in historical perspective'. Eric Williams, *Capitalism and Slavery* (1944; repr. London, 1964), ch. 4, at p. 211.

10 See Appendix 1 for the counterexamples and possible counterexamples of John Coakeley Lettsom, James Whitehorne, William Young Ottley and Bezsin King Reece.

11 E.g. Joseph Hume, who dismayed his radical colleagues by championing compensation for slave-owners, among whom his wife's brother, William Hardin Burnley, figured prominently.

12 Williams, *Capitalism and Slavery*, ch. 4.

13 Bernard Crick, 'Blair, Eric Arthur [pseud. George Orwell] (1905–1950), political writer and essayist', *ODNB*. This entry is unusual in its explicit recognition of slave-ownership, describing Charles Blair, Orwell's great-great grandfather and the founder of the family's fortune and of its transformed social position, as 'a plantation and slave owner in Jamaica'.

14 David Lambert, *White Creole Culture, Politics and Identity during the Age of Abolition* (Cambridge, 2005); Christer Petley, *Slaveholders in Jamaica: Colonial Society and Culture during the Era of Abolition* (London, 2009); Natalie Zacek, *Settler Society in the English Leeward Islands 1670–1776* (Cambridge, 2010); Christer Petley, 'Rethinking the fall of the planter class', *Atlantic Studies* 9 (1) (2012), 1–17.

15 Will of Nathaniel Snell Chauncy, merchant of Wilson Street Finsbury Square 28 July 1856 PROB 11/2235/334.

16 For difficulties of identification in an earlier period, see Kathy Chater, *Untold Stories, Black People in England and Wales during the Period of the British Slave-trade c. 1660–1807* (Manchester, 2009), pp. 24–5.

17 Susanne Seymour and Sheryllynne Haggerty, *Slavery Connections of Brodsworth Hall (1600–c.1830): Final Report for English Heritage* (English Heritage, 2010), at www.english-heritage.org.uk/publications/slavery-connections-brodsworth-hall/slavery-connections-brodsworth-hall.pdf, accessed 31 July 2013.

18 Nicholas Draper, *The Price of Emancipation. Slave-Ownership, Compensation and British Society at the End of Slavery* (Cambridge, 2010), pp. 100–7.

19 Julian Hoppit, 'Compulsion, compensation and property rights in Britain, 1688–1833', *Past & Present* 210 (2011), 93–128.

20 Gyan Prakash, 'Terms of servitude: the colonial discourse on slavery and bondage in India', in Martin A. Klein (ed.), *Breaking the Chains. Slavery, Bondage and Emancipation in Modern Africa and Asia* (Madison WI, 1993), pp. 131–49.

21 Marika Sherwood, *After Abolition: Britain and the Slave Trade since 1807* (London, 2007).

22 For the variety of forms of master and servant legislation see Douglas Hay and Paul Craven (eds.), *Masters, Servants, and Magistrates in Britain and the Empire, 1562–1955* (Chapel Hill, NC and London, 2004).

23 See Chapter 4.

24 See e.g. S. G. Checkland, *The Gladstones. A Family Biography 1764–1851* (Cambridge, 1971) and Madhavi Kale, *Fragments of Empire: Capital, Slavery, and Indian Indentured Labor Migration in the British Caribbean* (Philadelphia, 1998).

25 Matthew James Higgins inherited property in British Guiana from his mother Janet Higgins, who received compensation.

26 See Chapter 3.

27 See Chapter 5.

28 The book also includes other important theses that are not directly relevant to us here, notably that 'slavery was not born of racism: rather, racism was a consequence of slavery' (p. 7) and that abolition is to be understood primarily as an economic phenomenon.

29 Williams, *Capitalism and Slavery*, pp. 105–6.

30 *Ibid.*, p. 98.

31 *Ibid.*, p. 52.

32 *Ibid.*

33 David Eltis and Stanley L. Engerman, 'The importance of slavery and the slave trade to industrializing Britain', *Journal of Economic History* 60 (1) (2000), 123–44. Despite a lucid laying out of the spectrum of different positions on the relationship between slavery and industrialisation at the beginning of their article, Eltis and Engerman tend to revert to demolishing the straw man that the slave-trade or slavery caused the Industrial Revolution, and move between the slave-trade and 'the sugar industry' as proxies for the Atlantic slave-economy. It is noteworthy that the scholars who argue for the marginal nature of slavery in the eighteenth century are exactly those who argue that in the nineteenth century slavery was profitable and expanding and that it cost Britain economically to abolish it: slavery in their perspective thus becomes *more* important, the inverse of Williams' decline thesis.

34 E.g. R. P. Thomas and D. N. McCloskey, 'Overseas trade and empire, 1700–1860', in R. C. Floud and D. N. McCloskey (eds.), *The Economic History of Britain since 1700, Vol. I: 1700–1860* (Cambridge, 1981), pp. 87–102. For a balanced discussion of the historiography of these problems up to c. 2000, see Kenneth Morgan, *Slavery, Atlantic Trade and the British Economy, 1660–1800* (Cambridge, 2000).

35 Kenneth Pomeranz, *The Great Divergence. China, Europe and the Making of the Modern World Economy* (Princeton and Oxford, 2000).

36 Joseph E. Inikori, *Africans and the Industrial Revolution in England: A Study in International Trade and Economic Development* (Cambridge, 2002).

37 Joseph Inikori, Stephen D. Behrendt, Maxine Berg *et al.*, 'Roundtable: reviews of Joseph Inikori's *Africans and the Industrial Revolution in England: A Study in International Trade and Economic Development* with a response by Joseph Inikori', *International Journal of Maritime History*, 15 (2) (2003), 279–361. In

this collection, Maxine Berg rejects Inikori's use of the Import Substitution model but accepts the reinsertion of overseas trade, both Asian and Atlantic, into the history of industrialisation; for Asian connections with the slave-trade, see Maxine Berg, 'In pursuit of luxury: global history and British consumer goods in the eighteenth century', *Past & Present* 182 (2004), 85–142 and *Luxury and Pleasure in Eighteenth-Century Britain* (Oxford, 2005). The most sceptical contribution in Inikori *et al.*, 'Roundtable' was that of John Singleton, who developed a counterfactual argument that 'Britain's cotton industry could have managed without enslaved Africans' (p. 323).

38 William G. Clarence-Smith argued against Inikori and for 'autonomous technical factors' in Inikori *et al.*, 'Roundtable', but more recently there has been a return to explanations of technological change that stress its economic and commercial context; see e.g. R. C. Allen, 'Why the industrial revolution was British: commerce, induced invention and the scientific revolution', *Economic History Review* 64 (2) (2011), 357–84.

39 Pat Hudson, 'Slavery, the slave trade and economic growth: a contribution to the debate', in Catherine Hall, Nicholas Draper and Keith McClelland (eds.), *Emancipation and the Remaking of the British Imperial World* (Manchester, 2014), pp. 36–59.

40 Nuala Zahedieh, *The Capital and the Colonies: London and the Atlantic Economy 1660–1700* (Cambridge, 2010); T. M. Devine, 'Did slavery make Scotia great?', *Britain and the World* 4 (1) (2011), 40–64.

41 Williams, *Capitalism and Slavery*, pp. 85–97.

42 Simon Gikandi, *Slavery and the Culture of Taste* (Princeton, 2011).

43 Lowell Ragatz, *The Fall of the Planter Class in the British Caribbean 1763–1833: A Study in Social and Economic History* (New York and London, 1928).

44 Seymour Drescher, *Econocide: British Slavery in the Era of Abolition* (Pittsburgh, PA, 1977).

45 J. R. Ward, 'The profitability of sugar planting in the British West Indies, 1650–1834', *Economic History Review* 31 (2) (1978), 197–213.

46 Christopher Leslie Brown, *Moral Capital: Foundations of British Abolitionism* (Chapel Hill, 2006), 'Introduction', esp. pp. 13–16.

47 Nicholas Draper, 'The rise of a new planter class? Some countercurrents from British Guiana and Trinidad 1807–1833', *Atlantic Studies* 9 (1) (2012), 65–83.

48 Paul Sweezy, *The Theory of Capitalist Development* (New York and Oxford, 1942) and Maurice Dobb, *Studies in the Development of Capitalism* (London, 1946). The major modern Marxist interpretation of slavery has been the work of Robin Blackburn: *The Overthrow of Colonial Slavery 1776–1848* (London, 1988), *The Making of New World Slavery. From the Baroque to the Modern, 1492–1800* (London, 1997) and *The American Crucible. Slavery, Emancipation and Human Rights* (London, 2009).

49 Among other of his writings, see David Brion Davis, *The Problem of Slavery in Western Culture* (New York and Oxford, 1988).

50 Eugene D. Genovese, *The Political Economy of Slavery: Studies in the Economy and the Society of the Slave South* (New York, 1965) and *The World the Slaveholders Made: Two Essays in Interpretation* (New York, 1969); Eugene D. Genovese and Elizabeth Fox-Genovese, *Fruits of Merchant Capital: Slavery*

and Bourgeois Property in the Rise and Expansion of Capitalism (New York and Oxford, 1983) and *The Mind of the Master Class: History and Faith in the Southern Slaveholders'Worldview* (Cambridge, 2005).

51 P. J. Cain and A. G. Hopkins, *British Imperialism. Innovation and Expansion 1688–1914* (London, 1993). (A second volume covers the period 1914–90.)

52 *Ibid.*, p. 18.

53 His main essays have been collected as William D. Rubinstein, *Elites and the Wealthy in Modern British History* (London, 1987).

54 William D. Rubinstein, 'Wealth, elites and the class structure of Modern Britain', *Past & Present* 76 (1977), 99.

55 For Cain and Hopkins see especially M. J. Daunton, '"Gentlemanly capitalism" and British industry 1820–1914', *Past & Present* 122 (1989), 119–58; A. N. Porter, '"Gentlemanly capitalism" and empire: the British experience since 1750?', *Journal of Imperial and Commonwealth History* 18 (1990), 265–95; Raymond E. Dumett (ed.), *Gentlemanly Capitalism and British Imperialism* (London, 1999). For Rubinstein, see Daunton, '"Gentlemanly capitalism"' and also F. M. L. Thompson, 'Life after death: how successful nineteenth-century businessmen disposed of their fortunes', *Economic History Review* new series 43 (1) (1990), 40–61. Rubinstein replied with 'Cutting up rich: a reply to F. M. L. Thompson', *Economic History Review* new series 45 (2) (1992), 350–61 and Thompson responded with 'Stitching it together again', *Economic History Review* new series 45 (2) (1992), 362–75.

56 Clare Anderson, 'After Emancipation: empires and imperial formations', in Catherine Hall, Nicholas Draper and Keith McClelland (eds.), *Emancipation and the Remaking of the British ImperialWorld* (Manchester, 2014), pp. 113–27 is a very useful survey.

57 Perry Anderson, 'The figures of descent', in *English Questions* (London, 1992), pp. 121–92, at p. 20.

58 Bernard Cracroft, 'The analysis of the House of Commons, or indirect representation', in *Essays on Reform* (London, 1867), pp. 155–90, at 160, 173.

59 See, for a classic example, H. J. Perkin, *The Origins of Modern English Society 1780–1880* (London, 1969) or, for a Marxist view, John Saville, *1848. The British State and the Chartist Movement* (Cambridge, 1987) or his *The Consolidation of the Capitalist State, 1800–1850* (London, 1994).

60 See e.g. the work of Antoinette Burton, Kathleen Wilson, Mrinalini Sinha and Catherine Hall.

61 For discussion of some of this work see Catherine Hall and Sonya O. Rose, 'Introduction: being at home with the empire', in Hall and Rose (eds.), *At Home with the Empire. Metropolitan Culture and the ImperialWorld* (Cambridge, 2006), pp. 1–31. See also the Manchester University Press series *Studies in Imperialism*.

62 Kathleen Wilson, 'Introduction: histories, empires, modernities', in Wilson (ed.), *A New Imperial History. Culture, Identity and Modernity in Britain and the Empire 1660–1840* (Cambridge, 2004), pp. 1–28.

63 For discussion see e.g. Marcus Wood, 'Significant silence: where was slave agency in the popular imagery of 2007?' and Catherine Hall, 'Afterword: Britain 2007, problematising histories', in Cora Kaplan and John Oldfield

(eds.), *Imagining Transatlantic Slavery* (Basingstoke, 2010), pp. 162–90 and 191–201.

64 See Mrinalini Sinha, *Colonial Masculinity. The 'Manly Englishman' and the 'Effeminate Bengali' in the Late Nineteenth Century* (Manchester, 1995), 'Teaching imperialism as a social formation', *Radical History Review* 67 (1997), 175–86 and 'Mapping the imperial social formation: a modest proposal for feminist history' *Signs* 25 (4) (2000), 1077–82. See also, for related perspectives on imperial formations, Ann Laura Stoler, Carole McGranahan and Peter C. Perdue (eds.), *Imperial Formations* (Oxford, 2007), especially the introductory essay by Stoler and McGranahan, 'Introduction. Refiguring Imperial Terrains'.

65 Catherine Hall, *Civilising Subjects: Metropole and Colony in the English Imagination, 1830–1867* (Cambridge, 2002).

66 There are many issues that arise from work on imperial social formations, including, for instance, the complexities of the model and how the different levels of it are articulated together. Part of this arises from more general problems of causality, which will not be discussed here. While much of the new imperial history has been influenced by Marxism, among other things, what has not carried over into it has been a stress upon the ultimately determining weight of the economic.

67 A useful survey, reflective of much mainstream thinking, is Philip Harling, *The Modern British State. An Historical Introduction* (Cambridge, 2001), ch. 3; for the Poor Law see the classic analysis in Karl Polanyi, *The Great Transformation: The Political and Economic Origins of Our Time* (1945; repr. Boston, 1957), especially part 2.

68 Kathleen Wilson, 'Rethinking the colonial state: family, gender, and governmentality in eighteenth-century British frontiers', *American Historical Review* 116 (5) (2011), 1294–1322; Zoë Laidlaw, 'The Victorian state in its imperial contexts', in Martin Hewitt (ed.), *The Victorian World* (London and New York, 2012), pp. 329–45.

69 Laidlaw, 'Victorian state', p. 342.

70 On liberalism in its imperial context see Uday Singh Mehta, *Liberalism and Empire: A Study in Nineteenth-Century British Liberal Thought* (Chicago, 1999); Jennifer Pitts, *A Turn to Empire: The Rise of Imperial Liberalism in Britain and France* (Princeton, 2006); Catherine Hall, *Macaulay and Son. Architects of Imperial Britain* (New Haven and London, 2012).

71 Leonore Davidoff and Catherine Hall, *Family Fortunes. Men and Women of the English Middle Class 1780–1850*, 2nd ed. (London, 2002 [1987]).

72 See Chapter 6 of this book.

73 Sabean quoted in Leonore Davidoff, *Thicker than Water. Siblings and their Relations 1780–1920* (Oxford, 2012), p. 229.

74 *Ibid.*

75 Amy Erickson, *Women and Property in Early Modern England* (London, 1993), p. 168; R. J. Morris, *Men, Women and Property in England* (Edinburgh, 2005), p. 263.

76 Hannah Young, *Gender, Power and Slave-ownership: The Case of Anna Eliza Elletson* (MA thesis, University College London, 2012). See also the forthcoming work of Cassandra Pybus.

77 A West India Company, founded in the mid-1820s, appears to have been still-born. The West India Dock Company was the closest to a joint-stock vehicle to invest in slavery.

78 Draper, *Price of Emancipation*.

79 www.slavevoyages.org.

80 Parliamentary Papers 1837–8 (215) XLVIII: *Accounts of Slave Compensation Claims*; *Records Created and Inherited by HM Treasury: Office of Registry of Colonial Slavery and Slave Compensation Commission Records*. The underlying material in the National Archives is primarily in the T71 series. A full list of relevant material in the National Archives is in Draper, *Price of Emancipation*, pp. 370–1.

81 David Small, 'Huggins, Edward (1755?–1829), plantation owner', *ODNB*; G. P. Moriarty, rev. Christopher Fyfe, 'Hodge, Arthur (d. 1811), planter in the West Indies and murderer', *ODNB*.

2 Possessing people: absentee slave-owners within British society

Nicholas Draper

The ultimate failure of the West Indian slave-owners has been axiomatic since the work of Lowell Ragatz almost a century ago.[1] Eric Williams' subsequent characterisation of them by the 1830s as 'an outworn interest, whose bankruptcy smells to high heaven in historical perspective' has not been seriously contested.[2] The slave-owners themselves contributed to this dismal story through their continuous pleading of poverty. But Williams himself acknowledged a problem: how to account for the continued 'obstructionist and disruptive effect', 'the powerful defence put up by the West Indians', in the later years of slavery.[3] Partly this reflects his early dating (following Ragatz) of 'decline'. Drescher *et al.* have placed it after 1807, rather than after 1763 or 1783, where Williams variously situated the turning point,[4] but there has been consensus among all parties that decline did indeed occur after 1807, 'decline' embracing a deteriorating economic position and a diminished importance within the metropole in political, social and cultural terms. The evidence of the slave compensation records, however, provides a more complex story.[5] The slave-owners of the 1830s certainly afford plenty of examples of decaying fortunes and of overwhelming debts. Yet they also provide many counterexamples both of old wealth maintained and of new wealth generated. The welter of conflicting case studies risks creating only an indeterminate miasma. Yet beyond the contradictions there emerges a picture of a continuing series of contributions by slave-owners and from slave-ownership to the material and cultural formation of mid-nineteenth-century Britain. The argument here is not that the West Indians were economically as important in the 1830s or the 1860s as they had been, or had been perceived to be, in the 1760s or 1790s. Relative to the industrial weight of manufacturing industry and of a broader financial service sector, the slave-economy was clearly less important. Williams' connection of the abolition of slavery to declining economic significance is compatible with this relative as well as absolute decline. But the slave-economy was not trivial to Britain in the early decades of the nineteenth century. And beyond Emancipation, despite the reduced commitment to the West Indies by the British state and by many individual former absentee slave-owners, profitable exploitation of new forms of labour, both indentured and wage labour, was not only possible but demonstrably attained by former slave-owning families and firms. The proportion of the elites in Britain derived from 'West Indians' in the 1830s, the 1850s and the 1870s demonstrates the continuity and resilience of former slave-owners and their continuing importance to the fabric of metropolitan British society.

Against such a background, this chapter sets out to locate the overall population of absentee slave-owners in the context of early and mid-Victorian Britain, to analyse their wealth and the evidence such analysis provides for 'decline' or otherwise, and to highlight some of the cultural, physical and imperial legacies they bequeathed to Britain after the 1830s.[6]

Absentee slave-owners within British society

Some 3,000 individuals in the slave compensation process have been identified who were resident in Britain at the time of slave compensation or who came (or in many cases returned) to Britain from the Caribbean in subsequent decades, and it is this corpus of absentees whose legacies form the basis of this volume. In thus privileging absentee slave-owners and former slave-owners in our work, we are making a judgement that those slave-owners who lived in Britain at the time of Emancipation or came or returned to Britain thereafter constitute a separate category among slave-owners as a whole, and were distinct in their impact on metropolitan Britain society. This distinction has been challenged in the past, primarily in the context of gauging the impact of absentee ownership in the Caribbean. Douglas Hall made the case fifty years ago that not only absentee but also resident slave-owners shipped their commodity produce to Britain, drew on mercantile credit from British merchants, equipped their estates with British manufactures, spent their surplus income on British luxury goods and educated their children in Britain.[7] There was, he argued, no necessary distinction between absentee and resident slave-owners in their *systemic* roles in transmitting some of the effects of slavery into metropolitan Britain. Residency according to Hall was to some extent the product of a stage in a proprietor's life cycle, with people retiring to Britain when the profits from their West Indian investments allowed them to comfortably do so. 'Indeed, it is difficult to distinguish between resident and absentee owners except on the obvious difference that the former were, and the latter were not, resident in the colonies.'[8] Many white residents in the West Indies still viewed Britain as 'home' and, as David Lambert has demonstrated, both resident and absentee West Indian planters and merchants emphasised 'a shared British culture, common political traditions and their essential Englishness' as part of their pro-slavery political campaign.[9] We can accept these arguments while at the same time insisting on the immediacy of the specific impacts and specific legacies of slave-owners who lived (and died) in Britain itself. In order to hold political office in Britain, slave-owners by and large had to be resident in Britain at the time. Investments in country houses and influence on the urban built environment in Britain occurred mostly when people lived or were about to live there. Cultural accumulation and philanthropic activity in Britain were largely defined by local or regional physical proximities. Mercantile activity had mostly gravitated from the colonies to the metropole by the early nineteenth century. While we reiterate that the legacies of slave-ownership are only part of the legacies of slavery itself, we regard the individual *absentee* slave-owner as a vital and immediate agent in the diffusion of slavery into the fabric of Britain, through specific local interventions generated by his or her immediate presence that, in aggregate, become from a historical perspective cumulatively significant at the national level.

Certainly this is true in the cases of England and Scotland, for absentee slave-ownership was primarily an Anglo-Scottish phenomenon. Of all absentees for whom we have addresses, just under 20 per cent were in Scotland, fewer than 4 per cent in Ireland, fewer than 2 per cent in Wales and the remainder, just under three-quarters, in England. Wales' links to the slave-economy, as Evans has shown, were primarily at the level of the development of specific industries rather than that of slave-ownership.[10] Similarly, Ireland, whose own commercialisation and proto-industrialisation were bound up in its engagement in the Atlantic economy, had absentee slave-owners numbered in the low hundreds. Many of these were figures of local and regional importance, but, relative to its population and even relative to the size of its elites, Ireland was grossly under-represented among absentee slave-owners. Irish men and women embraced the opportunities of empire but appear to have been more inclined to emigrate permanently.[11] Slavery played a different role for Scots, and Scots played a different role in slavery. They left their home countries in larger numbers and returned to Britain more often than the Irish: the Scots were indeed sojourners.[12]

Of the total awards to absentees in Britain and Ireland, women represent just over 20 per cent of the awardees, lower than the average of approximately 40 per cent for female slave-owners overall. The discrepancy reflects first the smaller scale of holdings by women against the larger average scale of holding for absentees; second, the substitution of husbands for wives in compensation claims originating with married women in Britain, as with other forms of property in this period; and finally the greater tendency in Britain than in the colonies for men to be constituted (by other men) as trustees and executors of property belonging to widowed or unmarried women.

In saying that the absentees were 'a heterogeneous lot' – their only common features being that they were all estate owners, 'nearly all of them white' and many were or had at some time been wealthy – Douglas Hall highlighted the presence of important exceptions to the whiteness of the slave-owners.[13] The records of the Slave Compensation Commission are not structured by the slave-owners' race (although of course they are so structured for the enslaved people) but in a handful of cases of absentee slave-owners it is clear that they were people of mixed descent. Nathaniel Wells, sheriff of Monmouthshire, is perhaps the most famous example of these.[14] There are others, however. John Stewart, probably the first man of colour to become an MP, was a slave-owner in British Guiana and was awarded compensation for the enslaved people on his Annandale estate.[15] The Hopkinson family, the illegitimate sons and daughters of John Hopkinson (who died c.1822) and his brother Benjamin (who died in 1801), inherited several estates in British Guiana.[16] Such legacies of slavery and slave-ownership in the form of people of colour tend to be suppressed over time. In Diana Athill's memoir *Yesterday Morning*, which is largely about her mother's family, she says of her army officer father 'I have never in my life been attracted to a man of his physical type: fair haired, blue-eyed, pink-skinned.'[17] He was the son of a clergyman, the Rev. Herbert Athill (1851–1919).[18] Despite her emphasis on her father's quintessential whiteness, her paternal great-grandfather, George Athill, was almost certainly a man of colour, brother of the distinguished civil servant John Athill.[19] George Athill, a merchant who was awarded compensation for three enslaved people on Antigua, had a first family, born in the West Indies, and a second family, including Diana's grandfather Herbert, with the wife he married in Britain in 1845.

Slave-ownership permeated every tier of the elites, not only the aristocracy and gentry but also the more economically active sections. Among absentee slave-owners whose occupations are known, 'merchant' is by some distance the most common occupational classification, and as always hides as much as it discloses beyond registering an activity broadly in commerce (i.e. a business not involving manufacture or transformation of raw materials).[20] The second most frequent classification is 'lawyer' (whether solicitor, barrister or attorney), often attached to men (and members of the professions at the time were all men) who were awarded compensation as agents rather than principals – as trustees and executors of the underlying beneficiaries of slave compensation.[21] Judges, by definition senior lawyers, also figure in the compensation records, either as slave-owners and beneficiaries of compensation themselves, including Sir Edward Hyde East, Sir James Scarlett (Lord Abinger) and the chancellor of Ireland, Sir Anthony Hart (all born into slave-owning families in the Caribbean), or as representatives of slave-owners, such as Sir Nicholas Conyngham Tindal, the Chief Justice of the Court of Common Pleas, who was awarded two-thirds of the compensation for the Amsterdam estate in British Guiana as the trustee of a slave-owner called James Grant.[22]

Beyond the commercial classes, a number of other professions stand out. There is a striking frequency of senior naval officers among the slave-owners, some surprisingly small scale. In some cases their ownership flowed from their own origins in the slave-economy. Sir William Charles Fahie was born on St Kitts in 1763 and lived almost entirely in the West Indies in his intervals of half-pay and after his retirement, dying in Bermuda in 1833; his widowed daughter Arabella Louisa Burke (whose husband Michael Rowland Burke had died in London in 1831) received slave compensation on St Kitts for nineteen enslaved people.[23] In other cases, slave-ownership came from marriage into the families of slave-owners. Admiral John Carter Allen (who died in 1800) had married Stella Frances Freeman, co-heiress to her brother John Cope Freeman, owner of the Belvidere estate in St Thomas-in-the-East in Jamaica; compensation for the enslaved people was paid to the executors of the widowed Stella Frances Allen, who herself had died in 1821 at Langley House in Hertfordshire, which was sold after her death.[24] Sir Thomas Bladen Capel had married Harriet, the daughter of the absentee Jamaican slave-owner Francis George Smyth of Clifton; Smyth's estates were subject to his own marriage settlement and Capel was awarded the compensation for three enslaved people in St Elizabeth, Jamaica.[25] In a third category, ownership appears to have been a consequence of service in the West Indies station, during which individuals bought enslaved people as domestic servants or even invested directly in estates with larger groups of enslaved people attached. Thus Sir Thomas John Cochrane was awarded compensation for the Good Hope estate in Trinidad as heir-at-law of his father Sir Alexander Inglis Cochrane, who had served in the West Indies both during the American War of Independence and after Trafalgar (Sir Thomas John Cochrane's son was Alexander Dundas Ross Cochrane-Wishart-Baillie, a member of 'Young England').[26]

Another noteworthy concentration within the new professions in the generation after Emancipation was constituted by the connections between the offspring of slave-owning families and the London *Times*. Sir George Webbe Dasent, assistant editor of *The Times* for a quarter of a century from the mid-1840s, was the son of John Roche Dasent and Charlotte Martha Irwin, both St Vincent slave-owners.[27] Thomas Chenery (editor of *The Times* 1877–84, having earlier served as its Crimean correspondent)[28] and Mowbray Morris (its manager 1847–73) were both the sons of slave-owning West India merchants, John Chenery and John Ball Morris respectively.[29] Georgina Frances de Peyronnet, *The Times'* correspondent in Paris during the Franco-Prussian war, was the daughter of George Whitfield, 'a lawyer and West Indian sugar plantation proprietor'; her uncle, Henry James Ross, the trustee under her father's will, was awarded slave compensation for two estates on Grenada and St Vincent on behalf of Georgina Frances and her sister.[30] This nexus around *The Times* appears to have reflected the continued operation of networks of West Indians after the end of slavery.[31] There were other examples of journalists with West Indian connections – Jacob Abraham Franklin, proprietor and editor of the *Voice of Jacob*, was a partner until 1840 in the West India merchant firm established in Manchester in the 1820s by his father[32] – but it is less clear how representative *The Times'* coterie and Franklin were of the nascent profession of journalism as a whole.

Emancipation was an inflexion point in the healing of divisions over slavery within the British elites. Prior to 1834, slave-ownership had not been a consistent obstacle to social acceptance in Britain; it was in general ordinary, unexceptional and unexceptionable unless at times of crisis. Richard 'Conversation' Sharp, the famously well-connected society figure and key mover in the Friends of the People and then in the Whig King of Clubs, was a partner in the West India firm of Boddington, Philips, Sharp & Co., through which he became a mortgagee of enslaved people as well as 'one of London's most prominent merchants' with a reported £250,000 estate on his death in 1835.[33] But, at times of heightened anxiety about slavery, slave-ownership could bring social opprobrium from a vocal minority within and outside the elites. William Alers Hankey said in 1832 that he anticipated the end of slavery not only from the resistance of the enslaved but also from the social consequences for the slave-owners.[34]

Intermarriage had taken place, of course, between slave-owning families and opponents of slavery before Emancipation. In 1798, Favell Lee, sister of the London merchant Richard Lee and daughter of Robert Cooper Lee of Rose Hall, Jamaica and Bedford Square, had married the banker David Bevan, a partner in the Quaker firm of Barclay, Bevan & Co. (although not himself a Quaker); their son Robert Cooper Lee Bevan, born 1809 and bearing the name of his slave-owning grandfather, left almost £1 million at his death.[35] Richard Robert Madden, who served as special magistrate in Jamaica after Emancipation from a mixture of imperial careerism and ideological conviction, had married Harriet, daughter of John Elmslie of Jamaica in 1828.[36] But, among the abolitionists, there were impediments, famously Wilberforce's intervention to oppose the courtship of his daughter by Charles Pinney, the Bristol merchant.[37] After Emancipation, such barriers within the British elite dropped away. Ideological and political fault lines periodically re-emerged, notably over the Eyre crisis, but there is little evidence of social tensions as the identity of slave-owner disappeared and the wealth accrued from slavery lost its taint, just as a generation previously the slave-traders had been similarly cleansed. It is hard to imagine the marriage in 1847 of the evangelical John Griffith with Sarah Francis King, the daughter of a West Indies merchant (and slave-owner) William King and granddaughter of a slave-trader, occurring a generation earlier.[38]

Anxieties about class were freed to trump anxieties about slave-ownership once Emancipation had placed slavery firmly in the past. In his autobiography, Sir (George) Gilbert Scott was at pains to say of his mother that she was 'a particularly lady-like person, a hater of all vulgarity ... well-born, of a good old family ... related to persons of good position'. His mother was Euphemia Lynch (1785–1853), only daughter of Dr Lynch of Antigua 'and connected with the Gilberts, a family of West Indian planters', after whom Sir Gilbert Scott was named.[39] Scott acknowledged that '[m]y mother's family were West Indian. Of the family of her father Dr Lynch of the island of Antigua, I know but little, but her maternal grandfather was the possessor, at that time, of a valuable estate known as "Gilbert's Estate".'[40] The Rev. Thomas Scott of Wappenham (almost certainly Sir Gilbert Scott's father, but conceivably Sir Gilbert's brother) claimed for slave compensation as the sole representative of Elizabeth Gilbert (Euphemia Lynch's aunt and Sir Gilbert's great-aunt, who lived with the family at Gawcott when Sir Gilbert was growing up[41]), for a legacy of £1,800 under the will of Nathaniel Gilbert, Sir Gilbert's maternal great-grandfather.[42] 'She [Elizabeth Gilbert] and my grandmother were provided for by annuities upon their father's estate, then pretty good, but ever diminishing with the decline of West Indian property.'[43]

Absentee slave-owners and their wealth in the nineteenth century

Sir George Gilbert Scott's invocation of 'the decline of West India property' moves us to the wider question of wealth derived from slavery. There are controversies over both the origins of colonial wealth (conceived as systemic not individual wealth) and its progress over time.

Adam Smith (in a passage that itself perhaps reflected a mercantilist conception of wealth as locatable spatially as opposed to arising from relations of exchange) argued that the wealth of Britain 'over-flowed' onto
the colonies; Eric Williams and others argued that wealth extracted from
the labour of the enslaved was a material net contributor to Britain's
national wealth in the seventeenth and eighteenth centuries (although
in Williams' argument slavery later came to be seen not only as a drain
but also as an obstacle to the further development of Britain as the first
industrial nation).

Analysis of wealth at the micro-level can cast light on this debate about
the macro-economic importance of slavery, but not resolve it. Wealth-
generation from slavery for individuals, it seems clear, flowed from the
combination of the expropriation of labour in the colonies and the construction of a protected British market defended by a highly regressive taxation regime, in which the reliance of the state on consumption
taxes such as import duties raised the cost of staples such as sugar and
placed the burden of funding the British state disproportionately on the
poorer classes.[44] Unlike the East India Company, there were no collective
investment vehicles for the slave-economy, no equivalent of East India
Company stock.[45] Wealth therefore accrued to individuals and was held
directly by them. Our prosopographical approach is thus an appropriate
vehicle for analysing West Indian wealth.

Such an analysis of West Indian wealth has been hampered in the past
not only by the lack of comprehensive data but by the persistent efforts
of the slave-owners themselves, reproduced by subsequent commentators. For, in addition to the two conflicting broad narratives of rise and
then secular 'decline' outlined at the beginning of this chapter (the first
pivoted on 1763 or 1783, the second pivoted on 1807), there has been
a third version, sustained by slave-owners themselves, which is a story
of continuous financial difficulty and perennial hardship. This narrative
stresses the fragility, the transience, of slave-derived wealth. It is embedded but implicit in the *ODNB*, which records, for example, that in 1780
the political reformer Joseph Gerrald 'returned to the West Indies in order
to settle his inheritances. His father's extravagances during his lifetime,
however, had reduced the family fortune considerably and Gerrald's
own impulsions on taking possession of the bequest diminished the
estate further.'[46] In 1788, Sir William Young inherited four estates and
£110,000 debt, which eventually overwhelmed his efforts 'to save his
plantations from bankruptcy'.[47] In 1807 came the death of Ralph Payne,
Baron Lavington, whose 'career mirrored the meteoric rise and downfall
of absentee sugar planters in Britain'.[48] 'With the depreciation of West
Indian property in the early years of the nineteenth century, [Ralph]

Willett's collections were dispersed.'[49] In 1818 Henry Goulburn undertook 'vigorous domestic retrenchment' after his 'annual income from
his Jamaican estates halved to somewhere under £3000'.[50] In August
1836, Henry Barkly (who had joined his father Aeneas' West India merchant firm in 1832 and whose mother Susannah Louisa Ffrith was the
orphan daughter of a Jamaica planter) on his father's death 'inherited
both financial obligations towards his two sisters and a failing estate in
British Guiana ... Still in what he believed to be straitened circumstances
from West Indian losses and family obligations, he died ... on 29 October
1898.' As late as 1878, the decline of the West Indian income of Brooke
Lambert 'led to his resignation'.[51]

'West Indian property' (i.e. before 1834 slave-ownership and after
1834 estates almost invariably established originally under slavery)
is thus presented as consistently unreliable, shifting, transitory. The
disproportionate focus of the historiography on Jamaica partly feeds
these tropes, with the building and collapse of the younger William
Beckford's Fonthill Abbey its essential symbol.[52] The risk of West
Indian slave-owning is not in dispute. Slave-derived wealth *was* often
transient. Neither is the reduction in returns from sugar production
in many colonies post-1807 in any doubt.[53] It is clear that the 1846
equalisation of sugar duties significantly affected the sugar economy of
the British colonies of the Caribbean, especially the older colonies of
Jamaica and the Leeward Islands. The prices of plantations and of the
enslaved people upon them were falling in the early nineteenth century
in many colonies. The large presence of metropolitan British merchants
in the slave compensation records testifies to the build-up of debt on
the estates, often advanced by merchants and then secured by mortgage, although prior to Emancipation there were very few claims of
estates making operating losses. There are plenty of examples, however,
of the collapse of absentee West Indian fortunes after Emancipation.
When letters of administration of the estate of Francis George Smyth,
the owner of Goshill and Longhill Pen in St Elizabeth, were granted to
Dame Harriet Capel (the widow of Thomas Bladen Capel, referred to
above) after his death in 1839, his effects were no more than £20. The
will made in 1850 by Charles Nathaniel Bayly, who had married Lady
Sarah Villiers, the daughter of the fourth Earl of Jersey, in 1799 and was
the owner of four estates with almost 850 enslaved people in St Mary,
Jamaica, at the time of Emancipation, is a plaintive account of his fall
from financial grace, recounting that while under his marriage settlement ('now ... little better than a dead letter') he had settled a jointure
of £4,000 per annum on his wife and a £20,000 portion on his children
upon his death

the state of West India property occasioned in the first place by the abolition of slavery and in the next by the admission of foreign slave-grown sugar into British use has not only greatly impoverished me during the latter part of my life but has left me little or nothing to leave to my family from an income varying from 4 to 8000. So great have been the losses on the estate since 1838 ... that I am now reduced to an amount of £300 a year out of which I am obliged to provide for my oldest son and other things, which diminished it to [£]220 and even this I owe to the liberality and may I say charity of my merchant ... Samuel Baker Esq of Fenchurch Street.[54]

The history of the West Indian Encumbered Estates Commission suggests that (other perhaps than the liberality or charity of his merchant), Bayly's experience was not unusual for West Indian owners after the equalisation of the sugar duties from 1846. Established in 1854, the Encumbered Estates court ostensibly was to 'provide protection to West Indian planters and merchants residing in England ... but in actuality the Court served to transfer ownership of estates from the descendants of planters to the British commission houses', through consistent recognition of the priority of the consignee lien – that is, the right of the metropolitan merchant to be a preferred creditor for advances made on the estate.[55] By the end of 1868, the court had sold sixteen estates in Tobago; by the end of 1869, fifty estates in Jamaica; and, 'since 1864', thirty-five in Antigua, in each case mostly to London merchant houses, who increasingly were adopting incorporated status.[56] Ownership thus moved from (absentee and resident) individuals to (absentee) companies. At the same time many British merchants diversified away from the old sugar colonies.

But in Barbados the process of increasing corporate control was resisted politically and economically by resident planters.[57] And, in British Guiana and Trinidad, the Encumbered Estates Act did not apply at all. Nevertheless, narratives such as Charles Nathaniel Bayly's are established tropes that reflect the lived experience of many slave-owners after Emancipation (as the Encumbered Estates Commission Records make clear) but have come to stand for them all. However, material from the late eighteenth and early nineteenth centuries and, especially, the evidence of the slave compensation records also point to continued wealth-generation for other slave-owners. Anthony Morris Storer's fortunes had recovered after the American Revolution, and he left property worth £8,000 annually to his nephew Anthony Gilbert Storer.[58] The MP and collector Ralph Bernal spent a total of £66,000 on elections between 1815 and 1852 'after inheriting a large estate in the West Indies'; his granddaughter, the daughter of Ralph Bernal Osborne (also an MP and politician) married the tenth Duke of St Albans in 1874.[59]

The expectation of hardship and a predisposition to emphasise the difficulties faced by the slave-economy can make it hard to read the historical record when the evidence actually points to such continued generation of wealth under 'late slavery'. Alan Karras, for example, used the correspondence of Dr Colin MacLarty to record MacLarty's struggle to buy into a medical practice in Kingston in the 1790s, concluding, '[i]t is unclear how successful Colin MacLarty was ... no record of him has been found in the island's estate inventories, so it seems unlikely that he left property in the island when he died', and suggesting that MacLarty is an example of the export of capital from Britain to the colonial economy.[60] In fact, in 1819 'Dr Colin McLarty of Chestervale in the Island of Jamaica' (who was then residing in Sanda, later Macharioch, House, Kintyre, Scotland) had bought the estate of Samuel Omey at Keil, Kintyre, and substantially 'improved' it prior to his death in 1835.[61] MacLarty was awarded the slave compensation for the enslaved people on Chestervale as owner-in-fee in the year of his death, when it was paid to his acting executor.[62] Karras' narrative supports Adam Smith's argument that the wealth of Britain spilt over onto the colonies, but the whole story points rather to the generation of capital in the slave-economy itself, capital then returned to Britain.

Nor did wealth-generation from the colonial plantation economy cease upon Emancipation, or even with the removal of colonial preference, although it certainly became harder for the estate-owner than previously. This wealth, too, is in some real sense among the legacies of slavery. The markets the former slave-colonies served, above all the mass consumption of sugar, were the fruits of slavery. The estates, the production units, were generally constructed and planted in the years of slavery, and themselves represent major 'legacies of slave-ownership' in the colonies. Relations of production changed to wage labour and in certain colonies to indentured labour, in the movements of which former slave-owners were often prominent. Continuities of ownership are evident, even as ownership migrated slowly and partially from families to firms after Emancipation.[63]

Where there was such continuity of family ownership pre- and post-Emancipation, the legacy appears clear enough, even where the West Indian property was transmitted indirectly. Aretas Akers-Douglas, first Viscount Chilston, Tory chief whip in Salisbury's two governments between 1885 and 1892 and Balfour's Home Secretary 1902–5, inherited Chilston Park and land in Scotland, as well as his amended name, from James Douglas of Baads in 1875. Akers himself was descended from 'six generations of sugar planters and slave owners', as the *ODNB* comments with unusual candour,[64] but the Douglas legacy as well derived from the slave-ownership of George Douglas, who died in 1833. George Douglas left Chilston to his adopted daughter Margaret and her husband James Douglas Stoddart, who changed his name to James Douglas Stoddart Douglas and eventually James Douglas of Baads, and under his will, after the failure of both the Douglas line and that of George Douglas' nephew and niece Alexander and Elizabeth Houstoun-Douglas, George Douglas' estate passed to his cousin Aretas Akers.[65] Again, the Arctic yachtsman Sir James Lamont resigned from the army in 1849 'when his uncle left him a fortune'.[66] His uncle, John Lamont of Trinidad, had gone out as an overseer, then became a manager before becoming a proprietor himself, being awarded compensation for the enslaved people on the Canaan and River estates.[67] Sir George Benvenuto Buckley-Mathew, politician and diplomat, added the name Buckley in 1865 'on inheriting West Indian estates'.[68] The *ODNB* is silent on the nature of the inheritance but it was of Buckley's estate in St Kitts as well as land in Britain at The Lyth, Ellesmere, Shropshire from his kinsman Abednego Mathew.[69]

But in some cases, estate ownership in the Caribbean was entered into after Emancipation by those who had had only a toehold in slave-ownership beforehand. The artist, illustrator and collector Charles Paget Wade, son of Paget Augustus Wade and grandson of Solomon Abraham Wade, in 1911 'inherited a substantial interest in the family sugar estates, enabling him to devote the rest of his life to his own pursuits'.[70] Family ownership of the estates appears to have followed Emancipation. Solomon Abraham Wade, a dry-goods merchant on St Kitts, received slave compensation for nine enslaved people (his sisters were awarded compensation for thirteen more) and left £7,279 in personalty in England when he died at Beckenham, Kent, in 1881. His son Paget Augustus Wade was a partner in Sendall and Wade 'Colonial and West India merchants and shippers and agents for sellers of West India produce at 34 Fenchurch Street' and left personalty of £31,077.[71] The family thus appears to have taken advantage of the dislocation of Emancipation and its aftermath to buy estates, from which, in conjunction with its mercantile business in the post-slavery West Indian economy, it repatriated profits to England as capital accumulation. Charles Paget Wade's house Snowshill Manor is now a National Trust property; it is in essence conceived to be a legacy of slavery and of slave-ownership, but the descent is indirect and needs to be appropriately contextualised.[72] The origins of Booker Brothers, which came to dominate the Guyanese sugar industry until nationalisation in the 1970s, were similar.[73]

In order to provide a more systematic framework for analysing this whole problem of slave-derived wealth, we have cross-referenced our database with the work of William D. Rubinstein, which records all those dying in Britain after 1809 who left personalty of at least £100,000.[74] Individuals have been included in five categories: those rentiers whose overall wealth was significantly dependent on slave-ownership and those merchants whose overall wealth was significantly dependent upon the slave-economy and who owned or held mortgages over enslaved people; those who owned enslaved people but for whom slave-ownership appears to have been an ancillary form of wealth; those who married into slave-owning families; those who were the children of slave-owners or who had inherited wealth from slave-owners, slave-traders or merchants primarily involved in the slave-economy; and those who were not slave-owners but derived their wealth from activities directly connected with slavery, including slave-traders such as William Parry of London, but most notably in this period from the cotton industry, as manufacturers or merchants.[75] It is important to note that we have recorded *all* cotton brokers and merchants under the category of slavery-related wealth (because of the difficulty of differentiating individual patterns of cotton-sourcing), whereas slave-grown cotton accounted for five-sixths, rather than the whole, of Britain's cotton imports in the seven decades before the American Civil War.[76]

In some cases, individuals would qualify under more than one criterion (but are included only once) in this analysis of the Victorian rich. For example, Henry Metcalfe Ames is included by virtue of his marriage into the Cadogan family of Brinkburn Priory, bought in 1825 by the slave-owner Ward Cadogan, whose widow and son-in-law were awarded compensation for the enslaved people on the Pickering and Crab Hill estates in Barbados and whose granddaughter was Ames' wife; Ames might equally have been classified as a child and heir, or as other slave-related, by virtue of his own descent from the Bristol mercantile and banking dynasty with roots in the sugar and provisioning trades.[77]

Clearly we have exercised a degree of judgement in classifying a number of people, especially in relation to the materiality to individuals of slave-ownership and slavery. In general we are extremely sceptical of James Walvin's formulation that people were not rich because they were slave-owners but slave-owners because they were rich.[78] Very few people invested in slave-ownership as a portfolio investment: mostly, they invested because they were already aligned with the slave-economy and participating in it in various ways, as were the Lascelles, on whom Walvin's aphorism was based. However, in the case of the Dundas family, the original acquisition by Sir Laurence Dundas of Kerse (1712–81) of estates in Grenada and Dominica appears to have been part of a much wider programme of purchase of real estate and financial assets (including a major holding of East India Company stock) from the proceeds

Table 2.1 *Individuals with slave-derived wealth dying between 1809 and 1874.*

A	B	C	D	E	F	G	H
1809–19	235	7 rentiers; 8 merchants	3–4	4		12–18	34–41
1820–9	307	10 rentiers; 14–17 merchants	1	2–3		19–24	46–55
1830–9	359	9–10 rentiers; 9–10 merchants	5	5–7		15–22	43–54
1840–9	357	9 rentiers; 9–10 merchants	4	12	0–1	35–40	69–76
1850–9	442	9 rentiers; 12–15 merchants	3	7–8	8–9	35–52	74–96
1860–9	777	3 rentiers; 18–21 merchants	3–4	12–13	25–6	54–74	115–141
1870–4	640	3 rentiers; 6–7 merchants	5	8	13–14	61–92	96–129

A: Years
B: Number of people dying and leaving £100,000 or more
C: Number from column B for whom slave-owning was the primary source of wealth
D: Number from column B for whom slave-owning was an ancillary form of wealth
E: Number from column B who married into slave-owning families
F: Number of children or heirs of slave-owners (after 1850)
G: Number from column B in other slave-related activities (e.g. cotton trading or manufacture)
H: Total individuals with slave-derived wealth

of army contracting. One of the estates, Dougalston in Grenada, was passed to Sir Laurence's grandchildren, first to the naval officer George Heneage Lawrence Dundas and then to his brother and heir Lawrence Dundas, first Earl of Zetland, who was awarded the compensation for the enslaved people upon it in 1835. But slave-ownership does not appear to have been the central driver of the family's wealth.[79]

The numbers presented in Table 2.1 are ranges, which are particularly wide in the final category, those in slave-related activities. In a handful of cases this reflects uncertainty over the identity of the individual, but in the vast majority of cases it reflects uncertainty over the degree of importance of slave-derived wealth within a wider portfolio of activity or the precise nature of an individual's economic activity. Hence merchants trading with Brazil – a slave-economy throughout the period – are included in the higher number but not in the lower one, unless the commodity in which they dealt is known and is also known to have been exclusively or primarily slave-produced in this period (e.g. coffee). The lower number should thus be regarded as a firm number and the higher number as including all 'possibles'; the truth lies at a currently indeterminable point between the two.

There are general issues in using the probate data to address 'wealth' that are addressed in Appendix I. But there are particular issues relating to slave-owners. The first is the obvious one of periodisation: neither our data nor Rubinstein's work capture the slave-owners of the peak of the slave-system in the eighteenth century, unless they transmitted both enslaved people and personalty to people who do appear in Rubinstein's universe and in our database. The second limitation is the measure of wealth: the criterion is *personalty in Britain* – that is, non-real property in the metropole. Estates in the slave-colonies are doubly excluded, as real estate and as lying outside the 'province' (the jurisdiction of the clerical court): the enslaved people themselves, classed as personalty (as chattels) in most colonial jurisdictions, were similarly excluded as lying overseas – that is, outside the province. Hence, when Sir Simon Richard Brissett Taylor of Great Cumberland Place, London, the heir of his uncle Simon Taylor and supposedly the richest commoner in Britain, died in 1815, his personalty was valued at £100,000 'within province'; but, when his uncle (who lived and died in Jamaica and therefore falls outside the universe of both Rubinstein and ourselves) had died two years before, the 2,138 enslaved people alone on his Jamaican sugar estates and pens had been valued at £124,578 and his overall personalty in Jamaica at £226,609 (of which almost £200,000 was directly located on the estates and pens inherited by Sir Simon Richard Brissett Taylor).[80]

Hence, absentee slave-owners face a higher hurdle than other holders of non-landed wealth in Britain in order to be classified as 'wealthy': in order to appear in Rubinstein's lists, they needed to have converted a sufficient proportion of slave-derived wealth in the colonies into non-landed wealth in Britain by the time they died. Accordingly, the Rubinstein data exclude an unknown number of wealthy individuals dying in Britain whose wealth lay primarily in land and people in the slave-colonies. Given that slave-owners had a higher propensity to retain their colonial property (i.e. their slave-estates) on return (or moving) to Britain – by contrast with, for example, East India Company men whose wealth had been accumulated in service rather than physical assets in India – the figures in the table are likely to present a conservative estimate of the proportion of very wealthy men and women with slave-derived wealth.

With these provisos, the data in the table contain some important evidence for the significance of slave-derived wealth. First, for the whole period, the data suggest that between 8 and 8.5 per cent of all individuals dying in Britain between 1809 and 1874 and leaving at least £100,000 in personalty were slave-owners (or mortgagees of enslaved people), married into the families of slave-owners (or mortgagees) or were direct heirs of slave-owners (or mortgagees).[81] Second, a further 7 to 10 per cent in total were not slave-owners but derived their wealth from activities directly related to the slave-economy. Hence, around one in six of the wealthiest non-landed Britons of the first three-quarters of the nineteenth century had been embroiled in the slave-economy.[82]

This appears striking in at least two respects. For a source of wealth that has been essentially invisible in the history of nineteenth-century Britain, slavery appears to have made rather a significant contribution to the overall wealth of individuals. And, for an institution that had been finally dismantled by 1838 in the British colonies and placed firmly in the past tense, slave-derived wealth in Britain shows a notable resilience throughout a period in which the number of sources of wealth was increasing rapidly with the diversification of the economy from iron and cotton to a broader base of manufacturing and consumer industries.[83] In every decade, the total proportion of wealth attributed to slavery fluctuated within a fairly narrow band between 15 and 20 per cent.

This is not to say that the *composition* of slave-related wealth remained constant. After Emancipation, no new slave-owners were being created, so as time passed the population of slave-owners by definition died off. Wealth derived from slave-ownership was transmitted between generations (and in some cases new wealth was being created from legacies of slave-ownership) so that, as the last generation of slave-owners died off, it was replaced by its children and heirs, to an extent that is perhaps surprising given the accepted wisdom that 'West India property' was uniquely fragile. At the same time, the balance between slave-owners and their families on the one hand and other slave-related wealth on the other did alter as the British economy grew. The same number of 'core' rich slave-owners, about twenty, died in each decade, but the number of rich people overall dying increased sharply from around 1850 onwards, as did the number of fortunes made in slave-related businesses, especially cotton. The diminishing proportion of 'core' former slave-owners was an arithmetic inevitability.

The aggregate levels, however, have great value in establishing for the first time an explicit set of measures of slave-derived wealth (and within that, a narrower set of measures of wealth derived from slave-ownership specifically) in nineteenth-century Britain. There might be debate, as noted above, as to the classification of particular individuals, but the empirical data and its limitations are at least now there for examination, in large part because of Rubinstein's foundational work on the rich. Nevertheless, in many cases the specific workings of the wealth remain opaque. *Prima facie*, many of the rich individuals who married members of slave-owning families (especially male aristocrats marrying female members of slave-owning families) will have become or remained rich in part because of their access to slave-wealth through marriage settlements and legacies to their spouses, but we have not to date been able to demonstrate how many and how much. Family fortunes differ, too, in ways that remain unclear at present. James Law Stewart and Robert Stewart were both the sons of the Hon. James Stewart of Jamaica. James Law Stewart, the older son, died in 1869 leaving £600; Robert Stewart died in 1881, leaving over £113,000 in personalty. Both inherited slave-property and were awarded slave compensation. Neither appears to have had a profession. The disparity in their fortunes can only be reconciled by detailed work dependent on sources yet to be identified: all we can do is to highlight such cases for further work.

Cultural legacies I: philanthropy and institutions

Given the evidence of a richer and more resilient set of former slave-owners than previously was understood to exist, the remainder of this chapter explores some of the legacies of these slave-owners.

Education

The presence of West Indians as pupils at established British public schools and universities in the eighteenth and early nineteenth centuries has long been recognised. At least sixty of the slave-owners in the 1830s were educated at Eton and some two dozen at Harrow. Among the slave-owners for whom we have details of tertiary education, over a hundred had matriculated at each of Oxford and Cambridge. However, the decades spanning Emancipation also saw the formation of new institutions at secondary and tertiary levels, and slave-owners figured in the foundation, funding and development of these new schools and universities, both in England and Scotland.[84]

The nature of these legacies differs. Slave-owners had represented about ten per cent of the subscribers to King's College London in 1828, and William Manning served as one of the early Council members.[85] By contrast, relatively few of the founders of or subscribers to University College had been slave-owners, although the first council members included the mortgagee of enslaved people John Smith of Payne, Smith and Smith, and the slave-owner the Earl of Dudley.[86] A number of early professors, however, were from slave-owning families at each institution, most famously Edward Turner (1796–1837), inaugural professor of chemistry at University College and son of Dutton Smith Turner and his wife Mary Gale Turner née Redwar. An eminent scientist and author of 'one of the best of all nineteenth-century textbooks of chemistry', *Elements of Chemistry* (1827), Turner was involved in the compensation process as he held power of attorney for his brother William Dutton Turner.[87]

Among legacies at the secondary level, as part of the expansion of the public school system for a new middle class, St John's Leatherhead was founded in 1851 by the Rev. Ashby Haslewood of St Mark's Hamilton Terrace, St John's Wood in London; it moved several times before its final removal to Leatherhead, which was made possible by Henry Dawes, who gave £2,500 for the purchase of the land for the school at Leatherhead in 1867. The Henry Dawes Centre, the school's new classroom block named after the nineteenth-century donor, was opened in October 2010 by HRH The Duchess of Gloucester, the school's patron.[88] Henry Dawes was an East India Company servant who in the early 1820s inherited the Tufton Hall estate in Grenada from his brothers, and he was awarded the compensation for the ninety enslaved people on it in 1835.[89] This appears a relatively straightforward case of the move of money into Britain from imperial sources, but generated in unknown proportions between colonial slavery in the West Indies and colonial rule in India.

A more complex case is that of the Rev. David Laing, the secretary of the Governesses' Benevolent Institution from 1843 and a founder of Queen's College, Harley Street in 1848. Among the first attendees at Queen's College were Dorothea Beale (later principal of Cheltenham Ladies College for almost fifty years from 1858 until her death and founder of St Hilda's College [as St Hilda's Hall], Oxford[90]) and Frances Mary Buss, the founder (with her mother) and subsequently head of North London Collegiate School for over forty years from 1850. The latter 'was strongly influenced by the ideas and concerns of the Rev. David Laing (1800–60) … Laing as vicar of Holy Trinity, Haverstock Hill, taught divinity there [at North London Collegiate] and was a close adviser until his death.'[91] Frances Mary Buss established six Laing scholarships offering free education in his memory.[92] Laing, then, was deeply entwined in the birth of women's education in Britain. He was also the son and son-in-law of Jamaican slave-owners. He had been baptised at Marylebone on 29 October 1800, the son of David and Mary Laing.[93] David Laing senior died the same year. In 1817 and 1820 George Kinghorn, as attorney of the trustees of David Laing (Mary Laing, John West and Alexander Henry), registered thirty-three enslaved people in St George on their behalf: the enslaved people had been leased out in 1807 for seven years to Dugald Thomas and then recovered by Kinghorn; in

1820 they were leased to Thomas Pickersgill. The Rev. David Laing married Mary Elizabeth West, the daughter of another Jamaican slave-owner (John West), in 1824. Laing himself was awarded compensation for the Mount Lebanus estate in Jamaica as trustee with his brother-in-law the Rev. John West.[94] Laing signed at the National Debt Office for the compensation awarded to John West for the enslaved people on Betty's Hope in St Thomas-in-the-East (the Rev. John West was shown as the owner of Betty's Hope in 1817).[95]

Philanthropy

Williams established the nexus between slavery and philanthropy for the eighteenth century; examples such as James Dick's bequest clearly show the movement of money made in the colonial slave-economy into charitable activity in the metropole.[96] This continued in the nineteenth century. The Thomson Hankey charity was established in January 1854 by Thomson Hankey senior, who endowed it with £10,000 for the benefit of the widows, sons and daughters of Church of England clergymen 'being in poor circumstances'.[97] The charity continued until 1994. In 1808, 'owing to a heavy loss of property in the West Indies', Sir William Hillary, the son of a Quaker West India merchant in Liverpool, moved from Danbury Place in Essex to the Isle of Man, where he witnessed a number of wrecks. Hillary's pamphlet of February 1823, *An Appeal*, drew a response from George Hibbert and Thomas Wilson, and led to the foundation of the Royal National Institution for the Preservation of Life from Shipwreck (from 1854 the Royal National Lifeboat Institution).[98] The residue of Hillary's property in Jamaica (where his elder brother Richard, a member of the House of Assembly, died in 1803) is discernible in the slave compensation records, in the suits in the local courts of Hillary *v.* Winn and Hibbert *v.* Hillary, into which the compensation for the Adelphi estate in St James was paid. William Mackinnon, an MP and slave-owner who was entitled to one-third of the profits from the estate in Antigua bearing his name under the marriage settlement, chaired the SPCA (now the RSPCA, founded in 1824 by a group including Wilberforce) and said in 1837: 'I cannot but think that benevolence to our species, and humanity to the brute creation, go hand in hand, and that it is impossible for an individual to possess the one virtue without also possessing the other.'[99] Eleanora Atherton 'inherited the cumulative riches of her forebears, and became a prolific but unostentatious philanthropist'.[100] Her inheritance included both Manchester property and enslaved people in Jamaica, which she and her sister inherited from their uncle William Atherton of Jamaica. Eleanora Atherton and her brother-in-law Richard Willis were awarded half the compensation for Spring Vale Pen in St James and Green Park in Trelawny. After *in vivo* gifts estimated at £100,000 between 1838 and 1870 (including the building of Holy Trinity Church, Hulme, for £18,000 and the almshouses at Prescot for £10,000), she left £400,000 on her death, making her one of the richest British women of the nineteenth century.

John Kenyon appears through his patronage to be an exemplary absentee figure in the dissemination of money from slave-ownership into wider literary and cultural spheres, but the case also illustrates the difficulty of isolating wealth from slave-ownership. Kenyon was born in Jamaica and inherited Chester estate in Trelawney, Jamaica, for the enslaved people upon which he was paid slave compensation in two tranches in 1835 and 1836. His *in vivo* gifts are not known, but, after his death in 1856, *The Times* reported that

many a literary home has been made brighter this Christmas time by the noble sympathy of John Kenyon, the poet, whose death we recently announced. The poet was as rich as he was genial. Scarcely a man or woman distinguished in the world of letters with which he was familiar has passed unremembered in his will, and some poets and children of poets are endowed with a princely munificence. Among those who have shared most liberally in this harvest of goodwill we are happy to hear that Mr & Mrs Browning receive 10,000l, Mr Proctor (Barry Cornwall) 6000l and Dr Southey a very handsome sum, we think 8000l. We hear that there are eight legatees many of them the old literary friends of the deceased poet.

It added more details a month later, including £100 to Walter Savage Landor, £20,000 to Kenyon's executor Thomas Hawthorne and £5,000 to London University Hospital.[101] In total he left £180,000. Clearly his own fortune was derived from slave-ownership. Yet Kenyon is also known to have inherited part of his brother-in-law John Curteis' estate on the latter's death in 1849. Curteis was the last of his family, who had been London brewers; his father, also John, died in 1786 and his grandfather Thomas in 1787.[102]

Societies and clubs

Slave-owners participated in the formation of new cultural and social institutions of male sociability, as well as in the informal networks.[103] George Hibbert was also one of three London slave-owners among the first three dozen members of the Roxburghe Club, 'the oldest society of bibliophiles in the world'.[104] The Hon. Archibald Macdonald – who had married Jane, daughter and co-heiress of the slave-owner Duncan Campell of Ardneave, and who with his brother-in-law the Prince de

Polignac was the beneficiary of the compensation awarded to trustees of their marriage settlements for three estates on St Vincent – was a founding member of Arthur's, the first West End members' (as opposed to proprietary) club in 1811, the building for which is now the Carlton Club at 69–70 St James's Street.[105] The circle around John Sterling evolved into the Sterling Club in 1838. Sterling, an early Apostle at Cambridge and the subject of a biography by Thomas Carlyle after his death in 1844, had inherited a share in the Colonarie Vale estate on St Vincent and the 305 enslaved people tied to it from his uncle Walter Coningham.[106] The Roxburgh Club, Arthur's and the Sterling Club were elite metropolitan institutions, aimed at a select fraction of London society, but slave-owners also contributed to the foundation of organisations with wider and deeper reach, including the London Institution and the Liverpool Literary and Philosophical Society, which was co-founded in 1812 by Thomas Stewart Traill and Joseph Brooks Yates, who served as president for twelve years. The latter was a major mercantile figure, 'one of the leading reformers of Liverpool', and a significant mortgagee and slave-owner in Jamaica.[107] The early organisation of competitive chess features the slave-owners Alexander Macdonnell[108] and George Webb Medley as *de facto* British national champions. Generational transfers of wealth also supported the foundation of new institutions. William John Charles Moens, the son of Jacob Bernelot Moens (b. 1796), a Dutch West Indies merchant and slave-owner, was one of the twelve founders of the Huguenot Society.[109]

By contrast, the City livery companies or the freemasons were pre-existing institutions in which slave-ownership was inscribed because slave-owners were part of the elites from which membership was drawn: slave-ownership was not constitutive, in other words. In the Mercers' Company, the senior livery company, the West Indian merchant Edmund Francis Green (who later committed suicide) was Master in 1824, while later Masters included the East Indian merchants George Palmer (Master in 1820) and John Horsley Palmer (Master in 1826), who were recipients of slave compensation as mortgagees with Lestock Peach Wilson of Upper Lataute estate and as mortgagees-in-possession with William Jocelyn Palmer and Ralph Palmer of Springs and Mount Aire estates, all on Grenada. Together with Lestock Peach Wilson, the Palmers were awarded a total of £6,488 for 228 enslaved people on the three estates.[110]

Cultural legacies II: collections and connoisseurship

Recent scholarship has asserted or reasserted the links between eighteenth-century aesthetic sensibility and slavery in the Caribbean.[111]

Whether or not these arguments are accepted, the evidence appears irrefutable that British slave-owners participated at least proportionately in
the cultural accumulation by Britons that began in the early eighteenth
century but that was greatly accelerated by the destabilisation of continental European aristocracies by the French Revolution and its aftermath. As Chapter 6 shows, George Hibbert was a prime mover in this
form of opportunism but was also an example of a wider characteristic of
slave-owners. As with Hibbert's, few collections appear to have survived
intact, often dispersed in the immediate aftermath of the death of the
collector. Ralph Bernal, an MP and Jamaican slave-owner, was a serial
collector whose Dutch paintings were auctioned in 1824 but whose collection of glass, pottery and porcelain was sought in vain for the nation
by the Society of Arts after Bernal's death in 1854.[112] Joseph Marryat
the younger, West India merchant and pioneer of the iron industry in
South Wales, was also a connoisseur of china, and wrote an early authoritative guide.[113] The paintings of John Proctor Anderdon, a West India
merchant originally of Bristol and then London who owned 180 people
on Seaforth's in Antigua at the time of compensation, were dispersed
in 1847, and included Andrea del Sarto's *Charity* (now in the National
Gallery of Art Washington), which Anderdon had bought from Prince
Rospigliosi in Rome in 1827.[114] James Hughes Anderdon, John Proctor's
son and himself a recipient of slave compensation for 358 enslaved people
as one of the partners in the banking firm of Bosanquet Anderdon (a
predecessor firm of Lloyds Bank), acquired John Constable's *Malvern
Hall Warwickshire* (now in Tate Britain) in 1840; he also donated a large
number of drawings to the British Museum and a smaller number to
the Royal Academy.[115] Sir Simon Haughton Clarke's library was sold in
1840.[116] Philip John Miles in 1813 bought the collection of Old Masters
formed by the Bristol MP Richard Hart Davies, and added to it subsequently, especially from the collection of Henry Hope. His collection was
dispersed in two sales by Christies in 1884 (by Sir Philip Miles) and on
13 May 1899 (after the death of Sir Cecil Miles).[117]

However, some major collections reflexively associated with slavery,
notably the National Gallery and the Tate Gallery, are not the fruits of
slave-ownership, although both have various links with slavery that need
to be teased out. The collection formed by John Julius Angerstein and
purchased from (not donated by) his estate in 1824 was the foundation
of the National Gallery, and he is today frequently presented simply
as a slave-owner.[118] Recently, it has been argued that Angerstein sold
the estates that came with his marriage and that his continuing ownership was as a trustee.[119] His real link with slavery lies in the role of
maritime insurance and especially Lloyd's, where he made his fortune,

in underwriting the slave-trade. Neither slave-ownership nor the nexus of insurance and the slave-trade are mentioned in Angerstein's *ODNB* entry.[120] Henry Tate, whose collection formed the basis of the Tate Gallery (now the Tate Britain), was thirteen years old when slavery was abolished in the British colonies. The argument for tying his legacy to slavery must therefore proceed either from the general (and valid) assertion that the sugar economy as a whole and Britain's market for sugar in particular had developed from a slave-based system or from evidence of the consumption of slave-grown sugar from Brazil and Cuba in his refineries in Britain in the period from the early 1860s to the 1880s, when slavery was finally abolished in Brazil and Cuba.

Cultural legacies III: religious institutions and churches

The overwhelmingly Anglican nature of the slave-owners has been confirmed by the new data. 'Anglican' of course might be a default setting, but there is plenty of evidence of active engagement in the established church. There are over a hundred Anglican clergymen identified in the compensation process in capacities from owner-in-fee to trustee, including the slave-owners Renn Dickson Hampden,[121] later bishop of Hereford (owner of one enslaved person, presumably a domestic servant), and the Rev. Stephen Isaacson.[122] Stephen Isaacson was an anti-abolition polemicist who had been rector of St Paul's in Demerara and married the daughter of a slave-owner in Barbados. He was curate at Dorking, Surrey, at the time of Emancipation, when he was awarded the compensation for three enslaved people in Barbados and initially for a further single enslaved person in British Guiana, where the commissioners requested the return of the money after he was accused of mendacity. Both lay and clerical Anglican slave-owners bequeathed physical legacies to the Church. After the death of his sister Catherine Elizabeth Hyndman in June 1835, John Beckles Hyndman (a slave-owner in British Guiana and the father of the pioneering British Marxist H. M. Hyndman) provided £150,000 for the building of Anglican churches ('As low as possible') through the Hyndman Trustees. The Rev. John James Scott, son of two Jamaican slave-owning families and inheritor of the Clarendon Park estate there, spent £10,000 building the parish church of Holy Trinity at Barnstaple in Devon in the 1840s.[123]

Awareness of the minority of non-conformists among slave-owners was established by Eric Williams in his identification of the Unitarian Robert Hibbert, and there was a wider dissenting mercantile network in Manchester (including Sir George Philips from a family prominent among the trustees of Cross Street Chapel) linked to the Hibberts by marriage.[124] The commoditisation of slavery through annuities and legacies brought even Quaker abolitionists into the orbit of slavery, such as Alexander & Co., bankers of Ipswich, who claimed as assignees of an annuity of £200 on New Montpelier in St James, Jamaica.[125] James Barton Nottage of Lancaster, a merchant dealing with the Virgin Islands, appears to have been disowned by the Quakers in 1803.[126]

There are threads tying some slave-owners to the Catholic revival in England. Cardinal Manning's father, of course, was the West India merchant and mortgagee of enslaved people William Manning, but at least as important an influence on Henry Edward Manning was his brother-in-law John Lavicount Anderdon (also a partner with William Manning), his 'first real mentor', an example of 'industry and disciplined will-power' whose 'lively evangelical faith' greatly influenced the future cardinal. John Lavicount Anderdon's own son, William Henry Anderdon, trained as an Anglican priest but in 1850 converted to Catholicism, acted as his uncle's secretary for several years after 1863 and took first vows as a Jesuit in 1874.[127] Some legacies of John Hubert Washington Hibbert's Catholicism are discussed in Chapter 6.

There is no evidence of a disproportionate presence of Jews among the absentee slave-owners.[128] There are certainly Jewish London merchants (often connected to networks in Kingston, Jamaica) in the compensation records, but of the 200 London merchants there are no more than a dozen readily identifiable as Jewish. These include Emanuel Lousada, the High Sheriff of Devon 1842–3, 'apparently the first professing Jew to be made a provincial High Sheriff', who left £100,000 in 1855.[129] Judah Cohen of Mansell Street, an established West India merchant, was awarded the compensation in forty-five separate awards in Jamaica, many of them assigned to him by Nathan Joseph of Kingston: Nathan Joseph was almost certainly dealing in compensation claims. Henry Hyman Cohen (given as Henry Hymen Cohen in the compensation records), a partner in Henry H. Cohen of London and of H. & D. Cohen of Kingston, played a role in the administration of the Great Synagogue in the early 1840s but, by contrast to Emanuel Lousada, left only £50 on his death in 1865.[130] There were assimilated Jewish rentiers too among the slave-owners, including the MP Ralph Bernal and probably including the Franks family of Isleworth, whose representative Priscilla Franks died in 1823 leaving £400,000 and the Duckenfield Hall estate, bequeathed to her niece Lady Isabella Cooper. Finally, slave-owners and their children sometimes touched the wilder shores of religion. Henry James Prince, the founder of the Agapemonites, was the youngest son of Thomas Prince (1745–1816), a West Indian plantation owner.[131]

Physical legacies

Land in the metropole was predictably the destination for much West
India money since the beginning of British colonial slavery exemplified
in the history of the Drax family. In the 1690s, 'Col. Henry Drax was
looking for an estate of £10,000 p.a.' and he bought Ellerton Abbey near
Selby, Yorkshire, in the North Riding. His great-nephew Henry Drax
(who died in 1755) married an heiress, the only daughter of Sir Henry
Ernle and granddaughter of Sir Thomas Erle of Charborough, Dorset,
which became the Drax family seat. In 1768, the family had estates in
Lincolnshire (their original home), Dorset, Wiltshire, Yorkshire and
Barbados, where Drax Hall was the origins of the family fortune.[132] At
the time of Emancipation, the estate was held by John Samuel Wanley
Sawbridge Erle-Drax, who had married Jane Frances Erle-Drax and taken
her name. Their granddaughter Ernle Elizabeth Louisa Maria Grosvenor
Burton married John William Plunkett, seventeenth Baron Dunsany
(1853–99), and had in turn two sons, both in the *ODNB*, Edward John
Morton Drax Plunkett, eighteenth Baron Dunsany,[133] and Sir Reginald
Aylmer Ranfurly Plunkett-Ernle-Erle-Drax,[134] who took the additional
names on inheriting his mother's estates. In Scotland too, returning slave-
owners sought out land. The family of Sir James Grant of Grant between
1774 and 1785 sold sections of their estates in Inverness and Moray for
over £52,500 to near relations and to kinsmen 'returning from successful
careers in the East and West Indies'.[135] The difference between the latter
two types of career in this context was that generally the East Indians
retired from office and returned home with no continuing real property
in India, whereas the West Indians often retained their property in the
Caribbean at the same time as building up land in Britain.[136]

The eighteenth century is the classic period for locating the embodi-
ment of colonial wealth – East as well as West Indian – in the country
house, symbolised by Harewood House, which stands in the literature
for an unknown number of properties of which it is supposed to be representative. But the reworking of wealth into the purchase of land and the
purchase or building of country houses continued into the nineteenth
century. In analysing the landed estates in Britain and the country houses
built upon them, there are issues of classification and materiality to distinguish between the hundreds of such sites associated with nineteenth-
century slave-owners.[137] There appears to be a difference in the kind of
legacy represented by, for example, Camerton Court, built to designs of
George Repton by the former slave-owner John Jarrett in 1838–40 (the
family's money was indisputably from slavery); Peckforton Castle, built
by John Tollemache (né Halliday) at the cost of £60,000 in the 1840s,

the owner of six estates in Antigua for which he was awarded £12,000 in compensation, but also the inheritor of landed wealth in Britain;[138] and Lacock Abbey, where the slave-owner and MP John Rock Grosett was a long-term tenant rather than owner in the 1820s.

Centres of new forms of leisure were developed by slave-owners. Emanuel Lousada, noted above as a Jewish mercantile slave-owner, was the major developer of Sidmouth, where he lived at Peake House until his death in 1855.[139] Philanthropy took physical form, as it did with Eleanora Atherton's almshouses, or the Town Hall, almshouses and cemetery in Larne in County Antrim, Northern Ireland, which all bear the name of the slave-owner Charles McGarel. Anglican slave-owners built churches, as Eleanora Atherton and John Beckles Hyndman did, as noted previously. William Hudson Heaven purchased the island of Lundy in the Bristol Channel shortly after receiving compensation for four estates in Hanover, Jamaica, and developed the island as a private family retreat, building Millcombe House there. He continued to identify himself as a 'landowner and West India planter' until his death. He was the son of Thomas Heaven of Bristol, who had been in partnership as a wool wholesaler in the 1790s.[140] William Hudson Heaven inherited the Jamaican estates from his namesake William Hudson, presumably a relative by marriage or godfather, who died before 1811.[141]

Physical legacies might also be less direct. John Innes (1786–1869) was a West Indian merchant of Mincing Lane and Moorgate Street whose career spanned the slavery and post-slavery eras. He had been in partnership with Nathaniel Winter (who died in 1824) and was one of the Committee appointed in 1826 by London-based 'proprietors and mortgagees of estates' to oppose compulsory manumission (one of the key planks of amelioration) in Demerara and Berbice.[142] He was bankrupt in February 1833.[143] He appears, however, to have recovered somewhat, trading again under his own name and in partnership with his son James Innes, playing a leading role in the establishment of the British Guiana Bank, acting as secretary of the British West India Co. and leaving £12,000 on his death. His sons James and John junior set up as wine merchants in the late 1850s in Mincing Lane, and then founded the City of London Real Property Company (subsequently a subsidiary of Land Securities plc) in Mark Lane. James focused on the City company while John junior developed Merton Park between the early 1870s and 1904, and endowed the John Innes Horticultural Institution (now part of the John Innes Centre at Norwich); the John Innes compost is named after him.[144] Both the wife and mother of Henry Fauntleroy, the banker and forger who financed part of the development of the Portman estate, were from slave-owning families on St Kitts.[145]

Imperial legacies

Emancipation coincided with a critical period of developments in the 1830s of Britain's white settler colonies elsewhere in the world, and at the same time changed the posture of former slave-owners towards the former slave-colonies. In some newer colonies, former slave-owners recommitted to the production of tropical commodities, using wage labour or, in the case of British Guiana and Trinidad in particular, indentured labourers from south Asia, whose displacement to the Caribbean was and remains one of the major legacies of Emancipation, rather than of slave-ownership, in the region. But the evidence tends to point elsewhere in the Caribbean to patterns of movement away from the former slave-economies both by former slave-owners and their children, a withdrawal of human capital and in some cases the outright abandonment of the former slave-economies by erstwhile slave-owners, in favour of new opportunities in newer territories. This outflow appears to be a significant legacy of the end of slave-ownership and also of slave-ownership itself. Human capital developed in slave-owning families within the slave-economy was deployed outside its former boundaries in large enough numbers to be significant. The argument is not that such a movement in isolation represented an irreplaceable outflow of talent from the slave-colonies but that – in conjunction with a parallel movement of capital, the lack of any provision for the formerly enslaved people, the wider reduction in commitment by the British state and the structurally limited size of the potential markets in the former slave-colonies – this movement contributed to the underdevelopment of those colonies that marked their post-Emancipation history. At the same time, slave-owners and their children were among the early theorists, promoters and administrators of colonisation and migration. The case of James MacQueen is increasingly well known through the work of David Lambert,[146] while Sir Stephen Walcott (1807–87), born in Barbados and son of the slave-owner Robert J. Walcott (awarded the compensation for 202 enslaved people in May 1836), served between 1847 and 1878 as commissioner and secretary to the Colonial Land and Emigration Commission, which was established in 1840, subsuming the responsibilities of the Agent-General of Emigration and the Colonisation Commissioners for South Australia, and subsequently managing land sales in the settler colonies, using some of the proceeds to promote emigration.[147]

It is important to acknowledge, nevertheless, that 'imperial careering', involving elaborate patterns of movement between slave-colonies and other parts of the empire, preceded Emancipation. Sir Thomas Munro, first Bart. (1761–1827), was the son of a Glasgow Virginia merchant and had himself been apprenticed to the sugar importers Somerville and Gordon, but after his father was bankrupted he obtained a cadetship in the East India Company in 1779, and served as a soldier and administrator prior to his appointment in 1814 as judicial commissioner and then Governor of Madras.[148] Sir Alfred Stephen, the Australian judge and politician, followed his father John Stephen (the brother of the abolitionist James Stephen the elder) from St Kitts via England to New South Wales and Van Diemen's Land in 1824: anti-slavery, not Emancipation, drove them to leave the West Indies.[149] Sir Charles Cockerell and his son Charles Rushout Cockerell, who were mortgagees of enslaved people in Mauritius but whose fortunes were amassed primarily in India, came from a background of 'interests in the West Indies': Sir Charles Cockerell had followed his brother to Bengal in 1776.[150] Not all such moves were binary decisions in favour of other imperial opportunities at the expense of continued commitment to Caribbean slavery. The lawyer and Jamaica slave-owner Sir Edward Hyde East's successful pursuit of the post as chief justice of Bengal in 1813 did not qualify his commitment as 'a lifelong stalwart of the West Indian planter's committee', although his West Indian estates were supposedly 'an economic and political liability' after 1831.[151]

Even though the movement of slave-owning men (and these office-holders were men) had thus been a consistent part of the circuits of empire, anecdotal evidence suggests that there might have been a perceptible acceleration immediately prior to and following Emancipation in the flow of people from the former slave colonies to the white settler colonies. This parallels the appearance in London of former slave-owning merchants in the new joint-stock companies promoting imperial projects. In the case of Canada, for example, Andrew Colvile was the London-based governor of the Hudson Bay Company (the mining town of Colvile in British Columbia was named after him) and his son Eden Colvile (1819–93) became governor of Rupert's Land. Richard Clement Moody (son of Thomas Moody of Waltham Abbey, pro-slavery advocate and slave-owner in British Guinea) became lieutenant-governor of British Columbia in 1859–63, after serving as lieutenant-governor and then governor of the Falkland Islands between 1841 and 1848.[152] In British Columbia, the colonial administrator Sir James Douglas was a man of colour, the son of John Douglas of Glasgow who with his brothers held enslaved people in British Guiana.[153] Sir Anthony Musgrave (son of Dr Anthony Musgrave, Treasurer of Antigua 1824–52) became governor of Newfoundland in 1864 and of British Columbia in 1869–71, when he was instrumental in confederation; he later served as governor of Natal (1872–3) and South Australia (1873–7).[154]

The exchange of people and intermarriage between the East and West Indies was part of the wider patterns of colonial mobility in the late eighteenth and early nineteenth centuries. In India, there is also evidence of a 'swing east' from the West Indies. Henry Thomas Colebrooke, the Sanskrit scholar and administrator, the son of Sir George Colebrooke (chairman of the East India Company 1769–73) and Mary, daughter of Patrick Gaynor of Antigua, arrived in Calcutta in 1783, after his father's bankruptcy a few years previously. Henry Thomas Colebrooke's brother Sir James Edward Colebrooke (who died in 1838) sold the Antigua estates of his mother's family, the Gaynors, on 13 November 1835 to John Adams Wood, the 'owner' of Mary Prince.[155] The price was £10,000 and covered two plantations 'formerly called the Creek and Gaynor's Windward but now lately the Mangrove plantation, and Colebrooke's or the Windward estate and Brecknock', including the compensation money and the apprentice period.

The flow towards India perhaps accelerated in the early decades of the nineteenth century and further increased after Emancipation. Frederick Thesiger, first Baron Chelmsford and lord chancellor 1858–9, had come from a slave-owning family on St Vincent whose estate was destroyed in 1812; his son Frederick Augustus Thesiger became adjutant general in India 1869–74 and his grandson Frederick John Napier Thesiger was viceroy 1916–21.[156] Sir Richard Ottley, the son of Drewry Ottley of St Vincent (where Richard was born in 1782), served as chief justice of Grenada in 1814 but in 1819 became a puisne judge in Ceylon and subsequently chief justice of Ceylon.[157] Sir Stapleton Cotton, the commander-in-chief in India 1825–30, was the owner of estates on Nevis and St Kitts that he had inherited from his mother's family.[158] Again, the parents of the historian George William Cox, born in Benares in 1827, were Captain George Hamilton Cox of the East India Company and Eliza Kearton, daughter of John Horne, a 'planter' of St Vincent.[159] The judge Sir James William Colvile, appointed advocate general of Bengal in 1845, was the son of Andrew Colvile né Wedderburn (who died in 1856), a London merchant, major slave-owner, pioneer of indentured labour in post-Emancipation British Guiana 'founder of the Royal Mail Steam Packet Company' and, as mentioned above, chairman of the Hudson Bay Company. Colvile's maternal uncle George Eden had been governor-general in India 1835–41.[160] Sir Alexander Grant, tenth Bart., the Scottish university administrator, was the son of Robert Innes Grant and Judith Tower Battelle of Santa Cruz (St Croix) and the nephew of Sir Alexander Cray Grant. Both his father and uncle were major slave-owners before Emancipation, and Sir Alexander Grant, tenth Bart., himself lived in the West Indies as a boy in the mid-1830s. But Grant redomiciled to Britain and his own son, Sir (Alfred) Hamilton Grant, became an Indian administrator, serving in senior positions in the decade spanning the First World War.[161] The army officer William St Lucien Chase, who won a Victoria Cross in 1880 in the Second Anglo-Afghan War, was born in St Lucia, the son of Richard Henry Chase and Susan Ifill Chase, both born in Barbados at the time of apprenticeship; William St Lucien Chase was also grandson of the slave-owner Richard H. Chase of Barbados.[162]

In the early years of the Australian colonies, slave-derived capital financed settlers arriving both from England and from the West Indies. Fidelia Hill (née Munkhouse), the pioneering Australian poet, was the legatee of her uncle Arthur Savage, merchant and coffee planter of Kingston, Jamaica, who bequeathed her the Strawberry Hill estate in Port Royal. With her husband Richard Keate Hill, Fidelia Hill moved to Jamaica 'shortly after' their wedding in 1830 (although they were identified as of London in their claim), and in the mid-1830s, after compensation was paid, the couple travelled to Australia 'on the understanding that Robert Hill would be given a position in the new colony of South Australia'. They were in Adelaide 1836–8, then, Hill having died, Fidelia remarried in Tasmania, where she died in 1854. Hill's *Poems and Recollections of the Past* (Sydney, 1840) was the first volume of poetry by a woman published in Australia.[163] The London-born Montefiore brothers, sons of the slave-trader Eliezer Montefiore of Barbados and themselves recipients of slave compensation, shifted their focus to Australia when Joseph Barrow Montefiore sailed there in 1828 to invest £10,000 in the wool industry. He survived bankruptcy in New South Wales in 1841 to become an influential part of the business community in South Australia between 1844 and 1860; his brother and partner, the London-based Jacob, had been a member of the South Australian Commission between 1835 and 1839.[164] Archibald Stirling of Keir accelerated a planned legacy of £1,000 to his illegitimate son Edward Stirling in 1838 in order to fund the latter's departure to Australia; Edward Stirling (1804–73) became a significant figure in the development of South Australia and was the father of Sir John Lancelot Stirling and Sir Edward Charles Stirling.[165] Neill Malcolm, twelfth Laird of Poltalloch was a major recipient of slave compensation in Jamaica before his death in 1837. His two surviving sons, Neill (1797–1857) and John (1805–93), established the cattle station of Poltalloch in South Australia, sold with another station for £170,000 by John in June 1873.[166] The journalist and writer Mary Ann Broome followed an exemplary trajectory: born in Kingston, Jamaica, in 1831, the daughter of Walter George Stewart and Susan Hewitt (herself the daughter of William Hewitt 'the prosperous landowner'), she was educated in England, married an army officer in Jamaica and moved to be with him in India in 1860. After his death there in 1861, she returned to England and married Frederick Napier Broome (1842–96), then a sheep farmer in New Zealand, where the couple lived between 1866 and 1868 before Frederick began a series of colonial appointments as colonial secretary, lieutenant-governor and governor of Natal (1875–7), Mauritius (1877–80), Western Australia (1882–90) and Trinidad (1890–5).[167]

The cadre of colonial administrators in Australia was also formed in part by former colonial slave-owners and in particular their children. Sir Archibald Paull Burt (1810–79), the second son of the 'sugar planter', merchant and Speaker of the House of Assembly George Henry Burt (1787–1851) (and namesake of the London West Indian merchant and slave-owner Archibald Paull), moved to Australia in 1860 and became Western Australia's first chief justice in 1861. He retained his partnership with Francis Spencer Wigley, which had bought up estates on St Kitts in the dislocation of Emancipation, although, despite a mission by Burt to rescue them, the estates were bankrupt in 1873.[168] Sir Robert Dalrymple Ross (1828–87), the son of John Pemberton Ross of St Vincent, moved to South Australia via military and then administrative appointments on the Gold Coast in 1862 and served as treasurer of the state 1876–7 and Speaker of the House of Assembly 1881–7.[169] Sir James Fergusson, sixth Bart., governor of South Australia 1869–72, New Zealand 1873–4 and Bombay 1880–5, was the scion of an absentee slave-owning family. Of his father Sir Charles Dalrymple-Fergusson of Kilkerran, the *ODNB* says: 'a colonial proprietor, he condemned Peel's free trade policies as injurious to the colonies'.[170] Sir James Fergusson, fourth Bart., had owned the Rozelle estate in St Thomas-in-the-East and received slave compensation for the 198 enslaved people upon it with Sir David Hunter Blair as co-owner. In perhaps an emblematic encounter with different labour regimes across the empire at different imperial moments, John Price, the inspector-general of the Penal Department in Victoria and son of the slave-owner Rose Price (who had held 464 enslaved people on Worthy Park and 79 more on each of Mickleton Pen and Spring Garden) was murdered by convicts at Williamstown, Victoria, in 1857.[171]

Conclusion

Imperial legacies, as with other legacies of slave-ownership, were both direct and indirect and in some cases it is not always straightforward to identify such 'legacies' among the disparate connections of individuals to the slave-economy. Sir Henry Barkly – who was successively the governor of British Guiana 1848–53, of Jamaica 1853–6, of Victoria 1856–63, of Mauritius 1863–70 and of the Cape 1870–7 (and whose son, Arthur Cecil Stuart Barkly, was lieutenant-governor of the Falklands Islands 1886–7 and governor of Heligoland 1888–90) – had been a partner in his father's London mercantile firm at the time of Emancipation and was himself the awardee of slave compensation after the death of his father.[172] He certainly represents a series of imperial legacies. But the cases of Alfred Domett, the Prime Minister of New Zealand 1862–3, or the colonial governor Sir Ralph Darling are less clear cut. Alfred Domett was the son of Nathaniel Domett (1765–1849), a London ship-owner who appears in the slave compensation records as one of a group of five assignees of the failed West Indian mercantile firm of Plummer & Wilson. It is difficult to reconstruct, however, the rationale for his role as assignee. His shipping business was presumably part of a network to which Plummer & Wilson also belonged, but it is not known whether or not he was a major creditor of the bankrupt firm – that is, whether a significant part of Alfred Domett's material and personal formation was bound up with the slave-economy.[173] Again, Sir Ralph Darling, acting governor of Mauritius 1819–23 and governor of New South Wales 1825–31, had exposure to slavery in Grenada and elsewhere in the Caribbean as a young soldier in the 1790s, and his brother William Lindsay Darling was awarded slave compensation in Dominica both in his own name and through the trustee of his marriage settlement, but Sir Ralph Darling's conduct and attitudes in various imperial contexts were not legacies of slave-*ownership*, and probably not truly legacies even of slavery: his biographer places more emphasis on his military background in the authoritarianism of Wellington's armies.[174]

Each legacy of slave-ownership, therefore, requires first to be identified, then validated and finally evaluated. By its nature a summary of such legacies in total, as in the overview in this chapter, blurs the specificity of each individual legacy and risks aggregating non-comparable cases. But, taken together, the universe of absentee slave-owners gives overwhelming evidence that slave-ownership permeated the elites in mid-nineteenth-century Britain and that, despite an erosion of profitability of commodity production in many colonies before 1833 and in all colonies afterwards, old wealth was nevertheless preserved and new wealth generated in sufficient cases to make this strand of private riches a significant component of overall Victorian wealth. As a corollary, the wealth conferred by slave-ownership on the former slave-owners helped mould the cultural, social and physical fabric of Britain long after slavery itself had ended.

NOTES

1 Lowell J. Ragatz, *The Fall of the Planter Class in the British Caribbean, 1763–1833: A Study in Social and Economic History* (New York and London, 1928).
2 Eric Williams, *Capitalism and Slavery* (1944; repr. London, 1964), p. 211.

3 *Ibid.*

4 Seymour Drescher, *Econocide: British Slavery in the Era of Abolition* (Pittsburgh, 1977). For an unusually clear summary of the controversy surrounding 'decline' and of the wider conflict between humanitarian and economic determinist accounts of British abolition, see Christopher Leslie Brown, *Moral Capital: Foundations of British Abolitionism* (Chapel Hill, 2006), pp. 3–22.

5 See Nicholas Draper, 'The rise of a new planter class? Some countercurrents from British Guiana and Trinidad, 1807–1833', *Atlantic Studies* 9 (1) (2012), 65–83.

6 Commercial, political and historical legacies are addressed in Chapters 3–5.

7 Douglas Hall, 'Absentee proprietorship in the British West Indies, to about 1850', *Journal of Caribbean History* 35 (1) (2001), 97–121.

8 *Ibid.*, p. 113.

9 David Lambert, *White Creole Culture, Politics and Identity during the Age of Abolition* (Cambridge, 2005), p. 2.

10 Chris Evans, *Slave Wales: The Welsh and Atlantic Slavery 1660–1850* (Cardiff, 2010); Chris Evans, 'Slavery and Welsh industry before and after Emancipation', in Catherine Hall, Nicholas Draper and Keith McClelland (eds.), *Emancipation and the Remaking of the British Imperial World* (Manchester, 2014), pp. 60–73.

11 Nini Rodgers, *Ireland, Slavery and Anti-slavery: 1612–1865* (Basingstoke, 2007); Nicholas Draper, 'Research note: "Dependent on precarious subsistences": Ireland's slave-owners at the time of Emancipation', *Britain and the World* 6 (2) (2013), 220–42.

12 Alan L. Karras, *Sojourners in the Sun: Scottish Immigrants in Jamaica and the Chesapeake, 1740–1800* (Ithaca, 1992).

13 Hall, 'Absentee proprietorship', p. 101.

14 J. A. H. Evans, 'Wells, Nathaniel (1779–1852), slave owner and landowner', *ODNB*.

15 R. G. Thorne (ed.), *The House of Commons, 1790–1820*, (5 vols., London, 1986), V; T71/885 British Guiana no. 563. Stewart was also awarded compensation in Grenada as a trustee, T71/880 no. 449.

16 Benjamin James Hopkinson and his lunatic brother John Thomas Hopkinson, the sons of Benjamin Hopkinson and a woman of colour, Johanna, were awarded compensation for the East Hog estate, T71/885 British Guiana no. 616; Benjamin James Hopkinson himself was awarded part of the compensation for the enslaved people on John Cove and Craig Milne, T71/885 British Guiana no. 572. The children of John Hopkinson and two (possibly three) women of colour were awarded the compensation for the enslaved people on Bachelors Adventure and Clonbrook, T71/885 British Guiana nos. 568A&B and 577.

17 Diana Athill, *Yesterday Morning* (London, 2002), p. 118.

18 Ancestry.com, *London, England, Marriages and Banns, 1754–1921* (database online): 30 October 1916 marriage of Lawrence Francis Imbert Athill and Alice Katherine Carr at Christ Church, Lancaster Gate. Lawrence Athill's father's name is mis-transcribed as Hubert Athill but the underlying record clearly shows Herbert; *Oxford University Alumni, 1500–1886*, database online available through Ancestry.com 2007 shows Herbert Athill, third son of

George James of Bridge Kent matriculating at St John's 14 October 1876 aged twenty-four [sic]. The registration of his death in 1919 gave his age as seventy-two. In 1851, George Athill, aged forty-four, born in the West Indies, was living at Tonbridge with his wife Charlotte, aged thirty-four, and with four older children born in the West Indies and three in Britain.

19 Susan Lowes, *The Peculiar Class: The Formation, Collapse and Reformation of the Middle Class in Antigua, West Indies 1834–1940* (PhD thesis, Columbia University, 1994).

20 See Chapter 3 for an analysis of the commercial legacies of British mercantile slave-owners.

21 In assessing the legacies of slave-ownership, it is important to maintain the distinction between the roles of agent and principal in the slave compensation process; see Appendix 1.

22 H. J. Spencer, 'East, Sir Edward Hyde, first baronet (1764–1847), judge in India and legal writer', *ODNB*, which refers to Sir Edward Hyde East's great-grandfather taking part in the conquest of Jamaica and having obtained 'the sugar plantations there on which the family's fortunes were based'; G. F. R. Barker, rev. Elisabeth A. Cawthon, 'Scarlett, James, first baron Abinger (1769–1844), judge', *ODNB*, which refers to Scarlett's birth at Duckett Spring, Jamaica, without any further comment about the nature of the economy and society into which he was born; Daire Hogan, 'Hart, Sir Anthony (1757–1831), lord chancellor of Ireland', *ODNB*, which again refers to Hart's birth on St Kitts without further comment; J. A. Hamilton, rev. Hugh Mooney, 'Tindal, Sir Nicholas Conyngham (1776–1846), judge', *ODNB*; T71/887 British Guiana no. 2382A.

23 J. K. Laughton, rev. Andrew Lambert, 'Fahie, Sir William Charles (1763–1833), naval officer', *ODNB*. Fahie's second wife was Mary Esther Harvey, daughter of the Hon. Augustus William Harvey, member of council of Bermuda. This was almost certainly the Lady Mary Fahie who was awarded compensation for one enslaved person on Bermuda, T71/889 Bermuda no. 751; Fahie's daughter Arabella Louisa Burke was awarded compensation for nineteen enslaved people T71/879 St Kitts no. 624. George Augustus W. Fahie, probably Sir William Charles Fahie's nephew, also received compensation for fourteen enslaved people, T71/879 St Kitts nos. 508 and 509.

24 T71/867 St Thomas-in-the-East no. 508; *The Times*, 30 March 1822, p. 4.

25 J. K. Laughton, rev. Roger Morriss, 'Capel, Sir Thomas Bladen (1776–1853), naval officer', *ODNB*.

26 Stephen Howarth, 'Cochrane, Sir Alexander Inglis (1758–1832), naval officer and politician', *ODNB*; J. K. Laughton, rev. Roger T. Stearn, 'Cochrane, Sir Thomas John (1789–1872), naval officer', *ODNB*; M. G. Wiebe, 'Baillie, Alexander Dundas Ross Cochrane-Wishart, first Baron Lamington (1816–1890), politician and author', *ODNB*.

27 Thomas Seccombe, rev. John D. Haigh, 'Sir George Webbe Dasent (1817–1896), Scandinavian Scholar', *ODNB*. Dasent's family and writings are discussed in more detail in Chapter 5.

28 H. C. G. Matthew, 'Chenery, Thomas (1826–1884), newspaper editor', *ODNB*. Mrs William [sic] Ann Chenery, widow of John Chenery, was awarded slave compensation, T71/895 Barbados no. 386.

29 Hugh Brogan, 'Morris, Mowbray (1819–1874), newspaper executive', *ODNB*.

30 Martin Russell, 'Peyronnet, (Georgina) Frances de [née Georgina Frances Whitfield], Viscountess de Peyronnet in the French nobility (1815–1895), journalist', *ODNB*.

31 Matthew, 'Chenery' implicitly suggests this.

32 Hilary L. Rubinstein, 'Franklin, Jacob Abraham (1809–1877), newspaper proprietor and editor', *ODNB*.

33 David Knapman, 'Sharp, Richard [called Conversation Sharp] (1759–1835), politician and wit', *ODNB*. Sharp, however, does not appear among Rubinstein's lists of those dying with over £100,000 in personalty.

34 Parliamentary Papers 1831–2 (721) XX: *Report from the Select Committee on the Extinction of Slavery throughout the British Dominions*, p. 315.

35 Leslie Hannah, 'Bevan, Robert Cooper Lee (1809–1890), banker', *ODNB*. The entry states that his mother 'came from a prominent Caribbean slave-owning family'.

36 J. M. Rigg, rev. Lynn Milne, 'Madden, Richard Robert (1798–1886), author and colonial administrator', *ODNB*; Hilary Marland, 'Madden, Thomas More (1844–1902), gynaecologist', *ODNB*.

37 Anne Stott, *Wilberforce: Family and Friends* (Oxford, 2012).

38 Sian Rhiannon Williams, 'Griffith, John (1818–1885), Church of England clergyman', *ODNB*. The entry does not identify William King by name as Sarah Francis' father.

39 Sir George Gilbert Scott, *Personal and Professional Recollections by the late Sir George Gilbert Scott, R. A.*, ed. G. Gilbert Scott F. S. A. (London, 1879), p. 10; Gavin Stamp, 'Scott, George Gilbert (1811–1878), architect', *ODNB*.

40 Scott, *Recollections*, p. 2.

41 *Ibid.*, pp. 31–2.

42 T71/877 Antigua no. 131. The compensation was awarded to Nathaniel Gilbert, probably the cousin of Euphemia Scott née Lynch and son of the testator Nathaniel Gilbert.

43 Scott, *Recollections*, p. 32.

44 In the period of British colonial slavery there was income tax only between 1799 and 1815, although there were also periodic efforts to tax the more prosperous through levies on such items as windows, carriages and servants.

45 See Chapter 4 for a discussion of the West India Company, established in the joint-stock boom of 1825–6.

46 Michael T. Davis, 'Gerrald, Joseph (1763–1796), political reformer', *ODNB*.

47 E. I. Carlyle, rev. Richard B. Sheridan, 'Young, Sir William (1749–1815), second baronet, colonial governor and politician', *ODNB*.

48 W. P. Courtney, rev. Andrew J. O'Shaughnessy, 'Payne, Ralph, Baron Lavington (1739–1807), politician', *ODNB*.

49 Marc Vaubert de Chantilly, 'Willett, Ralph (1719–1795), book collector and connoisseur', *ODNB*.

50 G. F. R. Barker, rev. David Eastwood, 'Goulburn, Henry (1784–1856), politician', *ODNB*.

51 Ronald Bayne, rev. C. A. Creffield, 'Lambert, Brooke (1834–1901), social reformer and Church of England clergyman', *ODNB*.

52 Simon Gikandi, *Slavery and the Culture of Taste* (Princeton, 2011), p. 141.

53 Such dislocation in Antigua post-abolition was captured in Jane Austen's *Mansfield Park* (1814); see Edward W. Said, *Culture and Imperialism* (New York, 1993), pp. 100–16.

54 Will of Charles Nathaniel Bayly of Hampton Court Palace proved 16 February 1854, PROB 11/2185/345. Bayly lived in a grace-and-favour apartment at Hampton Court. (We are grateful to Alice Munro-Faure for providing a transcript of the will.) Samuel Baker, himself a recipient of slave compensation as a mortgagee of slave-property, was the father of Samuel White Baker, the African explorer and committee member of the Eyre Defence Fund in 1866; Thomas Paul Ofcansky, 'Baker, Sir Samuel White (1821–1893), traveller and explorer in Africa', *ODNB*.

55 Cecilia Karch, 'From the plantocracy to B. S. & T.: crisis and transformation of the Barbadian socioeconomy, 1865–1837', in Woodville Marshall (ed.), *Emancipation IV: Lectures Commemorating the 150th Anniversary of Emancipation, Delivered in February and March 1988* (Mona, Jamaica, 1993), pp. 29–46.

56 R. W. Beachey, cited in Karch, 'From the plantocracy', p. 32.

57 Karch, 'From the plantocracy', p. 34.

58 Ian K. R. Archer, 'Storer, Anthony Morris (1746–1799), politician and collector', *ODNB*.

59 Helen Davies, 'Bernal, Ralph (1783–1854), politician and art collector', *ODNB*; Derek Beales, 'Osborne, Ralph Bernal (1808?-1882), politician', *ODNB*.

60 Karras, *Sojourners*, pp. 55–60.

61 James Barbour, 'Keil through the ages', *The Kintyre Antiquarian and Natural History Society Magazine* 23 (Autumn 1988), at www.ralstongenealogy.com/number23kintmag.htm, accessed 20 August 2012.

62 T71/864 Port Royal no. 4.

63 R. W. Beachey, *The British West Indies Sugar Industry in the Late 19th Century* (Oxford, 1957).

64 Jane Ridley, 'Douglas, Aretas Akers- first Viscount Chilston (1851–1926), politician', *ODNB*.

65 Sir William Hodges, *Reports of Cases Argued and Determined in the Court of Common Pleas*, (2 vols., London, 1838), 2, pp. 235–9.

66 A. G. E. Jones, 'Sir James Lamont, first baronet (1828–1913), Arctic yachtsman', *ODNB*.

67 T71/893 Trinidad nos. 1075A, 1865 and 1869.

68 H. C. G. Matthew, 'Mathew, Sir George Benvenuto [formerly George Byam] Buckley (1807–1879), politician and diplomatist', *ODNB*.

69 *London Gazette*, 22,968, 12 May 1865, p. 2496.

70 Jonathan Howard, 'Wade, Charles Paget (1883–1956), collector and illustrator', *ODNB*.

71 *London Gazette*, 26,752, 26 June 1896, p. 3722; National Probate Calendar 1912. Both Paget Augustus Wade and Charles Paget Wade died on St Kitts, the latter in 1956 leaving £90,000.

72 www.nationaltrust.org.uk/snowshill-manor, accessed 29 October 2012.

73 Judy Slinn and Jennifer Tanburn, *The Booker Story* (London, 2003).

74 William D. Rubinstein, *Who Were the Rich? A Biographical Directory of British Wealth-holders, Vol. I: 1809–1839* (London, 2009). Professor Rubinstein has very generously shared his unpublished data for the years 1840–74. Some of the issues involved with the probate data are discussed in Appendix 1.

75 Parry left £120,000 when probate was granted for his estate in 1819; Rubinstein, *Who Were the Rich? Vol. I*, 1819/7 (which does not record Parry's activity as a slave-trader).

76 Ralph Davis, *The Industrial Revolution and British Overseas Trade* (Leicester, 1979), p. 41. Davis' table gives cotton imports by source for the middle years of each decade from 1784–6 onwards. The US alone accounts for 75 per cent on average between 1784–6 and 1854–6; the balance of the five-sixths figure for slave-grown cotton was derived by adding to the US the figures for the West Indies and Latin America, the latter identified in the text as Brazil.

77 John Charlton, *Hidden Chains: The Slavery Business and North East England 1600–1865* (Newcastle-upon-Tyne, 2008); T71/899 Barbados nos. 4726 and 4763. Ward Cadogan's widow was also awarded a share of the compensation for a third estate in Barbados as a judgment creditor, T71/897 Barbados no. 2959A&B.

78 James Walvin, 'The colonial origins of English wealth: the Harewoods of Yorkshire', *Journal of Caribbean History* 39 (1) (2005), 38–53.

79 R. P. Fereday, 'Dundas family of Fingask and Kerse (per. 1728/9–1820)', *ODNB*; T71/880 Grenada no. 604 Dougalston; Dundas also appears as an awardee in T71/881 Dominica no. 576A&B Castle Bruce, possibly as an executor; Helen Clifford, 'Aske Hall, Yorkshire: the Dundas property empire and Nabob taste', at http://blogs.ucl.ac.uk/eicah/aske-hall-yorkshire, accessed 8 August 2013.

80 Sir Simon Taylor left total personalty of £739,207, of which £380,680 was invested in the funds in England and a further £126,932 was due from merchants in Britain (a further ninety enslaved people were not included in the inventory valuation); his total estate including the value of the sugar plantations and pens is estimated to have been £1 million; R. B. Sheridan, 'Simon Taylor, sugar tycoon of Jamaica, 1740–1813', *Agricultural History* 45 (4) (1971), 285–96.

81 This is consistent with the previous analysis that between 5 and 10 per cent of the British elites were sufficiently close to the slave-economy to appear in the compensation records; Nicholas Draper, *The Price of Emancipation. Slave-Ownership, Compensation and British Society at the End of Slavery* (Cambridge, 2010), pp. 176–7, 273. However, that number was a one-time snapshot as of 1834, while the new data cover a period of sixty years.

82 This statistic holds whether or not the two dozen 'incidental' slave-owners are excluded, as they should be.

83 Participation in the foreign slave-trade was illegal, and ownership of enslaved people by British subjects was outlawed in the early 1840s. As Williams pointed out, however, British involvement (and individual wealth creation) in the international trade, shipping and finance of slave-grown commodities continued.

84 O'Shaughnessy stressed the importance of the traditions of educating successive generations of slave-owners in Britain in seeking to explain the loyalty of the Caribbean colonies in the American Revolution; Andrew O'Shaughnessy, *An Empire Divided: The American Revolution and the British Caribbean* (Philadelphia, 2000). The role of West Indians in founding Scottish schools has also been remarked: see e.g. for Inverness Academy, David Hamilton, *Scotland, the Caribbean and the Atlantic World, 1750–1820* (Manchester, 2005), pp. 205–7, 215.

85 Draper, *Price of Emancipation*, pp. 331–4.

86 *Statement by the Council of the University of London, Explanatory of the Nature and Objects of the Institution* (London, 1827).

87 W. H. Brock, 'Turner, Edward (1796–1837), chemist', *ODNB*. The entry gives his birth at Teak Pen, Clarendon, Jamaica, 'the second son of a Scottish sugar planter, Dutton Smith Turner (d. 1816) and his Creole wife, Mary Gale Redwar'.

88 An article by Richard Hughes, 'Who is Henry Dawes?', *The Old Johnian* (2011), www.stjohnsleatherhead.co.uk/Archives, accessed 1 November 2013, confirms the benefactor as the Henry Dawes of 6 Hyde Park Gardens, who gave anonymously through his solicitor William Phelps: http://open-charities.org/charities/251144, accessed 18 January 2012.

89 T71/880 Grenada no. 568.

90 Jacqueline Beaumont, 'Beale, Dorothea (1831–1906), headmistress', *ODNB*.

91 Elizabeth Coutts, 'Buss, Frances Mary (1827–1894), headmistress', *ODNB*.

92 Josephine Kamm, *How Different from Us: A Biography of Miss Buss and Miss Beale* (1958, repr. London, 2012), p. 41.

93 Ancestry.com, *London, England, Baptisms, Marriages and Burials, 1538–1812* (database online).

94 *The Times*, 16 April 1824, p. 3: Marriages: 'at Weymouth [Dorset], by the Rev. John West, M. A., the Rev. David Laing of St Peter's College [sic] Cambridge, younger son of the late David Laing Esq. of Jamaica, to Mary Elizabeth, second daughter of John West Esq. of the same island.'

95 *Jamaica Almanac 1817*.

96 Anita McConnell, 'Dick, James (bap. 1743 d. 1828), merchant and benefactor', *ODNB*.

97 Samuel Low jnr., *The Charities of London* (London, 1861). Hankey's address was given as Brunswick Square, Brighton, but that of the Thomson Hankey Charity as 7 Mincing Lane, the City counting house of the Hankey family firm of West India merchants. Thomson Hankey senior left £140,000 personalty in 1855.

98 Thomas Seccombe, rev. Sinead Agnew, 'Hillary, Sir William (1770–1847), founder of Royal National Lifeboat Institution', *ODNB*.

99 At the 1837 Annual Meeting of the Society; cited in Chien-hui Li, 'The animal cause and its greater traditions', *History & Policy*, at www.history-andpolicy.org/papers/policy-paper-19.html, accessed 8 August 2013.

100 Joyce F. Goodman, 'Atherton, Eleanora (1782–1870), philanthropist', *ODNB*.

101 *The Times*, 21 January 1822, p. 3: 'At St. Marylebone Church, by the Rev. Lucius Coghlan, D.D., John Kenyon, Esq., of the island of Jamaica, to Miss Caroline Curteis, of Devonshire-place'; *The Times*, 22 December 1856, p. 7; *The Times*, 27 January 1857, p. 9; Meredith B. Raymond, 'Kenyon, John (1784–1856), patron of the arts and poet', *ODNB*.

102 'The Monumental inscriptions in the churchyard of St Mary's Church, Lewisham, noted by Leland L. Duncan, typed up by Dawn Weeks', at www. kentarchaeology.org.uk/Research/Libr/MIs/MIsLewisham/01.htm, accessed 1 November 2013; will of John Curteis of St Marylebone proved 10 May 1849, PROB 11/2092/270. Caroline Curteis was Kenyon's second wife.

103 For an example of such informal networks, see Humphrey Gawthrop, 'George Ellis of Ellis Caymanas: a Caribbean link to Scott and the Bronte sisters', *Electronic British Library Journal*, 2005, at www.bl.uk/eblj/2005articles/article3.html, accessed 8 August 2013; J. M. Rigg, rev. Rebecca Mills, 'Ellis, George (1753–1815), writer', *ODNB*.

104 www.roxburgheclub.org.uk/membership, accessed 7 November 2012. A founding member in 1812 was Robert Lang, a London West India merchant who had been a slave factor in the West Indies; Hibbert was invited to join in 1816, and George Watson Taylor became the thirty-fourth member in 1822. James Heywood Markland, who as Treasurer of the Society for the Propagation of the Gospel was awarded the compensation for the the Society's Codrington estate in Barbados, was also a founder member. Hibbert is explored in depth in Chapter 6.

105 'St James's Street, west side, existing buildings', *Survey of London, Vols. XXIX and XXX: St James Westminster, Part 1* (1960), pp. 472–86, at www.british-history.ac.uk/report.aspx?compid=40623, accessed 29 March 2012.

106 T71/892 St Vincent no. 459.

107 C. W. Sutton, rev. Alan G. Crosby, 'Yates, Joseph Brooks (1780–1855), merchant and antiquary', *ODNB*. Yates was also president of the Liverpool Royal Institution in 1842–3 and was one of the founders of the Southern and Toxeth Hospital. The *ODNB* entry describes him as a partner in a West Indies merchant firm.

108 Thomas Seccombe, rev. Julian Lock, 'Macdonnell, Alexander (1798–1835), chess player', *ODNB*.

109 Charlotte Fell-Smith, rev. Elizabeth Baigent, 'Moens, William John Charles (1833–1904), antiquary', *ODNB*.

110 T71/880 Grenada nos. 455 and 859.

111 Gikandi, *Slavery and the Culture of Taste*; Catherine Molineux, *Faces of Perfect Ebony: Encountering Atlantic Slavery in Imperial Britain* (Cambridge, MA, 2012).

112 Helen Davies, 'Bernal, Ralph (1783–1854), politician and art collector', *ODNB*. The entry notes that Bernal spoke against 'the immediate abolition of the slave trade [sic]' in 1826; in fact he must have opposed immediate abolition of slavery.

113 Joseph Marryat, *A History of Pottery and Porcelain* (London, 1850).

114 National Gallery of Art Washington, at www.nga.gov/collection/gallery/gg21/gg21-43724-prov.html, accessed 5 November 2012. Somewhat eccentrically, the *ODNB* includes no entry for John Proctor Anderdon but

does include his son John Lavicount Anderdon as 'writer on angling and devotional subjects' (which also identifies John Lavicount Anderdon as a partner with his father-in-law William Manning in Manning and Anderdon, West Indies merchants, but does not mention slave-ownership or slavery) and for William Henry Anderdon, John Lavicount Anderdon's son, as 'Jesuit'; W. P. Courtney, rev. Wray Vamplew, 'Anderdon, John Lavicount (1792–1874), writer on angling and devotional subjects', *ODNB*; Thomas Cooper, rev. Rosemary Mitchell, 'Anderdon, William Henry (1816–1890), Jesuit', *ODNB*.

115 Royal Academy of Arts Collections – Persons, entry for James Hughes Anderdon (1790–1879), at www.racollection.org.uk, accessed 21 July 2013; the British Museum Collection database shows 728 items donated by James Hughes Anderdon.

116 'Notice of sale', *The Art-Union*, 14, 15 March 1840, p. 44.

117 www.christies.com/LotFinder/lot_details.aspx?intObjectID=5277781, accessed 9 April 2014. See also John Young, *A Catalogue of the Pictures at Leigh Court near Bristol, the Seat of Philip John Miles MP* (London, 1822).

118 E.g. Jackie Wullschager, 'Turner illuminated', *Financial Times*, 16 March 2012, at www.ft.com/cms/s/2/b6616f32-6d23-11e1-b6ff-00144feab49a. html#axzz2BSkMxRnv, accessed 6 November 2012.

119 Anthony Twist, *Widening Circles in Finance, Philanthropy and the Arts: A Study of the Life of John Julius Angerstein 1735–1823* (PhD thesis, University of Amsterdam, 2002).

120 Sarah Palmer, 'Angerstein, John Julius (*c.* 1732–1823), insurance broker and connoisseur of art', *ODNB*.

121 Richard Brent, 'Hampden, Renn Dickson (1793–1868), bishop of Hereford and theologian', *ODNB*.

122 Gordon Goodwin, rev. Mari G. Ellis, 'Isaacson, Stephen (1798–1849), writer', *ODNB*.

123 The church, originally built in 1843, was so badly constructed 'that in 1868 it became necessary to take the edifice, with the exception of the tower [built in 1847] down, and rebuild it on a somewhat different plan'; William White, *History, Gazetteer and Directory of the County of Devon including the City of Exeter* (2nd edn, London, 1878–9), p. 129.

124 Williams, *Capitalism and Slavery*, pp. 88–9, 156.

125 T71/873 St James no. 1.

126 Lancashire Record Office, Lancaster Society of Friends, Disownments FRL/2/1/5/117.

127 David Newsome, 'Manning, Henry Edward (1808–1892), Roman catholic convert and cardinal-archbishop of Westminster', *ODNB*; Thomson Cooper, rev. Rosemary Mitchell, 'Anderdon, William Henry (1816–1890), Jesuit', *ODNB*.

128 This is consistent with the findings of an analysis of Jewish participation in the slave-trade; Eli Faber, *Jews, Slaves and the Slave Trade: Setting the Record Straight* (New York, 1998).

129 William D. Rubinstein, *Who Were the Rich? Vol. II*, unpublished data for 1840–59, MS 1855/1.

130 Cecil Roth, *History of the Great Synagogue, London, 1690–1940* (1950), ch. 16, at www.jewishgen.org/jcr-uk/susser/roth/chsixteen.htm, accessed 8 August 2013; National Probate Calendar 1866.

131 Timothy C. F. Stunt, 'Prince, Henry James (1811–1899), founder of the Agapemonites', *ODNB*. It has not been possible to trace the family's ownership in the compensation records. A Thomas and Elizabeth Prince of 6 Blandford Place counterclaimed for the compensation on the Lower Diamond estate on St Vincent, T71/892 St Vincent no. 503; however, the Thomas in this counterclaim is probably the Thomas Prince shown as aged sixty-nine in the 1851 census born in the West Indies, too old to be Henry James Prince's brother, although conceivably a half-brother.

132 John Habakkuk, *Marriage, Debt and the Estate System: English Landownership 1650–1950* (Oxford, 1994), p. 455. Habakkuk describes Henry Drax (d. 1755) as the son (rather than great-nephew) of Col. Henry Drax, the purchaser of Ellerton Abbey. Erle-Drax's descendant, Richard Plunkett-Ernle-Erle-Drax, was elected as Conservative MP for South Dorset in the United Kingdom general election in 2010 using the truncated name Richard Drax. During the election campaign there was some controversy when the *Daily Mirror* wrote that Drax's ancestors had earned their fortune through slavery. In response, Drax replied in the *Dorset Echo* that 'I can't be held responsible for something that happened 300 or 400 years ago. They are using the old class thing and that is not what this election is about, it's not what I stand for, and I ignore it.' 'I think it shows how desperate they are if all they can do is pick at bits of my family history': *Daily Mirror*, 5 May 2010; *Dorset Echo*, 6 May 2010.

133 Leonard R. N. Ashley, 'Plunkett, Edward John Moreton Drax, eighteenth Baron Dunsany (1878–1957), writer', *ODNB*.

134 Peter Gretton, rev. Marc Brodie, 'Drax, Sir Reginald Aylmer Ranfurly Plunkett-Ernle-Erle- (1880–1967), naval officer', *ODNB*.

135 Andrew Mackillop, 'Grant, Sir James of Grant, eighth baronet (1738–1811), agricultural improver and politician', *ODNB*.

136 Margot Finn has pointed out that, because of restrictions on remittances to Britain and relatively attractive interest rates in India, retiring East India Company men often left their fortunes for several years in India after retirement. Private communication, February 2013.

137 Nicholas Draper, 'Slave ownership and the British country house: the records of the Slave Compensation Commission as evidence', in Madge Dresser and Andrew Hann (eds.), *Slavery and the British Country House* (Swindon, 2013), pp. 1–11.

138 Asa Briggs described John Tollemache as 'benevolent landlord and affable tory politician' in his *ODNB* entry for Tollemache's son, Lionel: Asa Briggs, 'Tollemache, Lionel Arthur (1838–1919), writer and man of leisure', *ODNB*.

139 See p. 57 above.

140 *London Gazette*, 13,579, 5 October 1793, p. 889.

141 *Jamaica Almanac 1811* shows Golden Grove etc. against 'Hudson, William, heirs of'.

142 *Proceedings before the Privy Council against Compulsory Manumission in the Colonies of Demerara and Berbice* (London, 1827).

143 *London Gazette*, 19,055, 4 June 1833, p. 1095; *The Times*, 16 July 1842, p. 6, described the Chancery case of Baillie *v.* Innes as 'one of the numerous proceedings arising out of the failure of Mr Innes, who was formerly in partnership with Mr Nathaniel Winter as West India merchants'.

144 Jenny West, 'Innes, John (1829–1904), property developer and philanthropist', *ODNB*. The connection between Nathaniel Winter and John Innes (1786–1869) is supported by the appearance of N. Winter as a witness at the marriage of John Innes and Mary Reid in 1817. The 1851 census shows John Innes and son James Innes as merchants of 46 Porchester Terrace. The John Innes of the East India Company is a different man.

145 Richard Davenport-Hines, 'Fauntleroy, Henry (1784–1824), banker and forger', *ODNB*.

146 David Lambert, *Mastering the Niger: James MacQueen's African Geography and the Struggle over Atlantic Slavery* (Chicago, 2013); David Lambert, 'The "Glasgow King of Billingsgate": James MacQueen and an Atlantic proslavery network', *Slavery & Abolition* 29 (3) (2008), 389–413.

147 The 1851 census shows Walcott at 17 Lansdowne Crescent, 'Sec. H. M. Col[o]n[ial] & E[migration] Commrs.', and the 1861 census as 'Colonial Land & Emigration Commissioner' (scored through by 'Civil servant'). In 1870 Stephen Walcott acted as executor of the will of his uncle William Alleyne Culpeper, also a slave-owner. The history of the commissioners is briefly sketched at the New South Wales State Records Archives Investigator site, Agency Number 3,050, at http://investigator.records.nsw.gov.au/Entity.aspx?Path=%5CAgency%5C3050, accessed 8 November 2012.

148 Martha McLaren, 'Munro, Sir Thomas, first baronet (1761–1827), army officer in the East India Company and administrator in India', *ODNB*.

149 Martha Rutledge, 'Stephen, Sir Alfred (1802–1894), judge and politician in Australia', *ODNB*.

150 P. J. Marshall and Willem G. J. Kuiters, 'Cockerell, Charles (1755–1837), banker', *ODNB*.

151 H. J. Spencer, 'East, Sir Edward Hyde, first baronet (1764–1847), judge in India and legal writer', *ODNB*.

152 John Sweetman, 'Moody, Richard Clement (1813–1887), army officer and colonial governor', *ODNB*.

153 Charlotte S. M. Girard, 'Sir James Douglas' mother and grandmother', *BC Studies* 44 (1979–80), 25–31; Adele Perry, '"Is your garden in England, sir?": James Douglas's archive and the politics of home', *History Workshop Journal* 70 (1) (2010), 67–85; Adele Perry, 'James Douglas, Canada and Guyana', *Stabroek News*, 4 April 2011, at www.stabroeknews.com/2011/features/in-the-diaspora/04/04/james-douglas-canada-and-guyana, accessed 20 April 2011.

154 Geoffrey Bolton, 'Musgrave, Sir Anthony (1828–1888), colonial governor', *ODNB*.

155 Vere Langford Oliver, *History of the Island of Antigua, Vol. II* (London, 1896), pp. 10–11; H. V. Bowen, rev. Anita McConnell, 'Colebrooke, Sir George, second baronet (1729–1809), banker', *ODNB*; Richard F. Gombrich,

'Colebrooke, Henry Thomas (1765–1837), colonial administrator and scholar', *ODNB*.

156 J. P. C. Laband, 'Thesiger, Frederick Augustus, second Baron Chelmsford (1825–1905), army officer and courtier', *ODNB*; P. G. Robb, 'Thesiger, Frederic John Napier, first viscount Chelmsford (1868–1933), viceroy of India', *ODNB*.

157 Ancestry.com, *Cambridge University Alumni 1261–1900* (database online), accessed 21 July 2013.

158 H. M. Chichester, rev. James Lunt, 'Cotton, Stapleton, first viscount Combermere (1773–1865), army officer', *ODNB*.

159 G. S. Woods, rev. Peter Hinchcliff, 'Cox, George William (1827–1902), historian', *ODNB*. The John Horne awarded slave compensation in the 1830s with his wife Frances Ottley Horne (*c.* 1803–74) was most likely the brother rather than father of Eliza Kearton Horne. No record of a marriage in England or Wales between George Hamilton Cox and Eliza Kearton Horne has been found. An Alexander Horne, son of John Horne of St Vincent, died in India in 1834; if as seems likely this was the brother of Eliza Kearton Horne, it would help explain her presence in India.

160 Katherine Prior, 'Colvile, Sir James William (1810–1880), judge in India', *ODNB*.

161 Katherine Prior, 'Grant, Sir (Alfred) Hamilton, twelfth baronet (1872–1937), administrator in India', *ODNB*.

162 H. G. Vibart, rev. M. G. M. Jones, 'Chase, William St Lucien (1856–1908), army officer', *ODNB*.

163 Australian Poetry Library, 'Fidelia S. T. Hill (1794–1854)', at www.poetrylibrary.edu.au/poets/hill-fidelia-s-t, accessed 9 May 2012. This site describes Robert Keate Hill as 'a captain in the service of the East India Company'.

164 Israel Getzler, 'Montefiore, Joseph Barrow (1803–1893)', *Australian Dictionary of Biography*, at http://adb.anu.edu.au/biography/montefiore-joseph-barrow-2472, accessed 21 July 2013.

165 Hans Mincham, 'Stirling, Sir John Lancelot (1849–1932), politician and Stirling, Sir Edward Charles (Ted) (1848–1919) surgeon, scientist and politician', *Australian Dictionary of Biography*, at http://adb.anu.edu.au/biography/stirling-sir-john-lancelot-4933, accessed 21 July 2013; Jude Skurray, 'Edward Stirling 1805–1873, son of Archibald Stirling of Keir and Cadder 1769–1847' (2007), at www.clanstirling.org/Main/bios/EdwardStirlingbyJudeSkurray.pdf, accessed 20 May 2012; Keir of Stirling Muniments 1338–*c.* 1940, Glasgow City Archives, Mitchell Library, GB243/T-SK; T-SK/13/13 Letters from Edward Stirling to his father Archibald Stirling of Keir include acknowledgment by Edward of the receipt of £1,000 from Archibald. We are grateful to Sonia Baker for this reference.

166 Stephen Coppel, 'Malcolm, John, of Poltalloch (1805–1893), art collector and landowner', *ODNB*.

167 Rosemary T. Van Arsdel, 'Barker [née Stewart] Mary Anne, Lady Barker [other married name Broome, Mary Anne, Lady Broome] (1831–1911), journalist and writer', *ODNB*; T71/852 St Catherine nos. 490 and 491 for Walter George Stewart's compensation for enslaved people on Bernard Lodge in Jamaica.

168 Chris Birch, 'Burt, Sir Archibald Paull (1810–1879), colonial judge', *ODNB*.

169 Marc Brodie, 'Sir Robert Dalrymple Ross (1828–1887), army officer and politician in Australia', *ODNB*.

170 G. B. Smith, rev. Roger T. Stearn, 'Fergusson, Sir Charles Dalrymple-, of Kilkerran [formerly Charles Fergusson of Kilkerran], fifth baronet (1800–1849), landowner', *ODNB*; Peter Harnetty, 'Fergusson, Sir James, of Kilkerran, sixth baronet (1832–1907), politician and colonial governor', *ODNB*.

171 *The Times*, 16 June 1857, p. 1.

172 John Benyon, 'Barkly, Sir Henry (1815–1898), colonial governor', *ODNB*.

173 Jeanine Grahame, 'Domett, Alfred (1811–1887), writer and premier of New Zealand', *ODNB*; T71/882 Nevis no. 20.

174 Brian H. Fletcher, 'Darling, Sir Ralph (1772–1858), army officer and colonial governor', *ODNB*.

3 Helping to make Britain great: the commercial legacies of slave-ownership in Britain

Nicholas Draper

In the decades following Emancipation, Britain's economy and in particular its financial and commercial structure continued to undergo significant changes that reflected its emergence as the world's first industrial nation: the apotheosis of cotton; the explosion of British overseas trade and within that dynamic growth the reorientation of British long-distance commerce towards Asia, Latin America and the settler colonies; the consolidation of the City of London as the centre of global capital flows with its concomitant growth in merchant banking, in financial services and in the professions supporting the City; the emergence of the joint-stock company; the increased integration of Britain through the railway and of the world through the steamship and telegraph; and the birth of the free-trade nation.

Together these changes were constitutive of a recognisably 'modern' economy, and each was seemingly the antithesis of the bounded colonial system, dominated by sugar, in which British slave-ownership had been embedded. To whatever extent colonial slavery had helped to create the preconditions for this transformation,[1] and notwithstanding recent scholarly scrutiny of the extent of compliance with the restrictions of the mercantile system, British slavery depended on colonial preference, on bilateral trade within a series of protective duties, on archaic forms of labour control and on personal proprietorship.[2] It might reasonably be supposed, therefore, that the slave-owners and the British merchants connected with them were part of the detritus swept away by the forces of modernity that overthrew slavery in the 1830s and colonial preference in the 1840s. This is certainly the way in which, to the extent they appear at all in the history of the British economy of the mid-nineteenth century, the 'West Indians' – the slave-owners and the merchants and financiers who handled their goods and advanced credit to them – have been presented, as the remnants of an outmoded and obstructive interest. Kynaston, for example, wrote of the opposition to free trade among 'the West India merchants, who were in any case in long-term decline', and classed them among 'the City's dead wood'.[3]

But the analysis of the 'commercial legacies' of the slave-owners and others financially interested in slavery at the time of its demise allows a re-examination of this received wisdom, and presents an altogether more complex picture that resituates many (former) slave-owners as important contributors to the transformation of the British economy between the 1830s and the 1870s, at the same time as it confirms that other slave-owners were indeed swept away by their inability to adapt to challenges originating both before and, especially, after Emancipation. Robin Pearson's notion of 'collective diversification' aptly describes the movement of sections of 'West Indians' as groups undertaking similar strategies to reduce the absolute or relative importance of the West Indies in their overall business activities.[4] This was part of what has come to be seen as a partial abandonment of the West Indies by the British state and British capital after the end of slavery, a characterisation that seems to have particular force in the case of Jamaica and the Leeward Islands colonies. At the same time, other groups recommitted successfully to the post-Emancipation West Indies, most markedly in the newer colonies. Such groups bequeathed a series of financial, institutional and corporate legacies explored in this chapter and collectively labelled as 'commercial' in order to reflect the fundamental importance of the mercantile sector in transmitting the fruits of slavery to the metropolitan British economy. Even where slave-derived wealth was invested in industrial projects in Britain, it was almost invariably mediated by merchants.[5] This summary chapter also emphasises the City of London at the expense of Glasgow, Liverpool and Bristol, the other port cities vital to slavery and for which in turn slavery was constitutive. Such emphasis on the City of London is not because these other cities are unimportant but because it is not possible to capture all the webs of connections embedded in our material in a single chapter. Work is underway elsewhere for some of Britain's main port cities, and it is hoped that further work for others will be undertaken, building on the foundations of the research to date.[6] For both the City of London and other port cities, the story of slave-wealth's transmission into Britain is also above all a story of mercantile capital, the merchants acting as channels for slave-derived wealth to flow into other areas of the economy, including investment in infrastructure and industry.

The lens through which the (partial) picture that follows is constructed, the lens of British colonial slave-ownership, is of course only part of the wider picture of the economic impact of the slave-system. First, British financial and human capital was active in many areas of the slave-economy beyond the British colonies, both before and after Emancipation.[7] For

example, the leading merchant bank Kleinwort Benson, a major force in
the City of London for more than a century, had one part of its origins in
the activity of Alexander Kleinwort in the cigar business in Cuba in the
1840s and 1850s. The other part of Kleinwort Benson's origins were in
the cotton-broking business: John Walter Cross of Dennistoun, Cross &
Co. (which had been established as part of an interlocking series of partnerships in Glasgow, New Orleans, Liverpool and London and traded
with the antebellum south) took on Robert Benson and put capital into
Cross, Benson & Co. in September 1875 after Robert Benson's earlier
bankruptcy (John Walter Cross later married the novelist George Eliot,
in May 1880).[8] Britain's cotton industry and the cotton-broking sector
in particular, as argued below, had an important part of its origins in the
West Indian slave-economy, but, by the time John Walter Cross rescued
Robert Benson, US cotton (slave-grown until the Civil War) had long
displaced West Indian cotton. Hence, Kleinwort Benson's origins were
not concerned with *British* colonial slavery but were certainly concerned
with Atlantic slavery as a whole.

Second, slave-*ownership* within the British colonies was only one form of
participation in the slave-economy. In processes that are well understood
and well documented, other forms of engagement in the slave-economy –
the advance of credit to slave-owners by mercantile consignees in Britain,
for example – often evolved into slave-ownership through mortgage and
foreclosure. Almost all of the London merchants identified as leaders
in the West Indian trade in the early 1830s appear in the compensation
records as owners or mortgagees of enslaved people. Only a handful do
not: Micholls & Lucas, the major London–Manchester trading house, is
a rare example of a metropolitan mercantile firm steeped in dealing in
produce of the slave-economy but of whom no trace has been found to
date in the slave compensation records, implying the firm eschewed both
slave-ownership and the extension of credit secured on enslaved people.
But trade in slave-grown sugar, indigo, mahogany, coffee and other slave-
produced commodities is not fully captured by data on slave-owning:
credit advances by metropolitan merchants to slave-owners whose produce they bought often led to involvement in mortgaging of 'slave-property' and ultimately to ownership, but this was not invariably the case. E.
D. & F. Man, the commodity broker that evolved into the Man Group plc
hedge fund management group (which in 2000 spun off the commodity business under its nineteenth-century name), was founded by James
Man as a sugar broker and barrel maker in 1783, and traded coffee and
cocoa as well as sugar from the early 1800s, but has not been found in
the slave compensation records.[9] Neither is the transformation of such
commodities in the metropole, above all sugar-refining, a major industrial sector, caught in the compensation records; nor is the consumption

in the slave-economy of goods manufactured in Britain, not only textiles for the clothing allowances of the enslaved people but also increasingly sophisticated machinery for sugar production. Finally, by definition our work does not capture the multiplier effects of any of these aspects of the colonial slave-economy. Focused as we are on slave-*ownership* within the overall slave-system, and not on its systemic effects, we therefore do not in any way present evidence concerning the totality of Britain's debt to slavery.

Nor does our reassessment of the place of slave-ownership imply that slave-owners (or even slavery itself) were central to all the changes that took place. Slave-ownership permeated British commercial life (and in itself that is an important conclusion), but it did not always determine the direction or the pace of change. There are numerous instances in our data where slave-ownership was clearly incidental to other activities, a consequence rather than a cause of commercial enterprise elsewhere. We have striven to be scrupulous in distinguishing the two.

Nevertheless, our conclusions qualify the prevailing story of 'decline' of the British slave-system after the abolition of the slave-trade in 1807 (a narrative shared by Williams and Drescher,[10] whose disagreement concerned whether or not decline was already underway *before* 1807 but who were equally convinced of decline *after* 1807), and point to continued contributions by former slave-owners to the transformation of British commerce. However, because we do seek to complicate the narrative of 'decline', it is important to acknowledge the reality of financial pressures on important sections of the slave-owners in the early nineteenth century. Slave-owners had consistently cried of distress, and had equally consistently secured substantial financial support from the British state throughout the eighteenth and nineteenth centuries. Abolitionists lost patience with these rhetorical tropes in the 1820s, at exactly the time when in some areas of the Caribbean slave-economy it is clear that the profitability of slave-ownership was indeed in structural decline, and that slave-owners' rhetoric and their reality had for once converged.

Hence it is necessary to set out evidence from our analysis of the slave-owners that supports 'decline', before we turn to evidence for the continued dynamism on the part of many slave-owners, which we argue went beyond successful reaction and adaptation to change and saw those slave-owners themselves as agents of change.

Failure

Risk and failure had been inherent in the mercantile and manufacturing economies of Britain in the eighteenth century.[11] The vulnerability of the typical business unit, organised as a partnership with limited recourse to outside capital, was exacerbated by the onset of successive cyclical crises in the nineteenth century, both before and after Emancipation.[12] The years 1825–6, 1837–8, 1847–8, 1856–7 and 1866 all saw multiple collapses across the spectrum of business activity in Britain. When Abel Lewes Gower had to resign from the directorate of the Bank of England after his firm failed in 1847 (because of excessive exposure to the Mauritius sugar economy), he became the sixth of the previous nine governors to have gone bankrupt. Within this overall context of heightened risk, the 'West Indian' merchants had still greater vulnerability occasioned by periodic crises in the underlying sugar market as well as by systemic credit crunches.

Part of the background to the Emancipation Act itself was the sugar crisis of 1830–1, which weakened the resistance to Emancipation of the West India interest, above all the Jamaican component of it, and hastened acquiescence in compensated Emancipation. This period saw the collapse of dozens of West India merchants in Britain, notably Manning & Anderdon, the firm of William Manning (the father of Cardinal Manning), a failure that in turn threatened Smith, Payne & Smith, the bank of the Evangelical Smith family.[13] The Smith bankers and their lawyers, Freshfields, were prominent in the compensation process seeking to secure the firm's capital by accessing compensation funds, which they succeeded in doing.

William Manning told his son that he had grown up with men for whom bankruptcy was synonymous with death.[14] For some, although not Manning himself, this remained the case.[15] In the early 1840s, Edmund Francis Green was found dead shortly after a fiat in bankruptcy was issued against him. The coroner reported: 'It had by some been rumoured that the deceased had taken poison, and by others that he died of a broken heart, owing to misfortune, he having lost a large fortune in mercantile pursuits, and become bankrupt.'[16] Nathaniel Snell Chauncy, the third generation of a London West India mercantile family whose father left £125,000 in 1809, is thought to have killed himself in 1856, a dozen years after he hit severe financial difficulties.[17]

Less fatally, the early 1840s also saw the bankruptcy of major former slave-owners, including Rowland Mitchell of the London merchant firm W. R. & S. Mitchell and Philip Protheroe of Bristol.[18] Emancipation in isolation did not destroy the West India merchants: it was the ending of the preference for colonial sugar from 1846 onwards that truly tested them. The 1847–8 crisis undermined Sir John Rae Reid (yet another governor of the Bank of England to fail) as well as Abel Lewes Gower: Reid's firm had, like that of Gower, heavily extended itself into lending to former slave-owners in Mauritius. The crisis was triggered by the failure on 15 November 1847 of Trueman & Cook, the leading colonial produce broker, and thirty-three significant houses failed, mostly East and West India houses dependent on the traditional protected system.[19]

Nor, of course, is failure always easy to read across generations. John Crosthwaite, a former slave-owner and West India merchant, went bankrupt in 1850; his son Arthur, a small child when his father failed, became a stockbroker, was Lord Mayor of Liverpool and left £70,000 on his death in 1925.[20] Shortly before the payment of slave compensation, the firm of D. H., J. A. and H. J. Rucker had failed: the compensation for the enslaved people over whom the firm had claims was paid to assignees. But J. A. Rucker's son, Daniel Henry Rucker, re-established himself and left £170,000 in 1890, and Daniel Henry Rucker's son Edward Augustus, who died in 1915, left over £192,000. He had been a founding director in 1888 of the London Produce Clearing House, a futures exchange and clearing house and part of the 'plumbing' of the City until the firm's sale to United Dominion Trust in 1950.[21]

The evidence is nevertheless clear for widespread sequential failures of former mercantile slave-owners, a litany that fits with the narrative of decline initiated or accelerated by the abolition of the slave-trade, compounded by the abolition of slavery and then completed by the end of the preferential sugar duties from 1846. These failures, visible to contemporaries, were real, and echo the pressures on the resident and absentee rentier slave-owners analysed in the previous chapter.

Survival

Given the risks of the environment and of the partnership structure (with the dissolution of the firm on retirement of a partner), given the frequency of bankruptcy for all businesses, given the particular challenges to the sugar economy and given the received wisdom of the decline and fall of the planter class and the mercantile community connected with it, there might reasonably be expected to be few if any among the formerly slave-owning mercantile firms that survived the commercial carnage prevalent in mid-century. But 'West India merchants' did not cease to exist after Emancipation: Dombey and Son in Dickens' 1846–8 novel were West India merchants. And in fact (in contrast to Dombey and Son), a striking number of such firms survived into the late nineteenth century, many into the twentieth and some into even the twenty-first century, including among the latter Booker plc (now solely a food wholesaler). Almost 200 merchant firms in London have been identified in the compensation records (of whom just under half were primarily West India merchants, the others more diversified international traders or specialists with an apparently anomalous single appearance in the compensation records). Two dozen or so had ceased to trade (or ceased to appear in the trade directories) by the mid-1830s, sometimes by virtue of retirement of the partners but more often as a result of bankruptcy: such latter firms appear in the compensation records because their assignees, trustees and creditors claimed or received compensation for enslaved people owned or mortgaged by the defunct firms before their demise. Of the London mercantile firms actively trading at the time of compensation, approximately twenty disappeared from the London trade directories by 1840, forty between 1840 and 1850 and a further forty between 1850 and 1863. Almost sixty of the original firms are thus still identifiable in the 1863 trade directories, and of these over a dozen were still extant after the First World War and still a dozen after the Second World War.

With many such surviving firms there is nevertheless a perceptible decline in scope and prominence. The West India merchant and slave-owner Boddington & Co., founded in the late eighteenth century and whose early partners included Richard 'Conversation' Sharp and the cotton magnate Sir George Philips, endured for a century and a half. The firm appeared at the same St Helens Place address between 1834 and 1902, and it was still listed in the London Post Office directory of 1927. Thomas Boddington left £120,000 in 1821. His nephew Samuel Boddington left £150,000 in 1843. Samuel's nephew Thomas Boddington the younger (son of Samuel's brother Thomas Boddington [1774–1862], who left £60,000), who rehabilitated Gunnersbury Lodge in West London, appears to have been the last member of the firm bearing the family name; he also served as a director of the Eagle Star insurance company.[22] By this stage, the family's fortunes were eroding: Thomas Boddington the younger left £12,000 in 1881. The firm, however, continued, at first with Ernest Luxmoore Marshall (who left almost £70,000 in 1947) and Sir John Alexander Hanham as partners in the 1880s and then with Ernest Luxmoore Marshall alone.[23] Similarly, the Sheddens were a well-established family of merchants in the mid-nineteenth-century City whose activities spanned more than a century but whose fortunes show a deterioration across that period. The founder of the dynasty, Robert Shedden (an American Loyalist who died in 1826) and two of his sons (the merchant George Shedden and the rentier Robert Shedden) were among the richest men of their respective generations.[24] Their brother John Shedden, an army officer, married the sister of Mathew 'Monk' Lewis, the Gothic novelist and slave-owner. George Shedden's son William George Shedden founded another West India merchant business, Hawthorn & Shedden, in the last years of slavery and left £45,000 in 1872. The latter firm, however, eventually failed

in 1895.[25] Again, the firm of Claud Neilson appeared in the London directories until 1927. The eponymous founder had been a partner in Hon.
William Fraser, Alexander, Neilson, a major recipient of slave compensation in the 1830s; Neilson died in 1872 leaving £25,000. His son, also
Claud, of 1 Jeffreys Square, died in 1898 leaving £6,768 14s.

Success

Hence, some former slave-owning firms that survived for a generation or
two after Emancipation had been and remained obscure firms operating
on a small scale, while a number had been prominent but declined in
significance over the nineteenth century. Still others, however, remained
significant forces in British business post-Emancipation.

For example, the firm of R. & T. Neave had been founded in the late
eighteenth century by Sir Richard Neave, first Bart., who died in 1814
leaving £150,000 after transforming his estate at Dagnam Park in Essex.
His son and successor Sir Thomas Neave was awarded material amounts
of slave compensation. The mercantile interests were pursued by Sheffield
Neave, a younger son of Sir Thomas Neave, second Bart., who became
governor of the Bank of England and left £100,000 in 1868. Until 1885,
the partners in R. & T. Neave, which had remained a West India merchant
house, were Sheffield Neave's sons Sheffield Henry Morier Neave and
Edward Strangways Neave, and Arthur Morier Lee.[26] Sheffield Henry
Morier Neave left £204,872 2s 7d on his death in 1936; his grandson
was Airy Neave, the Conservative politician killed by the IRA in 1979.
Edward Strangways Neave, who left the firm in 1889,[27] had a different
trajectory and left less than £1,000 on his death. These two were the last
family representatives in the firm (the title and estate continued in a line
to the current incumbent, Sir Paul Arundell Neave, seventh Bart., who
was himself a member of the London Stock Exchange and director of
the stockbroker Henderson Crosthwaite). Arthur Morier Lee, the son
of Sir George Philip Lee (who had been lieutenant of the Yeomen of
the Guard), grandson of London merchant and slave-mortgagee John
Ede of Upper Harley Street[28] and husband of the folk music archivist
Catharine Anne Lee née Spooner,[29] continued the firm after the departure of Edward Strangways Neave in 1889 as Lee & Crerar and then as
A. M. Lee & Co.[30]

Both sides of the Hankey family, bankers and merchants, flourished
in the City for a century after their slave-owning came to an end. The
banking side of the family had its origins in the colonial slave-economy of
the late seventeenth century, established as Houblon & Hankey, 'traders
to Jamaica, Antigua and the Leeward Islands' in 1674.[31] When William

Alers Hankey (who with his half-brother Thomas owned the enslaved people on the Arcadia estate in Jamaica) gave evidence to the 1832 Select Committee on the Extinction of Slavery (where he argued for compensation), he was careful to define himself as a banker against the mercantile activity of the other side of the family. Although one of his sons, also William Alers Hankey (d. 1866), was a 'colonial broker' (who left £18,000), others followed their father into the bank until its sale to the Consolidated Bank Ltd. of Manchester and London in 1865. The mercantile side of the family included the elder Thomson Hankey and his brother John Peter Hankey of Simmond & Hankey. Altogether the family accounted for around a dozen of the richest British individuals to die in the nineteenth century.[32] From such wealth, distinction followed. Thomson Hankey the younger was governor of the Bank of England; his great-nephew Sir Ernest Harvey was deputy governor between 1929 and 1936.[33] William Alers Hankey's grandson Robert Alers Hankey (1838–1906) was an Australian pastoralist whose own son was the civil servant Maurice Pascal Alers Hankey, first Baron Hankey.[34] Beatrice, the daughter of George Hankey (who died in 1893), was a pioneer of women's ministry *avant la lettre*, and is in the *ODNB* as 'evangelist', where her father is described as 'a wealthy merchant banker of an old Cheshire family'; in fact he was a partner in a mercantile firm with its roots firmly in colonial slavery.[35]

Almost a dozen partners of the Barings merchant banking firm feature among the richest Britons dying in the first two-thirds of the nineteenth century, and the family certainly represented the pinnacle of financial and social success well into the twentieth century.[36] Equally certainly, slave compensation was an important recourse for them in the 1830s after over-extension to the British Guiana slave-owner Wolfert Katz.[37] Similarly, Charles McGarel, a major mercantile slave-owner in British Guiana whose firm evolved into Curtis Campbell under the leadership of McGarel's brother-in-law Quintin Hogg (the founder of a twentieth-century Conservative political dynasty including two lord chancellors, each bearing McGarel's name), left £500,000 on his death in 1876.[38] At least ten other London mercantile firms furnished two or more individuals whose significant slave-derived mercantile wealth placed them in the realm of the very rich in Britain in the first three-quarters of the nineteenth century, eight of the firms spanning at least two generations.[39]

Similar slave-owning mercantile dynasties were established in Glasgow and Liverpool. In Glasgow, John Douglas (1768–1840), Thomas Dunlop Douglas (1776–1869) and Archibald Douglas (1778–1860) were partners in J., T. & A. Douglas of Glasgow and recipients of slave compensation in British Guiana as owners and mortgagees.[40] Thomas Dunlop Douglas, the last of the family in the firm, left almost a quarter of a million pounds in 1869.[41] Their sister Cecilia (1772–1862), who had married another West India merchant, Gilbert Douglas, 'left a large fortune, and a fine collection of paintings and sculptures, which she made during her extended residence in Italy and which was presented to the Corporation of Glasgow (who deposited them in their Galleries in Sauciehall Street) in accordance with her direction to deposit it "in some public institution in Scotland."'[42] She had been awarded half the compensation for the 231 enslaved people on the Mount Pleasant estate on St Vincent in 1836.[43] Her nephew John Douglas (1810–71), the son of Archibald, was an army officer wounded at the Charge of the Light Brigade and left £102,873.[44]

The firm that evolved into Sandbach Tinne in Liverpool was founded in 1782 (originally as McInroy, Sandbach & Co.) in Demerara, then under Dutch rule.[45] The Tinnes joined in 1813. The firm, 'the Rothschilds of Demerara', was a major recipient of slave compensation in the 1830s. The firm's partners at the beginning of the twentieth century were still recognisably from the same founding families: John Ernest Tinne (1845–1925), Charles Sandbach Parker (1864–1920), Evelyn Stuart Parker (1870–1936) and John Abraham Tinne (1877–1933). The final general meeting of the firm after its winding up was held at 34 Farringdon Street on 14 August 1975, two centuries after its inception.[46] The firm generated substantial wealth from slave-owning and trading in the slave-economy for the founding partners and from the sugar and shipping businesses for the generations who succeeded. At least ten family members featured among the richest people in Britain on their deaths, spanning more than a century.[47] Again, local distinction followed wealth. The Right Hon. Charles Stuart Parker (1829–1910) 'who inherited ample means' (as well as changing the spelling of his middle name to evoke a lineage from seventeenth-century royalty) was a politician, a Liberal MP who served on the public school commission and an important historian of the Peelites, endowing two Parker scholarships for Modern History at University College Oxford.[48] John Abraham Tinne (1877–1933), a partner in 1908, was MP for Wavertree 1924–31.[49]

For other mercantile firms in Britain that appear in the slave compensation records, the materiality of slave-*ownership* is open to question. For example, Joseph Travers & Sons was a significant wholesale grocer for two centuries, from 1728 until after the Second World War, originating as a sugar broker and then diversifying (the family gave rise to Ben Travers the farceur) into a produce merchant. At some point, the senior partner Joseph Travers became the owner of Harmony Hall estate in Trelawney; the compensation for the enslaved people on the estate was paid to John and Joseph Travers as trustees of Joseph Travers, who had died in 1820.[50] The firm was rooted in the slave-economy, more specif-ically in the sugar industry, but its slave-ownership appears to have been incidental to its participation in the wider slave-economy. However, for the firms discussed above as generating individual wealth for partners, slave-ownership or mortgaging of 'slave-property' *was* material. Such firms in aggregate left many significant commercial legacies in Britain, and the remainder of this chapter will present the evidence for these leg-acies under four headings: cotton; railways and shipping; overseas trade, the 'swing east' and the settler colonies; and 'the City'. As noted earlier, these legacies are by no means the only commercial legacies of slave-ownership, nor are the accounts of each of them exhaustive. Rather, what follows is intended to highlight some areas of particular importance to the transformation of the British economy and some areas of particularly intense links to slave-ownership.

Cotton

The slave-colonies of the West Indies, especially Grenada and British Guiana, were originally the main source of raw cotton for Britain, and, although cotton from the US south had long supplanted colonial cotton by the 1830s,[51] echoes of this earlier period can be found in the presence of Glasgow and especially Liverpool cotton brokers among the recipients of compensation. Stephen Mullen has traced the activity of Leitch and Smith of Glasgow in trading cotton with the Spanish in Grenada before 1786 and still importing cotton into Britain from Jamaica and Grenada in the 1820s.[52] In Liverpool, of the sixteen broking firms listed there by Ellison as the initial subscribers to the cotton trade's *General Circular* in 1832, and implicitly positioned by him as the core of the Liverpool cotton-broking community at that time, three appear directly in the com-pensation records: Nicholas Waterhouse and Sons, Ewart Myers, and Salisbury, Turner and Earle.[53] A fourth, Priestley, Griffiths and Cox, had traded until 1831 as Yates Brothers, which appears in the compensation records as an awardee in Trinidad.[54] A fifth (T. & H. Littledale) is known to have acted as the agent of the slave-owner John Bolton, while a sixth (Shand & Horsfall) appears to have been a partnership between two sons of slave-owners.[55] A seventh, Gladstone and Serjeantson, was a successor firm to Corrie, Gladstone and Bradshaw, corn-factors, John Gladstone's firm: the name partner was Thomas Steuart Gladstone. Members of this firm were steeped in the slave compensation process but the firm was not itself a slave-owner.[56]

Nicholas Waterhouse's firm was agent and mortgagee for Benjamin James Hopkinson on his cotton estates John & Cove and Craig Miln in

British Guiana, and Daniel, Rogers and Alfred Waterhouse and Thomas Bouch claimed a share in the compensation as holders of a lien for £17,007; the firm also counterclaimed as holders of two liens totalling £2,242 on the Clonbrook estate, which belonged to another free family of colour, the Rogers.[57] The partners of Ewart Myers were awarded the compensation for the enslaved people on Long Lane Delap's in Antigua as mortgagees-in-trust. Nicholas Salisbury & Co. had been established in 1808 or 1809. In 1812 the partnership was expanded to include John Hayward Turner and Hardman Earle, and the firm became Salisbury, Turner and Earle: 'Mr Earle attended to cotton, and the other partners to general produce.'[58] Nicholas Salisbury was awarded with the Lancaster solicitor John Taylor Wilson part of the compensation for the Broom Hall cotton estate in British Guiana.[59] His partners Hardman Earle (the son of the slave-trader Thomas Earle) and John Hayward Turner were significant awardees of compensation as trustees of Charles Turner, the West India merchant and slave-owner whose business in London failed in 1831.

The argument here is not that slave-ownership or even British colonial slave-grown cotton were material to these firms by the 1830s, although the £20,000 owed to Nicholas Waterhouse must have been significant in the context of the firm's capital.[60] What is argued is that slave-ownership in the 1830s was the residual evidence, first, of the prior importance of British colonial slave-grown cotton in the formative years of the Lancashire cotton industry and the associated development of the Liverpool cotton brokers who were so crucial a part of the cotton/US slavery nexus until the 1860s, and, second, of the continued importance of these early firms in the greatly expanded cotton-broking sector in the Liverpool of the antebellum years. The lens of the slave compensation process allows the recovery not only of the debt of Liverpool to British colonial cotton but also of specific continuities between the firms of the 1790s and 1800s that were trading in slave-grown cotton from the British colonies, and the most important firms of the 1830s and beyond, which consolidated Liverpool's position as the financial centre of the global slave-cotton industry.

The evidence suggests that, first, Liverpool cotton-broking was initially founded on West Indian cotton and, second, the early firms founded on British colonial slavery continued to thrive as important players even as new capital and men entered the industry as American slave-grown cotton overwhelmed West Indian cotton; in other words, these early firms adapted, and moved human and financial capital from the West Indian trade to the US trade. It may reasonably be objected that the mere fact of the existence of a firm in the 1790s does not demonstrate that it was trading in West Indian cotton. In fact, of the nine firms identified by Ellison as being founded between 1780 and 1800 (Holt Davies, N. Waterhouse, Ewart Rutson, William Peers, Thomas Tattersall, Edgar Corrie, Richard Dobson, Joseph Greaves, Thomas & Isaac Littledale), all of which were either still extant or had recognisable successor firms in the 1830s and 1840s,[61] Ellison gives specific evidence of all but Peers, Corrie and Greaves dealing in West Indian cotton.[62] T. & H. Littledale had been formed as Thomas & Isaac Littledale in 1795; in 1825 Isaac Littledale retired and Harold Littledale, nephew of Isaac, became partner. Ellison reports that the partnership was a consequence of the success of Harold Littledale in finding buyers at the top of the market on behalf of the slave-owner Colonel John Bolton for a consignment of Demerara cotton.[63] John Bolton originally left his country seat to Harold Littledale but then revised his will.[64] One of Thomas Littledale's sons was christened John Bolton Littledale. An early partner in Joseph Greaves between 1805 and 1816 was John Ashton Yates, who went on to found Yates Brothers.[65] Overall, of the first twenty presidents of the Cotton Brokers Association, half can be traced in their lineage to firms founded in the period of dependence on West Indian cotton sixty years before.[66]

Slave-owners were intertwined with cotton-manufacturing, as well as with cotton-broking. As noted above, Sir George Philips, Manchester cotton industrialist and free trader, had been a partner in Boddington, Sharp and Philips.[67] The firm was a major recipient of slave compensation and Philips himself appears in the compensation records counter-claiming with Thomas Boddington and Richard Davis as assignees of the equity of redemption for an estate in Hanover, Jamaica.[68] However, Philips' family firm, J. and N. Philips, had been 'deeply engaged in the West Indian trade' as early as 1749;[69] Philips drew over £250,000 from the firm between 1807 and 1831. Slave-owning in his case was not the source of capital for cotton-manufacturing but the result of him participating in parallel streams of business activity, all of which were based ultimately on slavery. Again, of the fifteen founding proprietors in 1837 of Clarke, Acramans, Maze & Co., the builders and owners of the Great Western Cotton Works in Bristol, eight appear in the slave compensation records and a further one was the son of a slave-owner.[70] In Scotland, Devine has argued that '[a]bove all, West India merchant capital was often vital for the big cotton-spinning firms which dominated the industry before 1815' and pointed among others to the shareholding of Leitch & Smith and Stirling Gordon in James Finlay & Co., to John Campbell sen. & Co., and to Dennistoun, Buchanan, all the recipients of slave compensation.[71] In fact, Dennistoun, Buchanan put £160,000 into a single cotton mill complex at Stanley in Perthshire in the 1820s,[72] while the Glaswegian merchant and slave-owner Archibald Douglas reportedly was a partner in Douglas, Brown & Co., cotton spinners.[73]

Railways and shipping

In a striking illustration of the withdrawal of British capital from the former slave-colonies after Emancipation, the will of the London merchant and former slave-owner (and possible suicide) Nathaniel Snell Chauncy, made in 1848, specified that his property in the Caribbean should be disposed of and all the money raised should be invested in railway or other companies '[i]n England, Wales, Scotland or Ireland or any of the British colonies'.[74] It is tempting to extrapolate a wider pattern of disinvestment from the Caribbean and reinvestment into the railways. Slave-owners and West India merchants had certainly been prominent in two of the iconic early railway schemes. John Moss, the Liverpool banker and slave-owner, was the chairman successively of the provisional (1822) and then permanent (1824) committee of the Liverpool and Manchester Railway and the initial shareholders included Lister Ellis (whose executors were awarded slave compensation for an estate in British Guiana) and Joseph Christopher Ewart (a mortgagee-in-trust on an estate in Antigua), although the holdings of all the commercial founding shareholders combined were dwarfed by those of the Marquis of Stafford.[75] Among the Gibbs family members prominent in the initiation of the Great Western Railway was George Gibbs, cousin of George Henry and senior partner of the West India firm Gibbs Son & Bright of Bristol and Liverpool. Anthony Cooke has argued from his close analysis of the wills and testaments of Glasgow West India merchants that these men 'were actively involved in the "second phase" of Scotland's economic transformation through substantial railway investment in the 1840s and 1860s.'[76]

Slave compensation itself clearly coincided with the beginning of the railway boom, an event that galvanised capital and mobilised investors in Britain. In order to assess how material the cross-over was between the infusion of liquidity to slave-owners and mortgagees, we have sought to analyse systematically the presence of slave-owners among those investors, through the 1837, 1845 and 1846 parliamentary returns of subscribers to railway contracts. There are issues with these lists. Not all of these railways were built, for example. There was some fraudulent use of names on such lists and it is not always clear that an individual was investing on his or her own account. But the lists constitute the most extensive set of records of railway investors extant. The amounts of capital represented were huge, dwarfing the slave compensation. In 1837 the lists have total subscriptions of £31.7 million; in 1845 £61.6million in investments over £2,000 and a further £21.4 million in smaller amounts; and in 1846 £121.2 million. Hence, in total, over £230 million in subscriptions was made. By definition, slave compensation was only a small fragment of that total. Again, there are tens of thousands of subscribers listed, and, while several hundred slave-owners permeate these lists, these necessarily constitute a minority of the whole.

But the evidence suggests, first, that slave-owners were often among the most active of the subscribers, and, second, that in some railway companies, but a distinct minority, slave-owners subscribed a significant part of the total. For example, the Glasgow, Paisley, Kilmarnock and Ayr Railway Company was one of the focal points of slave-owning investment. In 1837, some 10 per cent of the total of £452,900 raised can be attributed to slave-owners: the lists are headed by Theodore Walrond, William Leckie Ewing, John Miller and his wife Mary Robinson Miller, all slave-owners and three of them Glasgow merchants. Mary Robinson Miller née McCook was born in Jamaica and moved to Scotland when her husband, who had been a merchant in Kingston, returned to Glasgow around 1816. It is not yet clear whether and how the cluster of slave-owners operated as a network in forming and driving this company. But John Fairfull Smith, Writer to the Signet and secretary of (and investor in) the Glasgow, Paisley, Kilmarnock and Ayr Railway Company was the recipient of slave compensation: he had married Caroline Turner, the daughter of a Jamaica slave-owner and as it happens the sister of Edward Turner, the first Professor of Chemistry at University College London. And, in 1846, the Glasgow merchant Thomas Dunlop Douglas, the recipient with partners of slave compensation for British Guiana, is shown as subscribing an extraordinary £336,100 to eleven railway contracts, all in Scotland, including several companies that were additions and amendments to the Glasgow, Paisley, Kilmarnock and Ayr Railway. In general, the significance of the slave-owners as investors appears to increase between the lists. In 1837, for example, a number of the companies have no identifiable links with slave-owners and, where there are concentrations, they are relatively modest, as with the Glasgow, Paisley, Kilmarnock and Ayr and its 10 per cent from slave-owners. By the mid-1840s, slave-owners were more prominent. In 1845, the Edinburgh and Northern, for example, had a marked concentration of slave-owners, both in Scotland and among the Scottish diaspora, drawing on networks in Liverpool but also in London: we estimate that over £80,000 or 40 per cent of the total subscriptions were from slave-owners, both from Scots and from the diaspora. Individual diasporic Scottish slave-owners were also prominent. In 1845 again, Patrick Maxwell Stewart, the

London-based Tobago slave-owner who with John Moss of Liverpool had handled the negotiation over compensation for the slave-owners with the British government in the 1830s, subscribed £153,730 to ten companies in England and Scotland, including £100,000 to the East & West India Docks & Birmingham Junction company. The overall picture is of uneven importance, high in some railway companies but incidental in many. The Glasgow, Paisley, Kilmarnock and Ayr and the Edinburgh and Northern are exceptions, not the rule.

The advent of steam technology coincided with the later days of slavery, and the technology was rapidly deployed in an effort spearheaded by slave-owners seeking to integrate the Caribbean and in turn to connect the region more closely to Britain. The Jamaica Steamship Co., founded in April 1836 with paid-up capital of £40,000, operated briefly between August 1837 and January 1838 before collapsing amid recrimination. Of the seven directors, four were slave-owners and a fifth the son or nephew of a slave-owner.[77] The Royal Mail Steam Packet Company was a more durable business. It was 'projected and organised' by James MacQueen, the geographer, pro-slavery polemicist and slave-owner.[78] Of the twelve original directors, nine were former slave-owners or recipients of slave compensation in another capacity.[79] The *ODNB* says of Alfred Booth (1834–1914), who was the son of the corn-factor Charles Booth (1799–1860) and Emily Fletcher (1803–53) and with his brother Charles Booth (1840–1916) became a major Liverpool ship owner, that 'his mother's side descended from West Indies merchants.'[80] His grandfather was Thomas Fletcher, a partner with Joseph Brooks Yates and a recipient of slave compensation. The Liverpool shipping companies Holts and the Ocean Steamship Company had their origins not in slave-ownership but in Liverpool's cotton-broking community and in the post-Emancipation Caribbean: Alfred Holt (1829–1991), the founder of the Ocean Steamship Company and son of the cotton broker George Holt (1790–1861), had been apprenticed to Samuel Hope, a leading Liverpool cotton broker, and ran a fleet in the West India trade from 1855 to 1864. Alfred Holt's nephew, Richard Durning Holt (1868–1941), who took the business on into the twentieth century, was also the son of another Liverpool cotton broker.[81]

Overseas trade, the 'swing east' and the settler colonies[82]

One of the corollaries of the explosive increase in Britain's international trade, the volume of which rose by a factor of five between 1840 and 1870, was the culmination of the prolonged emergence of new intermediaries between producer and customer. The century before 1870 was the 'crucial formative stage of British multinational merchant enterprise … From the heterogeneous and changing population of merchant houses, a number of larger and more stable firms had emerged by 1870.'[83] Many of these were oriented towards the East, towards Asia, African and Australasia, and others towards Latin America.[84] Their raison d'etre was to connect sellers and buyers, and thus in principle they inherently undermined their own existence.[85] In fact, such groups proved more durable than theoretically should have been the case. However, since they depended on local knowledge of markets, by definition they could be expected to have been specific to time and place, and to have shown zero correlation with West Indian slave-owners. Yet there are notable examples of slave-owners redeploying capital into trades in the East. John Gladstone is a well-known case, with his fundamental role in the founding of Oglivy Gillanders & Co.,[86] but the evidence suggests he was not alone.

James Campbell of Moore Park (1792–1874) and Colin Campbell of Colgrain (1782–1863) were sons of the major Glasgow West India merchant John Campbell senior (1735–1808). The firm became a mortgagee and in turn owner of enslaved people. At the time of Emancipation, the partners in John Campbell sen. & Co. were awarded at least £73,565 in compensation.[87] The firm itself was held to have 'faded away' in the late 1850s.[88] But, while some of the family continued its involvement in the post-Emancipation sugar economy regime through Curtis Campbell in London (where William Middleton Campbell, grandson of Colin Campbell, first of Colgrain, was a partner, leaving £711,000 in personalty on his death in 1919),[89] James Campbell and a number of his nephews reoriented themselves towards the East. James Campbell was described as

[t]he last survivor of the family of John Campbell senior: a man of fine presence and stately manners, and familiarly known as 'Dignity'. He was latterly in the East India trade, first in the Glasgow house of Campbell, Bogle & Douglas, and afterwards along with his nephews, sons to Colgrain, in the great Bombay house of Finlay Campbell & Co. He married Elizabeth Bogle of Gilmorehill and had a numerous family.[90]

The Campbell family remained plantation owners in British Guiana and, in the twentieth century, John Middleton 'Jock' Campbell (the great-great-grandson of Colin Campbell, first of Colgrain, partner in John Campbell sen. & Co.), of Curtis Campbell, the successor to Quintin Hogg's firm, went on to chair Booker after the merger of the companies in 1934.[91]

The firm of Blyth, Greene and Jourdain exemplified both the pull of slavery in Mauritius as part of the opportunity set offered by the East and the redeployment of human and financial capital from the Caribbean. James and Henry David Blyth had in 1826 joined their father in Thomas Blyth and Sons, a business established in Limehouse as a sail maker and ship chandler and later extending into whaling gear and investment in whaling voyages. James Blyth, having earlier visited Mauritius himself, went in September 1830 to run Thomas Blyth, Sons and Co. there and to undo the damage done by the initial inept performance of his brother Philip. He had a ten-year horizon, intending to return to Britain after a decade. He made £25,000 from the firm's Slave Indemnity Department, trading in slave compensation claims (Mauritian slave-owners were awarded government stock, not cash). Blyth and others founded the Mauritius Commercial Bank in 1838 (against the rival project of the Banque de Maurice).[92] In 1846 Henry David and James' brother-in-law Benjamin Buck Greene (who had married their sister Isabella in 1837) joined the partnership. Benjamin Buck Greene was the son of Benjamin Greene, the brewer, merchant and slave-owner in St Kitts. When Henry David Blyth died in 1864, he left personalty of £400,000.[93] James Blyth left £250,000 in 1873.[94] The firm continued past its 150th anniversary.

The evidence, then, is real for the shift East by some former slave-owners. But it should not be overstated. The majority of the Asian trading houses were founded between 1840 and 1860, and the bulk were not capital-intensive but grew from modest beginnings by entrepreneurial Britons, especially Scots. Of the sixteen firms trading to India, China and the Far East identified by Chapman, three appear in the slave compensation records: Ogilvy, Gillanders & Co., Palmer & Co. and James Finlay & Co. The last's involvement illustrates the embedding of long-standing businesses in the slave-economy as a by-product of their global trading links. James Finlay was founded in Glasgow in 1745, 'originally strong in the cotton trade and industry', before shifting in the 1860s from cotton to tea under Sir John Muir.[95] As noted above, cotton in the eighteenth century largely though not exclusively meant the West Indies. In the nineteenth century, the Glasgow West India firm of Leitch and Smith as a partnership was a member of both James Finlay of Glasgow and of Finlay Hodgson in London until 1823, and individual members of Leitch and Smith (James Smith and John Ryburn) continued as partners in both James Finlay and Finlay Hodgson until John Ryburn's retirement in 1834.[96] The partners in Leitch and Smith and its successors were recipients of slave compensation in Grenada. But underlying these specific ties to slave-ownership at the time of slave compensation was a wider move of redeployment from the Atlantic economy to Asia. In the case of John Swire & Co., there is no evidence of slave-ownership, but John Swire's father was a merchant who opened a merchant house in Liverpool in 1816 that imported raw cotton from New Orleans and exported cotton piece goods.[97] The Dent family were an important factor in early British trade with China, with the brothers Thomas (1796–1872), Lancelot (1799–1853) and Wilkinson Dent (1800–86) all involved.[98] Thomas, the key driver, was in Canton before 1820 and changed the name of W. S. Davidson's firm to Thomas Dent & Co. By 1824 he was back in London to join Rickards Mackintosh and in 1835 he joined Palmer Mackillop Dent & Co.; both firms appear in the slave compensation records, but West Indian slave-ownership was not their principal business. Lancelot was a partner in Messrs Keirs & Co. of Madeira, while Wilkinson Dent, 'a lesser man of business … unsuccessful in Europe' was a slave-owner prior to reorienting himself to the Far East.[99]

The palm oil trade in West Africa, 'legitimate' trade, was intertwined in complex ways with the slave-trade. There was at the time and remains controversy over the role of Matthew Forster in the 1820s and 1830s. Sir Frederick Pedler of Unilever understandably sought to distance the precursors of his company from the slave-trade. It was not possible for him to make this argument in the case of F. and A. Swanzy, rooted in service on the Gold Coast with the Company of Merchants Trading to Africa and with James Swanzy (the father of the eponymous Francis and Andrew Swanzy) continuing from surgeon on slave ships through governorships of two forts to his position as a leading slave-trader based in Austin Friars in London.[100] Pedler's argument in his chapter on the firm of R. & W. King – one of the few traders before 1807 – that its predecessors consciously held themselves apart from the slave-trade is largely supported by the evidence now available, but Sydenham Teast, whom Pedler characterised as 'a "legitimate" trader who would have nothing to do with slaving' nevertheless appears as a co-owner of a single slaving voyage in 1765 while Thomas King of Bristol (1759–1841), 'not engaged in the slave-trade', appears as the owner (with unknown others) of the *African Queen*, captained by Richard Buckle on a slave voyage in 1799.[101] James Swanzy's daughter-in-law petitioned the Colonial Office in 1841 to oppose the ending of domestic slavery on the Gold Coast.[102] James Finlay & Co. had been a shareholder in the Bathurst Trading Company Limited, purchased in 1917 by Lever Brothers to gain access to supplies of groundnuts from Gambia. But there is no evidence of slave-ownership in the Caribbean by members of the founding firms of the United Africa Company. The connections between the three members (including John Senhouse Goldie Taubman) of the Taubman family who represented the Central African Company on the board of the predecessor United African Company on its formation in 1879 and the slave-owning Senhouse family of Barbados are too remote to support an argument of connectivity.[103] Miller Brothers, which absorbed the business in West Africa of F.

and A. Swanzy in the early 1900s, had its origins in the involvement of Alexander and George Miller's disappointment with their participation in the West India trade, from which they turned away in 1868. The sons were born after Emancipation: it is implied by Pedler that James Miller, the father, 'a soft goods merchant in Glasgow', had no involvement in the West Indian trade prior to the sons' participation.[104]

While the links between West Indian slave-owners and West African trade before and after Emancipation, although real, were limited, London-based slave-owners played a more significant role in the commercial enterprises set up to develop and exploit the white settler colonies, especially Australia and Canada, in the 1820s and 1830s. Charles Bosanquet (formerly a partner in Manning and Anderdon) was 'governor of the Canadian Land Company and instrumental in bringing vast tracts of land in western Canada into cultivation'.[105] Sir Richard Neave was one of the nine of the Hudson Bay Company directors in 1802 and 1808.[106] By 1839, Andrew Colvile and Edward Ellice were on the board; Colvile was deputy governor in 1845 (when Ellice was still on the board); by 1863, Edward Ellice was deputy governor and Andrew Colvile's son Eden Colvile was on the board; Eden Colvile was deputy governor in 1879.[107] The British American Land Company was incorporated in 1834 and claimed to own one million acres of land by 1839, when its board included Russell Ellice and Patrick Maxwell Stewart, as well as Alexander Gillespie junior (probably the son of the Alexander Gillespie who acted as trustee of Inglis Ellice after its failure). By 1845, John Bloxam Elin had joined the board. Bloxam Elin, together with James Bogle Smith, was also a director of the Union Bank of Australia in 1845.[108] Among the two dozen directors of the Australian Agricultural Company (incorporated under 5 Geo. IV c. 86) in 1827 were William Manning of Manning & Anderdon as deputy governor, Richard Hart Davis the Bristol MP, Simon Halliday and Joseph Hume, who (notwithstanding his political radicalism) had married into a Trinidadian slave-owning family. The Bank of Queensland, formed under the joint-stock acts of 1857 and 1858, displayed a tripartite pattern of West Indian, East Indian and metropolitan connections: its board in 1863 included Joshua Rowe, former Chief Justice of Jamaica; Henry Brockett, late council member of Jamaica; J. B. Darvall, a slave-owner and recipient of slave compensation; N. B. Acworth of Madras; Arthur Hodgson of Drayton Hall and Queensland; two English provincial bankers; and two London bankers, including John Alers Hankey.[109]

Finally, there is evidence of British capital remaining active in the slave-trade after 1807 and in slavery after 1834 in the mining sector in South America.[110] John Irving was chairman of the National Brazilian

Mining Association in 1839. The company was not, despite its name, a trade association but the owner and operator of the Mocaubas and Cocaes mines, and rented enslaved people to another British-controlled mine, Morro Velho, in 1861.[111] Ambrose Humphrys of Upper Wimpole Street, a solicitor and a financier of slave-owners, was on the board of the United Mexican Mining Association in 1845, with the recipients of slave compensation John Hibbert, James Mackillop and John Biddulph. The Mexico Co. in 1827 was chaired by John Mitchell, and its thirteen directors included Philip Monoux Lucas, John Mitchell junior and James Deacon Hume, all (or their heirs) again recipients of slave compensation.

'The City'

In tracing the legacies of slavery and slave-ownership in the development of the nineteenth-century City of London, this section will focus on identified links between slavery and the City: the composition of one set of the City elites as expressed in the Bank of England; the evolution of banking more widely; new joint-stock company formation, notably in the insurance sector; and the development of the professional service sector within the City.

Recent scholarship has complicated the narrative of the Bank of England directorate as the summit of the City of London's mercantile elite. Of twenty-three directors elected between 1833 and 1847, half died leaving less than £100,000.[112] The directors were exposed to risk in their own businesses, and failure (as mentioned previously) was endemic. Nevertheless, of all the marks of acceptance, a directorship of the Bank weighed heavily, and the position was often accompanied by power elsewhere: ten of its directors in 1863, for example, were also MPs. Slave-owners and their descendants participated fully in this nexus of power.

The Bank had a 'particular bias' among its directorate towards Russia and West India merchants in the second quarter of the nineteenth century, according to Kynaston.[113] In fact, slave-owners and their direct descendants were prominent in the Bank's directorate throughout the century. Of twenty-six directors in 1801, five were West India merchants (Thomas Boddington, Beeston Long, Ebenezer Maitland, William Manning and Sir Richard Neave) while Peter Isaac Thellusson had been a major slave-owner in Grenada. By 1827, William Manning and Sir Richard Neave were still *in situ* and there were a further three West India merchants (William Mitchell, Samuel Hibbert and Sir John Rae Reid); John Horsley Palmer, who would later collect slave compensation, was also among the directors.

Of the 1839 directorate, three were West India merchants (Sir John Rae Reid, by that time deputy governor; Henry Davidson; and Thomson Hankey junior) and two had received slave compensation although their primary business was elsewhere (Alfred Latham of Arbuthnot Latham and Humphrey St John-Mildmay of Barings), while John Horsley Palmer was still in post. In 1863, when Alfred Latham was governor, the shadow of slavery persisted in the shape of Benjamin Buck Greene, who had spent his formative years managing slaves owned by his father Benjamin or by clients of the latter on St Kitts; Thomson Hankey junior; Bonamy Dobree; and three other sons of mortgagees of slave-property who had collected compensation in the 1830s, Edward Howley Palmer, Sheffield Neave and Charles Frederick Huth. Henry Huck Gibbs was the son of Henry Gibbs and nephew of William Gibbs of Anthony Gibbs & Sons, the sister firm of which, Gibbs, Bright (headed for many years by Henry and William's cousin George Gibbs), owned slaves in Jamaica (and later the SS *Great Britain*) and was eventually folded into Anthony Gibbs & Co. in 1881.[114]

The two slave-owning or mortgagee governors most active in the struggle to define and redefine the Bank of England's role in mid-century, John Horsley Palmer and Thomson Hankey, were on the wrong side of important debates from an historical point of view. The 'Palmer rule', governing the role of bullion in the Bank's reserves, was held by Samuel Jones Loyd and other influential bankers to have contributed to the financial crises of the late 1830s, and Palmer unsuccessfully resisted the Bank Charter Act of 1844.[115] Thomson Hankey opposed the development of the Bank of England as the lender of last resort.[116] The two men therefore support a view of the West Indians as regressive. But other West Indians and their descendants active in the Bank of England were by no means reactionary. In the 'American' financial crisis of 1857 the governor was Sheffield Neave, the deputy governor Bonamy Dobree and the chancellor Sir George Cornewall Lewis, all sons or nephews of slave-owners.[117] Two of the three 'capable governors' of the 1870s, Benjamin Buck Greene, John William Birch and Edward Howley Palmer, were also the sons of slave-owners.[118] The Greene–Gibbs policy of 1873–5 was articulated by two sons of slave-owners, and, in the 1890 Barings crisis, the government turned to Benjamin Buck Greene to determine the solvency of Barings prior to the launch of a lifeboat among City firms.[119] And the slave-owners cast a long shadow over the directorate of the Bank of England: as noted above, Sir Ernest Harvey, deputy governor in the 1930s, was the great-nephew of Thomson Hankey and the nephew of Richard Musgrave Harvey, a partner in Hankey's firm post-Emancipation.[120]

The middle decades of the century, as the Bank of England found its new role, also saw the decline of the London private banks and the rise of the joint-stock banks, and indeed the rise of joint-stock companies more generally, the corollary of which was the emergence of a professional class of managers and directors. This separation of ownership and control was novel and controversial. Timothy Abraham Curtis, a former governor of the Bank of England who was awarded slave compensation as a trustee of James Wilson, the slave-owner and MP, makes a cameo appearance in *Das Kapital*, in which Marx cites the commentary from *The City or the Physiology of London Business; With Sketches on Change, and the Coffee Houses* (London, 1845) on the details in Curtis' 'private balance sheet' of his income of between £800 and £900 a year from directorships, presented to the Court of Bankruptcy after his failure, which Marx cited as evidence of 'a new swindle' in the form of boards of numerous managers and directors being placed above the actual director, 'for whom supervision and management serve only as a pretext to plunder the stockholders and amass wealth'.[121] Slave-owners, unlike East Indians, had no prior involvement in joint-stock vehicles in their original enterprises, but they filled the new forums in large numbers, focused on banking, insurance and (as seen above) new colonial enterprises.

Of the fifty-two private banks that were members of the clearing house in 1810, only twenty-nine remained by 1841.[122] Many of the early joint-stock banks that challenged the private banks were metropolitan (London & Westminster; London Joint Stock; Union Bank of London; London & County; Commercial of London) and in 1854 were admitted to the clearing house.[123] So valuable was such access that the National Provincial Bank gave up provincial note-issuing in 1866 in order to secure a London base, forfeiting £500,000 per annum, while Lloyds gained a London presence and a seat on the London clearing house in 1884 by buying up Barnetts Hoares and Bosanquet, both Lombard Street private banks and both appearing in the slave compensation records, the former as an agent and the latter as a beneficiary.[124] Henry Luard, the influential general manager of the London and County bank between 1841 and 1856 (when his career ended in scandal), was awarded slave compensation in St Kitts as trustee under the will of his father, Peter John Luard (1755–1830) of Blyborough Hall: the house had been bought in 1747 by Peter John Luard's grandfather Zachariah Bourryau, a West Indian planter. John Stewart, a slave-owner in British Guiana and the first man of colour to be elected an MP, was a director of the London and Westminster joint-stock bank.[125] James Hughes Anderdon, a retired private banker, held shares in the Bank of London in 1856. Archibald Paull was a director of the National Provincial Bank of England until 1844.

The slave compensation records suggest that lending against enslaved people permeated provincial banking, not only in areas of predictable concentration – London, Liverpool, Bristol – but also throughout Britain. The partners in Alexander & Co., the Ipswich bank embedded in Quaker networks in East Anglia, counterclaimed unsuccessfully as assignees of an annuity of £200 per annum secured on the New Montpelier estate of Lord Seaford.[126] In some cases, a City of London bank tied its associated provincial banking networks into slavery. The importance of slave compensation to the banking firm of Smith, Payne & Smith has previously been noted.[127] Smith, Payne & Smith was of course the centre of a nineteenth-century City dynasty. John Abel Smith retired from the London firm on 31 December 1842, and from the Nottingham bank and Magniac Jardine & Co. on the same day, 30 June 1843.[128] Hugh Colin Smith, son of John Abel Smith, was involved in Hay's Wharf and became a director of the Bank of England in 1876.[129]

As private banks declined, so 'merchant banks' became central to the evolution of the Victorian City of London as the global financial centre and remained dominant until the 'Big Bang' in the 1980s unleashed US and European competition on the City. As the name implies, merchant banks developed from mercantile firms shipping physical commodities. They did not take deposits or have branch networks but were intermediaries like US investment banks but (until the Big Bang) without the stock-broking function of the integrated US houses. They financed trade and they secured capital for the world, for US railroads or for South American states, as the nineteenth century saw the City move from a national to a global role as a mobiliser and allocator of capital, 'the pivot of the world's entire commercial system'.[130] In the early loans, for example the loans to France of 1817 and 1818, and to Prussia of 1818, the City was an agent for continental money but subsequently the finance organised by the City increasingly reflected and reproduced Britain's position as the leading and eventually dominant exporter of capital.[131] For over a century, Britain celebrated this status and feted the merchant banks who sustained this system; but it has been suggested that its long-term results were that Britain remained characterised by small family firms for far too long and that competitors abroad were brought into being and sustained, as the patronage of merchant banks was not confined to British companies but extended to free international markets.[132]

The origins of merchant banking, the evolution of merchants into bankers, was bound up with the Atlantic world and specifically the need for credit instruments in the flow of tropical produce and of slaves.[133] The system of bills of exchange and acceptance credits centred on London accepting houses was the fruit of the Atlantic economy of long-distance trade of the eighteenth century. In the nineteenth century, there was an escape from commodity dealing by 'merchant banks'[134] and specialised houses gave way to 'internationally minded' firms as the volume of international trade expanded by a factor of five between 1840 and 1870.[135] At the same time, successive waves of 'cosmopolitan plutocrats' arrived in London from continental Europe and established new merchant banking firms. Hence, the sector's very existence was intimately bound up with slavery and specifically the slave-trade, but it evolved away from its initial intimate dependence.

The importance or otherwise of continuities of slave-ownership and slavery in this sector in the nineteenth- (and twentieth-)century City can be analysed by examining the position on the eve of the First World War. In 1914 (eighty years after the Abolition Act became effective), twenty-one London firms came together to form the Accepting Houses Committee. Of the twenty-one, twelve had their origins in Germany and ten had been established in London before 1834.[136] Of these ten firms in existence in London in 1834, partners of the firm or the firm itself received slave compensation in four cases (Arbuthnot Latham, Barings, F. Huth & Co., N. M. Rothschild). The materiality varies: Barings had bet one-third of the firm's total capital on credit to Wolfert Katz, the largest slave-owner in Berbice (and later boosted its capital by a merger with Finlay Hodgson, the firm into which James Campbell of John Campbell sen. & Co. redeployed slave-wealth);[137] whereas N. M. Rothschild and Frederick Huth each pursued compensation in a single case. Arbuthnot Latham was a hybrid case, exemplifying the 'swing to the East' in the form of Alfred Latham's decision in 1833 to join as the London partner of John Alves Arbuthnot, who was from an established East India mercantile family and had based himself in Madras. Alfred Latham came from a London-based mercantile family, originally wine merchants in partnership with the Pulsford family, the firm of Latham and Pulsford subsequently diversifying into the West India trade and into slave-ownership.[138]

So the analysis of the original Accepting Houses Committee would appear to suggest that slave-ownership had seeped into the merchant banking sector (which still bore its traces almost a century later) but was not its foundation. Yet slave-ownership of course was not the only kind of link to slavery. Of the merchant banks in the compensation records, cotton and sugar were a material part of the trade of F. Huth. Of the five firms established in London by 1834 and *not* receiving slave compensation, one (Brown Shipley) was a major trader in slave-grown cotton and two (Schroders and Fruhling & Goschen) can be identified in secondary histories as involved in the sugar and tobacco economies in the period of slavery (shipping colonial sugar from Britain to Europe and Russia and tobacco from Cuba to continental Europe), while a fourth, Anthony Gibbs, though making its fortune in guano, was intimately entwined with the Bristol–Liverpool slave-owning firm of Gibbs and Bright, which it absorbed in the 1880s.[139] Moreover, Kleinwort, as mentioned above, the best capitalised of all the accepting houses in 1914, had its origins in sugar and cigar business in the slave-economy of Cuba undertaken by Alexander Friedrich Kleinwort, who went to Havana in 1838, joined the major sugar exporter Drake's in 1840 and operated independently in the cigar trade throughout his time there.[140] Furthermore, not all the merchant banking firms that were significant to the City of London in the nineteenth century made it to the formation of the Accepting Houses Committee in 1914. McCalmont Brothers, a power in Atlantic finance in mid-century, whose eponymous partners were among the richest men to die in the nineteenth century, had its origins in the mid-1830s when Hugh McCalmont, an owner of property in Berbice, lent two of his sons, Robert and Hugh, £50,000 as their initial capital.[141] Overall, it is noticeable that the Asian houses that emerged did not give rise to a proportionate contribution to merchant banking, which (Arbuthnot Latham notwithstanding) was ultimately the fruit of continental Europe and of the Atlantic economy.

The ties between the Atlantic slave-system and the development of marine insurance in the eighteenth century have tended to be assumed rather than documented, with the notable exception of Joseph Inikori's estimates, drawn from data from A. H. John for the London Assurance Company (one of two joint-stock companies holding an effective monopoly on marine insurance alongside Lloyds until 1824), which suggested that in the 1790s premia for the slave-trade and the West Indies trade together amounted to 63 per cent of the whole marine insurance market in Great Britain. Subsequent reworking of the same data by Draper yielded a share of risks insured of 15 per cent and of premium income closer to one-third.[142] Both analyses suggest that the slave-economy was either critical (Inikori) or the most important single sector (Draper); but both are limited as authoritative estimates by the tiny fraction of overall marine business written by the London Assurance (and the Royal Exchange Assurance), both dwarfed by private insurers grouped together in Lloyds of London. There is no equivalent figure for the importance of the slave-trade and the West India trade in the development of Lloyds, nor has a systematic analysis yet been undertaken of the seventy-nine underwriters each putting up £100 to found 'New Lloyds' in 1771. What can be said is that close ties between slave-traders and London's marine insurance market existed in the eighteenth century and traces of this slavery–insurance nexus continue into the nineteenth century. James

Mather and John Shoolbred were known large-scale London slave-traders among the seventy-nine subscribers in New Lloyds. West India merchants had a consistent presence both in the governing body of Lloyds and on the boards of the two joint-stock insurers, the Royal Exchange and London Assurance. Joseph Marryat, absentee slave-owner and merchant, succeeded John Julius Angerstein as chairman of Lloyds in 1811 and served in that capacity until 1824; when he took the chair in 1811, the managing committee of Lloyds included James Swanzy, active in the London slave-trade as late as 1806. By 1801, two of twenty-seven directors of the Royal Exchange (Richard Lee of Old Broad Street, and William Vaughan of Dunsters Court Mincing Lane) and two of twenty-five directors of London Assurance (Deputy Governor Samuel Turner and his son Samuel Turner junior, both of 6 New City Chambers) were West India merchants while their co-director Robert Hankey of 7 Fenchurch Street was a banker in a firm with mortgages over 'West India property'.[143] These ties endured. In 1845, four or five (William Davidson, possibly John Deacon, William Tetlow Hibbert, John Ede and Charles J. Manning) of twenty-five directors of the Royal Exchange were West India merchants who had been beneficiaries of slave compensation ten years earlier, while two further directors, Edward Howley Palmer and Abraham George Robarts, were the sons of such beneficiaries.[144]

In the case of fire insurance, sugar-refining had been the basis for the Phoenix, which had seized a quarter of the British market within fifteen years of its founding in 1782. 'For the first twenty-five years of its life, this company was governed virtually exclusively by the sugar-refiners.'[145] The founding shareholders were also overwhelmingly sugar-refiners but included Sir Richard Neave. Subsequently 'financiers' arrived, including two men who were large-scale slave-traders, Alexander Anderson (elected in 1806 and forced off in 1814 for financial failure) and Richard Miles, 'with the sheen of operators' hot money', who served between 1810 and 1812 and was then similarly forced off for financial failure.[146]

In the first half of the nineteenth century, insurance-company formation was a significant element in the periodic manias of company promotion, but beneath the speculative bubbles there was strong secular growth in both the life and the fire insurance sectors. Sums assured in the life business increased more than tenfold between 1800 and 1852, from an estimated £10–12 million (of which the Equitable accounted for £5 million) to £150 million, and doubled again to £290 million in 1870.[147] It is striking against this background of rapid growth of the metropolitan industry, however, that neither insurance of enslaved people nor investment in West Indian assets (including enslaved people) feature in the history of British insurance. No evidence has yet been found of group insurance of enslaved people of the kind undertaken by some American insurance companies. Group insurance as a product appears in Britain to have post-dated Emancipation: in 1854, the Pelican underwrote the pioneering Post Office scheme for its employees as well as a policy covering the ballast men in Cardiff Docks, while in 1855 the company insured 'French Government coolies in transit from India to the West Indies'.[148]

Nor were insurance companies inclined to invest in mortgages on West Indian property. This appears to have reflected risk aversion rather than principled anti-slavery. British insurance companies in the eighteenth century invested primarily in government stock, in 'the funds', and turned to investment in mortgages at various times: the Phoenix had no investments outside the funds before 1816 and the Royal Exchange none in the eighteenth century, but Sun and the Equitable were active buyers of mortgages, the former with half to two-thirds of its investment assets in mortgages in the late eighteenth century. However, throughout the period, companies would barely lend against Irish estates, regarding them as novel and exotic forms of security: the Phoenix rejected four in five Irish proposals between 1823 and 1870, accepting only some of those in the Dublin Pale. In this context, investment in West Indian mortgages was a step too far.[149]

Again, this is not to say that the insurance companies did not lend indirectly against slavery by lending to slave-owners in Britain. The first loan against a life annuity by the Pelican (the life assurance offshoot of the Phoenix set up in 1797), in which it put up a lump sum in exchange for regular payments from the recipient, was of £8,000 on 21 May 1812 to John Anthony Storer of Purley, Berkshire, against an annuity of £1,000.[150] In 1820, 80 per cent of the Pelican's total portfolio was of such annuity loans, secured on landed estates in England. The Royal Exchange, generally a small player in the annuity market, lent £57,000 to the Marquis of Chandos in 1827 as an annuity loan.[151] The West Indies were also the site of other early innovations in insurance. The first non-European life assurance policy of the Pelican was written for Charles Douglas to travel from Jamaica to St Domingo for three guineas per £100, on 10 September 1799.[152] The firm's first co-insurance policy was written for Major-General Marcus Beresford, who died in Barbados in March 1803 with claims for £5,000 on Royal Exchange Assurance and £4,000 on Pelican.[153]

But the West Indies were limited in their significance as a market both for fire and life by the relatively small size of the white population and of the urban infrastructure. In 1805, the year in which twelve new agencies were opened by firms in the West Indies, its Caribbean business accounted for only 1 per cent of all Phoenix's foreign premia, and by 1826–35 it accounted for just over 3 per cent, against 69 per cent from

Europe in 1826–35.[154] The Caribbean was also a risky area for insurers, both fire and life. The conflagration of St Thomas in December 1806 was nearly catastrophic for the Phoenix (costing it £200,000), and was closely followed by the destruction of Port of Spain in Trinidad by fire in 1808.[155] Already by 1803, the Royal Exchange Assurance was rejecting proposals from the West Indies having 'resolved sometime since not to accept any further insurances there'.[156]

The main legacy of slave-ownership in the insurance sector was therefore neither market expansion nor investment returns. It was rather the role of slave-owners in the formation and conduct of the early insurance companies. The City of London was central to the development of such companies but did not have a monopoly. The share of London offices in fire insurance nationally fell from 85 per cent in 1810 to two-thirds by 1850.[157] After 1850, 'some of the most enterprising developments in insurance ... were not metropolitan at all.'[158] The fastest expansions of market share in the 1850s and 1860s and those that led the great boom in insurance exports of the 1860s and 1870s were by the Royal of Liverpool, the Liverpool and London and Globe, and the Glasgow-based North British (which built a 20 per cent market share). Both in London and elsewhere, a number of these newly established leading companies in life and fire, especially those with global ambitions, were clearly the product of a West Indian slave nexus.[159] The Imperial (established as a fire insurer as an offshoot of the West India Dock Company with seven of twenty-one directors appointed by Company, and a room in the Dock House) grew rapidly from its initial capital base of £1.2 million, setting up or acquiring eighty domestic agencies, especially in the industrial north, and bought the St George company in Liverpool in 1805.[160] Of twenty-one directors in 1808, eleven are identifiable as West India merchants.[161] In 1820, the Imperial formed a sister company, Imperial Life, and for another half-century the two companies' interlocking directorates were heavily populated with West India merchants. By 1839 both were chaired by former slave-owners (Imperial Fire by Samuel Hibbert and Imperial Life by Andrew Colvile) and Imperial Fire had ten of twenty-one directors and Imperial Life four of sixteen directors who had been beneficiaries of slave compensation, while the former directors listed included the slave-owners Charles Porcher Lang and Charles McGarel. In 1863, eight of twenty directors of Imperial Fire and five of fifteen in Imperial Life were identifiable as slave-owners or sons of slave-owners. The Imperial companies were acquired by Alliance Assurance in 1902.

Alliance Assurance itself was famously founded in 1824, at the end of the Lloyds/Royal Exchange/London Assurance monopoly in marine insurance. Of the five presidents of Alliance Assurance in 1827, two (John Irving and Francis Baring) had substantial involvement in the slave-economy (the other three were Nathan Mayer Rothschild, the Quaker Samuel Gurney and Moses Montefiore). The sixteen directors included two West India merchants and slave-owners (John Innes and David Lyon junior) and a third, Arch. Campbell, who was probably the Archibald Campbell of Campbell, Dent who owned enslaved people in British Guiana. By 1845, Irving, Gurney and Montefiore remained presidents and among their sixteen colleagues on the board were William Gladstone, John Irving junior and Melvil Wilson (all of whom appear in the slave compensation records) and Louis Lucas of the West India merchant Lucas & Micholls.[162] By 1863, the echo of slavery had almost died away: William Gladstone and Samuel Lucas of Lucas & Micholls were the last remaining directors with identifiable ties to slave-ownership or the slave-economy.[163] Alliance Assurance merged with Sun in 1959 and today forms part of the RSA Insurance Group after the merger of Sun Alliance and Royal Insurance in 1996.

The Indemnity Mutual Marine Assurance Co. was the first specialist company to enter the marine insurance business after the end of the monopoly of Lloyds, the Royal Exchange and London Assurance in 1824. The first policy was taken out by George Hibbert junior, who was a director. Of the twenty-five initial directors, six are identifiable as slave-owners or beneficiaries of slave compensation (the chairman Robert Rickards, George Hibbert junior, Edward Ellice, Ellis Ellis, John Innes and John Horsley Palmer).[164] Richard Hart Davis, the Bristol MP and anti-abolition campaigner, was also a director. The company, which abandoned mutuality after its first three years, was bought in 1917 by Northern Assurance, which in turn was acquired by Commercial Union in 1968 and is thus a predecessor firm of Aviva.[165] The Marine Insurance Co., which appeared briefly in the mid-1840s, had as its chairman James Bogle Smith; among the fifteeen directors were the former slave-owners Andrew Colvile, Benjamin Greene and Patrick Maxwell Stewart.

Crown Life was established in 1825, under the initial chairmanship of William Peat Litt, a slave-trader and slave-owner. The board of fifteen in 1827 included two other slave-owners ('Major Moody' and A[lexander] Stewart), the merchant George Henry Hooper (who appears as a counterclaimant and agent for slave compensation) and James Colquhoun (who was the agent for St Vincent, St Kitts, Dominica, Nevis and the Virgin Islands).[166] Moody, Colquhoun and Alexander Stewart remained on the board until at least 1845. The company merged in 1891 with the Law Union Fire & Life company; in turn, the combined company was acquired by the London and Lancashire Fire Insurance Company, and then by the Royal Insurance Company Limited.[167] Palladium Life was

established in 1824. Of the twenty-one directors in 1827, Sir Edward
Hyde East, John L[avicount] Anderdon, Samuel Bosanquet, W. R. K.
Douglas, Patrick Maxwell Stewart and Sir William Young were all slave-
owners or mortgagees of 'slave-property'.[168] The company, together with
the Albion, was absorbed by Eagle in the late 1850s.[169] Royal Insurance,
founded in 1845, had dual London and Liverpool boards. The London
Board in 1863 had only one director (Daniel Henry Rucker) with identifiable slave connections but the Liverpool board included three such directors: George Booker, Thomas Bouch as deputy chairman and George
H[enry] Horsfall. The Scottish insurers had in some instances London
boards. Scottish Union had an elaborate structure of a president, two
vice presidents, twelve honorary directors and twelve ordinary directors; among the honorary directors was Thomas Gladstone and among
the ordinary directors James Gordon Duff, John Kingston and Divie
Robertson as well as the solicitor Richard Oliverson.[170] The company
was another predecessor firm of the RSA Insurance Group.

The middle decades of the nineteenth century saw not only the explosion of the insurance sector but also the consolidation of some extant
professions aligned to business (such as commercial lawyers) and the rise
of new professions, most notably accountancy. These professions served
the slave-economy alongside many other sectors and it is hard to isolate
the proportion of the business of such professional firms attributable
to slavery or to slave-ownership. Rather, it is possible to see some firms
demonstrably embedded in the nexus of slave-ownership and others
where there is little or no evidence for such ties. This is not to say that
slavery did not touch these firms, only that no evidence is provided by
the compensation records. In addition, individuals with backgrounds in
the slave-economy joined the new professions, some in areas that have
marked commercial legacies even today.

Dozens of British solicitors, especially in London, are evident in the
slave compensation process, mainly but not exclusively in an agency capacity. William Henry Clapham, a London solicitor, was awarded slave
compensation as an assignee of John Henry Clapham, for many years
rector of the Port of Spain and rector of Isfield, Sussex ('to which he was
collated by Abp Moore in 1792'); John Henry Clapham died in Trinidad
aged seventy-six around 1835, and it is reasonable to infer that William
Henry Clapham or members of his immediate family were beneficiaries.[171] But in most cases solicitors shown as awardees were acting as
trustees or executors rather than as beneficiaries. Many of these firms
exhibited long continuity. Jonathan Brundrett, of Brundrett, Randall,
was awarded compensation as a trustee of John Graham Clark; the firm
he founded was taken over by 1972 by Edgley & Co., itself later absorbed

by Lawrence Graham & Co., continuing to practice as Lawrence Graham LLP (and itself founded before 1730; the firm's George Herbert Kinderley was appointed a trustee in a claim by Maria Dowager Countess of Carhampton).[172] Of the five leading law firms commonly known today as the 'Magic Circle' in the City of London, only two were extant at the beginning of the slave compensation process in the 1830s.[173] The role of one of these, Freshfields, as the solicitor to Smith, Payne & Smith and as an agent for slave-owners in the compensation process has been highlighted elsewhere.[174] In addition, 'Mr Freshfield' (James William Freshfield senior) was secretary to the West India Company as it sought a charter in 1825.[175] George Stephen, the abolitionist violently opposed to compensation and a partner in Freshfields, himself appears acting on behalf of a counterclaimant in pursuit of compensation.[176] Among smaller firms still practising today, Oliver Farrer of the royal solicitors Farrer & Co. was a trustee for George Watson Taylor, a major Jamaican slave-owner, probably by virtue of Farrer & Co.'s relationship with Coutts & Co. Other law firms heavily involved in slave compensation do not appear to have great continuity. John Hopton Forbes, senior partner of the London law firm of Forbes, Hale and Boys, appeared as an awardee in eight separate claims across the Caribbean; in almost all he is identifiable as a trustee. He was sufficiently embedded in the slave-economy to subscribe to the hurricane relief fund for Jamaica in 1832. The partnership appears to have ended around 1840: Matthew Hale died in 1848 and Forbes in 1873.[177]

In the middle years of the nineteenth century, the accountancy profession in England and Wales evolved from a first generation of accountants who had been insolvency specialists through a public accounting function towards major auditing firms supporting the growth of joint-stock companies. A major figure in the first phase was Peter Harriss Abbott, himself born in the West Indies.[178] Abbott was one of the first official assignees appointed after the reform of the bankruptcy process in 1831. In that capacity, he was awarded compensation in Trinidad as assignee of Turnbull Forbes; he was also one of three assignees of Edward Gale Boldero, partner in a London bank that had collapsed twenty years before. In the 1830s he also emerged as an authority on state finance, publishing *On the Public Debt: With a Plan for its Final Extinction* in 1839, shortly before he fled abroad amid his own financial difficulties.

Two of the founders of today's big four global accounting firms were from slave-owning families or from families with loans secured on the enslaved.[179] William Welch Deloitte's mother was the daughter of a West Indies planter named Welch.[180] Deloitte initially trained as an assistant to the official assignee before founding his eponymous firm (the firms operating as a network under the 'Deloitte' brand are now all members of Deloitte Touche Tohmatsu Limited) in 1845.[181] Edwin Waterhouse (1841–1917), who formed Price, Holyland Waterhouse (now Price Waterhouse Coopers) in 1865 was the son of Alfred Waterhouse (1798–1893), the Liverpool cotton broker, partner in the firm of Nicholas Waterhouse & Sons 'merchants and brokers of Liverpool' (and with his wife 'committed members of the Society of Friends'), who counter-claimed apparently unsuccessfully for the compensation for the enslaved people on two cotton estates in British Guiana, Plantation John Cove and Craig Miln, and Plantation Clonbrook, on which they held liens for more than £20,000.[182] These connections are separate from the impact of 'plantation' (i.e. slave-system) accounting on the development of management accounting tools more generally, which recent scholarship has emphasised in the context of the separation of ownership and management inherent in British absentee slave-ownership.[183]

The growth of the joint-stock company drove not only accounting but also stockbroking, which developed from its base in dealing mainly in government stock. The foundation of the modern stock exchange in London had clearly predated the period of Emancipation. Its membership was in the high hundreds by the decade of Emancipation, with an early peak of 804 in April 1826, and subsequently 637 in April 1833 and 675 in 1838.[184] Given our argument that slave-ownership permeated the British elites by the 1830s, it is to be expected that some of these members of the Stock Exchange would appear in the compensation records and that is indeed the case. For example, George Bowley Medley, who was married in 1825 at St John Hackney to Hester Webb (1804–49), reputed daughter of John Racker Webb and Mary Wint ('a free quadroon') of Jamaica, and moved to Jamaica for a period c. 1830, had been a stockbroker of Threadneedle Street in 1826, and with his brothers-in-law was awarded compensation as co-owner of the Keynsham estate in Manchester. He was back in London by 1841 and in 1845 appeared as a railway subscriber of Austin Friars to the extent of £45,000, mobilised presumably from clients. He became a Lloyds underwriter and was bankrupted in 1854: although discharged, on his death he left only a modest estate. His son George Webb Medley (1826–98), however, also a stockbroker – and a free trader, writer for the Cobden Club, chairman of Assam Tea Co. and chess pioneer – flourished and left net personalty of £252,038 5s 7d in 1898. William Henry Cooper, described as 'head of the stock exchange', was executor and residuary devisee of his father-in-law, the slave-owner Rowland Edward Williams, and gifted Newlands at Weston Green in Surrey (which he had inherited under Rowland Edward Williams' will) to his brother-in-law, Rowland Edward

Louis Charles Williams (who had inherited the West Indian estates) before Cooper's death in 1840. Provincial stockbrokers also appear in the slave compensation records. George Bowley Medley's brother-in-law and co-beneficiary of the Keynsham estate, Robert Podmore Clarke of Bristol, also became a 'stock and share broker' in the 1840s, having been a ship broker in 1841.[185]

However, the evidence does not suggest that the development of the London Stock Exchange or of the provincial markets was being driven by the capital or talent of former slave-owners. George Bowley Medley and Robert Podmore Clark were unusual among stockbrokers in appearing in the compensation records as slave-*owners*. Robert Hichens, founder of the oldest stockbroker in the City, Hichens Harrison (bought in 2008 by Religare of India) and a major City figure in his day, was with his brother William a trustee for the Stapleton family.[186] Again, Capel Cure, the grandfather of Arthur Capel Cure of Capel Cure & Terry (the stockbroking firm that later became Capel Cure Myers), was the trustee of Stella Frances Allen, a role he had inherited from his father, while John Hasler, a very successful stockbroker of 4 Church Court Clements Lane who left £160,000 at his death in 1850, was a trustee for Judith Guterres.[187] Outside London, Andrew Sievwright of Edinburgh, who was awarded slave compensation as trustee and executor of Elizabeth Wightman, was described as 'Stockbroker and General Agent in Edinburgh' in her inventory of 1837.[188] Such trustee roles reflected, and in turn reinforced, the status of the trustee, conferring considerable discretionary power upon him (women trustees are very rare in the compensation records) and confirming the interweaving of slave-ownership with other forms of wealth; but such roles also appear different from direct beneficial slave-ownership in the context of our overall argument.

Conclusion

Of the five exemplary 'outsiders' whom Kynaston uses to introduce his history of the City (John Julius Angerstein; William Hancock of Smith, Payne & Smith; the Goldsmid brothers; Nathan Mayer Rothschild; and John James Ruskin of Gordon, Murphy & Co.), four individually or through their firms can be linked to slave-ownership,[189] although this is unacknowledged by Kynaston and slavery remains invisible throughout the volume. However, the nature of the links with slave-ownership is different in each of the four cases. The evidence from the slave compensation records suggests that slavery permeated the City but also that it could in some cases be a relatively shallow involvement, in others a deep

and deeply important one. To say that slavery was not solely responsible for the formation of the City is not to say that the City would have
developed in the same way and at the same pace without it. The role
of slavery in the development of the City in the seventeenth and eighteenth centuries has not been explored systematically, although suggest-
ive and sometimes brilliant work has been done on aspects of the links
of slavery and the City.[190] The importance of the City to slavery has been
analysed more thoroughly for these earlier periods than has the importance of slavery to the City.[191] And it remains possible for general histories of the eighteenth-century City to neglect the question of slavery
and its role altogether.[192] But the evidence of slave-ownership should
make it impossible any longer to consider the nineteenth-century City
without reference to it. Beyond the City, the picture is again one of
uneven development. Predictably, Glasgow and Liverpool have the most
profound commercial legacies of slave-ownership, but few commercial
communities were untouched by the slave compensation process. And
this was indeed commercial, in the sense of mercantile as opposed to
industrial, capital. Industrialists did not invest in slave-ownership but
slave-owners, above all mercantile slave-owners, did invest in industry.
In some important and dynamic sectors – shipbuilding, engineering and
metal fabrication – slave-owners appear conspicuously absent, but in
others, notably cotton and railways, they were significant. The patterns
illuminated by Eric Williams for the eighteenth century were repeated
in the nineteenth.

NOTES

1 See pp. 9–11 above.
2 Julian Hoppit, 'Smith versus Keynes: the mercantile system versus mercantilism', public lecture at University College London, 19 November 2012;
I am grateful to Professor Hoppit for providing the text of his lecture. For
the political underpinning of the British slave-system and the emphasis the
slave-owners placed on sustaining protection through preferential duties,
see e.g. Douglas Hall, 'Absentee proprietorship in the British West Indies, to
about 1850', *Journal of Caribbean History* 35 (1) (2001), 97–121 and Andrew
O'Shaughnessy, 'The formation of a commercial lobby: the West India interest, British colonial policy and the American Revolution', *Historical Journal* 40
(1) (1997), 71–95. There were no collective vehicles for investment in slavery
comparable to the East India Company, or to the joint-stock companies that
were founded to develop the white settler colonies, prior to the West India
Company, conceived as a means of funnelling capital to beleaguered plantation economies and established in the joint-stock boom of 1825–6, which was
itself stillborn.
3 David Kynaston, *The City of London, Vol. I: A World of Its Own 1815–1890*
(London, 1994), pp. 82, 166.

4 Robin Pearson, 'Collective diversification: Manchester cotton merchants and the insurance business in the early 19th century', *Business History Review* 65 (2) (1991), 379–414.

5 The distinctive form of organisation of the mercantile involvement in slavery was the consigneeship, the agency relationship of a London merchant with a slave-owner for one or more estates in which the London merchant was granted an exclusive agreement to ship and sell the tropical produce of the estate and was responsible in turn for procuring supplies for the estate. These relationships, which might appear more characteristic of the eighteenth century, endured until and beyond Emancipation. They were usually embedded in credit relationships, the London merchant running an open account for the slave-owner and moving to secure the account against the estate if indebtedness ballooned beyond the level that would be self-liquidating. Consigneeships were formalised in various ways. Marmaduke Trattle, for example, a London merchant and pioneering numismatist, was granted an annuity of £500 by Sir Christopher Bethell Codrington in 1829 as an inducement to him to give up the sole consigneeship guaranteed to him under the will of Codrington's uncle Sir William Codrington thirty-seven years earlier, in 1792; Codrington Papers, RP 2616/1–37.

6 E.g. Anthony Cooke, 'An elite revisited: Glasgow West India merchants, 1783–1877', *Journal of Scottish Historical Studies* 32 (2) (2012), 127–65; Stephen Mullen, 'A Glasgow-West India merchant house and the imperial dividend 1779–1867', *Journal of Scottish Historical Studies* 33 (2) (2013), 196–233 (I am grateful to Stephen Mullen for supplying a draft copy of the text prior to publication).

7 Marika Sherwood, *After Abolition: Britain and the Slave Trade since 1807* (London, 2007); Chris Evans, *Slave Wales: The Welsh and Atlantic Slavery 1660–1850* (Cardiff, 2010), pp. 113–29.

8 John Walter Cross was a partner in Dennistoun Cross & Co. from at least 1867; a William Cross, possibly his father (who was certainly of the same name), was a partner until his retirement from the firm in 1847; *London Gazette*, 23,205, 4 January 1867, p. 108 and *London Gazette*, 20,728, 27 April 1847, p. 1558. It is not known whether the William Cross who was a partner with the recipient of slave compensation James Robert Dennistoun in the firms Dennistoun, M'Gregor of Glasgow and Dennistoun & Co. of Trinidad (apparently unconnected with Dennistoun, Cross) until he withdrew in 1834 was the same man; *London Gazette*, 19,729, 12 June 1835, p. 1133.

9 www.edfman.com/about-us/history, accessed 30 April 2014. The firm's website features an advertisement from the *Public Ledger* 1805, in which James Man was selling at Garraway's Coffee House '200 Hhds. British Plantation coffee, 150 bags pimento, 3 puncheons lime juice, 4 casks honey'. The firm was described as 'West India brokers' in an announcement in 1819 of a transition of the partnership from James Man and Sons to Edward and James Man; *London Gazette*, 17,491, 3 July 1819, p. 1156.

10 Eric Williams, *Capitalism and Slavery* (1944; repr. London, 1964); Seymour Drescher, *Econocide: British Slavery in the Era of Abolition* (Pittsburgh, 1977).

11 Julian Hoppit, *Risk and Failure in English Business 1700–1800* (Cambridge, 1987).

12 V. Markham Lester, *Victorian Insolvency: Bankruptcy, Imprisonment for Debt, and Company Winding-Up in Nineteenth-Century England* (Oxford, 1995).

13 R. B. Sheridan, 'The West India sugar crisis and the British slave Emancipation, 1830–1833', *Journal of Economic History* 21 (4) (1961), 539–51.

14 Martin Daunton, 'Manning, William (1763–1835), merchant', *ODNB*.

15 Draper, *The Price of Emancipation*, p. 265.

16 The verdict was deceased from natural causes; *London Gazette*, 20,441, 14 July 1842, p. 409; *London Gazette*, 21,461, 26 July 1853, p. 2071; *The Times*, 24 October 1842, p. 7.

17 Jackie Morris, 'The Chauncys of Little Munden', at www.mundens.net/genealogy/chauncy.htm, accessed 8 August 2013. The partnership of Nathaniel Snell Chauncy and Nathaniel Bannerman Chauncy was dissolved in 1843; *London Gazette*, 20,271, 20 October 1843, p. 3404.

18 Rowland Mitchell of Lime Street; *London Gazette*, 20,036, 9 November 1841, p. 2773.

19 Kynaston, *City of London*, pp. 156–7.

20 *London Gazette*, 21,082, 2 April 1850, p. 974; *National Probate Calendar* 1883 and 1926.

21 Peter Norman, *The Risk Controllers: Central Counterparty Clearing in Globalised Financial Markets* (London, 2011); *London Gazette*, 22,768, 4 September 1863, p. 4348. Among the other nine founder-directors were Henry John Jourdain of Blyth Jourdain and Robert Ryrie, a partner in Gladstone Latham and Gladstone Ewart.

22 For Gunnersbury Lodge, see 'Ealing and Brentford: growth of Ealing', *A History of the County of Middlesex, Vol. VII: Acton, Chiswick, Ealing and Brentford, West Twyford, Willesden* (London, 1982), pp. 105–13.

23 *London Gazette*, 25,594, 4 June 1886, p. 270.

24 William D. Rubinstein, *Who Were the Rich? A Biographical Directory of British Wealth-holders, Vol. I: 1809–1839* (London, 2009). Robert Shedden (1826/16) left £120,000; William D. Rubinstein, *Who Were the Rich? Vol. II*, unpublished data for 1840–59: Robert Shedden 1850/1 and George Shedden 1855/4.

25 *London Gazette*, 26,640, 5 July 1895, p. 3848.

26 *London Gazette*, 25,506, 28 August 1885, p. 4100.

27 *London Gazette*, 25,950, 2 July 1889, p. 3550.

28 Charles R. Dod, *The Peerage, Baronetage and Knightage of Great Britain and Ireland* (London, 1848), p. 287; John Ede had been a partner with Henry Pearse and John Bond the younger in the West India merchant firm of Ede, Bond and Pearse until his retirement in 1833; *London Gazette*, 19,020, 8 February 1833, p. 282. The then partners of the firm were awarded compensation both as mortgagees and as owners-in-fee in 1835 and 1836 for enslaved people on Cedar Valley and Amity Hall in Jamaica; T71/865 St Andrew no. 336 and T71/867 St Thomas-in-the-East nos. 605 and 606.

29 C. J. Bearman, 'Lee [née Spooner], Catharine Anna [Kate] (1859–1904), singer and folksong collector', *ODNB*.

30 *London Gazette*, 27,150, 2 January 1900, p. 32; on his death in 1909, when he was shown as 'of Bendals estate Antigua', Arthur Morier Lee left £38,858 (resworn at £43,817), National Probate Calendar 1909.

31 'Hankey & Co', RBS Heritage Hub, at http://heritagearchives.rbs.com/companies/list/hankey-and-co.html, accessed 11 October 2012.

32 Rubinstein, *Who Were the Rich? Vol. II*; *Who Were the Rich? Vol. III*, unpublished data for 1860–74: from the bank, William Alers Hankey 1859/50, his sons John Alers Hankey 1872/45 and Thomas Alers Hankey 1872/46, and Thomas Alers Hankey's sons Frederick Alers (d. 1892) and Edward Alers (d. 1896). Thomas Hankey, who died in 1878, left £50,000 on his death in 1879. From the mercantile firm, Thomson Hankey 1855/7 left £140,000 'within province'; John Alexander Hankey (d. 1881) left £154,982 16s 4d; Thomson Hankey (d. 1893) £133,482 0s 8d; and George Hankey (also d. 1893) £197,092 15s 8d. Other later partners in Thomson Hankey & Co. included Blake Alexander Hankey, who left £96,243 12s 7d in 1899; Thomson Hankey's nephew Richard Musgrave Harvey, who left £42,829 16s 4d in 1899; Rodolphe Alexander Hankey, who left £95,501 13s 10d in 1906; and Beaumont Hankey, who left £68,996 0s 1d in 1909. Walter Hankey, who died young in 1871, left under £10,000. John Barnard Hankey 1869/42 (the son of Thomas Hankey d. 1793), who left £140,000, and his son George James Barnard Hankey (who died in 1875, leaving £90,000) appear to have been rentiers, while Stephen Alers Hankey (who died in 1878, possibly the son of William Alers Hankey) was a white-lead manufacturer who left £250,000.

33 W. P. Courtney, rev. A. C. Howe, 'Hankey, Thomson (1805–1893), politician and political economist', *ODNB*.

34 John F. Naylor, 'Hankey, Maurice Pascal Alers, first Baron Hankey (1877–1963), civil servant', *ODNB*.

35 Mark Pottle, 'Hankey, Beatrice [called Help] (1858–1933), evangelist', *ODNB*.

36 Rubinstein, *Who Were the Rich?* (Vols. 1–3). Francis Baring 1810/10; Charles Wall 1815/4; Alexander 1848/6; Henry 1848/18; Humphrey St John Mildmay 1853/32; Joshua Bates 1864/5; second Baron Ashburton 1864/2; third Baron Ashburton 1868/7; Rev. Frederick Baring 1868/10; Humphrey Francis Mildmay 1867/49; Henry Bingham Baring 1869/6.

37 Draper, *Price of Emancipation*, p. 246.

38 John Ramsden, 'Hogg, Douglas McGarel, first viscount Hailsham (1872–1950), lawyer and politician', *ODNB*; National Probate Calendar 1876 (the estate was resworn in January 1877 from £600,000 at probate).

39 Rubinstein, *Who Were the Rich? Vol. I*; *Who Were the Rich? Vol. II*; *Who Were the Rich? Vol. III*: Charles Snell Chauncy 1809/18 and John Snell 1847/36; Alexander Ellice 1811/2, Edward Ellice 1864/24 and Russell Ellice (d. 1873) £70,000; Thomas King 1824/5 and William King 1861 (omitted from Rubinstein but leaving £140,000); David Lyon 1827/21 and David Lyon 1872/70; James Baillie 1828/29, David Baillie 1861/4 and James Evan Baillie 1863/2; Robert Hibbert 1835/14 and William Hibbert 1844/10; William Pulsford 1834/17 and Robert Pulsford 1836/33; Thomas Daniel 1854/10 and Thomas Daniel 1872/29; James Cavan 1859/7 and Philip Charles Cavan 1870/7.

40 Charlotte S. M. Girard, 'Some further notes on the Douglas family', *BC Studies* 72 (1986–7), 3–27.

41 Rubinstein, *Who Were the Rich? Vol. II*, 1869/86.

42 John Guthrie Smith and John Oswald Mitchell, *The Old Country Houses of the Old Glasgow Gentry* (2nd edn., Glasgow, 1878), lxxix (Orbiston House).

43 T71/892 St Vincent nos. 490A&B.

44 Rubinstein, *Who Were the Rich? Vol. III*, 1871/97.

45 Institute of Commonwealth Studies, 'Archive collections – Sandbach, Tinne & Co.' (8 September 2010), at http://icommlibrary.blogspot.co.uk/2010/09/archive-collections-sandbach-tinne-co.html, accessed 11 October 2012.

46 *London Gazette*, 46,624, 4 July 1975, p. 8644.

47 Rubinstein, *Who Were the Rich? Vol. I*; *Who Were the Rich? Vol. II; Who Were the Rich? Vol. III*: James McInroy 1825/37; Charles Stewart Parker 1829/34; Samuel Sandbach 1851/2; George Rainy 1863/49; George Haygarth Rainy 1872/92; John Abraham Tinne (d. 1884) £121,586 18s 2d (resworn from £107,744 8s 2d); Alfred Traill Parker (d. 1900) £225,631 18s 9d; Samuel Sandbach Parker (d. 1905) £275,302 10s 4d; John Ernest Tinne (d. 1925) £161,830 18s 11d; Evelyn Stuart Parker (d. 1936, £295,621 4s 8d). Other slightly less wealthy family members included Gilbert Robertson Sandbach (d. 1907) £78,965 2s 6d and Charles Sandbach Parker (d. 1920) £80,223 6s 3d.

48 [Anon], rev. H. C. G. Matthew, 'Parker, Charles Stuart (1829–1910), politician and biographer', *ODNB*, which describes his father Charles Stewart Parker as a partner in Sandbach Tinne 'merchants for the West Indies'.

49 The Tinne family are described as 'Dutch sugar merchants and ship owners, who first came to Liverpool in 1813 from Demerara in Guyana', in the Liverpool Museums site devoted to Sudley House, where members of the family lived in the twentieth century (www.liverpoolmuseums.org.uk/sudley/exhibitions/tinne/family.aspx, accessed 11 October 2012).

50 The *Jamaica Almanacs* show Harmony Hall against Joseph Travers in 1818, 1820, 1821 and 1822, and 'heirs of Joseph Travers' in 1823; T71/874 Trelawney no. 101; Will of Joseph Travers, Grocer of Swithin's Lane, City of London proved 14 June 1821, PROB 11/1645; Anon, *Chronicles of Cannon Street, a Few Records of an Old Firm* (London, n.d. [1957]). Benjamin and Joseph Travers also appear as trustees of Martha Fleming Ottley for the Marble Hill estate in Antigua; T71/877 Antigua no. 38.

51 Thomas Ellison, *The Cotton Trade of Great Britain* (London, 1886). Total raw cotton imports rose twenty-fold between 1786–90 and 1836–40. According to Ellison (p. 86), the West Indies accounted for 70 per cent of British imports 1786–90, 35 per cent 1796–1800, 16 per cent 1806–10, 7 per cent 1816–20, 2 per cent 1826–30 and below 1 per cent thereafter, while the US rose from less than 1 per cent 1786–90 to 80 per cent 1836–40; the figures in Ralph Davis, *The Industrial Revolution and British Overseas Trade* (Leicester, 1979), p. 41, show the West Indies as less dominant in the earliest period, at 51 per cent 1784–6 but continuing at a more significant level thereafter at 44 per cent 1794–6, 33 per cent 1804–6 and 20 per cent 1814–16, before declining to 3 per cent 1824–6 and below thereafter.

52 Mullen, 'A Glasgow-West India merchant house'.

53 Ellison, *Cotton Trade*, p. 181.

54 *Ibid.*, pp. 233–4. T71/894 Trinidad nos. 1831A & B, 1893 and 1895. John Ashton Yates had retired in 1831. Cotton-broking was not in the early years always the only business of these firms: Priestley, Griffiths and Cox had departments dealing with cotton, 'sugar, coffee and other colonials' and drysalteries. The evidence suggests nevertheless that in most cases it was cotton that tied the firms to the slave-economy.

55 The partnership between John Shand and Robert Horsfall was dissolved 31 March 1833; *London Gazette*, 19,036, 5 April 1833, p. 674. Ellison, *Cotton Trade* describes both partners as 'related to eminent firms of the same name', although Ellis appears to give 'Robert H. Horsfall' as the name of the man who went on to become a partner in Bateson & Horsfall until 1845, when he 'left the cotton market for the Stock Exchange' (pp. 220, 269). Robert Horsfall (1807–81), the son of the slave-owner Charles Horsfall, fits all parts of this description other than the 'Robert H.'. John Shand's cousin William Walcott Shand (b. 1820, the son of the slave-owner William Shand) took over John Shand's cotton business in 1840 (Ellison, *Cotton Trade*, p. 220) and hence John Shand appears to have been the son of William Shand's brother Charles (who had a son John baptised 4 September 1824, ostensibly born 1 December 1804: Ancestry.com, *Liverpool, Lancashire, England, Baptisms, 1813–1906* (database online). This John Shand 'the son of a Liverpool cotton broker' was active in New Zealand, where he died in 1874.

56 Thomas Steuart Gladstone was paid slave compensation along with his brothers William and Robert for their father's estate in Jamaica. Edgar Corrie, the son of the original Corrie, was based in London in the 1820s and 1830s and signed at the National Debt Office for the compensation for the Lower Quarter estate on Tobago on behalf of Thomas Corrie of Edinburgh, presumably a relative; T71/891 Tobago nos. 30A & B.

57 T71/885 British Guiana nos. 572 and 577. In the latter case, where the liens were for £1,241 3s 4d and £1,180 18s 3d, Thomas Bouch signed for the compensation at the National Debt Office in London.

58 Ellison, *Cotton Trade*, p. 228. 'The firm held a leading position on 'Change for over half a century.'

59 British Guiana nos. 608A & B. Nicholas Salisbury also counterclaimed on two estates in St Lucia as assignee of Wm Coupland & Co., which had failed 1 November 1823; T71/884 St Lucia nos. 844 and 845; *London Gazette*, 18,410, 2 November 1827, p. 2264.

60 Waterhouse's firm had capital of £13,092 on 1 January 1800 and £22,642 on 1 January 1802; Nicholas Waterhouse died in 1823 'worth well over £100,000'; Francis E. Hyde, Bradbury B. Parkinson, Sheila Marriner, 'The cotton broker and the rise of the Liverpool cotton market', *Economic History Review* new series 8 (1) (1955), 75–83. Waterhouse is not in Rubinstein, *Who Were the Rich? Vol. I*: Hyde *et al.* clarify that the value of Waterhouse's personal estate was under £100,000 but that 'he died possessed of considerable real estate' (p. 80).

61 Ellison, *Cotton Trade*, p. 197. Holt Davies gave rise to Cooke and Comer, but Ellison stresses that Comer, a partner in Holt Davies, had closed that firm and opened a new partnership.

62 *Ibid.*, p. 167 (Holt Davies) and p. 179 (Tattersall and Dobson).

63 *Ibid.*, p. 213.
64 John Hughes, *Liverpool Banks & Bankers 1760–1837* (Liverpool, 1906), p. 130.
65 Ellison, *Cotton Trade*, p. 230.
66 Those with such a connection are italicised in the following (the dates in brackets signify when each person first took up a directorship): *George Holt* (1842) was an apprentice to Samuel Hope, in turn an apprentice to Nicholas Waterhouse until he set up on his own in 1805. Holt became a partner with Hope in 1812 and in 1821 took up the cotton business under his own name; James H. Wrigley's (1843) firm was founded by his father in Liverpool *c.* 1810; *John Marriott* (1844) was originally a partner in Messrs John Fisher of Manchester but formed a partnership in 1821 with Thomas Rogers, an apprentice in Ewart Rutson. *William Clare* (1845) became a partner in Thomas Tattersall in 1825; *Peter Serjeantson* (1846) was a partner with Thomas Steuart Gladstone but in a firm (not a cotton broker) descended from that of the first Edgar Corrie; *Robert Gill* (partner in Richard Dobson since 1813); James Ryley (1848) set up with Adam Hodgson (1824); *Hardman Earle* (Salisbury, Turner & Earle); John Stock (1850, James Stock *c.* 1800); Miles Barton (1851) (Henry and Miles Barton 1810); *Jacques Myers* (1852), Ewart Myers; *William Bower*'s (1853) father, also William Bower, had his apprenticeship in Ewart Myers until becoming a partner in Kearsley & Bower in 1816; James Buchanan 1854 came from Glasgow in 1826; *Isaac B. Cooke* 1855 (who came from Manchester in 1795, entered into the family and counting house of Nicholas Waterhouse, partner 1803, retired 1819 and set up Isaac Cooke and William Comer with a former partner in Holt Davies); Thomas B. Blackburne 1856 (connected with Swainson, 'although not actually a partner'); *Thomas Haigh* 1857 ('son of an extensive Manchester merchant'), entered 1834 into partnership with Edward Franceys, an apprentice in Isaac Cooke; Matthew Jee 1858 (founded somewhere about 1800); *Rogers Waterhouse* 1859 (fourth son of Nicholas Waterhouse, partner in the family firm 1833 or 1834; James Hardy Macrae 1860 (John Wrigley, founded *c.* 1810); Samuel Gath 1861 (1823 partner in Edward Emmet, founded 1818); John Swainson 1862 (Swainson and sons, founded 'at the opening of the present century').
67 A. C. Howe, 'Philips, Sir George, first baronet (1766–1847), textile industrialist and politician', *ODNB.*
68 T71/872 Hanover no. 66.
69 Williams, *Capitalism and Slavery*, p. 156. Williams gives the firm as J. N. Philips.
70 Thomas Kington, Peter Maze, George Gibbs, Robert Bright, Charles Pinney, Robert Edward Case, George Henry Ames and Henry Bush. Philip William Skynner Miles was the son of P. J. Miles; another son, John William Miles, was a partner by 1845. Four of the six members of the first committee (Maze, Bright, Kington and Pinney) came from among these men; Bristol Record Office, Great Western Cotton Company 12142/1 28 February 1837; 12141/10a–b 24 June 1845.
71 T. M. Devine, 'Did slavery help to make Scotia great?', *Britain and the World* 4 (1) (2011), 40–64, at 52.

72 Anthony Cooke, 'An elite revisited: Glasgow West India merchants, 1783–1877', *Journal of Scottish Historical Studies* 32 (2) (2012), 127–65, at 145.

73 T. M. Devine, 'An eighteenth-century business elite: Glasgow-West India merchants *c.* 1780–1815', *Scottish Historical Review* 57 (1) (1978), 40–67, at 59. This article was more qualified about the importance to the cotton-spinning industry of capital derived from slavery than Devine, 'Did slavery help?.

74 Will of Nathaniel Snell Chauncy, merchant of Wilson Street Finsbury Square, 28 July 1856 PROB 11/2235/334; http://archive.museumoflondon.org.uk/ LSS/Map/Enslavement/People/31.htm, accessed 30 April 2014.

75 Graham Trust, *John Moss of Otterspool (1782–1858), Railway Pioneer, Slave Owner, Banker* (Milton Keynes, 2010); T71/885 British Guiana no. 631; T71/877 Antigua no. 86.

76 Cooke, 'Elite revisited', 153.

77 Henry Pinckard, *Observations on the Management and Extraordinary Losses of the Jamaica Steam Navigation Company. By Henry Pinckard Esq., an Auditor of the Company* (London, 1838). The directors were Edmund Francis Green and Charles Green of 147 Leadenhall St[reet]; William Elmslie of 24 York St[reet] Portman Square; James Daly of Lambeth Lodge, Commercial Road (who was excepted from Pinckard's strictures); Arthur Timperon of 26 Philpot Lane; and two men apparently unconnected with slave-owning, Adolphus Pugh Johnson of Lloyds and Capt. John Rees of Blackheath. The secretary was Adam W. Elmslie. Pinckard, *Observations*, pp. 3, 5, 6.

78 Gordon Goodwin, rev. Elizabeth Baigent, 'MacQueen, James (1778–1870), geographer', *ODNB*; David Lambert, 'The "Glasgow King of Billingsgate": James MacQueen and an Atlantic proslavery network', *Slavery & Abolition* 29 (3) (2008) 389–413.

79 The directors in 1839 were John Irving (chairman), Andrew Colvile (deputy chairman), Thomas Baring, James Cavan, Henry Davidson, Russell Ellice, George Hibbert, John Irving junior, Patrick Maxwell Stewart and three men apparently unconnected with slave-ownership, George Brown, Robert Cotesworth and W. S. Marshall. I am grateful to Anyaa Anim-Addo of the University of Leeds, for the list of names of the original directors. It has not proved possible to determine the source of the capital invested in the firm. Of a list (again provided by Anyaa Amin-Addo) of eighteen people attending the first general meeting of the company and therefore likely to have held shares, three (Joseph Liggins and Owen Pell – both connected with Antigua – and Joseph Marryat) appear in the slave compensation records.

80 Robert G. Greenhill, 'Booth, Alfred (1834–1914), merchant and shipowner', *ODNB*; Jose Harris, 'Booth, Charles (1840–1916), shipowner and social investigator', *ODNB*.

81 J. Gordon Read, 'Holt, Alfred (1829–1911), engineer and shipowner', *ODNB*.

82 Marshall argued for an initial 'swing to the South' after 1783 – i.e. a move from the American colonies towards the Caribbean; P. J. Marshall, *Remaking the British Atlantic: The United States and the British Empire after American Independence* (Oxford, 2012), ch. 9.

83 Geoffrey Jones, *Merchants to Multinationals: British Trading Companies in the Nineteenth and Twentieth Centuries* (Oxford, 2000), p. 17.

84 Chapman listed sixteen such groups in India, China and the Far East; three in Latin America; two in both Latin America and Russia; five in Russia; and five in South Africa; Stanley D. Chapman, 'British-based investment groups before 1914', *Economic History Review* 38 (2) (1985), 230–51, at 249–51.

85 Jones, *Merchants to Multinationals*, p. 9; Stanley D. Chapman, 'British marketing enterprise: the changing roles of merchants, manufacturers and financiers, 1700–1860', *Business History Review* 53 (2) (1979), 205–34 is an attempt to refute the 'gross oversimplification' by Buck that manufacturers assumed the initiative from merchants after 1815, to set out the overlapping periods of different structures and to locate the rise of commission agents and accepting houses in the period 1800–60.

86 S. G. Checkland, *The Gladstones*, p. 181.

87 Draper, *Price of Emancipation*, p. 236.

88 Smith and Mitchell, *Old Country* Houses, lxxxiii (Possil). 'They [the Campbells of John Campbell sen. & Co.] are not one of our old families: they were here just three generations, coming with the West India trade, and, when it went, vanishing'; Draper, *Price of Emancipation*, p. 266.

89 National Probate Calendar 1919.

90 Smith and Mitchell, *Old Country Houses*, lxxxiii (Possil).

91 Jonathan F. Taylor, 'Campbell, John Middleton [Jock], Baron Campbell of Eskan (1912–1994), businessman', *ODNB*.

92 Augustus Muir, *Blyth, Greene, Jourdain & Company Limited 1810–1960* (London, 1961).

93 National Probate Calendar 1865; Rubinstein, *Who Were the Rich? Vol. III*, 1865/18.

94 National Probate Calendar 1873.

95 Chapman, 'British-based investment groups', 234.

96 *London Gazette*, 17,999, 7 February 1824, p. 217; *London Gazette*, 19,355, 12 February 1836, p. 296.

97 Jones, *Merchants to Multinationals*, pp. 36–7.

98 The firm collapsed in 1867 but had played a major role in the foundation of HSBC.

99 Philip K. Law, 'Dent family (per. c. 1820–1927), Far East merchants', *ODNB*.

100 'James Swanzy' or 'Swanzy' appears as the vessel owner in eight slave-voyages between 1801 and 1806, all purchasing enslaved people on the Gold Coast, www.slavevoyages.org, accessed 7 June 2014.

101 The Trans-Atlantic Slave Trade Database, voyage IDs 17,583 (which gives the name as 'Sydenham Teaste') and 18,221; www.slavevoyages.org, accessed 8 September 2012. Thomas King of Bristol is not to be confused with the major London slave-trader of the same name.

102 Frederick Pedler, *The Lion and the Unicorn in Africa, a History of the Origins of the United Africa Company 1787–1931* (London, 1974), p. 32.

103 John Senhouse Goldie Taubman was the son of John Taubman Goldie Taubman and Ellen Senhouse. Ellen Senhouse was the daughter of

Humphrey Senhouse of Netherall (d. 1814) and cousin of Samuel Edward Hooper and Humphrey Fleming Senhouse, who all appear in the compensation records for Barbados.

104 Pedler, *Lion and Unicorn*, pp. 12–13.

105 Andrew J. O'Shaughnessy, 'Bosanquet, Charles (1769–1850), merchant and writer', *ODNB*.

106 For Richard Neave see p. 85 above.

107 For Andrew Colvile see p. 61 above. Edward Ellice was the Whig power-broker with significant interests in North America and the West Indies, including slave-property.

108 Bloxam Elin was also a director of the Alliance Bank of London & Liverpool in 1863. He was a West India merchant who had lived in Jamaica in the 1820s. He left £160,000 in personalty.

109 *Post Office Directory* 1863.

110 Marshall C. Eakin, *A British Enterprise in Brazil: The St John D'el Rey Mining Company and the Morro Velho Gold Mine, 1830–1960* (Durham, NC, 1989); Evans, *Slave Wales*, pp. 113–29.

111 Eakin, *British Enterprise*, p. 34.

112 Anthony Howe, 'From "old corruption" to "new probity": the Bank of England and its directors in the age of reform', *Financial History Review* 1 (1994), 23–41.

113 Kynaston, *City of London*, p. 84.

114 Martin Daunton, 'Gibbs, Henry Huck, first baron Aldenham (1819–1907), merchant and merchant banker', *ODNB*.

115 A. C. Howe, 'Palmer (John) Horsley (1779–1858), merchant banker', *ODNB*.

116 Kynaston, *City of London*, pp. 242–3.

117 *Ibid.*, p. 263.

118 *Ibid.*, p. 297, which acknowledges the 'West Indian' business of Benjamin Buck Greene's father.

119 John Orbell, 'Greene, Benjamin Buck (1808–1902), merchant', *ODNB*.

120 Kynaston, *City of London*, p. 332.

121 Karl Marx, *Capital* (1867; repr. London, 1974), Vol. III, pp. 389–90.

122 Kynaston, *City of London*, p. 121.

123 *Ibid.*, pp. 181–2.

124 *Ibid.*, pp. 226, 333; Draper, *Price of Emancipation*, pp. 348–9.

125 Stephen Lees, 'Stewart, John', in *History of Parliament, 1832–1868* (forthcoming). We are grateful to the History of Parliament project for access to this before publication.

126 T71/873 St James no. 1 (New Montpelier), counterclaim by Dykes Alexander junior, his brother Samuel Alexander and his son Henry Alexander. Dykes Alexander (1763–1849) was the son of Dykes Alexander senior and his wife Martha née Biddle, who were both part of a network of East Anglian Quaker banking families. His son Richard Dykes Alexander made some land in Ipswich available for development in the 1850s and stipulated that some of the streets should be named after leading abolitionists; www.pennyghael.org.uk/Alexander2.pdf, accessed 3 July 2012; Margaret Dawes, *Women Who Made Money: Women Partners in British Private Banks,*

1752–1906 (Bloomington, IN, 2010), pp. 85–7, at http://ipswich-lettering.org/streetsabolitionists.html, accessed 3 July 2012.

127 Draper, *Price of Emancipation*, p. 244.

128 *London Gazette*, 20,238, 30 June 2012, p. 2203

129 Kynaston, *City of London*, p. 295.

130 Kynaston, *City of London*, frontispiece.

131 *Ibid.*, p. 46.

132 Chapman, 'British marketing enterprise', 232.

133 Kynaston, *City of London*, p. 12.

134 *Ibid.*, p. 309.

135 *Ibid.*, p. 167.

136 Stanley D. Chapman, *The Rise of Merchant Banking* (London, 1984).

137 The merger of Barings and Finlay Hodgson took place in 1867. The capital of Barings, which had been over £760,000 on Bates' death, rose to £1,390,000 on the merger.

138 David Lascelles, *Arbuthnot Latham, from Merchant Bank to Private Bank 1833–2013* (London, 2013). This official history is unusual in its candour in acknowledging the slave-ownership of the Lathams (pp. 30–1), although it is silent on the possible involvement of members of the Arbuthnot family in the slave-economy of Mauritius: both J. E. Arbuthnot and the firm of Hunter Arbuthnot, who appear in the slave compensation records as owners and agents, are possibly connected to the James Arbuthnot whom Lascelles shows as active in Mauritius at the time of Arbuthnot's bankruptcy in the mid-1840s.

139 *The Law Journal for the Year 1833, Comprising Reports of Cases in the Courts of Equity … Vol. XI* (London, 1833), p. 160; Thomas J. Spinner jun., 'Goschen, George Joachim, first Viscount Goschen (1831–1907), politician and financier', *ODNB*.

140 Jehanne Wake, *Kleinwort Benson – The History of Two Families in Banking* (Oxford, 1997), pp. 65–6, 72–3; see p. 80 above.

141 Will of Hugh McCalmont of Carnmoney Co. Antrim proved 5 December 1838, PROB 11/1904/160.

142 Joseph E. Inikori, *Africans and the Industrial Revolution in England: A Study in International Trade and Economic Development* (Cambridge, 2002), p. 356; Nicholas Draper 'The City of London and slavery: evidence from the first docks companies 1785–1800', *Economic History Review* 61 (1) (2008), 432–66.

143 *Kent's Directory* 1802, pp. 224–5, 226.

144 John Ede counterclaimed with John Bond the younger and Henry Pearse on Manchester no. 337.

145 Clive Trebilcock, *Phoenix Assurance and the Development of British Insurance, Vol. I: 1782–1870* (Cambridge, 1985), pp. 109–35.

146 *Ibid.*, pp. 45, 122.

147 Barry Supple, *The Royal Exchange Assurance: A History of British Assurance 1720–1970* (Cambridge, 1970), pp. 111–12.

148 Trebilcock, *Phoenix*, pp. 591–2.

149 Supple, *Royal Exchange Assurance*, pp. 74–5; Trebilcock, *Phoenix*, pp. 566–8, 596, 646–9; Robin Pearson, *Insuring the Industrial Revolution: Fire Insurance*

in Great Britain, 1700–1850 (Aldershot, 2004), pp. 328–62, especially p. 340.

150 Trebilcock, *Phoenix*, p. 632.
151 Supple, *Royal Exchange Assurance*, pp. 317–19.
152 Trebilcock, *Phoenix*, p. 554.
153 *Ibid.*, p. 574.
154 *Ibid.*, pp. 186, 190, 198, 226. Including North America, the whole Atlantic region accounted for was 18 per cent of the business in 1826–35 (down from 33.3 per cent in the years of the Napoleonic wars).
155 Trebilcock, *Phoenix*, pp. 115–17, 203–4, 208.
156 *Ibid.*, p. 555.
157 Pearson, *Insuring the Industrial Revolution*, p. 17.
158 Trebilcock, *Phoenix*, p.670.
159 For the global aspirations of the second generation of companies (Imperial, Global, Atlas etc.), see Trebilcock, *Phoenix*, p. 166.
160 Pearson, *Insuring the Industrial Revolution*, p. 157.
161 Thomas Plummer, Henry Davidson, Thomas Gowland, Thomas Hughan, Richard Lee, Eben[ezer] Maitland, David Mitchell, Thomas Reid, Ab[raham] W. Rutherford, Joseph Timperon and Andrew Wedderburn, *Holden's Triennial, 1808*. In 1827, six of twenty directors of Imperial Fire were West Indian merchants and/or mortgagees of slave property (the deputy chairman John Horsley Palmer, Aeneas Barkly, John Henry Deffell, Robert Lang, Richard Lee and David Lyon), as were three of fifteen directors of Imperial Life (Andrew Colvile, John Henry Deffell and Richard Lee). In 1839 Imperial Fire was chaired by Samuel Hibbert and Imperial Life by Andrew Colvile; Imperial Fire's directors included Samuel Hibbert, Andrew Colvile, Henry Davidson, George Hibbert, Richard Lee, Claud Neilson, John Horsley Palmer, George Reid, Martin Tucker Smith and Joseph Timperon, while Imperial Life's directors included Andrew Colvile, John Henry Deffell, Samuel Hibbert, George Hibbert and George Reid; the former directors listed included the slave-owners Charles Porcher Lang and Charles McGarel. In 1845, the Deputy Chairman of Imperial Fire was Henry Pearse; he also sat on the board of Imperial Life. By 1863, of twenty directors of Imperial Fire, eight (Robert Cooper Lee Bevan, Augustus Henry Bosanquet, Charles Cave, George William Cottam, Henry Davidson, Samuel Hibbert, Claud Neilson and George Hibbert) can be identified as beneficiaries of slave compensation or direct descendants of such beneficiaries; the equivalent figure for Imperial Life was five (Henry Davidson, Charles Cave, Samuel Hibbert, George Hibbert and Martin Tucker Smith out of fifteen.
162 William Gladstone was the son of Robert Gladstone and cousin of the prime minister; with two brothers he was awarded the compensation for his father's estate in Jamaica. Louis Lucas (d. 1851) is identified as president of the Jews' Free School, active in other communal institutions and 'head of the firm of Lucas & Micholls, West Indian merchants, of London & Manchester' in *Catalogue of Anglo-Jewish Historical Exhibition 1887 Royal Albert Hall* (London, 1887), No. 1060 (presumably a portrait) painted in 1839. Lucas & Micholls (or Micholls & Lucas) has not been found in the slave compensation records, as noted on p. 80, above.

163 Sampson Lucas is identified as of Lucas, Micholls & Co. in e.g. *Melbourne Argus*, 9 June 1866, p. 7.
164 Ellis Ellis of Lloyds London counterclaimed as mortgagee for £4,058 2s 9d against Henry Edward Sharpe as receiver on Grenada nos. 862 and 863; Ellis Ellis (possibly a different man) was awarded compensation as assignee of Inglis Ellice for Trinidad no. 1345.
165 www.aviva.com/about-us/heritage/companies/indemnity-marine-assurance-company, accessed 9 May 2010. George Hibbert junior (1796–1882) was the son of George Hibbert (1757–1837) the slave-owner.
166 George Henry Hooper of 11 Coleman St Buildings counterclaimed 'assignment £5000' against the Mary's Hope estate (British Guiana no. 313). He or his firm also appear as London attorney under British Guiana no. 90 (T71/1610 letter 2 March 1837 from G. H. Hooper on behalf of A. R Hollingsworth and Edward Hicks) and British Guiana no. 93 (T71/885 counterclaim from Mary Gwillim late Reynolds by her attorney George Henry Hooper), and A. Denoon of George Henry Hooper and A. Denoon signed for the compensation awarded to William Ross and Robert Robertson under British Guiana no. 5 (NDO4). Lillian M. Penson, *The Colonial Agents of the British West Indies: A Study in Colonial Administration Mainly in the Eighteenth Century* (London, 1924), pp. 252–4.
167 *London Gazette*, 26,220, 6 November 1891, p. 5789; London Metropolitan Archives GB 0074 CLC/B/192–22, 'Law Union and Crown Insurance Company'.
168 Samuel Bosanquet counterclaimed successfully with his partners James Hughes Anderdon, Charles Franks and James Whatman Bosanquet as assignees or 'parties interested in the compensation money' in Nevis nos. 42, 76 and 132 for a total of £5,971 11s 0d for 358 enslaved people. T71/882; T71/1609 letter to Commissioners from Samuel Bosanquet & Co., 21 October 1835.
169 Trebilcock, *Phoenix*, p. 600.
170 James Gordon Duff of London, together with James Gordon of Madeira and others, was awarded the compensation for Barbados no. 1,710 as a judgment creditor. John Kingston is possibly the merchant of Copthall Chambers who was awarded the compensation for British Guiana no. 2421, together with John Kingston of Gloucester Place executor of John Kingston decd., and Edward Egan (on behalf of his wife, Divie Robertson) was John Gladstone's brother-in-law; with John Gladstone and others, he was awarded part of the compensation for St Elizabeth no. 535 and St Thomas-in-the-East no. 1.
171 T71/893 Trinidad no. 1,192; *Gentleman's Magazine*, 3 January 1835, p. 441.
172 East Sussex Record Office, Additional Manuscripts, Catalogue Z AMS6417 'Brundrett & Co. of 10 Kings Bench Walk, solicitors: clients' papers'. The summary, although unclear, suggests that Brundrett may have split from Brundrett, Randall around the time of slave compensation. The University of Aberdeen Gordon of Cluny Papers include correspondence between Captain John Gordon of Cluny, former slave-owner, and Alexander Martin of Brundrett, Randall in the early 1860s; University of Aberdeen Special Libraries and Archives, MS 3600 Gordon of Cluny Papers.

173 The five firms are Allen & Overy (founded 1930), Clifford Chance (founded 1802), Freshfields Bruckhaus Deringer (founded 1743), Linklaters (founded 1838) and Slaughter & May (founded 1889).

174 Draper, *Price of Emancipation*, pp. 262–3.

175 CO 137/161 115 2 November 1825, George Hibbert to Robert J. Wilmot Horton. I am grateful to Katie Donington for this reference.

176 T71/871 Westmoreland no. 182. T71/1594 p. 15, 13 March 1837 letter from the commissioners to Geo. Stephen, 19 King's Arms Yard, concerning the appropriate process and returning to Stephen a declaration he had submitted on behalf of a client as inadequate as a counterclaim.

177 Will of Matthew Hale gentleman Ely Place proved 2 October 1848, PROB 11/2082/27; the National Probate Calendar record for John Hopton Forbes (1873) shows him leaving effects 'under £80,000'.

178 John Richard Edwards, 'Accounting regulation and the professionalization process: an historical essay concerning the significance of P. H. Abbott', *Critical Perspectives on Accounting* 12 (6) (2001), 675–96.

179 The other two firms are KPMG, of which the London component traces its roots back to Robert Fletcher in 1867 and William Barclay Peat in 1870, and Ernst & Young, which traces its English roots to the foundation of Harding and Pullein and the arrival in the firm of Frederick Whinney, both in 1849.

180 Edgar Jones, 'Deloitte, William Welch (1818–1898), accountant', *ODNB*. The *ODNB* entry does not identify her but a Mary Mercy Welch was baptised 3 June 1794, St Michael Barbados, daughter of William and Ann Welch. This fits with the death record of William Welch Deloitte's mother Mary Mercy Deloitte, of Paragon Place, aged forty, buried at St George the Martyr Southwark, 18 August 1835; Ancestry.com, *London, England, Deaths and Burials, 1813–1980* (database online).

181 www.deloitte.com/view/en_GB/uk/about/our-history/index.htm, accessed 30 April 2014.

182 British Guiana T71/885 nos. 572 (John Cove and Craig Miln) and 577 (Clonbrook). Edwin Waterhouse was president of the Institute of Chartered Accountants of England and Wales 1892–4; his son Sir Nicholas Edwin Waterhouse was president 1928–9; www.icaew.com/~/media/Files/Library/subjects/accounting-history/past-presidents-of-the-institute-of-chartered-accountants-in-england-and-wales.pdf, accessed 23 July 2013; Edgar Jones, 'Waterhouse, Edwin (1841–1917), accountant', *ODNB*. His brother Alfred designed Manchester Town Hall and the Natural History Museum; Colin Cunningham, 'Waterhouse, Alfred (1830–1905) architect', *ODNB*, which describes Alfred Waterhouse senior correctly as 'cotton broker of Liverpool'.

183 Richard K. Fleischman, David Oldroyd and Thomas N. Tyson, 'Plantation accounting and management practice in the US and the British West Indies at the end of their slavery eras', *Economic History Review* 64 (3) (2011), 765–97.

184 Ranald C. Michie, *The London Stock Exchange: A History* (Oxford, 1999), pp. 57, 59.

185 1841 and 1851 censuses online.

186 Michie, *London Stock Exchange*, p. 67.
187 Capel-Cure Myers was purchased in 1997 by the South African financial conglomerate Old Mutual and merged with Albert Sharp in 1998; www. oldmutual.com/about/heritage.jsp, accessed 6 September 2012.
188 Inventory of Elizabeth Wightman née Cooper 1837, Edinburgh Sheriff Court Inventories SC70/1/56.
189 Kynaston, *City of London*, pp. 2–8.
190 David Hancock, *Citizens of the World: London Merchants and the Integration of the British Atlantic Community 1735–1785* (Cambridge, 1995); Madge Dresser, 'Set in stone? Statues and slavery in London', *History Workshop Journal* 64 (2007), 162–99.
191 S. G. Checkland, 'Finance for the West Indies, 1780–1815', *Economic History Review* 10 (3) (1958), 461–9; Richard B. Sheridan 'The commercial and financial organization of the British slave trade 1750–1807', *Economic History Review* 11 (2) (1958), 249–63.
192 See e.g. Perry Gauci, *Emporium of the World: The Merchants of London 1660–1800* (London and New York, 2007).

4 Redefining the West India interest: politics and the legacies of slave-ownership

Keith McClelland

In *Capitalism and Slavery*, Eric Williams argued that the political defeat of the West India interest was a drama with three acts. First came the abolition of the slave-trade in 1807; second, the abolition of slavery itself in 1833; and third, the abolition of the protection of Caribbean sugar producers in 1846. What resulted in Britain was the triumph of the bourgeoisie under the banner of free trade, the consolidation of modern capitalism and the defeat of atavistic 'mercantilist' fractions. Industrial capitalism 'turned round and destroyed the power of commercial capitalism, slavery, and all its works'.[1] Williams' story of tripartite catastrophic defeat reflected an undeniable shift in the relative position and power of the slave-owners and former slave-owners as a whole, but his frame of reference was too narrowly drawn to summarise adequately the balance of failure and success for the 'West Indians' in the nineteenth century. In important parts of the former slave-colonies, the erstwhile slave-owners successfully evolved a new system of labour, based on a revival of the instrument of indenture in the face of opposition from many of the former abolitionists. At the same time, as Catherine Hall shows in Chapter 5, the former slave-owners led the rethinking of slavery and Emancipation in order to legitimate the new labour regimes. These efforts were led, politically and culturally, by absentee former slave-owners in Britain, especially by mercantile slave-owners. Williams' contention (and one followed by some other historians since) that the West India merchants were a kind of 'residual lumpen element of capitalism' has also been challenged: as Nicholas Draper shows in Chapter 3, those who received compensation following abolition were enmeshed in the circuits of later nineteenth-century finance capitalism. The essentially Marxist narrative that framed Williams' argument has also been complicated on the political level by recent work on the sugar duties controversies. Rather than this being a story of the triumph of the political representatives of the bourgeoisie over the regressive protectionists, Duncan Rice and, much more recently, Richard Huzzey have shown that the debates and agitations over the sugar question in Britain in the

1840s reveal a more complex pattern of argument and political alliance than Williams suggested.[2]

Hence, while the West Indian interest changed shape and direction as it lost its anti-abolition cohesion (just as the abolitionist alliance lost coherence post-Emancipation), its political representatives are visible at work through to the Eyre controversy and beyond. The cadre of MPs among the former slave-owners naturally died off over successive decades, but strikingly another generation of MPs, drawn from the sons, nephews and sons-in-law of the original West India MPs, emerged. While less moored in slavery, some were palpably shaped by the struggles of the earlier generation. This chapter re-explores, therefore, the political demise of the West Indians, not to refute it but to present a more complete picture than in Williams' brilliant starkness. We should see this as a process not of decline but of transformation.

This chapter examines some of those who appear in the compensation records in relation to the institutions and practices of political power between 1833 and the 1860s. Many of them belonged to the political elites that exercised local power, such as urban and county political offices including lord lieutenancies and the magistracy. For example, Rear Admiral Sir Charles Adam was both MP for Clackmannan and Kinross and Lord Lieutenant Kinross-shire 1839–53; Sir Thomas Birch was MP for Liverpool, 1847–52, high sheriff of Lancashire from 1841 and deputy-lieutenant for the county from 1847; and Charles Horsfall was mayor of Liverpool in 1832–3. They are also evident in the networks of voluntary political association within a relatively powerfully developed civil society.

Others belonged to those many aristocratic families who were bound into slavery. For example, the Balcarres family, part of the Scottish peerage since the early seventeenth century, came to be founded on slavery, land and coal, situated in that characteristic nexus of Scotland, England and the Caribbean. Alexander Lindsay, sixth Earl of Balcarres (1752–1825), was governor of Jamaica 1795–1801. His son, James Lindsay (1783–1869), seventh earl, was an awardee on eleven compensation claims in Jamaica. At the same time, the family developed extensive coal-mining interests in Lancashire, where James was MP for Wigan (1820–5) before inheriting the earldom on his father's death. Similarly, Stapleton Cotton (1773–1865), created Baron Combermere in 1814 and then the first viscount in 1827, was awarded compensation for enslaved people in Nevis. An army officer, he was appointed governor of Barbados and commander-in-chief for the Leeward Islands (1817–20), commander-in-chief in Ireland (1822–5) and commander-in-chief in India (1825–30). In Britain, as a peer he devoted himself to opposing 'innovative' political reforms such as Catholic Emancipation, the Reform Act and the repeal of the Corn Laws.[3]

The peerage included those who were particularly active in the defence of slave-owning interests. Charles Rose Ellis (1771–1845), Lord Seaford, for example, came from a family whose fortune had been established in Jamaica from 1665. Charles Rose Ellis had been brought up as the foster brother of Elizabeth Vassall, who was to become Lady Holland in 1797. An MP for various constituencies between 1793 and 1826, he was highly active in the West India Committee, of which he became the permanent chair, and a leading spokesman for the West India interest in Parliament.[4] As Lord Seaford, he became the leading spokesman in the House of Lords for the interest, speaking on its behalf on the protection of sugar, apprenticeship, the government of Jamaica and other issues.[5] Similarly, Henry Lascelles, second Earl of Harewood (1767–1841), scion of a family whose power and wealth derived from slavery in the Caribbean, landholdings and political office in Yorkshire, was an insistent voice of the West India lobby, both as an MP for various constituencies between 1796 and 1820 and as a member of the House of Lords from 1820 until his death.[6]

However, this chapter focuses largely on those who were in the House of Commons in the period. While there were important figures in the Lords, after 1832 the locus of parliamentary power had shifted decisively to the Commons and it was there that the key legislative decisions were made and where the most important political figures of the West India interest were to be found. Concentrating on the Commons, this chapter examines, first, the composition of the core MPs and, second, their engagement with three critically important issues: apprenticeship in the 1830s; sugar duties in the 1840s; and the question of indentured labour.

The group of MPs identified by Nicholas Draper in his analysis of MPs and compensation fall into four categories: first are those who appeared in the slave compensation records, either as direct beneficiaries or counterclaimants or who appear by virtue of other connections to particular claims; second are those whose immediate families appear in the records; third are those 'West India interest' MPs who did not appear in the compensation records but who held seats after the Reform Act of 1832; and fourth are those other MPs who were aligned to the West India interest over Emancipation and who were still active in the 1840s.[7] This analysis very significantly extended that drawn by earlier historians as to the nature and composition of what has generally been called, as it was at the time, 'the West India interest' or 'the West Indians'. To make sense of this, it is necessary to look at Higman's earlier analysis.[8]

Higman showed that in structure there were three layers or 'rings' of support for the West India interest in the eighteenth and early nineteenth centuries. First there was the inner ring of 'real' West Indians, resident planters born in the West Indies, who resided there for at least part of their lives or held political office there. Second was the 'outer ring' of absentee planters and merchants. Third, there were those colonial agents, relatives and friends, military men and others who sat for the 'old Tory interest' in London or in Bristol, Liverpool or Glasgow. Higman's definition of the interest includes the first two as the core group.

Within this structure, the composition and character of the group was changing in the period before 1832. It was not a wholly unified group. There were divisions both in Caribbean economic interests and political leanings and, to some extent, as a consequence of distinct regional concerns evident in the tensions between those in London and the key ports of Bristol, Liverpool and Glasgow.

There were two especially important shifts that occurred in the period leading up to 1832–3. First, and partly as a consequence of the changing political economy of the slave-colonies in the Caribbean, by the 1820s the predominance of the merchants over the planters was much more evident within the interest. The second was that the number of West Indian MPs was diminishing, though unevenly so. In sheer numbers the MPs were at their strongest in 1826–7, while after 1827 their numerical strength rapidly diminished. Hit by economic decline, they were also politically weakened by the 1832 Reform Act.

After 1832–3 this parliamentary group contracted further, as Figure 4.1 illustrates. The basis of these figures is to include those who were directly involved in the compensation process in various capacities (including as awardees, beneficiaries, mortgagees, executors or trustees, or as unsuccessful claimants).[9]

It should also be noted that the number of 'West Indian' MPs in the narrowest sense – that is, those identified by Judd[10] as belonging to the West India interest and who also appear in the compensation records – shrank drastically after 1832. Only three remained after the 1832 election, and, while the numbers increased between 1841 and 1846, even then the maximum number at any one point in the Commons was nine, in 1842–3. After 1846, only three remained: Ralph Bernal (1783–1854), a Whig but a staunch defender of slavery and of the West India interest throughout, who ceased to be an MP in 1852; Rt. Hon. Edward Ellice (1783–1863), a key figure in the Whig party, especially from the 1830s, and who remained an MP until his death; and Henry Goulburn (1784–1856), Peel's Chancellor of the Exchequer (1841–6), who likewise remained in the Commons until his death.[11]

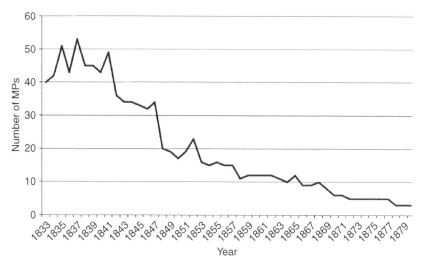

Figure 4.1 Number of West Indian MPs, 1833–80.

Death accounts for a large part of the decline in numbers: of eighty-seven MPs within our cohort, almost a quarter were dead by the end of the 1840s, almost half by the end of the 1850s and almost three-quarters by the end of the 1860s.

Many of these MPs represented more than one constituency in the course of their careers. Some might have been MPs for geographically quite dispersed areas but they overwhelmingly represented English constituencies (and English boroughs). (Given the electoral system this is not very surprising.) What is more striking is that some regions figure more commonly than others. In particular, there is a disproportionate weighting towards constituencies in the south-west of England, in Dorset, Hampshire, Somerset and Wiltshire, and, if one adds in Devon and Cornwall, the relative prominence of these areas becomes more pronounced. While other areas of England are certainly represented, the north of England (taking that as Lancashire, Yorkshire, Cumberland, Westmorland, Northumberland and Durham) does not figure significantly. Indeed, there was not a single such MP occupying a borough or county seat in Northumberland or Durham. Elsewhere in Britain, in Scotland the distribution roughly reflects the balance between burghs and counties; not a single West Indian MP sat for a Welsh constituency, while nine men sat, at one point or another, for an Irish constituency.

If this was an identifiable political grouping, the political alignments of its members were not fixed. While the bulk of these MPs were Tories, slave-owning 'crossed the spectrum of British politics'.[12] As Draper shows, in an analysis that complements those of others, there was no absolute correlation between slave-owning and anti-abolitionism, though there was in many cases and most slave-owners were seen as Tory enemies of reform. There were also those, such as some associated with one of the great centres of Whig power, the Holland House coterie, who were abolitionists even if Holland himself was not.[13]

Gross and Franzmann have argued that there was no direct correspondence between the stance taken on abolition and this group's voting on a number of key issues of the early 1830s. They suggest that there was no clear-cut association between, for instance, those who voted for or against abolition, parliamentary reform or the New Poor Law of 1834, a measure widely condemned by both some working-class radicals and significant popular Tories as exemplifying the same rule of Whig liberalism as had brought about abolition. The fundamental point here is that party political divisions were cut across by those beneficiaries of compensation: there was no straightforward association between party affiliation and a stake in slave compensation nor was there a straightforward class divide.[14]

This was not then a 'West Indian bloc acting unilaterally', as Higman put it.[15] However, on the issue of protecting the interests of those MPs who appear in the compensation records, there was a high degree of cohesion, of correlation between economic and ideological interest and political stance.

Just as there was no single political affiliation before 1832–3, so too in the 1840s. Political affiliations tended to be Conservative (disregarding the distinctions between Peelites, or those who aligned with the Tory leader Sir Robert Peel after the debacle over the Corn Laws and the split in the Tory party) and the Tories were increasingly dominant within the group as a whole by the 1840s. Thus, if the political affiliations of this group in 1835 were weighted towards the Tories, they was not dramatically so. But by the 1840s something like 60 per cent of them were labelled (by themselves and such documenters of them as *Dod's Parliamentary Companion*) as Conservative.

One way of testing their political affiliations is to use parliamentary division lists. The analysis that follows is based on voting on four key issues: the 1832 Reform Act; the motion by Sir George Strickland, a leading abolitionist, on 29 March 1838 that apprenticeship be abolished on 1 August 1838;[16] sugar duties in June 1844; and the repeal of the Corn Laws in 1846.[17]

It is clear from the voting records that in 1832 people generally voted with their parties regardless of any special interest arising from connections to slave-ownership. In 1838, the voting pattern on Strickland's motion was a little more complex. A little over half the MPs identified in compensation records voted on the issue. Those who were Whigs were fairly evenly divided but the Tories were much more clearly against: only two voted with Strickland on the abolition of apprenticeship – the Marquis of Chandos and W. A. Mackinnon. Neither spoke on the issue, so it is not entirely clear why they should have voted with Strickland, though Mackinnon was certainly on the liberal side of Toryism and Chandos had abandoned the West India Committee and committed himself to abolition in 1833, even if he remained strongly protectionist.[18]

On the other hand, in 1844, MPs were mainly voting from motives of special interest as having a stake in the maintenance of the duties protecting sugar. Between 1840 and 1850 there were thirty-four divisions recorded on sugar duties in the House of Commons. The analysis is based on three of these at a crucial point in the debates on sugar – namely 3, 14 and 17 June 1844. The resolutions are complex, but the central issue concerned whether or not the West Indian sugar producers were to maintain, as Robert Stewart has put it, 'a clear market advantage over their foreign rivals when parliament had raised their labour costs by abolishing slavery in 1833'.[19] Most of the MPs who had received compensation voted in at least one of these debates but they were not always consistent in their voting. However, it is fair to say that there was a bloc of sugar protectionists. Their voting records on the sugar question overrode, with few exceptions, their nominal party affiliations. Thus, in the voting on resolutions in the House of Commons in June 1844, only nine of these men voted consistently with the government, though they included two crucial figures for the government side, the Chancellor of the Exchequer, Henry Goulburn, and the President of the Board of Trade, W. E. Gladstone, as well as one or two far less important figures including William Mackinnon and John Samuel Wanley Sawbridge Erle-Drax (whose sole contribution to parliamentary debate throughout thirty-six years as an MP in three different periods amounted to asking the Speaker whether a window could be opened in the chamber of the House). On the opposite side of the government were ranged twenty-six Conservatives and Whigs acting as a more or less unified bloc. On the question of sugar, those who voted against the government were not all strident advocates of the protectionist cause; indeed, one or two of these who were beneficiaries, notably the liberal William Ewart, were vocal in their opposition to it. Yet the great majority of those in the larger grouping were hostile, and typically implacably so, to the movement towards freer and then free trade in sugar and the opening up of the Caribbean economy to greater competition from elsewhere.

Finally, on the repeal of the Corn Laws in 1846 there is again a pattern of voting with one's party rather than as a sectional interest. One might expect that those advocating protection for sugar would also be corn protectionists. But, in fact, there is no obvious correlation between those voting against Corn Law repeal and those voting for the protection of sugar, at least on the Whig side.

While party affiliation is one way of characterising the MPs, there was a larger social context that can be indicated by reference to a few individuals. Taken as a whole, this is a group that, economically, straddled the landed, mercantile and financial sectors of capital; some were also evidently moving into industrial capital. Sociologically they belonged to a larger world of economic, cultural and political power, linked through not only economic interests but also often family and friendship.

Some who were aligned to the world of the Whig grandees were bound into both the centres of state power and the fluid social and economic networks of an imperial formation. Edward Ellice, for instance, benefited as a mortgagee of two estates in Grenada and as an executor of the former owner of an estate in Tobago.[20] Extending geographically and economically the very considerable wealth built up by his father's business in London, New York and Canada, he became a prominent merchant banker and ship owner who traded in furs, fish, sugar, cotton and general merchandise in North and South America, the East and West Indies, and Europe. He was also a key player in effecting the union in Canada of the North-West Company and the Hudson's Bay Company in 1821, subsequently selling his interest in 1863 at great personal profit. In 1809 Ellice married Lady Hannah Althea Grey, daughter of Charles Grey, later the second earl, who was a central figure in the Whig party from the 1790s and a primary architect of the 1832 Reform Act. Ellice's insertion into the Whig elites was consolidated in the 1830s by his role, above all, as a political manager, *éminence grise* and organiser of political corruption (through the purchase of seats and distribution of honours). His connections to both political elites and those with economic interests in the Caribbean were further extended by a short-lived second marriage (1833–44) – Hannah had died in 1832 – to Lady Anne Coke, daughter of the fourth Earl of Albemarle and widow of Thomas William Coke, first Earl of Leicester, agricultural improver, committed Whig and opponent of the slave-trade who, nonetheless, had a tangential relationship to slave-ownership through an unsuccessful claim with a number of other aristocrats on a plantation in Barbados.[21]

There were those whose political affiliations were Tory and whose social location, while connected into the imperial world, belonged less to the metropolitan world and the highest of political elites and more to regionally and locally based places of power and influence. Thus, the Tudways of Somerset were significant landowners and had been since the early eighteenth century. As such they held office as magistrates and other local government roles. Their influence and local power rested, in part, on the creation of a political dynasty and the exercise of bribery and corruption, of that 'Old Corruption' characteristic of British politics in the period. Three successive generations, Clement, John and Robert, effectively owned the seat at Wells in the Tory interest for most of the period between 1761 and 1855. Indeed their elite connections were extended through business, politics and, in their case, the military, into the early twentieth century. Robert's son, Charles Clement (1847–1926), married, first of all, Lord Nelson's daughter, Edith, and then through a second marriage to Alice Hervey-Bathurst became brother-in law to the wife of the third Baron Methuen, who served in the army in Egypt and South Africa, becoming commander-in-chief in the latter in 1908 and later governor of Malta.[22]

The importance of such people is also to be found in the key provincial ports of Bristol, Liverpool and Glasgow, which had serviced and bene-fited from the slave-trade and slavery. One prominent voice in the sugar debates was Philip William Skynner Miles, a Conservative who described himself in elections as 'protectionist' and who was an important figure in the building of a parliamentary alliance opposed to the Peel govern-ment proposals on sugar in 1844. He was part of an established elite family within Bristol with a network of connections between Jamaica and Britain. His grandfather, William, had acquired a fortune in Jamaica as a planter in the eighteenth century and then set up in Bristol as a merchant and with substantial landownership in Somerset. His father, Philip John, was the primary claimant on sixteen claims, thirteen in Jamaica and three in Trinidad, whose total value amounted to almost £50,000. Philip John Miles expanded the family's wealth and became a millionaire through his activities as a merchant, ship owner and banker and, as with the Tudways, extended the range of the family's activities through politics. As MP for variously Westbury in Wiltshire (1820–6), Corfe Castle in Dorset (1829–32) and then Bristol (1835–7), he established one of those minor pol-itical dynasties that can be found quite often in the nineteenth-century House of Commons. Philip William Skynner Miles succeeded him as MP for Bristol 1837–52; another son (by his first marriage), William, was MP for Chippenham 1818–20, New Romney 1830–2 and East Somerset 1834–65; and, in turn, William's son – another Philip – became

Conservative MP for East Somerset 1878–85. Further, Miles extended the family business interests through financing the building of the railway and docks at Avonmouth, Bristol, and also owned two very substantial country houses close to the city.[23]

Illustrating the nexus of relations between London, the Caribbean and the important group of slave-owning families in Scotland and at the heart of Britain's financial hegemony in the City of London stood figures such as Patrick Maxwell Stewart. A London merchant and investor in insurance companies, he was also a prominent member of the West India Association Committee, sat on the select committees investigating apprenticeship in 1836 and 1837, was agent for Tobago in the 1840s and was associated with claims in Tobago worth £4,600. He was to be a prominent advocate of the West Indians' cause in the sugar debates in the 1840s. His family's wealth derived from not only their Tobago interests but also their landholdings in Renfrewshire, Scotland, where they had been entrenched since the mid-seventeenth century. For such men, politics was a natural arena in which to manifest power. Patrick Maxwell Stewart was Whig MP for Renfrewshire 1841–6, following his father, Sir Michael Shaw Stewart, who was one of the Whigs who attended a City meeting of the West India interest in May 1833.[24]

Many were imbricated within the wider circuits of empire, either through commercial connections like Ellice, through military careers like Sir Edward Cust or through roles in imperial government. An example is Henry Barkly (1815–98), son of Aeneas Barkly. He joined Davidson & Barkly and was MP for Leominster 1845–8; was knighted in 1853; was appointed governor and commander-in-chief of British Guiana in 1849 and then of Jamaica in 1853, Victoria in 1856 and Mauritius in 1863; and, in August 1870, was sent to the Cape of Good Hope as governor and British High Commissioner in South Africa until 1877. In 1879 he was a member of the Royal Commission on Colonial Defence. A Fellow of the Royal Society from 1864 and of the Royal Geographical Society from 1870, in retirement he devoted himself to scientific pursuits and to committee work for the London Library.[25]

Such individuals should be seen as parts of networks of association and sociability that might embrace not only several generations of a family and families by marriage but also others in a region, connected through common interests in land, merchanting, banking or other economic activities; through political activities (in both parliamentary and local politics); and through forms of friendship and special-interest associations. Forms of sociability were usually highly masculinised. For instance, the Glasgow Western Club was established in 1825 as a gentlemen's club in the heart of the merchants' district of central Glasgow (and it is a club that still exists). Something like half of the founding members of the Club had direct connections with compensation and, as with the Miles family in Bristol, one can see their connections – economic, cultural, political – threaded through the elites of Glasgow in the nineteenth century, not least in such associations as the Glasgow West India Association, established to defend and promote the interests of the city's sugar merchants and that mutated from a defence of the slave-economy to being, later in the nineteenth century, an organisation to promote the interests of the sugar business.[26]

These examples are only examples. They suggest some of the tentacles that stretch out – culturally, social and politically – into the world of the British ruling class of the nineteenth century. More particularly, these were people whose political representation was to be manifest in the debates over apprenticeship, sugar and indentured labour in the 1830s and 1840s.

While some of the politicians who appear in the compensation records were aligned with Whiggery, the Tories' defence of planter interests was bound up with a wider defence of empire. As Anna Gambles has shown, empire was 'an integral feature of Tory economic discourse in the first half of the nineteenth century'.[27] 'National interests', they believed, were defined by the particular historical development of individual nations and lay at the centre of both trade and international relations. The protection of the economy through such instruments as preference, navigation laws, Corn Laws and sugar duties was appropriate both to the distinctive historical circumstances of Britain and to the maintenance of imperial politics and power. At the same time, empire was of central importance politically and economically: it was seen by Tory commentators as necessary for the sustenance of political power and for economic development. A key mechanism of this was the need to maintain domestic and colonial markets for British trade and manufactures. The periodic crises in the economy were to be largely explained as under-consumption at home: sustaining and protecting imperial markets was central to avoiding such crises because they provided a more stable base for industry than reliance on non-colonial foreign markets.

This was also a political argument in that protection and preference were not only fiscal instruments but also, as Gambles puts it, 'political structures which bound together the diffuse elements of … empire'.[28] Concerned with the threat, as they saw it, of the equalisation of the duties on East and West Indian sugar in the 1820s, 'West Indians' such as Joseph Marryat, William Manning and James MacQueen – men embedded in the slavery business – were vocal and public advocates of such views.[29]

The political argument was also one about domestic political institutions and who was to be represented. For conservative critics of the 1832 Reform Act, not the least of its putatively damaging consequences was the weakening of the political representation of colonial interest.

In the early 1830s, Conservative defenders of the colonial empire did not separate their responses to Whig–Liberal–Radical arguments for retrenchment and free trade from issues surrounding the 1832 Reform Act. The dilution of virtual representation by 1832 was understood as a measure that would weaken the cohesion of the empire. This was the case put, for instance, by those, like Sir George Staunton, who argued that it was difficult if not impossible to 'conceive any argument that sustained Manchester, Birmingham, and Leeds representatives, and denied the same privileges to Canada, Jamaica, and Calcutta'.[30] Similarly, Archibald Alison, historian, lawyer, sheriff in Glasgow, high Tory writer on politics and political economy and one who appears as a trustee if not direct beneficiary of compensation, insisted that the numerical strength of small urban property in reformed Parliament would swamp and extinguish the virtual representation of imperial interests.[31]

This defence of the national and colonial was posited against liberal 'cosmopolitanism', associated above all by the 1830s with liberal politicians and thinkers such as Richard Cobden. Free trade would, it was believed, not only lead to a weakening of Britain's economic position but also have deleterious effects on the consumption and living standards of the poor and the working class. Liberalism was defined in terms of abstract notions of rights and principles. It was essential, Tories argued in contrast, to ground policy in history and past national experience. Failure to do so could be catastrophic. Why, for example, had the French West Indian empire declined? James MacQueen, beneficiary of compensation for slave-ownership in St Kitts, pro-slavery polemicist and geographer, ascribed French decline to the application of the 'unhistorical principles' of 1789 and notions of abstract rights to both slavery and the government of colonies. Civil and economic liberties might be desirable, but the abolition of slavery had not been driven by due attention to the distinctive social, moral and economic conditions that ought to govern such policies but rather had been the consequence of abstract notions.[32]

So what was at stake here after Emancipation was not only a particular economic interest – the defence of protection of sugar and the wider economy of imperialism in the Caribbean – but also a fundamental disagreement about Britain's whole political–economic framework. The political terrain had shifted irrevocably after 1833. If the interest had fought campaigns over the abolition of the trade in 1807 and of slavery in 1833, it was obviously no longer possible to defend slavery after

1833. Some before 1833, such as Goulburn, had come to realise that in the face of the anti-slavery campaigns of the 1820s they must do something to ameliorate the conditions of the enslaved on their estates. After 1833–8 the framework in which they sought to defend their interests changed fundamentally as they sought to deal with a 'free' labour regime and new market conditions.

Apprenticeship

The introduction of the apprenticeship system across the colonies, except for Antigua and Bermuda, on 1 August 1834 inaugurated a new, harsh system of forced labour upon the formerly enslaved, a transitional point that combined the effective maintenance of relations between master and slave with those between employee and employer. Children under six were to be freed immediately, field hands were to serve a period of six years and domestic servants were to serve four years. Both field and domestic servants would be compelled to devote seventy-five per cent of their time to working for their former owners, for which they would receive no wages except for any overtime worked. The system also effected changes in the forms of the local state, which was strengthened through extending institutions and forms of policing and punishment such as the use of treadmills and workhouses. In some respects the 'ameliorationist' measures that some planters had introduced in the 1820s to attempt to stave off abolition were set back. The supervision of the system by special magistrates appointed from London called into question the relationship between the local, central state and the institutions of government in the Caribbean such as the Houses of Assembly. The failures and weaknesses of the system were evident in both planter obstructions to the work of the special magistrates and in apprentice resistance to the system, for example in riots in St Kitts, St Vincent and elsewhere.[33]

In Britain, the introduction of apprenticeship led to a great revival of the anti-slavery movement against the system (led by Joseph Sturge, T. F. Buxton and others during 1836–8) and a renewed demand for an immediate end to it. In large part in response to this, two select committees reported (in 1836 and 1837) and debates were held in Parliament in 1838.[34]

The select committee of 1836 included not only prominent abolitionists, such as Thomas Foxwell Buxton and Daniel O'Connell, but also, as representative of the West India interest, Patrick Maxwell Stewart and W. E. Gladstone. Stewart also sat on the 1837 committee. The witnesses included a small number of former slave-owners, notably Augustus Hardin Beaumont – a curious and contradictory figure who by 1836–8 had become a leading radical in the north-east of England – and William Burge, MP for Eye, formerly attorney general for Jamaica and a staunch defender of slavery before abolition. Gladstone, Edward Ellice, William James and others associated with slave-owning spoke in the debates in Parliament on the issue between March and May 1838. These investigations and debates came to turn on the key question of whether apprenticeship ought to be ended early.

Three aspects of the arguments made by the erstwhile slave-owners and their allies are striking: first, the stress upon the need to maintain the system because of the 'contract' undertaken in passing abolition in 1833; second, how well the system of apprenticeship was allegedly working; and, flowing from this, third, the representation of the view that this was a transitional state to a regime of free labour, which was accompanied by an elevation of the moral state of the apprentices. The debates marked the effective repudiation of the pro-slavery argument and helped to lay the foundations of an assimilation to what was to become the hegemonic view of Britain as a nation committed to anti-slavery.

That a 'contract' had been made with the planters in 1833 was emphasised. The 1833 Act consisted of several contracts, argued Sir Charles Grey, and while 'he was not so extravagant as to suppose that the condition of the negroes in the 20 colonies had been free from complaint; but let it be as bad as it might, the proprietors who were resident out of the country ought not to lose ... the benefit to which they were entitled by the contract'.[35] Such views sought, with considerable success, to place planter interests at the centre of the question, highlighting the damage to the planters and to the wider economy if they were not allowed the full six years. This was to become part of the rhetoric of defence of the planters as the victims of Emancipation, as we shall see.

That apprenticeship was working well was stressed in many quarters. Sir George Grey may have believed, as he told the House in introducing the debate on 28 May, that the formerly enslaved were 'now in a state of transition from that state [of oppression] to the possession of the rights and privileges of British subjects and freemen'. The evidence that such a 'transition' was being managed successfully was as central to the defence of planter interests as it was to the Whig government's desire to prevent early termination of apprenticeship. Thus, Lord Stanley cited a communication from Sir James Carmichael Smyth to the effect that in British Guiana the colony had improved; there was 'increased moral and religious feeling, evidenced by the number of marriages, by the communicants at the sacraments, by the children who attended the schools'. And, above all, the conditions of the labouring classes had markedly improved, as demonstrated by 'the quantity of manufactures exported' and, Smyth claimed, 'the transition from the dejected and almost naked slave to the cheerful and decently clad labourer could only be believed by those who had recently revisited the colony after an absence of several years. The apprenticeship system was to teach the negroes to depend on their own industry.' This optimistic view of the success and benefits of apprenticeship was echoed in the extensive evidence of William Burge to the select committee of 1836.[36]

Such an account meshed with a key element of the 'transitional stage' argument, that the apprentices were learning the habits of wage labour even before they had actually become 'free labourers'. In its 1836 report, the select committee noted, for example, that:

The system of apprenticeship in Jamaica is working in a manner not unfavourable to the momentous change from Slavery to Freedom which is now going on there. They perceive undoubtedly many traces of those evils which are scarcely separable from a state of society confessedly defective and anomalous, and which can only be defended as one of preparation and transition.

However, the committee believed that the apprentices were not only conducting themselves well and were willing to work for wages when treated fairly by employers but also that there were productivity gains as compared with slave labour. Moreover, 'industrious habits, and the desire of moral and physical improvement, seem to be gaining ground'.[37] Anxiety about the likely future of the former slave-colonies informed the debates. Would they survive and prosper in a post-slavery state or would the ending of slavery bring about the ruin of the planters, the decline of the economy and a weakening of the British imperial system?

For some, it was because of such anxieties that the full term of apprenticeship had to be sustained, so that the apprentices would learn the disciplines of wage labour. Expressing doubts that the end of apprenticeship would lead to an improvement in the economies of the islands, Lord Seaford, for example, claimed that:

They adopted the course to prepare the apprentice, by gradually emancipating him; which afforded him an opportunity, by improving his moral condition, and by accustoming him to a limited state of freedom, to prepare himself for the unqualified exercise of his civil liberties. That intermediate state was important, by placing at his disposal a portion of his time, and teaching him the habit of labouring for wages, and thus bringing him into the condition of a free labourer; and it was important, also, by rendering his condition satisfactory and comfortable, to temper the change to liberty. For these reasons, also, he thought that the few remaining years of the apprenticeship were of the greatest importance, both to the welfare of the apprentice, and of the master. He considered it the duty of every master so to employ the interval, and it had been so employed in no inconsiderable number of instances, as to prepare the apprentice for the great change which was about to take place.[38]

In the event, apprenticeship was brought to an end in the Caribbean by 31 July 1838, partly because the system was effectively being abandoned in the Caribbean (encouraged by the Whig Colonial Secretary, Lord Glenelg) and partly because of a parliamentary muddle. Following the end of apprenticeship, doubts about the future of the sugar colonies were to become increasingly insistent in the 1840s, not least in regard to conditions in the market for sugar – including concerns about fiscal regulation and competition from slave-based economies – and the conditions of production.

There was a general belief by the 1840s that the sugar economies were in deep trouble. Though Antigua, Barbados and St Kitts remained relatively prosperous and production costs rose only modestly in the period, following abolition all the sugar economies were facing some common structural problems, to greater or lesser extents –the abandonment of estates; the increasingly seasonal nature of sugar production; and the shortage of capital as the region became a high-risk economy for new capital investment – all of which made the economies more susceptible to seasonal fluctuations in crop yields. They were also vulnerable to the general international economic crisis of 1847–8, when they were particularly exposed to rising levels of bankruptcies and lack of credit. And they were, of course, particularly vulnerable to competition from the slave-based sugar economies, especially those of Brazil and Cuba.[39]

Above all, the fundamental problem of the post-abolition economies concerned labour, especially in Jamaica (which always figured large in metropolitan understandings of the British West Indies), British Guiana and Trinidad; these were characterised by Green as 'low density' colonies – that is, where the ratio of population to arable land was lowest. The ending of slavery and apprenticeship was followed by the withdrawal of labour from estates as many of the freed worked as much as possible on their own account on their own modest land holdings, strengthening the position of the 'proto-peasantry'. It was particularly marked that formerly enslaved women field labourers, and to a lesser degree children, withdrew their labour from the estates. Flight from the plantations partly took the form of the establishment of 'free villages' but the problems, from the point of view of the planters, were compounded by a variety of forms of resistance to the attempted imposition of the new capitalist regime of free labour, including struggles over wages and conditions and what was widely seen as a failure in the ability to control and discipline labour.[40] Faced by rising production costs, lower output and reduced profits, the planters made attempts to raise productivity through the introduction of new machinery and new techniques and to impose tighter labour controls.[41] But what was seen as crucial if the future of the colonies was to be assured was that the state should protect the colonies both through the maintenance of sugar duties and by enabling planters to import immigrant labour.

Sugar duties

Originally introduced in the seventeenth century in order to raise revenue and protect colonial markets through preferential treatment, sugar duties were a central pillar of the West India interest by the early nineteenth century. After 1833 their defence came to occupy a much more prominent place. The ending of apprenticeship in 1838 had been bought at the cost of expectation among the planters and their allies that the duties would be maintained. Faced by competition from slave-grown economies and weakened by economic problems within the West Indian colonies, it is difficult to underestimate how important the sustainment of the duties was to the post-Emancipation West India interest.

By 1825 there were three levels of duty in play: the duties paid on sugar from the British West Indies, which were the lowest; a higher rate applied to sugar from the rest of the British Empire; and a very considerably higher duty paid on foreign sugar.[42] Between 1825 and 1835 the West Indian monopoly was broken by enacting the same rate of duty for sugar from Mauritius (1825) and the East Indies (1835). In May 1841 the Whig government proposed that foreign sugar, whether slave- or free-grown, should be admitted on more favourable terms. While this proposal was defeated, in 1844, Peel's Tory government brought forward their own proposals to admit foreign sugar that was certified as being free-grown. It was defeated in the 1846 election, but in 1846 the succeeding Whig–Liberal government introduced the Sugar Duties Act, which had the effect of reducing protection in the British market by reducing the differential on all sugars, admitting all foreign sugars at only a modestly higher duty than West Indian, regardless of whether it was slave- or free-grown. By 1851 the Sugar Equalization Duties Act had put all sugar imports into the empire on a par, with full equalisation coming into effect in 1854.

There were three key political positions on the sugar duties. The protection of West Indian interests, it was maintained by out-and-out protectionists, meant sustaining the defence against both foreign free labour-grown sugar and, most importantly, the slave-grown sugars of Brazil and Cuba, in particular. The Peel government in 1844 argued that the distinction against slave-grown sugar should be maintained while the duties on free-grown sugar were reduced. The 'pure' free traders, on the other hand, sought to remove *all* differentiation between sugars of different provenance, whether free-grown or slave-grown, colonial or foreign.

The opposition to the dilution or abandonment of protective duties for the West Indians broke into two political groupings: the protectionists who wanted a defence of West Indian planters and merchant interests through the maintenance of duties, and those, including the abolitionists of the British and Foreign Anti-Slavery Society, for whom moves towards free trade in sugar would entail a betrayal of the anti-slavery cause because they would mean opening up to slave-grown sugar from Brazil and Cuba and would also neglect a central concern of theirs, the conditions of the emancipated in the West Indies.[43]

For the 'pure' free traders, only complete free trade could bring about the ultimate dissolution of slavery. Full abolition would follow free trade, argued William Ewart – whose father, a major Liverpool merchant, was godfather of W. E. Gladstone: 'commerce [was] the great emancipator. By throwing open our commerce with all parts of the world we should be more likely to put an end to slavery than by any enactments which that House could frame. Open the markets of the world and free labour might boldly enter into competition with slave labour.'[44]

The 1844 debates were introduced by Henry Goulburn, Chancellor of the Exchequer. He brought to the debates not only a set of political arguments but also a personal experience of being a slave-owner and a participation in the shared experience articulated by his opponents.[45]

Since the beginning of the nineteenth century, Goulburn's primary source of income was his estate at Amity Hall, Jamaica, an income that had 'assured him of his social and political position'.[46] On Emancipation he received almost £5,000 for the ownership of 242 enslaved. His absentee ownership and management of the estate, maintained through correspondence with his attorneys and managers, was marked by two impulses: an attempt to make the estate profitable and his evangelical Christian conscience. At the heart of the problems of his estate both before and after Emancipation was the problem of labour. 'If', he wrote to his attorney in 1838, 'the negroes will work when emancipated [following the abolition of apprenticeship] we shall all ultimately benefit by the change. If they will not our prospects are poor indeed.'[47] His cast of mind was to see enslaved people as naturally both promiscuous and indolent. He struggled with the resistance of freedmen to working in the manner he and his managers expected. His attempts to restore the profitability of his estate and his family's income through both encouraging the birth rate and importing labour, and attempting to attach labour to the estate through investment in food, clothing and the disciplines of religion and education, largely failed. His income from the estate declined.

Despite his evangelical Christian conscience, only in the mid-1820s had he come to recognise the necessity of both amelioration of slave conditions and eventual Emancipation. Though he had for too long failed to recognise the stain of slavery, his conscience was troubled by slavery and its legacies for him, and his attempts to rectify this after Emancipation were marked by regret that slavery had existed. However, it is striking that, if he could not and did not forget slavery, when it came to the public debates in the House of Commons about protecting the interests of the West Indians, he effectively suppressed his own engagement. His apparently dispassionate presentation of the fiscal case for changing the sugar duties entailed a displacement of his own involvement with slavery. Indeed, he was reminded of this by one of his opponents, Philip Miles, who demanded of him that he visit his own estates – and that he should take Gladstone with him.[48]

Government strategy was driven by a number of different elements, not least the fiscal problems of the state. It was necessary to increase revenues by imposing income tax, beginning to shift the burden of taxation from indirect to direct taxes and, at the same time, keeping income tax low through increasing revenues by lowering duties on consumption goods and thus boosting, in particular, working-class consumption. This has to be seen in the broader context of, on the one hand, dealing with Chartist insurgency by attempting to attach the working class to the state through encouraging consumption and some measures of social reform, and, on the other, of dealing with the interests of manufacturing and the effects of the economic depression of 1837–42 through attacking the Corn Law problem. The latter would also entail addressing the crisis in Ireland by moving towards free trade as the putative solution.

Within this wider framework, Goulburn situated his aims so far as sugar was concerned. Sugar had become an essential element of working-class consumption so his aim was 'to secure to the people of this country an ample supply of sugar'. But he also wished to make that supply 'consistent with a continued resistance to the Slave Trade, and with the encouragement of the abolition of slavery'. Finally, he sought 'to reconcile both with a due consideration to the interests of those who have vested their property in our Colonial possessions'.[49]

The dryly expressed objectives that Goulburn outlined were framed within a debate as a whole that exemplified Disraeli's view that sugar was caught in a 'maze of conflicting interests and contending emotions'.[50] All were agreed that this was another opportunity to reaffirm the moral weight and value of having made the break with slavery. 'We shall show the world', said Goulburn, 'that we have not forgotten the principles on which this country has always acted.'[51] Such sentiments echoed across the debates. Thus, said the Whig politician Henry Labouchere, 'the emancipation of that race was the brightest page in our history. We might have been sometimes mistaken, and suffered disappointment, but it was that conduct regulated by moral and religious feelings which was the source of England's greatness.'[52] Ranged against Goulburn and the government was an opposition that included a pretty solid phalanx of MPs who had benefited from compensation. Three overarching themes can be discerned in their claims. They presented themselves as the effective victims of the post-Emancipation situation, as those who had suffered and for whom the compensation they had received was wholly inadequate. At the same time they sought to draw a line against their own involvement with slavery, not least by embracing the cause of and moral value of abolition itself. They sought remedies that focused especially on the question of labour.

Patrick Maxwell Stewart was not only an MP but also an agent for Tobago and a key member of the West India Committee. Stewart claimed that 'the West India Colonies were the victims of the legislature of this country' and that

many of the estates in the West Indies had already been abandoned, and that, in consequence of the circumstances to which he had just adverted many persons were plunged into the deepest suffering. More estates would be, he was afraid, abandoned, and more persons would be exposed to suffer from the extraordinary step which the Government now proposed to adopt.[53]

For Philip Miles, the government's actions in reducing protection would be a betrayal of the 'long course of fidelity and loyalty, and [of] our great sacrifices in endeavouring to co-operate with your Majesty's Government in carrying out the benevolent scheme of Negro Emancipation'.[54]

Such views were enlarged by William James, whose family had made a fortune as Liverpool-based merchants and as estate owners. Though describing himself in elections as a 'Radical' and advocate of universal manhood suffrage and free trade in corn, he was an implacable defender of the need for protection of sugar.[55] In a quite personal and angry statement he claimed that he had only become a proprietor by accident:

He was, unfortunately, one of those persons called West India proprietors, and he was not so through any fault of his own. He was a West India proprietor because, somewhere about a century since, an ancestor of his, relying on the faith of the Government of that day, did invest a considerable amount of capital in the purchase of a West India estate in the island of Jamaica; and he did so, perhaps, under the impression that future Governments would not interfere to injure, much less to utterly destroy, the value of that property.

This rhetorical disavowal of responsibility for slavery was then complemented by the claim that, for all he had done to make his estate more
profitable through economy of labour and improved modes of cultivation, proprietors like him had:

been most cruelly and unjustly treated – they had been treated worse than ever
the slaves had been treated by the West India planters in the worst times of slavery. At all times they gave them a sufficiency of good and wholesome food. What
had been done to those who depended on property in the West Indies for their
support? Widows and orphans had been driven to the greatest distress, the bread
had been taken from them, and they had been driven to destitution.

While he welcomed Emancipation, with 'cordial satisfaction', that 'greatest, the most hazardous, and ... the most successful experiment which has
ever been made in civilized society', it was also an experiment attended
by danger. Society in the colonies 'is staggering under the shock of that
experiment' and if protection is to be reduced, then 'you take a step which
may decide for ever that sugar shall no longer be produced at a profit by
free labour in those Colonies'; it will 'give a great additional stimulus to
slavery and the Slave Trade'. But, concluded a gloomy James, in the face
of the various assaults upon the planters and their allies, 'he had learned
to look upon the cause of the West India proprietors as hopeless.'[56]

What supported such arguments was the notion that the compensation they had been paid was wholly inadequate. Ralph Bernal even
opined that really the proprietors might have done better not to accept it,
'for it had been of very little real benefit to them'.[57] For his part Stewart
did not reject the notion of compensation in such terms; but was it
really sufficient to cover the losses of 'property' – that is, of the enslaved,
though he forbore to mention the fact – and the suffering that attended
the proprietors, especially when faced with the additional burdens of
apprenticeship?

The Legislature at first had proceeded, in regard to the West India Colonies,
upon the principle of encouraging their cultivation by slave labour, and pre-
vented the Emancipation of slaves; then they took it into their heads (very properly he admitted) to emancipate the slaves, and to compensate the colonists for
the loss; but how was that compensation settled? They had heard much of the
munificent grant of £20,000,000 (and he admitted it was munificent); but that
was by no means a sufficient compensation for property which, as estimated by
the valuers of the Government, amounted to £100,000,000; but, in addition to
the £20,000,000, they instituted a term of apprenticeship, which was also to go
as part of the compensation due to the planters. It, however, was soon urged that
they should not stop in the progress of emancipation, and the apprenticeship was
abolished, and then, while the £20,000,000 proved to be only £17,000,000 in
actual payment, the twelve years apprenticeship turned out to be only six.[58]

The repudiation of slavery and of connections to it, the effect of drawing a line against their own and the nation's engagement with it, were of central importance to the ways in which the West India interest represented themselves. One example of this was when the West India Association, the extra-parliamentary instrument of the interest, sent a deputation to the government in 1848 to lobby on the state of the Caribbean colonies. Their mixture of special pleading, complaint and assertion of moral integrity was typical of the deliberations of the Association throughout the 1840s. Its reworking of the argument about slavery was indicative of what was to give a very particular cast to the history.[59]

In presenting its address to the colonial secretary, Sir Henry Grey, the Association spoke of the 'atrocious slave trade' and the 'evils which are inevitably associated with production on a large scale, through the compulsory, the unrequited, the whip-extorted drudgery of slaves'. Moreover, the Association represented an alliance. While it included those with connections to the West Indies as proprietors and residents, it was stressed that it also included those who,

having no personal interest in the West Indies, are led by feelings of patriotism and humanity deeply to deplore the actual distress and the probable ruin of these once important dependencies of the British empire. It is also supported by those who, through a long series of years, have struggled for the universal abolition of the slaver trade and the complete extinction of slavery.

Thus they set up a position in which they could be seen to belong to that moral revulsion against slavery. Positioning themselves among those who had come to sympathise with enslaved negroes, a result of 'the unwearied labours of our Sharpes, our Clarksons, and our Wilberforces' – and note the appropriative use of 'our'– they moved into a different set of claims, primarily focused on a defence of the planter interest against competition from other slave-based producers. They spoke with 'pleasure' of 'the payment of millions for [the] redemption of the enslaved', as if the purpose of compensation had been to enable the enslaved to be freed rather than a means of compensating slave-owners for the loss of their property. What was needed now, they claimed, was the introduction of measures to discourage production by slave labour and the strengthening of the West Indian economy by encouraging immigration of capital, skill and labour. If such measures were to be undertaken by the government then 'the British West Indies may again take the lead in their respective productions, and prove to the civilized world that it has been the true policy, as well as the duty and honour of England to maintain the cause of the slave and make no compromise with the oppressor'.[60]

The belief that it had been the moral impulses of the nation that had been mobilised was a major cultural as well as political shift and was a crucial thread in the reconfiguration of the sense of the nation, of what constituted 'Britishness'. In his address to the electors of Tamworth in 1841, Robert Peel captured much of this new narrative:

The character of this country in respect to slavery is thus spoken of by one of the most eloquent writers and statesmen of another country. It is Dr. Channing, of the United States, that speaks, and he speaks in these terms: –

'Great Britain, loaded with an unprecedented debt and with a grinding taxation, contracted a new debt of a hundred millions of dollars [sic] to give freedom, not to Englishmen, but to the degraded African. I know not that history records an act so disinterested, so sublime. In the progress of ages England's naval triumphs will shrink into a more and more narrow space in the records of our race – this moral triumph will fill a broader, brighter page.'

Gentlemen, let us take care that this 'brighter page' be not sullied by the admission of slave sugar into the consumption of this country by our unnecessary encouragement of slavery and the slave trade.[61]

Such views were echoed by some who had originally opposed abolition. For example, Grantley Berkeley, MP for West Gloucestershire, violent, disputatious and a generally extremely unpleasant man, was to claim that 'I held the abolition of slavery in the West Indies to be a religious and moral duty.' However, abolition required the reciprocal exchange of protection and that was the responsibility of others, most specifically of government. Though referring particularly to free trade in corn, he was clearly thinking of the effects of moves towards free trade in sugar. It was the state that should have carried out its obligations to those who suffered; and those who suffered should have had their property and labour supply assured:

[B]ut, if the Government fails in adapting the great interests of the nation to receive and to work well under so vast a change as free trade forces on our political economy, why the misery that ensues is not so much the fault of the measure; the blame more aptly rests with him who misconducted the affairs intrusted to his charge, and the sooner the false step is retrieved the better.

Ere slavery had been abolished and the West India interest endangered, new colonial laws should have been framed for the protection of property, and an industrial supply of labour established.[62]

The issue of the supply of labour was a key aspect of the protectionist case. Pre-1833, debate about labour in the Caribbean had focused on demographics and problems of supply, modes of discipline and punishment of the enslaved, and the cultural qualities and characteristics of labour and the culture – familial, religious and moral – of the enslaved. By the 1840s the terrain had altered. Were the formerly enslaved potentially adequate as labourers? The movement towards nominally free labour and the question of immigration turned not only on numbers but also on cultural questions and, typically, was cast in terms of a racialised view of labour. Thus, for instance, Peel remarked:

You are making a great experiment in the West Indies – it has hitherto been more successful than all the circumstances of the case warranted – the industry of those colonies has been somewhat paralyzed by the gift of freedom to the slaves. There is now some difficulty, natural enough, in finding for the present a sufficient supply of free labour; and there is, therefore, rather a diminution in our supply of sugar, for the negroes have not yet come round to regular habits of working. It is, however, a diminution and difficulty only temporary, I apprehend, which will soon, therefore, be at an end.[63]

The 'gift of freedom' as Peel put it was for the protectionists a problem – the problem of labour. It was an issue that ran through the protectionists' arguments in Parliament and through the deliberations of the West India Committee, and it received renewed emphasis as a consequence of the reduction of duties with the passing of the Act of 1846. Before then there were repeated references to the necessity of ensuring an adequate supply of labour through immigration to the West Indian colonies, typically couched as complaint. State schemes to help the colonies with this had been inadequate for being, in essence, too little and too late. Patrick Maxwell Stewart, for instance, complained that an 'ample supply of labourers' should have been afforded. Proposing the importing of 'Chinese coolies' as Lord John Russell had proposed in 1841 or further importing African and Chinese labour was inadequate, indeed 'un-English'. The complaint was uttered in a tone of the kind that could only be heard from someone who saw himself as a victim. One can almost hear the squeal of self-pity as Stewart declared that 'Such treatment was not fair – it was un-English'.[64]

After the Sugar Duties Act of 1846 the protectionists continued to argue, unsuccessfully, for the restoration of the sugar duties as a means of defence. Their preoccupations rested on an analysis of what the problem of labour in the Caribbean was and the conditions that pertained in a post-apprenticeship regime.

In general, what was needed was more labour and labour of sufficient quality so that it could be inserted into a fully developed capitalist regime able to compete with slave-based economies. The trouble with labour in the Caribbean was, it was claimed, that the free labourers did not work hard enough.[65] In Barbados the 'free Negro' worked, it was claimed, eight to nine hours a day and did so at a 'moderate' pace. In Jamaica, British Guiana and Trinidad the labourers only worked five to six hours per day. By contrast, in Brazil and Cuba slaves had to work never less than twelve hours a day and typically sixteen, including Sundays.

This argument was reinforced by the ex-slaves' allegedly 'natural' indolence, insufficient acculturation to the disciplines of wage labour and ability to resist the demands of 'their masters'. In this respect it was a scarcely veiled belief that slave labour had distinct advantages over free. In colonies such as Jamaica, 'the free labourer is much more independent, and naturally dictates his terms of employment' and the efforts of planters against resistance were to no avail: the labourer 'performs the work in his own way and at his own time, the master having practically little control'.[66] Or, as Andrew Colvile, West Indian proprietor, merchant and recipient of large amounts of compensation for claims in Antigua, British Guiana and Jamaica, put it to the Select Committee on Sugar and Coffee Planting in 1848:

It is difficult to suppose that free labour should be so abundant and so much at the command of the employer in a tropical climate as to make him equally secure of the continuous labour and attention of his people at the manufactory as one can naturally conceive to be the case where the labour is under his actual control as a slave. In the present position of the West India colonies, the population is so far from being in that dense state, that a labourer, in point of fact, conducts himself as he pleases, and the employer has very little, if any, control over him at all, so that if the employer complains of his manufacture being badly done, the answer is, 'If you are not satisfied I will go away.'[67]

That they did not work enough was because they were a mix of peasants and wage-labourers. Able to sustain a combination of self-subsistence and wage labour, these peasant-labourers did not produce a sufficient surplus of value for the planter to cover his costs in employing them. The consequences would be ruinous for all the contending parties, whose interests were, it was claimed, conjoined:

Although they [the peasantry] have hitherto been eminently prosperous, because they have hitherto been able to exact more for their labour than what its produce has yielded, they cannot be exempted from all participation in the fate of those by whom they are employed. The interests of both are, in fact, identical, though for a time their adjustment may be deferred.[68]

They needed the disciplines of competition and the market that were to be found in British labour. Drawing a comparison between the conditions of labour in Britain and the colonies, the West India Committee argued that free labour in Britain was generally superior but it was so because of the disciplines of the free market and of competition:

The vigorous 'free labour' which we witness in this country, and upon which observation the general confidence in the efficacy of freedom over slavery is founded, is a result of circumstances entirely different [from the colonies] – it is stimulated by a competition for employment which is unknown in the Colonies, and which not only reduces wages to the lowest scale of subsistence on which such labour can be sustained, but also secures the most seasonable and perfect performance of the work.[69]

These conditions of labour necessarily meant that labour in Brazil and Cuba, or in regimes such as Java where labour was compulsory, was necessarily cheaper and more productive. There may be continual waste of life inherent in slave systems but labour would always be cheaper: 'the whole cost is less than the most reasonable wages for which the free Negro can as yet be induced to labour'.[70]

For the West India interest the solution to the labour problem was more labour. By the late 1840s this had crystallised into the view that there must be unrestricted immigration to the West Indies, not least from Africa: 'Without an abundant supply of free labour it is impossible to contend with an unlimited supply of slaves. In order to secure that abundance it will not suffice merely to permit emigration from Africa – it must be openly and zealously encouraged.'[71] At the same time, the government must maintain and extend its suppression of the slave-trade elsewhere through military force and the deployment of naval squadrons. This entailed acting in two zones. The state had to act both in the face of the 'bold defiance and calumnies of the Slave Trader' of West Africa and to suppress the Brazilian and Cuban slave-trades.[72]

For many abolitionists and political radicals, the question of military intervention was the subject of renewed debate in 1848–50, not least in response to the House of Commons Select Committees on the Slave Trade, which deliberated during 1848–9. The issue produced renewed turmoil among the abolitionists and radicals about not only how the slave-trade might be suppressed but also the extent to which state force should or could be used to enforce liberal, humanitarian policies.[73] For the West India interest, the central question was about ensuring the supply of labour for the Caribbean. Yet the terms in which they addressed this ultimately resolved themselves into a stance that betrayed their own casting of themselves as people in need of redress because of Emancipation, as people who could deliver freedom and as people who shared in the continuing work of 'the great Emancipation'. Without any apparent sense of historical irony, they claimed that the importing of African labour would bring benefit to the Africans themselves. To enable the liberation and settlement of Africans from Sierra Leone, in particular, in the West Indian colonies would greatly improve their lives as free people. For it was in the free British West Indies that 'it would be well for the African, in every point of view, to find himself a free labourer ... enjoying there ...

higher advantages of every kind than have fallen to the lot of the negro race in any other portion of the globe.'[74]

Bound into this view was the attachment of the proprietors to the great project of abolition:

The suppression of the Slave Trade – the abolition of Slavery throughout the world – the condition of the emancipated Negroes – and the existence of the colonial Proprietors are all dependent upon each other. These questions cannot be separated, and the more they are investigated the more it will appear evident that the true remedy for the Slave Trade is to discourage the produce of slave labour, and to encourage the cultivation of our own Free Colonies.[75]

With the failure to protect the sugar duties, the representatives of the planters and merchants fought a rearguard action, led by Lord George Bentinck,[76] to not only attempt to restore the protection of the sugar duties but also to press the government on the general problems of the sugar colonies and to seek redress through the recruitment of immigrant labour. A major vehicle they adopted for putting forward their views was a series of parliamentary enquiries in the 1840s that were the occasion, not surprisingly, for a barrage of lamentations and complaints about the state of the Caribbean economies and related matters. Most importantly, in the wake of the Sugar Duties Act of 1846, Bentinck led the setting up of the Select Committee on Sugar and Coffee Planting, which met in the spring of 1848.[77]

Somewhere over a third of the eighty-one witnesses called before the Select Committee on Sugar and Coffee Planting were recipients of compensation or closely related to people who were and they were supported by the advocacy of the West India Committee, notably in London, through its meeting with and lobbying of government.

Among the themes that dominated the reports were that the sugar economies were in a parlous and even desperate state; that fundamental to this was the problem of 'continuous labour', of regular and disciplined work; that the removal of the sugar duties had removed an essential protective shield from the colonies and that this not only embodied the removal of a particular measure but also was indicative of the whole treatment of the colonies since Emancipation; and that, without the twin strategies of a renewal of protection and the encouragement of immigration, the future of the colonies was profoundly bleak. As well as special pleading, this was an early articulation of a particular narrative of what had happened in the region after abolition and one that was to become part of the common sense of subsequent years: while no one was prepared to defend slavery (although one or two came quite close to it), the location of the problem was the transition from slave labour to supposedly free labour within a regime of free trade. Just as in the sugar debates the 'real' victims of Emancipation had been projected as the planters, here those who were suffering most were the owners. They wanted capitalism but with state protection and the institutionalisation of forms of labour that were not slavery but were, nonetheless, forms of coerced labour. The emphasis on immigration was not on simply 'free labour' but on labour brought in to work under coercive conditions.[78]

Throughout the 1830s and 1840s there had been various schemes to import labour into the Caribbean. Initially, attempts had included bringing in labour from Europe (including from Germany and Madeira), but there were also proposals to migrate labour to Trinidad and British Guiana from the Leewards and Barbados in the Caribbean, from Africa (especially liberated Africans who had been rescued from slave ships and sent to Sierra Leone) and even from free blacks from the United States. But, above all, it meant importing labour from India.[79]

The introduction of immigrant, indentured labour depended critically upon the willingness or otherwise of the British state to back schemes. Following abolition, the first scheme was initiated by John Gladstone and his associates from 1836 onwards. They developed a plan to import labour from India into British Guiana under five-year contracts of indenture. There was also the implementation of Indian migration to Mauritius. These schemes provoked a wave of indignation and protest both in India and among anti-slavery humanitarians and evangelicals in Britain.[80] Subsequent investigations of the Mauritius labour trade in 1839 and of conditions in British Guiana showed that there had been coercion and misrepresentation in recruitment and cases of systematic abuse on some plantations. This and the initial hostility to such schemes from within government – particularly Lord Glenelg as colonial secretary and James Stephen, the highly influential civil servant at the Colonial Office – led to the suspension of all overseas labour migration in May 1839.[81]

The end of apprenticeship and the need for new sources of labour, coupled with the creation of an effective alliance between those representing West Indian interests and the state, meant that the pressure to devise acceptable new emigration schemes was maintained. By the end of 1842, new schemes had been developed that enabled the ban on emigration to Mauritius to be lifted and then made possible the extension of Indian migration to the Caribbean. In November 1844, legalisation permitted Indian emigration to Jamaica, British Guiana and Trinidad, with the first migrants travelling from Calcutta in January 1845.

Lord John Russell had been fearful in February 1840 that schemes for migrating labour from India to British Guiana might lead to, as he famously declared, 'a new system of slavery'.[82] James Stephen had worried about both the possibilities of the revival of the slave-trade and, in a racially charged manner, the potentially deleterious consequences of renewed African immigration, which might lead to a revival of obeah and other 'dangerous' practices.[83] Nonetheless, the 1840s saw a major shift in state policy. With Lord Stanley as colonial secretary in Peel's Conservative government from 1841 and Earl Grey in the same role in Russell's Whig government from 1846, government support for immigration schemes was strengthened. At the same time, Russell's government responded to Bentinck's select committee of 1848 by offering modifications to the sugar duties, increasing the rate of colonial preference, postponing the full equalisation of duties from 1851 to 1854 and offering state support for capital investment in infrastructure and immigration schemes. While the measures did not meet the support of the planters, these shifts represented a partial victory for the advocates of indentured, immigrant labour and protection. Whereas in British Guiana and Trinidad immigrant labour came to be decisive in sustaining these countries' economies, in Jamaica, where there was relatively little immigration, the economy continued to be locked into the doldrums.

If the parliamentary representatives of the West India interest largely disappeared in the latter half of the nineteenth century, the preoccupations of their lobby with labour and the colonial economies certainly did not. The long decline of slavery and slave-owners and the creation of the 'anti-slavery nation' may have been accomplished in very important respects with defeat over abolition and the sugar duties, but this was by no means an unqualified victory. Those who see only the victory of liberal market capitalism and a culture of anti-slavery need to see, as well, that the spread of the coercive practices of indentured labour as part of the spectrum of forms of labour mobilised within Britain's global empire was a critically important dimension of the legacies of slave-ownership. To a considerable extent those owners and their political allies who had pressed for this in the 1840s very largely won (even if it did not rescue the whole of the British Caribbean). Further, and equally importantly, the arguments that the problems with labour in post-slavery societies lay at the heart of the long-term deterioration of the sugar colonies had by the 1870s become, as Kale has argued, 'routine assumptions among government administrators throughout the empire'. Such beliefs were to continue into the twentieth century. As Kale shows, the Sanderson Committee of 1910, established to investigate the possibilities of extending indentured labour schemes from India to parts of the empire hitherto not participating in the scheme, echoed the inclination to blame the 'inadequacies and ill-discipline' of the freed slaves for the general problems of the Caribbean economies.[84]

The issue of the condition and character of labour in the British West Indies was also to be drawn into a wider discourse about the nature and characteristics of labour: the relative worth of slave versus free labour and the racialised distinctions between free black West Indian labour and white labour in Britain and between Irish and English labour were among the issues that had visibility within a culture of the mid-Victorian decades in which debate about the value of work was central.[85]

In imperial politics and cultural life too, the traces of slave-owners continue to be found. One index of this is in responses to the Governor Eyre case in 1866. Like responses to the Indian rebellion of 1857 and the US Civil War, the Eyre case was a moment in which boundaries were drawn around race, nation and 'otherness' within British society and the increasing legitimacy of overtly racist discourses was shown.[86] In some cases, the link to slave-ownership was direct. Thus, of the 594 clearly identifiable individuals who were committee members or subscribers to the Eyre Defence and Aid Fund in 1866, at least sixty-five appear to have been directly connected with people appearing in the compensation records.[87] In the case of the American Civil War, the connection is less obvious. While there was certainly pro-Southern sympathy and support during the American Civil War, direct links between slave-owners and pro-Confederacy politics appear to have been marginal. For example, John Welsford Cowell, banker and awardee of almost £7,250 for 333 enslaved people in Jamaica, was a pro-South advocate.[88] Similarly, the Rev. Frederick William Tremlett – the Anglican Vicar of St Peter's, Belsize Park, London, and the second husband of Jamaican slave-owner Josephine Catherine Bonella Ware (née Scarlett), the daughter of Philip Anglin Scarlett (1763–1823) and niece of Sir James Scarlett, first Baron Abinger – was co-founder in 1863 with the Confederate Matthew Maury of 'The Society for Promoting the Cessation of Hostilities in America'. The Society ostensibly existed for the purposes of bringing pressure on British and European governments to end the war. As secretary of the organisation, Tremlett was the main force behind it. His vicarage was known as the 'Rebel's Roost'. A meeting was held in July 1864 between a small delegation, including Tremlett, and Lord Palmerston. Palmerston flatly rejected their proposals and the Society closed down, although Tremlett's sermons calling for an end to the war were quite widely distributed.[89]

These continuing reverberations are hardly surprising given the connections between people appearing in the compensation process and other politicians. It was frequently the case within the political system as a whole that sons followed fathers as MPs. Some indication of this can be seen in Appendix 5. This list is indicative rather than comprehensive and a simple listing cannot account for the complexities of shifting political and cultural attitudes. But the connections do indicate some of the ways in which those with historical links to or experience of slave-ownership were part of later generations of elite circles in Britain.[90]

NOTES

I am very grateful to Chris Robinson for all her help.

1 Eric Williams, *Capitalism and Slavery* (1944, repr. London, 1964), pp. 136, 210.

2 C. Duncan Rice, '"Humanity sold for sugar!" The British abolitionist response to free trade in slave-grown sugar', *Historical Journal* 13 (3) (1970), 402–18; Richard Huzzey, 'Free trade, free labour, and slave sugar in Victorian Britain', *Historical Journal* 53 (2) (2010), 359–79; Richard Huzzey, *Freedom Burning. Anti-slavery and Empire in Victorian Britain* (Ithaca and London, 2012), ch. 5.

3 H. M. Chichester, rev. James Lunt, 'Cotton, Stapleton, first Viscount Combermere (1773–1865)', *ODNB*.

4 The West India Committee of planters and merchants was created in 1775. It was central to mobilising and articulating its members' extra-parliamentary interests. For its history see Douglas Hall, *A Brief History of the West India Committee* (St Lawrence, Barbados, 1971) and Alexandra Franklin, *Enterprise and Advantage: The West India Interest in Britain, 1774–1840* (PhD thesis, University of Pennsylvania, 1992).

5 For Seaford's speeches in the Lords after 1833, see *House of Lords Debates*, 27 February 1835, cols. 422–3; 2 June 1836, cols. 1333–5; 29 March 1838, cols. 11–16; 18 March 1839, cols. 790–1; 2 July 1839, cols. 1148–51; 12 March 1840, cols. 1151–2.

6 For the Lascelles family see especially Simon D. Smith, *Slavery, Family and Gentry Capitalism in the British Atlantic: The World of the Lascelles, 1648–1834* (Cambridge, 2006).

7 Nicholas Draper, *The Price of Emancipation. Slave-Ownership, Compensation and British Society at the End of Slavery* (Cambridge, 2010), Appendices 1–4.

8 The following draws from B. W. Higman, 'The West India "interest" in Parliament, 1807–1833', *Australian Historical Studies* 13 (49) (1967), 1–19.

9 For further details, see Appendix 1.

10 Gerrit P. Judd IV, *Members of Parliament 1734–1832* (New Haven, 1955).

11 Only two others in Judd's West India interest list remained after 1848: William Saunders Sebright Lascelles (1798–1851), who was Whig MP for Wakefield 1837–41 and 1847–51 and the son of Henry Lascelles, second Earl of Harewood; and George Nugent-Grenville, Whig-radical MP for Aylesbury, 1847–50.

12 Draper, *Price of Emancipation*, p. 159.

13 Draper, *Price of Emancipation*, pp. 156–60.

14 Izhak Gross, 'The abolition of negro slavery and British parliamentary politics 1832–3', *Historical Journal* 23 (1) (1980), 63–85; Tom L. Franzmann, 'Antislavery and political economy in the early Victorian House of Commons:

a research note on "capitalist hegemony"', *Journal of Social History* 27 (3) (1994), 579–93.

15 Higman, 'The West India "interest" in Parliament, 1807–1833', 18.

16 Strickland's motion, which arose from a rising tide of abolitionist protest against the conditions of apprenticeship, was proposed against the government's desire to avoid immediate abolition and avoid upsetting the planters. See Izhak Gross, 'Parliament and the abolition of negro apprenticeship 1835–1838', *English Historical Review* 96 (1981), 560–76.

17 Voting lists used are: on the third Reading of the Reform Bill (England): *House of Commons Debates* (hereafter, *HC Deb*), 22 March 1832, cols. 780–5. The vote on Strickland's motion: *HC Deb*, 30 March 1838, cols. 257–61. Sugar duties: *HC Deb*, 3 June 1844, cols. 219–22; *HC Deb*, 14 June 1844, cols. 968–72; *HC Deb*, 17 June 1844, cols. 1082–6. The third reading of the Corn Law repeal: *HC Deb*, 15 May 1846, cols. 721–6.

18 For Chandos: Franklin, *Enterprise and Advantage*, p. 269; F. M. L. Thompson, 'Grenville, Richard Plantagenet Temple-Nugent-Brydges-Chandos, second duke of Buckingham and Chandos (1797–1861)', *ODNB*.

19 Robert Stewart, *The Foundation of the Conservative Party, 1830–1867* (London and New York, 1978), p. 187.

20 T71/880 Grenada claim nos. 439, 440 and 758A & B; T71/891 Tobago claim no. 15.

21 For Ellice see Gordon F. Millar, 'Ellice, Edward (1783–1863)', *ODNB*; R. H. Fleming, 'Phyn, Ellice and Company of Schenectady', *Contributions to Canadian Economics* 4 (1932), 7–41; James M. Colthart, 'Ellice, Alexander', *Dictionary of Canadian Biography*, at www.biographi.ca/en/bio/ellice_alexander_5E.html, accessed 23 July 2013; James M. Colthart, 'Ellice, Edward', *Dictionary of Canadian Biography*, at www.biographi.ca/en/bio/ellice_edward_9E.html, accessed 23 July 2013.

22 Material on the Tudways includes R. G. Thorne (ed.), *The House of Commons, 1790–1820, Vol. V* (5 vols., London, 1986), p. 417; family papers for the sixteenth to the twentieth centuries are held by the Somerset Archive and Record Service: Tudway of Wells Manuscripts. These include estate records for the family properties in Antigua. Some details are included in a website, 'Historical Sketches Dulcote Wells Somerset', at www.dulcote.com/webpages/dulcote_in_georgian_times.htm, accessed 23 July 2013.

23 His son and heir, also Philip, was to become a musician, composer and reasonably important musical patron of the early twentieth century. Surprisingly little has been produced on the Miles family. William D. Rubinstein in his unpublished wealth files documenting the rich in nineteenth-century Britain, which he has kindly made available to us, includes Philip John in his file for 1845/17.

24 Draper, *Price of Emancipation*, p. 157.

25 For overviews of Barkly see B. A. Knox, 'Barkly, Sir Henry (1815–1898)', *Australian Dictionary of Biography*, http://adb.anu.edu.au/biography/barkly-sir-henry-2936/text4251, accessed 23 April 2014 ; John Benyon, 'Barkly, Sir Henry (1815–1898)', *ODNB*.

26 For the Western Club see T. F. Donald, *Centenary History of the Western Club* (Glasgow, 1925). Stephen Mullen is undertaking a PhD at Glasgow University

on the history of the Glasgow-West India Association. Some insight into its history can be gleaned from, among others, *Glasgow Herald*, 1 June 1883.

27 Anna Gambles, *Protection and Politics: Conservative Economic Discourse 1815–1852* (Woodbridge, 1999), p. 149.

28 Gambles, *Protection and Politics*, p. 156.

29 Joseph Marryat, *A Reply to the Arguments Contained in Various Publications Recommending an Equalization of the Duties on East and West Indian Sugar* (London, 1823); Anon., *A Statement of the Claims of the West India Colonies to a Protecting Duty against East India Sugar, Dedicated to William Manning, Esq., MP* (London, 1823); James MacQueen, *The West India Colonies; the Calumnies and Misrepresentations Circulated against Them by the* Edinburgh Review, *Mr Clarkson, Mr Cropper, &c. &c., Examined and Refuted* ... (London, 1824).

30 *HC Deb*, 16 August 1831, col. 130.

31 Cited in Gambles, *Protection and Politics*, p. 180; cf. Miles Taylor on the issue of empire and 1832: Miles Taylor, 'Empire and the 1832 parliamentary Reform Act revisited', in Arthur Burns and Joanna Innes (eds.), *Rethinking the Age of Reform: Britain 1780–1850* (Cambridge, 2003), pp. 295–311 and Miles Taylor, 'Colonial representation at Westminster, *c.* 1800–65', in Julian Hoppit (ed.), *Parliaments, Nations and Identities in Britain and Ireland, 1660–1860* (Manchester, 2003), pp. 206–20.

32 For MacQueen on 1789 and especially the revolt of St Domingue see his *West India Colonies*; see also David Lambert, 'The "Glasgow King of Billingsgate": James Macqueen and an Atlantic proslavery network', *Slavery & Abolition* 29 (3) (2008), 389–413; David Lambert, *Mastering the Niger: James MacQueen's African Geography and the Struggle over Atlantic Slavery* (Chicago, 2013).

33 For overviews of apprenticeship see, among others, William A. Green, *British Slave Emancipation. The Sugar Colonies and the Great Experiment* (Oxford, 1976), ch. 5; Thomas C. Holt, *The Problem of Freedom: Race, Labor, and Politics in Jamaica and Britain, 1832–1938* (Baltimore, 1992), ch. 2; Mary Turner, 'The British Caribbean, 1823–1838: the transition from slave to free legal status', in Douglas Hay and Paul Craven (eds.), *Masters, Servants, and Magistrates in Britain and the Empire, 1562–1955* (Chapel Hill, NC and London, 2004), pp. 303–22.

34 Parliamentary Papers (hereafter PP) 1836 (560) XV: *Report from the Select Committee on Negro Apprenticeship in the Colonies*; PP1837 (510) VII: *Report from the Select Committee on Negro Apprenticeship in the Colonies*.

35 *The Times*, 29 May 1838, p. 5.

36 All quotations in this paragraph are from *The Times'* report of the debate, 29 May 1838, pp. 2, 3 and 5; for Burge's evidence see PP1836 (560) XV, pp. 247–75, 301–16, 317–26, 327, 438–42, 458–9, 511–25.

37 PP1836 (560) XV, p. viii.

38 *House of Lords Debates*, 29 March 1838.

39 For an overview, Green, *British Slave Emancipation*, esp. ch. 7.

40 For context see, among others, Michael Craton, *Empire, Enslavement and Freedom in the Caribbean* (Kingston, Jamaica, 1970), ch. 18; Michael Craton, 'The transition from slavery to free wage labour in the Caribbean, 1780–1890: a survey with particular reference to recent scholarship', *Slavery & Abolition* 13 (2) (1992), 37–67.

41 See e.g. the *Rules to be strictly observed in the management of Mr Tollemache's estates ... 4 January 1847*, which the MP John Tollemache introduced: PP1847–8 (167) XXIII Pt. I. *Third Report Select Committee Sugar and Coffee Planting*, pp. 260–2.

42 For the details of the duties see especially Philip D. Curtin, 'The British sugar duties and West Indian prosperity', *Journal of Economic History* 14 (2) (1954), 157–64; for a tabulation of the duties 1830–65, see Green, *British Slave Emancipation*, p. 416; complete details of the duties are to be found in PP1898 [C.8706] LXXXV: *Customs Tariffs of the United Kingdom, from 1800 to 1897*, pp. 209–28.

43 For the abolitionists see especially Rice, '"Humanity sold for sugar!"' and Huzzey, 'Free trade, free labour'.

44 *HC Deb*, 10 June 1844, col. 432.

45 For Goulburn as a slave owner see Brian Jenkins, *Henry Goulburn, 1784–1856: A Political Biography* (Liverpool, 1996), esp. ch. 4: 'Slavery and empire'.

46 Jenkins, *Henry Goulburn*, p. 356.

47 *Ibid.*, pp. 276–7.

48 *HC Deb*, 14 June 1844, col. 918.

49 *HC Deb*, 3 June 1844, col. 154.

50 Benjamin Disraeli, *Lord George Bentinck: A Political Biography* (4th edn., London, 1852), p. 530.

51 *HC Deb*, 3 June 1844, cols. 166–7.

52 *HC Deb*, 3 June 1844, col. 206.

53 *HC Deb*, 10 June 1844, col. 450.

54 *HC Deb*, 14 June 1844, col. 911.

55 D. R. Fisher (ed.), *The House of Commons 1820–1832, Vol. V* (7 vols., Cambridge, 2009), pp. 839–44; *The Times*, 12 July 1841, p. 5.

56 *HC Deb*, 10 June 1844, col. 423.

57 *HC Deb*, 10 June 1844, col. 456.

58 *HC Deb*, 10 June 1844, col. 451.

59 For the deputation and address, see *Morning Chronicle*, 31 January 1848, p. 1.

60 *Ibid.*

61 Sir Robert Peel, *Tamworth Election: Speech of Sir Robert Peel, June 28, 1841* (London, 1841), p. 6.

62 The Hon. George Charles Grantley Fitzhardinge Berkeley, *Two Letters Addressed to the Landed and Manufacturing Interests of Great Britain and Ireland, on the Just Maintenance of Free Trade* (London, 1850), p. 5. Berkeley, beneficiary with other family members of compensation for holdings in British Guiana, was also a member of the Select Committee on West India Colonies, 1842. Its Report is in PP1842 (479) XIII. For an account of his political life see his *My Life and Recollections* (4 vols., London, 1865–6).

63 Peel, *Tamworth Election*, p. 7.

64 *HC Deb*, 3 June 1844, cols. 212–13.

65 *Report of the Acting Committee to the Standing Committee of West India Planters and Merchants ... January 1848* (London, 1848).

66 *Report of the Acting Committee*, p. 10.

67 PP1847–8 *Select Committee on Sugar and Coffee Planting*, Third Report, p. 121.

68 *Report of the Acting Committee*, p. 16.

69 *Report of the Acting Committee*, p. 11.

70 *Report of the Acting Committee*, p. 10.

71 *Report of the Acting Committee*, p. 18.

72 *Ibid.*

73 See, among others, Miles Taylor, *The Decline of British Radicalism 1847–1860* (Oxford, 1995), pp. 179–83.

74 *Report of the Acting Committee*, p. 18.

75 *Report of the Acting Committee*, p. 41.

76 Bentinck, nephew of Lord William Henry Cavendish Bentinck, a slave-owner, had emerged as the leader of the Tory protectionists in the wake of the repeal of the Corn Laws in 1846; for a brief survey see Angus Macintyre, 'Bentinck, Lord (William) George Frederic Cavendish-Scott- (1802–1848)', *ODNB*; and see Disraeli 's fawning biography, *Lord George Bentinck*.

77 There were eight reports of the *Select Committee on Sugar and Coffee Planting*. Reports and paper numbers are: first (123); second (137); third (167); fourth (184); fifth (206); sixth (230); seventh (245); eighth (361) (361-II).

78 See Madhavi Kale, *Fragments of Empire. Capital, Slavery, and Indentured Labor Migration in the British Caribbean* (Philadelphia, 1998); Clare Anderson, 'Convicts and coolies: rethinking indentured labour in the nineteenth century', *Slavery & Abolition* 30 (1) (2009), 93–109. Contrast the neo-classical views of one economic historian, Pieter Emmer, that the failings of the post-Emancipation economies were not least 'that slavery failed to educate the slaves for the market economy after slavery' and that Indians who 'chose' to migrate to the Caribbean were really earnest 'self-improvers': Pieter C. Emmer, 'The big disappointment. The economic consequences of the abolition of slavery in the Caribbean, 1833–1888', *History in Focus: The Guide to Historical Resources* [Institute of Historical Research], 12 (2007), at www.history.ac.uk/ihr/Focus/Slavery/articles/emmer.html, accessed 8 August 2013; see also Pieter C. Emmer, 'Scholarship or solidarity? The post-Emancipation era in the Caribbean reconsidered', *New West Indian Guide/Nieuwe West-Indische Gids* 69 (3/4) (1995), 277–90. His views have been effectively rebuffed by Michael Craton in his response in the same issue, 291–7.

79 Hugh Tinker, *A New System of Slavery: The Export of Indian Labour Overseas, 1830–1920* (Oxford, 1974); Green, *British Slave Emancipation*, ch. 9; David Northrup, *Indentured Labor in the Age of Imperialism, 1834–1922* (Cambridge, 1995); Kale, *Fragments of Empire*.

80 See Kale, *Fragments of Empire*, ch. 1 and especially pp. 13–26 for Gladstone's scheme.

81 For condemnation, see John Scoble, *Hill Coolies: A Brief Exposure of the Deplorable Condition of the Hill Coolies in British Guiana and Mauritius* (London, 1840). For the parliamentary report, published in 1840, PP1841 (45) XVI; see also PP1840 (151) XXXIV: *British Guiana. Copies of Correspondence between the Secretary of State for the Colonies and the Governor of British Guiana,*

Respecting the Immigration of Labourers into That Colony. I. M. Cumpston, *Indians Overseas in British Territories* (London, 1953), pp. 19–27.

82 Cited in Tinker, *New System of Slavery*, p. vi.

83 Green, *British Slave Emancipation*, p. 267.

84 Kale, *Fragments of Empire*, pp. 82–5.

85 Work bearing upon these issues includes Catherine Hall, Keith McClelland and Jane Rendall, *Defining the Victorian Nation: Class, Race, Gender and the British Reform Act of 1867* (Cambridge, 2000); Huzzey, *Freedom Burning*.

86 See especially Catherine Hall, *Civilising Subjects: Metropole and Colony in the English Imagination, 1830–1867* (Cambridge, 2002).

87 The numbers were possibly higher although without more substantial genealogical information about many of the signatories certainty is not possible. For the committee members and subscribers, see the lists in *The Eyre Defence and Aid Fund* (London, 1866), pp. 4, 25–31. Draper, *Price of Emancipation*, p. 337 identifies ten of the signatories.

88 His claims were for Jamaica St Ann no. 467 (Llandovery Estate) and St Ann no. 468 (Flat Point Estate); he wrote pro-South pamphlets including *Southern Secession: A Letter Addressed to Captain T. Maury Confederate States Navy, on his Letter to Admiral Fitzroy* (London, 1862); *Lancashire's Wrongs and the Remedy* (London, 1863); and *La France et les États Confédérés* (Paris and London, 1865). Cf. Charles Priestley, '"France's opportunity": an Englishman's plea for French intervention', at www.acwrt.org.uk/uk-heritage_Frances-Opportunity-an-Englishmans-Plea-for-French-Intervention.asp, accessed 8 August 2013.

89 R. J. M. Blackett, *Divided Hearts. Britain and the American Civil War* (Baton Rouge, 2001), pp. 74, 104, 154, 164–5.

90 See Appendix 2.

5 Reconfiguring race: the stories the slave-owners told

Catherine Hall

In this chapter I explore the varied writing strategies of the slave-owners and their descendants as they grappled with a world of otherness in which chattel slavery was no longer acceptable. Some of these writers are well known though their connections with slave-ownership are rarely discussed; others have been identified through our prosopographical work. Between them they had a lot to say and a powerful impulse to tell, to give witness to various forms of testimony, to weigh in with their versions of the past and their expectations of the present and future, and to counter the narratives of humanitarians and abolitionists. They believed in the power of writing and they believed they could make a difference to how the past was understood and in so doing would shape the present. In the eyes of almost all of them, racial hierarchy was essential to social order: slavery might be over but difference must be maintained. This was their most important message.

In the late 1820s pro-slavery writers were busy promoting their beliefs, desperately hoping as anti-slavery activities mushroomed that they would be able to at least delay abolition. In 1829 an anonymous author started to publish a series of picaresque naval adventures set in the West Indies in *Blackwood's Magazine*, that favoured journal of conservatives. The tales, which were not completed until 1833, were an immediate hit and were soon published in book form as *Tom Cringle's Log*. The *Quarterly Review* was lavish in its praise of the series while Coleridge regarded the book as 'excellent' and as close to Smollett as anything he could remember. *Tom Cringle* became a point of reference for many subsequent authors from Trollope to Froude, while a great cotton tree on the Spanish Town Road in Jamaica is still named after him. Michael Scott, the youngest son of a Glasgow merchant and the author of *Tom Cringle*, had lived for more than twenty years in Jamaica, following in the footsteps of many young Glaswegians, learning the management of estates and working in business in Kingston. He had returned permanently to Scotland in 1822 and was made a partner in his father-in-law's firm, a firm that had slave-owning interests and received compensation.[1] *Tom Cringle*, packed full of adventures from the press gang to pirates and privateers, from war and rape to men overboard eaten by sharks, represented Jamaica as a benevolent patriarchy and slavery as a civilising institution. 'I had pictured to myself the slaves', recorded Tom,

a miserable, squalid, half-fed, ill-clothed, over-worked race – and their masters, and the white inhabitants generally, as an unwholesome-looking crew of saffron-faced tyrants, who wore straw hats with umbrella brims, wide trousers, and calico jackets, living on pepper-pots and land crabs, and drinking sangaree and smoking cigars the whole day – in a word that all that Bryan Edwards and others had written regarding the civilisation of the West Indies was a fable. But I was agreeably undeceived.[2]

Not only were the West Indian islands a source of great wealth to Britain but also, notwithstanding anti-slavery propaganda, Jamaican planters were kindly and hospitable, and 'blackie' was happy and contented, well dressed and well fed, enjoying good dinners and time off from work to eat them, with Christmas holiday festivities crowning the year. But the 'demon of change' was abroad and part of Scott's work was to counter Messrs Wilberforce and Macaulay and warn against the serious political blunders that threatened. It was a profound injustice to ask the West Indians to free their slaves; Emancipation must be a work of time. As Aaron Bang, the jovial Jamaican planter, put it, 'I don't defend slavery – I sincerely wish we could do without it … I am a planter, but I did not plant slavery. I found it growing and flourishing, and fostered by the Government.' Now the government was fanatically 'intermeddling' with the colonies but 'black savages' were not ready for freedom.[3]

This chapter concerns the ways in which slave-owners and their descendants who received compensation wrote about race and slavery in the aftermath of Emancipation. But what differences were there between their representations before and after 1833? Prior to abolition, pro-slavery writers did not hesitate to represent Africans as semi-barbarians who should be grateful for the gift of civilisation that their enslavement offered them. Captain Frederick Marryat was another naval writer, just making his name, who defended the institution right up to the moment of Emancipation. His father was Joseph Marryat, a merchant and ship owner with interests across the Caribbean and North America. Marryat senior, a prominent member of the Society of West Indian Planters and Merchants, served as the agent representing the interests of planters in Trinidad, then Grenada. In 1807 he petitioned Parliament against the abolition of the slave-trade. He was in the House of Commons for two periods and spoke in defence of the trade and of slavery. He published pamphlets, the most widely circulated of which was his *Thoughts on the Abolition of the Slave Trade and Civilization of Africa* (1816). This

Figure 5.1 William Blake after John Gabriel Stedman, *A Suriname Planter in His Morning Dress*, engraving, 1793.

was part of a long-running controversy with the leading abolitionists James Stephen and Zachary Macaulay. In that pamphlet he insisted that Africans would only work under the whip, that talk of legislation was stirring up trouble in the West Indies and threatened repeats of the French and Haitian revolutions, that planters were simply the instruments of government-sanctioned slavery, that the planters' property was inviolate and that threats to the planters' freedom might well result in another American Revolution.[4]

Frederick, the second son of Joseph Marryat, went to sea as a midshipman in 1808 when he was sixteen. He was in the navy during the Napoleonic Wars, fighting in the East and West Indies and Burma, glorying in adventure and danger. After leaving the navy he started writing in the late 1820s, recognising the enthusiasm of the new reading public for heroic tales of the navy that would sustain the spirit of Nelson and Trafalgar. He drew on his experience to write rollicking adventures that enchanted his audience. Marryat sometimes illustrated his own books. His friend George Cruickshank, the celebrated cartoonist, did some illustrations for him and made prints of Marryat's drawings. 'Puzzled which to choose!! Or the King of Tombuctoo offering one of his daughters in marriage to Capt. ——' is one of their early collaborations and first circulated in 1818. The women being offered in marriage to the naval officer (Marryat himself according to his daughter Florence) are represented as horribly obese and squat, with huge bottoms similar to that of Sara Baartmann, the Southern African woman named 'the Hottentot Venus' who was being exhibited in London at this time to the dismay and outrage of the abolitionists.[5] The chief is smiling blandly, wearing a huge nose ring, a plume of ostrich feathers and a sword for which his left ear serves as a hilt. Immediately behind him is a bodyguard of four warriors holding four spears on each of which a skull is transfixed. These are savage figures but to be laughed at – scarcely human. Such racialised images were repeated in Marryat's early naval novels, which told of the 'cheerfulness of the slaves whom our morbid philanthropists wish to render happy by making discontented', the 'gabble of a West Indian market', the poisonously jealous nature of mulatto women and the frightful and violent superstitions of Hindus.[6]

In 1832, the year before abolition, Marryat published *Newton Forster*, which was an explicit defence of slavery and an intervention in the national debate over Emancipation and compensation. He stood unsuccessfully for the House of Commons that same year, at the height of debates over reform, aiming to represent 'ships, commerce and colonies'. Asked for his position on abolition, he averred that 'He detested slavery as heartily as any man could', for few pro-slavers would admit to being positively in favour of the institution by the 1830s though it was commonplace to argue that slavery was a necessary step on the road to civilisation. He continued, however, using well-tested pro-slavery arguments,

He could never consent to give his whole attention to the negro across the Atlantic, while he knew that his own countryman was dragged into slavery, and the wife and children of his bosom were left to pine in wretchedness and want. He would redress that grievance and protect the British seaman before he thrust his philanthropy on the African negro.[7]

The novel included the visit of the young Newton, represented as having imbibed foolish philanthropic ideas of the wrongs associated with

Figure 5.2 George Cruikshank after Captain Frederick Marryat, *Puzzled which to choose!! Or the King of Tombuctoo offering one of his daughters in marriage to Capt. ——*, hand-coloured etching, 1818.

slavery, to a Barbadian plantation. There he discovered the error of his ways: the 'old gentleman' who owned the plantation was kind to 'his people', patting their 'woolly heads', feeding them well, caring for his 'breeding women', allowing them to buy their freedom if and when they wished, but finding that none of them did since he provided care through sickness and old age. 'I assert', he told Newton,

that my property in slaves is … as legally mine as my property in land or money; and that any attempt to deprive me of either is equally a robbery, whether it be made by the nation or by an individual … Let the country take our estates and negroes at a fair valuation, and we shall be most happy to surrender them.[8]

Marryat continued to campaign for the West India interest and early the following year, when abolition was being debated in Parliament, he reviewed Mrs Carmichael's *Domestic Manners and Social Condition of the White, Coloured and Negro Population of the West Indies* (1833) in the *Metropolitan Magazine*, which he edited. Mrs Carmichael had written a pro-slavery account of the time that she had spent in St Vincent and Trinidad. Marryat's long panegyric opened with 'SLAVERY!',

where is the truly British bosom that does not, at that fearful word, inflate with indignant feelings, and heave, as it were, to fling from it afar even the idea of a state so degrading? This commiseration for the enslaved, this scorn for the enslaver, is a pure, a holy sentiment, holy almost as religion herself.

Yet this 'holy sentiment' should not mislead. It was fated, he pronounced,

like religion, too often to be put to many vile purposes – to be made the self-sounding trumpet of fanaticism – the cloak for hypocrisy – the plea for robbery – and a herald to a state of anarchy, the flames of whose torch will be quenched but in blood, and peace be purchased only by universal desolation. The besetting sin of England is her proneness to legislate overmuch and overquickly.

The legislators should pause before it was too late, recognise the legitimacy of eye-witness accounts, abandon wild schemes that would make the West Indian islands into little Africas. The negro was 'not a slave to the oppression of the white, but to his own ignorance, to his own ferocity, and to his own inaptitude to value the blessing of civilization'. Only time could do the work of preparing him for freedom.[9]

Archibald Alison, the Scottish lawyer, historian and committed Tory, began to write regularly in the Tory magazine *Blackwood's* in 1830. His interventions warned of the dangers of reform and defended slavery. An essay on 'The West India question' in February 1832, prior to abolition, foresaw that the colonists would abandon the mother country and turn to the US if the government did not abandon its 'incessant efforts ... to interfere with the management of the slaves'. Slavery, he averred, was not an evil in an uncivilised society; rather it was a necessary step on the road to progress and a form of protection for the weak and the vulnerable. Africans were

incapable of understanding what freedom is, the duties with which it is attended, the restraint which it imposes, and the labour which it induces. They have none of the artificial wants which reconcile men to the severe and uninterrupted toil which constitutes the basis of civilized prosperity, nor of the power of voluntary restraint upon inclination and coercion of passion ... To them, freedom conveys the idea of the immediate cessation of all restraint, the termination of every species of labour, the undisguised indulgence of every passion.

African negroes could not 'conduct themselves as freemen'.[10] The evidence for this was clear in San Domingue, which had collapsed into savagery; Britons should learn the lessons of history.

In 1833, however, Parliament did abolish slavery in the West Indies, Mauritius and the Cape. How were the slave-owners and their descendants to respond? Having fought hard for the maximum amount of compensation and the maximum term of apprenticeship they could secure, they bowed to the inevitable. Once Britain had defined itself as an anti-slavery nation, they speedily aligned themselves with that position, rewrote and disavowed their own histories and were actively involved in the remaking of racial hierarchies. Enthusiasm for the ending of 'the stain' upon the nation could provide a way of screening disturbing associations, partially forgetting and rewriting a long history of British involvement in the slavery business and at the same time reconfiguring race now that enslavement could no longer be the defining mark of the African. The historians, essayists, travel writers, novelists and poets among them worked on their own memories and imaginatively reconstructed their own relation to their West Indian connections, significantly contributing to contemporary debates on race. Their personal memories and family histories were interwoven with more public forms of remembering and forgetting. Silencing, as the Haitian historian Michel-Rolphe Trouillot argues, is a practice. Questions of silence always raise questions of memory.[11] Who and what has been forgotten? Which peoples and events downplayed? There is 'no memory without forgetfulness, no forgetfulness without memory' and memory is a site of conflict, 'in which many contrary forces converge and in which the interactions between memory and forgetting are contingent as much as they are systematic'.[12] Having established moral frameworks through which they could legitimate their slave-holding, very few of the West Indian proprietors or their descendants seem to have suffered guilt as perpetrators, or trauma associated with their actions. They exhibited a remarkable capacity for denial and disavowal: they knew but chose not to know the truths of the plantation. They had the facts but chose not to interpret them.[13] After abolition they subscribed to the orthodoxy that slavery was an anathema, an institution that it now seemed ought not to have happened, or alternatively that slavery had been a benign institution, totally misrepresented by its enemies, an essential tool in the difficult work of civilising Africans. The cruelties and atrocities associated with slavery – the everyday practices of violence, of punishment and of humiliation – were sectioned off as if having nothing to do with them. At the same time they constructed themselves as the unfortunate victims of Emancipation and denigrated the African. The horrors of slavery were erased, all excoriation reserved for foreigners who continued to trade in slaves. Working with a variety of genres that allowed different foci, these authors explored their entanglements in slavery and the Caribbean with a variety of voices. The authoritative historian, the imaginative novelist, the romantic travel writer, the troubled poet each in their different ways and working within the framework of their own genres wrote the past and the present. Michael Scott went on to write *The Cruise of the Midge* (1835), a picaresque adventure spliced with cruel humour, representing the slave-trade as totally un-British, while Africa was a place of savagery, cannibalism and fetishism.[14] Marryat had a long and successful literary career, playing his part in the reconfiguration of racial hierarchies in the process. Alison's histories became the bible of the Tories.

The historians

History-writing was one of the genres chosen by some of the men. The dramatic transformations of the late eighteenth and early nineteenth centuries had inspired a new historical consciousness, an awareness of the contrast between past and present. Sir Walter Scott's influence was pervasive with his depiction of the past as another country. There was a huge appetite for history, a hunger to grasp the new world in which readers now found themselves. Historians could select their material, tell stories, offer causal explanations, provide what appeared to be authoritative narratives based on fact. William Mackinnon, chief of the Clan Mackinnon and a Tory MP for much of the period from the 1820s to 1865, wrote extensively on public opinion and its central place in civilisation. His lengthy volume in 1828 argued that liberty was intimately connected to the rise of the middle class and a public opinion that acted as a bulwark against revolution. He benefited from the wealth his father had accumulated in the West Indies and received nearly £4,000 in compensation for

276 enslaved men and women in Antigua.[15] His more extensive account of the progress of civilisation, published in 1846, traced the growth of liberty in England from ancient times to the Hanoverians. Slavery figured as degradation, in ancient Egypt, in Greece and Rome and in feudal England. Savage nations, he argued, have the most cruel and abject slavery. He travelled the world finding slavery and degradation everywhere yet despite his West Indian wealth New World slavery was banished from his text, the only reference to the British slave-trade provided by a quotation from Pitt's speech arguing for abolition.[16] This was a quite deliberate forgetting.

Something similar can be found in the memoirs of Lord Holland, leader of the Whigs during the long years they were excluded from power. His marriage to Elizabeth Vassall had brought him the estates of Sweet River and Friendship in Jamaica, said to be worth £7,000 a year. He took on the Vassall name in order to secure the West Indian properties for himself and her children.[17] The protégé of his uncle Charles James Fox, he followed Fox in his opposition to the slave-trade despite being a West Indian proprietor. When it came to slavery, however, his efforts were focused on mediating between the West Indians, the colonial legislatures and the Whig government of which he was a part. His anxiety was always to uphold 'the various orders of society without which property cannot subsist' and to secure the maximum amount of compensation for the slave-owners.[18] Three claims were made in the names of Lord and Lady Holland, one of which was contested. The compensation money was divided and the Hollands got over £2,200.[19] In the wake of Emancipation, Holland tried to ensure that the plantations were conducted on paternalistic lines and to influence the Jamaica Assembly.

How then did he construct the slave-trade and slavery in his *Memoirs of the Whig Party*, which dealt with the period up to 1821? This was not a work aimed at the new reading public – rather it was for those cognoscenti who were fascinated by Whig policy. There was a remarkable silence on slavery. Issues of foreign politics, which had long been a major preoccupation for Holland, were dealt with at great length, while the colonies were ignored. Yet we know from his diary and correspondence that West Indian matters at times occupied much space in his mind. In his history, however, the abolition of the slave-trade merited half a paragraph. There was no need to record anything about it, he noted, since it had been extensively dealt with; it could be taken for granted. He merely remarked that it 'put an end to one of the greatest evils to which the human race has ever been exposed, or at least to our share in the guilt of it'.[20] And, when it came to considering the failure of efforts to get abolition of the continental slave-trade into the peace treaty of 1814, an issue to which Wilberforce and his allies devoted much time and energy, he simply blamed the Tories.[21] In this well-chronicled history, the memories of plantation slavery and the struggles over it had been entirely marginalised. Holland chose not to bring slavery, a disturbing thought, into the present. Amnesia was a less troubling condition.

If Mackinnon and Lord Holland worked hard at refusing connections and strategically forgetting, Archibald Alison followed a different trajectory. He did not himself benefit from compensation but acted as a trustee for his deceased brother-in-law's claim on his property in 152 enslaved people in Antigua.[22] As a young man he had decided that he would write a history of Europe and this was published in ten volumes between 1833 and 1842 while his essays in *Blackwood's* on matters of the day were conceived as his intervention 'in the great Parliament of the nations'.[23] The *History* was relatively successful, welcomed by Marryat in his *Metropolitan Magazine*, a godsend for every Tory faced with the dominance of Whig history. It was republished in special editions first for the middle classes and then, with a print run of 10,000, for the working classes. It was confidently asserted that Alison had made £20,000 from it, a figure that enabled him to claim comparison with the popularity of Macaulay.[24] Though the volumes were dominated by accounts of the wars, Alison was keen that his work should be read 'in the cottage or by the fireside'.[25] It was satirised by Disraeli, whose Mr Rigby (widely believed to be based on the Tory John Wilson Croker) urged Coningsby to 'make himself master of Mr Wordy's History of the late War, in twenty volumes, a capital work, which proves that Providence was on the side of the Tories'.[26]

Reacting against his clerical father's over-optimistic view of human nature, Alison traced the misery of the world to 'the wickedness and selfishness of man'.[27] To his mind it was the French Revolution that had unleashed horror on Europe and his writerly efforts were to demonstrate this fully to his reading public. The example of France should ensure that nothing similar could happen in England. Alison hammered home his message as to the dangers of political innovation and the 'terrible evils of democratic oppression'.[28] All great changes needed time. His account of the 'dreadful insurrection' in San Domingue dwelt on 'the dissimulation and cruelty of the savage character', the vile crimes that the 'unchained' Africans had committed and the collapse into 'savage life' that had followed the uprising.[29] Look what happens when Africans are free, his text demanded; reflect on their essential nature, their violence that needs to be controlled. His eight-volume continuation of his original work covered the period from 1815 to 1852 and was published between 1852 and 1859. By this time there was a widespread feeling that Emancipation had not worked, that the West Indies were seriously in decline and that freed

Africans were not prepared for continuous labour. Alison's views on race and slavery, uncomfortable for many in the heyday of abolitionism and reform, were now part of a more acceptable discourse, signalled by Carlyle's *Occasional Discourse on the Negro Question* (1853), an essay that explicitly regretted 'the great experiment' of Emancipation and raged at black men refusing to labour.[30] It had marked a public break with humanitarian discourses of 'the negro' and legitimated more open and explicit forms of racism. The slave-trade, Alison maintained, had been a vital branch of British commerce, authorised and regulated by crown and Parliament, 'a step unavoidable in the progress of improvement', affording 'the best prospect of effecting the ultimate civilisation of the negro race'. It had extracted the negro from the 'impenetrable veil' of Africa and exposed him to civilisation. The ex-slaves' condition in the West Indies was 'eminently prosperous', infinitely better than it had been in their native land, and far better than that of the European peasantry. Slavery was a necessity and if it had been left to do its slow work the murder, conflagration and crime seen in Jamaica in 1831 would have been avoided. But the nation had 'run wild'; 'reason and experience' were disregarded in the rush to abolition, the effects of which had been fatal both to the 'sable race' and to the proprietors. 'Savage habits and pleasures' had 'resumed their ascendancy' and total freedom had 'completed the ruin of the West Indies'.[31] Alison was an undisguised apologist for slavery, a position that was once more possible in public discourse by the 1850s. Not surprisingly, he was an avowed supporter of the South in the American Civil War, insisting that 'in certain climates and with certain races of mankind', slavery was 'part of the system of nature'. It was a hopeless illusion 'that all men are equal' maintained this 'most unbending Conservative in Great Britain'.[32]

Family histories

While Alison took the history of Europe as his grand subject, George Webbe Dasent was more preoccupied with the history of his own family. Born in 1773 in St Vincent, the third son of the then attorney general of the island, he came from a long line of prominent West Indian slave-owners. Educated in England, he became part of a London literary circle including John Sterling and Carlyle. Returning to England after a period in Stockholm in the early 1840s, when he had met the brothers Grimm and become fascinated by Icelandic sagas (which he famously went on to translate), he joined his friend and soon to be brother-in-law John Delane, the editor of *The Times*, as an assistant editor, a position that he occupied until 1870. While there the many editorials on the West

Indies – with their judgements on 'untutored Africans' 'liberated from restraint', sentimental philanthropists more concerned with the plight of those far distant than with poverty at home, and irresponsible absentees – undoubtedly drew on his expertise.[33]

Dasent's semi-autobiographical *Annals of an Eventful Life* (1870), a very successful work that went through several editions, fictionalised the plight of West Indian proprietors, the victims of Emancipation, who longed for the good old days. Once again, the date of publication was significant: *Annals* appeared thirty-seven years after abolition, when the bitterness of the economic losses had somewhat faded and could be represented as comedy while the 'Indian Mutiny', the American Civil War and the black uprising at Morant Bay in Jamaica had all hardened Britons' opinions on race. Narrated in humorous mode, it was replete with garbled African speech from 'Sambo' and his like that was designed to entertain and denigrate. The story was presented as that of a planter who is the author's father, a man who had the foolish dream of making his estate profitable after Emancipation. Yet he was caught between the grasping hands of merchants and bankers (Messrs Claw, Tooth and Nail of Vulture Yard, who sold him machinery that did not work and trapped him in loans and mortgages from which he could not escape) and the lazy Africans, 'busy doing nothing'. In the olden days, when the price of sugar was high, the family estate, Two Rivers, had been an 'earthly paradise' and 'the slaves were good people. Grown children, black Irishmen, call them anything you please … they were well fed, well clothed, and not over-worked'.[34] There was no defence for the slave-trade but it should never be confused with slavery. 'His' people were happy and contented, singing as they worked. But then amelioration had been imposed, which did 'everything to deteriorate the position of the planter'; profits were down, Messrs Claw, Tooth and Nail tightened their grip and 'real ruin came with Emancipation'. 'Slavery', he opined, 'was, no doubt, a great evil – greater to the proprietors than to any one else; but the way in which it was done away with was the first step to that great march of sentimental humbug which has been going on in England ever since'.[35] What was more, Claw, Tooth and Nail got all the compensation money. The 'Great Dismal Swamp' became worse and worse:

The slaves had passed from apprenticeship to complete freedom, for which they were about as fit as children to keep house. In any temperate clime they would have been forced to work for existence, but in the West Indies a man can sit down for a month and supply himself with food by mere tickling the soil with a hoe for a half-a-day. Then too, wife-working is a great institution, especially for a negro, and very often the men did no work at all, but made their wives put in their provisions.[36]

This was a picture of a retreat to barbarism: men living without labour, women forced to carry the burden of work.

George Webbe Dasent's son, John Roche Dasent, devoted himself in his later years to writing his family's history. The Dasents had been in the West Indies since the 1690s and some of the men had occupied senior legal positions in Nevis and St Vincent. He followed his father in judging Emancipation to have ruined the planters, blaming 'the premature and ill-considered Act of Emancipation, by which was to be swept away at one stroke at least one-half of the capital of the West Indian proprietors, whilst the very inadequate compensation voted by parliament went practically into the pockets of the merchants'.[37] Messrs Boddington and Davis were the winners, receiving between them the compensation on the Dasent properties.[38] This period was 'probably the darkest in the history of the family'; they were compelled to leave St Vincent and move into a small house in London.[39] A distant cousin looked after the estates but 'the great difficulty of course, after 1838 was the want of labour, as the negroes, though remaining on their provision grounds on the estates, practically refused to do any work for wages, preferring to lie under their bread-fruit trees'. In an attempt to solve this, 'a shipload of indentured Portuguese from Madeira' was brought in but this was only temporarily successful and foreclosure followed in 1843, 'and complete extinction of the interests of the nominal proprietors'.[40] The planters were the victims – of grasping merchants, of thoughtless legislators and of lazy negroes. Those slave-owners and their descendants who wrote family histories could claim eye-witness status for the veracity of their accounts: their selective rememberings and rewritings were hard to challenge. There was no space in the metropolis for the voices of the free men and women of the Dasent estates.

The novelists

If histories were beloved by the Victorians so too was the novel. The pleasures of reading and living in imagined worlds were extending to wider audiences as literacy increased, cheaper editions were published, serials appeared in magazines and circulating libraries expanded. This was the heyday of the nineteenth-century novel, when the three-decker dominated the market and was enjoyed by all who read, and when the distinction between 'light' and 'serious' had not been fixed.[41] While histories sought to present authoritative truths, novels gave play to fantasy and imagination. They allowed for multiple voices, even black voices, through characterisation; could tell stories grounded in romance and adventure; not simply describe but imaginatively recreate; and provide plots and magical resolutions. Fiction was, as Cora Kaplan has argued, 'a discursive mode where both the utopian and dystopian sides of imperial relations' could be elaborated. The slave-owners took full advantage of these freedoms to tell their stories.[42] 'As the world, or a great part of it, now choose to be instructed rather by novels, than either by sermons or moral essays', wrote Marryat, 'books of fiction have become of a paramount importance.'[43] A number of slave-owners and their descendants were fiction writers, among whom Marryat himself was undoubtedly the most successful, writing between the 1820s and his death in 1848. He was the first to serialise his novels and he was widely read, published and republished in popular editions, a bestseller on W. H. Smith's first station bookstalls. He strongly defended his reputation as a popular writer for in the new times 'the mass ... required instruction'.[44]

Marryat put his naval experience to work in his first fiction, creating tales of ordinary lads learning to be men through war and adventure. He revived the naval tradition, building on earlier tales of piracy and desert islands, on Defoe and Smollett, and on Southey and Coleridge's heroic naval biographies.[45] He wrote in praise of empire: in his two most popular novels, written in the early 1830s, *Mr Midshipman Easy* and *Peter Simple*, he celebrated the glories of British history and the navy as the protector and pride of England. His boy heroes were simple swashbuckling lads who saw life as a series of adventures and who were part of a triumphalist narrative celebrating authoritarian and anti-egalitarian values laced with patriotism and martial valour.[46] War was a lark: 'the life of a man consists in getting into scrapes and getting out of them.'[47] All would turn out right in the end – marriage, family and property would be secured. This was a genre of writing very different from the silver-fork novels of fashion of the 1820s and 1830s and the social reform novels of the late 1830s to 1850s, troubled by the 'condition of England'. Marryat's 'national story' told how Britain's imperial power was based on white men's valiant deeds and actions across the globe. One Englishman was worth three Frenchmen and 'natives' were another thing entirely. For Joseph Conrad, Marryat's naval adventures 'created a priceless legend'. 'There is an air of fable about his work', he wrote, 'Its loss would be irreparable, like the curtailment of a national story, or the loss of an historical document ... His adventures are enthralling ... He was the enslaver of youth.'[48] These 'enthralling adventures', however, systematically racialised others, particularly Africans.

Marryat senior had died shortly before abolition but his eldest son – Joseph (aforementioned), who was born in Grenada – carried on the family traditions, entering the business and later putting his money into the Welsh iron industry and banking. He, together with his brother

Charles, who was also in the family business, received compensation money of over £44,000 for 700 enslaved men and women in Trinidad, Grenada, Jamaica and St Lucia.[49] Captain Frederick Marryat clearly drew income from the West Indian estates and was to claim in later years that his money troubles were due to Emancipation and the ruin of the plantations.[50] Once the battle over Emancipation was lost and compensation won, Frederick Marryat quickly shifted ground: abolition was now a triumph and all Britons were united in their pride in the 'anti-slavery nation'.[51] This in no way affected his denigration of Africans or of philanthropists. *Peter Simple* caricatured both abolitionists, 'distributing prints of a black man kneeling in chains and saying "Am not I your brother" to sailors who ridiculed him and knocked him down for insinuating such a thing', and black preachers, one of whom reminded Peter of 'a monkey imitating a man'.[52] French and Spanish slavers were represented as cruel and tyrannical for they continued to practice the trade. The British of course could no longer be accused of such cruelties. Marryat ridiculed free blacks too, distorting their speech, patronising their claims to freedom. A 'dignity ball' in Barbados – an occasion when the 'most consequential of the coloured people' gave a ball, provided him with an opportunity to define the hierarchies of race – 'mulattos, quadroons, sambos and niggers' – and to caricature the absurd notions of gentility associated with those of paler skin and their aping of European manners.[53] Africans, it was clear, would never be anything other than other.

Marryat's *Mr Midshipman Easy* told the story of Jack, the tall, manly, honest and bold hero, reared by his foolish and deluded gentleman father to believe the rhetoric of liberty and equality. Jack went to sea seeking to put these ideas into action but gradually learnt that authority and order were essential and that racial hierarchies were to be rigidly maintained. On board he befriended an African, 'Mesty', short for Mephistopheles, once an African prince, seized and sold to owners in New York, who 'having been told that there was no slavery in England' escaped to an English merchant vessel and then entered the navy. He thus owed his deliverance to the British. Serving as cook on a British man-of-war, he talked of equality and was entranced by Jack's rhetoric. But Mesty remained a 'savage' at heart, true to his Ashantee warrior origins, proud of the skulls he had won and ready to kill when need be. At the same time he was childlike in his characteristics, followed Jack through thick and thin, and abandoned any notion of the value of equality once he had risen from the lowest ranks and was able to issue orders to others. He is represented as a figure to mock with his broken speech and his mimicry of a man of fashion, frizzing his 'woolly hair' and sporting his white neck cloth, gloves and cane. Equality, he came to believe, is 'all stuff'. 'Damn equality'.[54]

Jack, meanwhile, has been convinced through hard-won experience that inequality cements society. It was inequality that 'enabled [us] to live in peace and happiness, protected by just laws, each doing his duty in that state of life to which he is called, rising above or sinking in the scale of society according as he has been entrusted with the five talents or the one. Equality can and does exist nowhere'.[55]

In the late 1830s, Marryat had travelled in North America and like so many of his contemporaries he published his diary. His 'object was to view the Western world, and ascertain what might be the effects produced upon the English character and temperament by a different climate, different circumstances, and a different form of government from those which they had been accustomed to.'[56] He travelled in the northern and eastern states but never went to the South. He did not condemn slavery and concluded that northern blacks would never have the same intellectual power as whites since 'the race are not formed for it by the Almighty'.[57] He could not abide 'fanatical' abolitionists and was deeply disturbed by miscegenation and the spectre of democracy. He hoped that his book would expose its dangers: 'If I have in any way assisted the cause of Conservatism, I am content', he wrote.[58] In Canada he bought some land and while there in 1838 was horrified to hear of the troubles in the Upper and Lower provinces and volunteered to fight with the British army, serving under Sir John Colbourne in two of his expeditions against the rebels. He had, after all, grown up with the French as *the* enemy.

Marryat constructed a brutal account of racial antagonism in *Percival Keene* (1842), written after his American sojourn. The novel opened as a familiar story of a wild youth going into the navy but took an unusual turn. Percival, the hero, was captured by pirates in West Indian waters but, astonishingly, they turned out to be all black. The captain, 'gigantic in stature' with a 'fierce, severe, determined-looking countenance' ordered him to be immediately thrown overboard but the lad's sparky responses saved him. 'Very proper you have white slave boy', as one of the pirates said, but they blacked him up so that he would be like them. They captured a slaver and the captain was in a fierce rage with the white men on board. Percival, locked below, heard terrible noises and sounds of preparation on deck. 'The countenances of the negroes who were thus employed appeared inflamed, as if their wrath was excited; now and then they laughed at each other, and looked more like demons than men.' Then he heard terrible screams and shrieks followed by the most appalling smell. He discovered that they had roasted all the white men alive, then thrown them overboard. He pondered over the fact,

That I really did not feel so much horror as perhaps I ought to have done. Had this dreadful punishment been inflicted upon any *other* persons than slave dealers, and *by* any other parties than negroes, I should not have been able to look at the captain without abhorrence expressed in my countenance; but I knew well the horrors of the slave trade ... and I had imbibed such a hatred against the parties who had carried it on, that it appeared to me to be an act of retaliation almost allied to justice. Had the negro captain only warred against slave dealers, I do not think I should have cared about remaining in the vessel; but he had told me, and fully proved to me, that he detested all white men, and had never spared them except in my own instance.[59]

The captain told Percival his story: he had been born free in the US, 'but a free black in America is even worse treated and more despised than a slave'. There was no justice there for men of colour. He had been enslaved, horribly flogged and escaped to turn pirate but his experience had taught him to hate all white men. Percival and the captain became friends but Percival tired of murder and bloodshed and declared that he did not want such a life. The captain responded: 'And who should be pirates if the blacks are not? ... Have they not the curse of Cain? Are they not branded? Ought not their hands to be against every one but their own race?'. Percival recalled the terrible battle that then took place between the pirate ship and an English frigate: 'the negroes, most of them intoxicated, fought with rage and fury indescribable – their shouts, their screams – their cursing and blasphemy, mingled with the loud report of the guns, the crashing of the spars and bulwarks, the occasional cry of the wounded.' Many were killed, and the captain eventually blew up his ship, destroying himself and his crew. Percival of course escaped to tell his English friends: 'I've been playing the nigger for the last three months.'[60] Marryat used his cast of characters to voice various perspectives, yet it was all too clear where his identifications lay. The roots of the captain's hatred of all white men lay in their treatment of him. But the pious recognition of the horrors of the slave-trade and the ways in which white Americans could blight the lives of Africans was juxtaposed with a terrifying picture of black cruelty and race hatred sitting alongside a representation of the British as untouched by any such history.

By the 1840s Marryat had lost his lead in the field of popular adult fiction to his friend Dickens, was less preoccupied with the Caribbean and had run out of naval themes. He turned to writing books for children, ranging more widely across the empire: the colonies were his oyster, racial difference a central theme. Children's books, he believed, had a particular duty to instruct and should be based on truth, and colonisers should turn to pastures new. His first effort, *Masterman Ready* (1841), was a reworking of *Robinson Crusoe* and *The Swiss Family Robinson*. It featured the family of a former colonial official in New South Wales, returning from time in England to take up a new career as a farmer on the several thousand acres he had bought for sheep and cattle. Mr Seagrave was the source of all patriarchal knowledge and authority, Mrs Seagrave a thoroughly domesticated and practical wife and mother. Wrecked just off the coast of the Cape, the family, helped and supported by the deferential Masterman Ready, a weather-beaten old seaman with grizzled locks but a wealth of experience, created a perfect colony on a desert island: here was a model for colonising the world. They built a shelter and made a home, found goats and milked them, saved seeds from the wreck and planted them. Their African servant girl Juno – a name that Marryat used for a dog in another novel and that was indeed the name of one of his own dogs – had been saved from enslavement to the Boers and was free, as Mrs Seagrave told her, because she had been to England and 'whoever puts his foot on shore in England becomes from that moment free'. (This was an implicit reference to the popular but mistaken view of the Mansfield decision.) She was 'a good girl' with a 'thick woolly coat' on her head, who always put her young charge Albert first, was capable of endless hard work and was only allowed to speak a few words, and then in crude mimicry.[61] Mr Seagrave gave his son Willy lessons on colonialism: colonies, just like sons, grow up and want independence, he told him, empires too come and go. The Romans thought that Britons were barbarians and who knew what the 'barbarians and savages' of Africa might become? 'But the negroes, Father – they are blacks', responds Willy. 'Very true', he replies, 'but that is no reason to the contrary.'[62] Juno and the history lesson sit at odds with each other in the text: Marryat was claiming that skin colour did not matter and once again the form of the novel facilitated multiple voices. Yet the direction of his tales told a different story. Mr Seagrave ruled the roost; Mrs Seagrave was tearful and anxious, prayed and read her Bible; and Masterman Ready and Juno did much of the heavy work – the gender, class and racial hierarchies were firmly in place. Dickens loved *Masterman*: 'famous', he enthused, 'I have been chuckling and grinning and clenching my fists and becoming warlike for three whole days.'[63] This was a book to feed imperial minds and inspire settlers with the will to conquer.

Marryat's Canadian novel, *The Settlers*, published in 1844, was again a blueprint for British colonialism and represented 'Indians' as confined in an archaic culture that would not survive. The future was a Canada dominated by the British, who were Christian and industrious, domesticated and literate, committed to progress. They would struggle, unsuccessfully for the most part, to civilise the native population. Marryat had one last foray into the empire with *The Mission*, published in 1845. This combined a critique of slavery – 'the greatest of all curses ... nothing demoralizes so much' – with a horror at the savagery of Africans and its potentially polluting effects on Europeans.[64] The repudiation of slavery was unproblematically combined with ugly racial stereotypes and explicit fear of miscegenation. Africa was represented primarily as a hunting ground – a place to kill every possible variety of wild animal and to triumph in this defeat of nature. With its teeming black populations, imagined as both warlike and docile, it was less fertile ground for colonial settlement than the 'empty lands' of Canada.

Theodora Lynch shared Marryat's range across adult and children's fiction. In every other respect, excepting her interest in the Caribbean, she could not have been more different. She turned from wars, pirates, naval heroes and colonial adventures to the domestic lives of white West Indians, and in a series of books written over twenty years she evoked the past as a time of harmony, and slavery, while regrettable, as a benevolent institution. Her father, Arthur Foulks, lived between Bristol and Jamaica. As was the case with many absentees, they were a transatlantic family. Foulks ran the Lodge Estate sugar plantation near Old Harbour on the south side of Jamaica, flat lands where heavy sugar production was possible. In 1836 he was awarded £8,911 2s 10d for 426 enslaved men and women on the estate.[65] The previous year Theodora had married a lawyer, Henry Lynch, at her father's plantation. He died ten years later. She settled in England and like many respectable widows turned to writing presumably at least partly for financial reasons. Her chosen genres, poetry, adult and children's fiction and a travel book about the West Indies, all informed by her evangelical Christianity and strong didactic purpose, were all deemed appropriate arenas for a female author. She drew heavily on her Jamaican experience and was concerned to paint a benign picture of the island and its society. After 1838, when apprenticeship was abolished, the West Indies slipped out of public consciousness in Britain, no longer an area of central political concern. It came back into focus in the mid-1840s when the planters were fighting, unsuccessfully in the end, to retain the protective sugar duties that they enjoyed. They mounted campaigns, stressing the decline of the plantations since Emancipation, the reluctance of freed slaves to work and their need for more labour to be imported, either from Africa or from the East Indies. Africans were represented as indolent and lacking in discipline and ambition, threatening to return what had once been wealth-producing economies to barbarism and subsistence.

It was in this context that *Jane Eyre* was published in 1847 with its picture of a dangerously degenerate and polluting West Indian society centred on the terrifying figure of the mad monster, Bertha Mason, an animalised figure, racialised as creole and white. The picture of the Caribbean as a place of failure and decline into barbarism was becoming more widely accepted. Theodora Lynch was responding to those currents. Slavery, as she narrated it, was a benign institution: Africans were simple but good people when properly guided by their white masters and mistresses. 'Little English reader', she instructed her audience in *The Cotton-Tree: or Emily, the Little West Indian*, published the same year as *Jane Eyre*, 'my first recollections are those of ... kind black faces ... there were smiles from these sable nurses that filled my infant heart with happiness'.[66] 'Trusty negroes' would safely guide ladies 'pale with terror' through the rushing mountain streams that sprang up in the wake of the 'rainy season'.[67] Faithful domestics would greet their masters and mistresses returning from England with unalloyed joy, workers would merrily sing 'wild snatches of African song' on their way to the cane fields, 'negroes ... in the true spirit of feudal attachment' cared for their 'massas', ruined and dispossessed by creditors.[68]

Lynch's writing was an attempt to redeem the West Indian creole for an English audience; her women were not Bertha Masons – they were represented as gentle and responsible. While Bronte's Caribbean was horrible, a phobic place, Lynch evoked a paradise. Pro-slavery discourse had long insisted on the benevolent and paternalistic nature of plantation slavery, the good relations between masters and 'their' people; this was her story too. Yet there was the occasional recognition of a disjunction. Her *Years Ago* (1865), the imagined tale of a young girl, Dorothy, growing up in Jamaica in the late eighteenth century, constructed the father as the harsh voice of white authority, the women as more recognising of the common humanity of white and black.

'Good, kind papa who never says a harsh word to any of [his children], changes his voice and manner when he addresses a slave. It vexes me so to hear him call them "lazy brutes", "idle dogs" etc., and almost in the same breath he will lavish words of tenderness on us'. Fortunately Aunt Ellie would say, 'Doth a fountain send forth at the same time sweet water and bitter' ... What is there in the black skin that seems to set every man's heart and hand against it?[69]

At other points, however, it was all too clear that black skin denoted difference; illiterate negroes were 'semi-barbarous', 'uncouth', 'half-civilized'.[70] In describing the effects of the uprising in San Domingue on the white population of Jamaica, Dorothy commented that 'certainly there is something very alarming in being in the midst of a wild people, who, if they were to act with energy, and skill, and courage, could soon make themselves masters of the whole island'.[71] There were no whips in Lynch's picture of the past, no cruel punishments, no separation of mothers and children or excruciatingly long hours of labour, no resistance or rebellion, only the haunting fear of it that occasionally surfaced. The 'deformities of vice' that she addressed were lack of real religion, not the contradiction between Christianity and slavery. The four young black boys who fanned the family with orange boughs while they ate their breakfast were well fed and well dressed; the women who cleaned the mahogany floors with orange juice before polishing it with the husks of the cocoa nut were content with their labour. Indeed, slavery was scarcely named, the realities of the plantations veiled by the extraordinary tropical luxuriance that was depicted so extensively. Lynch's memories of a Jamaican childhood were uniformly rosy – her tales of the past airbrushed out any but the most fleeting references to enslavement. A black nurse would understand a child's fears and calm her terrors, Jamaican planters never punished their slaves cruelly, family parties on the plantations were happy and the constant reiteration of the beauty of the surroundings masked the ugly relations of enslavement.

Charles Kingsley was haunted by his West Indian past in a different way. He was an Anglican clergyman; a Christian Socialist; a friend of F. D. Maurice and Tom Hughes; a novelist and poet; a sanitary reformer; a professor of English at Queens' College, Cambridge, the college established by the Christian Socialists to provide some education for women, and later professor of History at Cambridge; and a patriot and an imperialist, concerned about the 'condition of England' and Chartism. A much more intellectual figure than Marryat and part of the literary intellectual elite of the Victorian world, Kingsley was serious in his Christianity and his enthusiasm for Christian manliness. His maternal grandfather was part of the Lucas family, who had been in the West Indies for five generations. Nathan Lucas, his grandfather, was a judge in Barbados. His main estate was Mt Clapham and he also had estates in Demerara. Charles' mother, Mary Lucas, married his father, Charles (a clergyman) in 1813. Their son Charles was born in 1819 when Marryat was a young man, already ridiculing Africans. Nathan Lucas had died by 1834, and his estate was administered by Thomas Louis, who was resident in London but dealt with a number of claims in Barbados. Thomas received £3,410 for 157 enslaved people in 1836 but there is evidence of indebtedness and it seems likely that a private arrangement was made whereby some of the money went to the debtors.[72] Many years later Kingsley told his friend Thomas Hughes that Emancipation had been a financial disaster for him.

Kingsley was very influenced by Darwin and convinced of the power of heredity. Francis Galton wrote to Fanny Kingsley after her husband's death that Galton's judgement, 'partly on your husband's own verbal account to me', was that it was Kingsley's descent on his mother's side from a 'pure West Indian family' of many generations that had been crucial to his makeup. He had 'instinctive' connections with the tropics.[73] As a boy Charles loved his grandfather's stories and they made a great impression, particularly the tale of a major earthquake in St Vincent that terrified the Barbadians: 'his' negroes were in panic, shrieking in the streets, the whites all busy praying 'as they had never prayed before', but his grandfather remained 'rational and self-possessed' and studied his scientific books.[74] These qualities – manliness, self-possession, reason, belief in the wonders of nature (which he regarded as providential) – were among the ones that Kingsley most valued and that he propagandised in his work. His grandfather had been on *HMS Formidable* with his friend Admiral Rodney when Rodney won his great victory against the French in 1782 and saved the British West Indies. It was this picture of the English as conquerors and naval heroes that Kingsley returned to in his patriotic novel *Westward Ho!* (1855), written to encourage a sense of national pride in the context of the Crimean War, hoping to energise a nation he regarded as effete.

Kingsley's lifelong friend and brother-in-law was the historian and biographer of Thomas Carlyle, James Antony Froude. Froude, like Kingsley, was heavily influenced by Carlyle. They were all disturbed by the lack of energy and masculine vigour in society; effete manliness was an evil to be attacked. In 1852 Froude wrote an essay in the *Westminster Review*, 'England's forgotten worthies', that celebrated Hakluyt's accounts of his voyages as 'the prose epic of the modern English nation', England's *Iliad*. These volumes, Froude argued, contained the 'heroic tales of the exploits of the great men in whom the new era was inaugurated', an epic for 'the common people'.[75] Froude's essay contained the seeds of the twelve-volume *History of England* that he wrote over the next fifteen years, a history that challenged Macaulay's epic account. While Macaulay and the Whig historians focused on 1688 and the Glorious Revolution as the turning point in English history, Froude saw the sixteenth century as the formative period for English imperial power. He explicitly celebrated empire and the seamen who 'went out across the unknown seas, fighting, discovering, colonising' and preparing the routes through which the commerce and enterprise of England flowed out, sowing 'its colonies over the globe'. His heroes were Drake, Raleigh and Hawkins, who suffered 'none of that weak watery talk of "protection of aborigines"'. These were men of honour (a strange term particularly for Hawkins, who was a key instigator of the slave-trade) who, in Froude's view, 'never committed a single crime against the savages' – unlike the cruel Spaniards.[76] This was the story that Kingsley elaborated in *Westward Ho!* It was his fictional version of Elizabethan colonial adventure and it was an extraordinary success, reprinted thirty-eight times by the end of the nineteenth century. Kingsley told his readers that it was to Drake, Hawkins and Raleigh that England owed its commerce, colonies and very existence. His hero Amyas was a manly West Country lad, a 'symbol of brave young England longing to wing its way out of its island prison, to discover and to traffic, to colonise and to civilise until no wind can sweep the earth which does not bear the echoes of an English voice'.[77]

Amyas sailed for the New World, keen to attack the cruel Spanish and their dreaded tool, the Jesuit Inquisition. Kingsley's history was an attempt to counter contemporary disenchantment with a declining Caribbean by invoking older narratives of conquest and possession.[78] He was fiercely anti-Catholic: but for the glorious victory against the Spanish Armada of 1588 'we would have been a Popish appanage of a world-tyranny'.[79] He denounced the slave-trade and slavery, the frightful harm it had done, not only for the Spanish but also, to their shame, for the English, evoking 'the groans of those stolen negroes' ... 'a national curse for generations yet unborn'.[80] His racial ambivalence was expressed in the novel through various characters – Yeo, who despised black men, was reproved by the authoritative Grenville. But negroes were depicted as 'savages', shouting and 'jabbering' while Indian 'natives', despite the cruelty of the Spanish to them, had nothing noble about them; rather they were dirty and primitive, practising cannibalism.[81] The heroine, Ayacanora, originally understood to be half Spanish, half Indian, turned out to be white and learnt self-restraint and a gentler femininity through her training by Amyas' mother. The novel ended with the defeat of the Armada and a utopian vision of the future of the British Empire, an empire built on freedom that would not decay as others had before. 'A shout of holy joy' greeted 'a germ of new life, liberty and civilisation ... the seed of future virtue and greatness ... of free commerce and free colonialism' across 'North America, Australia, New Zealand, the Pacific Islands'. [82]

Kingsley was to support the South in the American Civil War: slavery, he thought, was an abomination but probably the best way of ruling people who were incapable of self-government. He wrote to his friend Hughes in the aftermath of the war, questioning him as to why he was supporting Freedman's Aid. 'What do they ask our money for over and over', he wrote; 'I am personally shy of giving mine. The negro has had all I ever possessed; for emancipation ruined me. I am no slave-holder at heart. But I have paid my share of the great bill in Barbados and Demerara, with a vengeance.'[83]

In 1865 he famously became associated with the defence of Governor Eyre's conduct in Jamaica in the wake of the rebellion at Morant Bay, an issue that split the British public between those who welcomed his authoritarian response and those who were horrified by the abandonment of due legal process. Kingsley, the man who was 'no slave-holder at heart', came to believe that 'there are congenital differences and hereditary tendencies which defy all education'.[84] Kingsley was no simple biological racist. Like most Victorians he drew on stadial theory and by the late 1860s it was in its post-Darwinian moment, a harsher evolutionary version that saw the timing of the civilising process as glacial. Negroes were like Europeans in the Middle Ages; they had been locked in stagnant Africa for centuries and it was only their encounter with Europe that made progress possible. Yet, as was so common, Kingsley's evolutionary assumptions jostled with harsher registers; culture and biology were both in play, essentialist notions of physical differences between the races entangled with visions of improvement under European tuition.

Kingsley's younger brother Henry also became a writer, though he never enjoyed the success or notoriety of his brother. It was not the West Indies and the stories of his grandfather, however, that preoccupied him; rather it was his experience as a colonist in Australia that he drew on for two of his novels. As younger sons in his time headed for the new colonies of white settlement rather than the West Indies as their ancestors had done, he was preoccupied with the settler identity and its relation to Englishness.[85] After in inauspicious time as an undergraduate in Oxford, Henry had set out for New South Wales seeking his fortune. He landed at Port Philip in 1853, just after it had gained independence from New South Wales and when the dispossession of indigenous people and the assertion of settler rights were going on apace. He stayed there for five years, mainly in Victoria, working on a sheep farm for a period and trying his hand, with very little success, at gold-digging. In 1858 he returned to England with a half-finished novel that was completed while living with his parents in a cottage in the grounds of his brother Charles' rectory at Eversley. *The Recollections of Geoffrey Hamlyn* was published in 1859 and did well, with sales of over 7,000 and 500 bought by Mudies, the circulating library. *Geoffrey Hamlyn* purported to be the memories of an old bachelor who had spent years in Victoria but had now returned to his home county of Devon. It was written in the voice of a successful pastoralist and offered a romanticised and idealised picture of first-generation squatters. It 'initiated the line of colonial romance' and 'probably influenced the writing of Australian fiction more than any other single work of fiction about Australia during the nineteenth century'.[86]

Australia was represented as 'land with millions of acres of fertile soil … calling aloud for some one to come and cultivate them', a land of opportunity, 'a new heaven and a new earth'.[87] The fictional English settlers all prospered, occupying thousands of acres with their sheep and living the lives of the West Country gentry, transposed into New South Wales. A series of dramatic episodes evoked station life – a bushfire, a kangaroo hunt, a child lost in the bush, conflicts with bushrangers. The major villains were the ex-convicts who had not reformed and the bushrangers, the dregs of society, who oiled the wheels of the melodramatic and exceedingly far-fetched plot. Aboriginal people were not erased. In the writings of the colonists dispossession was both known and not known, disavowed.[88] The 'savages' made fleeting appearances – sometimes labouring on the farms, 'jabbering' among themselves, 'gorging' meat, unable to eat in a civilised manner, swimming 'in Mother Nature's full dress'. Occasionally a young boy, somewhat more assimilated to European ways, was allowed to demonstrate his loyalty to his masters. An aboriginal cattle raid provided a moment of danger in the text, when shouting like devils and brandishing their spears 'the blacks' briefly spread terror, until the superior arms and strategy of the tiny band of settlers left the 'discomfited savages' slinking away. Henry Kingsley held to a belief in the universal family of man, yet at the very same time he pointed his readers to the impossibility of civilising these 'savages'.

Kingsley's second Australian novel, *The Hillyars and the Burtons*, was published in 1865, the year of the Morant Bay rebellion in Jamaica. Both convicts and 'blackfellows' were entirely marginalised. The fictional colony was no longer in the first phase of settlement; now the preoccupations were mining companies and land sales, supported emigration and labour costs, local politics and the conflicts between the squatters and the radical Irish. Dispossession had happened and 'the blacks' had been 'tamed'.[89] Yet the bush was a dangerous place; nature had not yet been conquered and aboriginal people still haunted the white imagination. That same year Kingsley published a two-part essay about Edward John Eyre in *Macmillan's Magazine*. At the time of publication he did not know that Eyre was still alive, or what had just happened in Jamaica. The essay was a celebration of Eyre the explorer who had crossed the great Australian Bight in a terrible journey. Eyre had spent several years in Australia in the 1830s and 1840s as a young man. According to Kingsley, he 'knew more about the aboriginal tribes, their habits, language, and so on, than any man before or since'. He had been appointed Black Protector for the Lower Murray, and was 'eminently kind, generous, and just'. He defended 'the natives' from the depredations of

the squatters (the great pastoral aristocracy) at a time when to do so was social ostracism … He pleaded for the black, and tried to stop the war of extermination which was, is, and I suppose will be, carried on by the colonists against the natives in the unsettled districts beyond reach of the public eye. His task was hopeless. It was easier for him to find water in the desert than to find mercy for the savages. Honour to him for attempting it, however.[90]

This passage was to be quoted as evidence of Eyre's good character in the controversy as to the rights and wrongs of his actions in Jamaica.[91]

Kingsley admired what he saw as Eyre's paternalism in relation to 'the natives'. Yet his own conception of those 'natives' and their role in the great exploration of the Bight was profoundly negative. They were 'savages', variously described as 'sneaking', 'crawling', 'crouching' and 'whining'. Wylie, who stayed with Eyre through the worst passages of the expedition, had, he wrote, 'some feeling of a faithful doglike devotion in the darkened soul of him ... something more in the inside of the man than any marmoset or monkey ever had got ... This fellow Wylie was a *man* after all.'[92] But Eyre, the 'lover and protector of the blacks', whose life had been devoted to 'the protection of these savages against the whites', knew that 'doomed race better than any man has done before or since'. Directly addressing his readers, Kingsley commented, 'Now you know these people must *go*. God never made the Portland District for *them*. All one asks is, that the thing should be done with decency, and with every sort of indulgence; whereas it is not, but in a scandalous and disgraceful manner.'[93] This was not dispossession, for these people had no rights of possession – the land was there for the settlers to make fertile. Aboriginal people were men, but men locked in savagery and doomed to extinction. Henry Kingsley joined the Eyre Defence Committee along with a number of others whose families had received compensation but he was reluctant to positively defend Eyre's actions and remained critical of those squatters who made fortunes out of Australian soil, 'drenched with the blood of the natives'.[94] But his criticism of others did not inspire him to reflect on his own assumptions. 'The most lethal aspect of extinction discourse', writes Patrick Brantlinger, 'has probably been its stress on the inevitability of [primeval others] vanishing.' In claiming Eyre as one whose life had been devoted to protecting 'savages' against the whites while at the same time accepting the doomed nature of those people, Kingsley was fully participating in that discourse.[95]

Travel writers

Travel writing was another very popular form for the Victorians and offered innumerable possibilities for denoting 'the radical difference between metropolitan and colonial subjects' while affirming 'the centrality of the other in the cognitive maps of Englishness'.[96] If the historian could claim to stand above the events he narrated, the travel writer was the eye-witness par excellence, not claiming to be neutral but drawing the reader into the experience, offering an intimacy, evoking the shock of the tropics for those at home. James Mursell Phillippo's *Jamaica: Its Past and Present State* had been published in 1843. This enthusiastic account of the wondrous transformation that had been effected by Emancipation was written by a Baptist missionary who had been on the island since the 1820s. With its optimistic account of a prosperous Christian future peopled by industrious and domesticated black men and women led by their ministers, it was a modest success among the abolitionist and missionary publics.[97] *The Wonders of the West Indies* told a rather different story. It was Theodora Lynch's effort to represent the Caribbean islands as a wonderfully inviting region. As the Lord Bishop of Jamaica put it in the preface, it was remarkable that an area 'so distinguished by novelty, and so exuberant in beauty' should be so little known; Lynch's 'poetic chronicle' would provide the remedy. Memories of the Antilles were still 'darkened by the deep shadows of a great though not wholly expiated national crime' but 'the natural endowments' of the region would enrapture all.[98] Ranging across the islands from the 'flying fish, mountains, magnificent cedars and mahogany, blue skies, [to the] sheet-lightning most sublime', Lynch concluded, as did more distinguished later writers, that 'there is little interesting or exciting in the history of the West India Islands'. Yet it was slavery and conquest that haunted this landscape for her, its 'whole history' represented as one of 'Power trampling on Weakness'. Jamaica stayed in her mind as 'the resting places of our loved and dead', though these same loved ones were slave-owners. Post-Emancipation Africans were represented as having 'great simplicity of manner, and an affectionate and forgiving spirit', and while 'comparatively an enlightened set' were 'listless and idle, and almost entirely devoid of enterprise', a very different story from that of Phillippo.[99]

Fifteen years later, and in the wake of Trollope's *The West Indies and the Spanish Main* (1859), which simultaneously used irony to undermine the binaries of the colonial relation while confirming white superiority and African inferiority, Charles Kingsley published *At Last*, the journal of his visit to the West Indies.[100] He *knew* the West Indies, had always dreamed of the romances, histories and tragedies of the Caribbean. 'From childhood I had studied their Natural History, their charts, their Romances, and alas! Their Tragedies,' he wrote: now he would compare books with facts. This was a place already known and possessed through the familial and imperial archive, fictionalised by Kingsley himself and its history reworked by Froude.[101] But the stories he had been told and the texts he had read were not enough; he needed to see it for himself, to claim the status of eye-witness for his observations and classifications, to reflect on the parlous state of aspects of his own civilisation from the distant Caribbean while reaffirming the clear superiority of English culture, albeit an affirmation tinged with anxiety. In the olden days, travel had been for adventure; now it could deliver moral improvement. His enthusiasm as a naturalist, his lengthy depictions of the glories of tropical forests and plant life, sat alongside a dread of otherness, the swamps of brown foul water next to white sand, the flowers that contained deadly poison, the 'wonderful wealth' of nature and then the 'scene which we would fain forget' of the black women, half-civilised creatures 'doing men's work' and loading coal.[102]

Kingsley hoped to make an intervention in the post-Morant Bay debates on race and the Caribbean. Britain had neglected the West Indies, he thought, locked in its guilt over slavery, subject to 'dark shadows and ghosts' from the imperial past, 'too ignorant and helpless to govern ... now slavery is gone'.[103] Yet he was also nervous, shocked by the hostility that he had encountered as a result of the support he had offered to Eyre and reminding himself to be cautious in his public judgements, to emphasise his scientific rather than his ethnographic authority, to reflect on black rebellion through historical tales rather than too-present concerns. His representation of the African was animalistic but he claimed their 'brutality' was a result of being 'half-civilised' not from 'deliberate depravity'.[104] They screamed, jabbered and gnawed sugar-cane with their strong incisors, but they might be able to progress. Like Carlyle he regretted that tropical luxuriance meant that Africans had to work little to gain a subsistence. He was disgusted and excited by the physicality of both men and women. The women with their masculine, ungainly figures, coarse and loud, and their independence shocked and intrigued him. He stopped himself complaining too much about Africans being 'fat and comfortable' and enjoying themselves, like the 'lizard on the wall', however, by reminding himself of the poverty and misery at home.[105] 'We must remember that we are very seriously in debt to the Negro ... After all we brought him here, and we have no right to complain of our own work. If, like Frankenstein, we have tried to make a man and made him badly; we must, like Frankenstein, pay the penalty.'[106] Privately he concluded, 'I am afraid I don't like the negroes, especially the women', but 'I delight in the coolies', who would be the saving of the West Indies.[107] Coolies were graceful and well-mannered, brought as indentured labour to fill the gap left by freed Africans who preferred subsistence farming to staying on the plantations of their former masters; they thus offered hope. They were industrious and docile, locked it was true in awful superstitions, but coming from an old civilisation and capable of being educated

Figure 5.3 'Coolie family' in *At Last: A Christmas in the West Indies*, Charles Kingsley (1905).

into a new. Indenture was Kingsley's solution to labour problems. He knew that feudalism was dead but hoped for a moral bond combining the best of patriarchalism and feudalism with free labour. The 'coolies' would teach 'the negro' thrift and industry by their example and their competition.

Kingsley's main hope was for more emigration of white Britons: each married couple could be 'a little centre of civilization for the Negro, the coolie'.[108] Kingsley mapped difference between the races in his writing: negroes, coolies, coloureds, the Irish – all were placed on a complex hierarchical ladder topped by the white, but painfully flawed, Englishman.

Poetry

Poetic writing from the slave-owners was mainly by women and ranged from conservative to feminist, from expressive lyrics mourning the death of beloved ones in the Caribbean to a strident polemic. Theodora Lynch and Fidelia Hill (Australia's first white woman poet) both produced texts reflecting on their experience as the descendants of slave-owners, but by far the most significant voice was that of Elizabeth Barrett Browning. The daughter of a long line of slave-owners in Jamaica, she was both deeply troubled by and profoundly identified with that heritage.[109] The Barrett family had been in Jamaica since 1655 and were major landowners on the north coast. Elizabeth had contact with the island from her earliest childhood. Her mother, Mary Graham-Clarke, came from a rich merchant family in Newcastle and they too had property in Jamaica.[110] Elizabeth's grandmother, who had spent much of her life in Jamaica, had a companion, Mary Trepsack, known in the family as Treppy and a familiar of the Barrett children. She was the daughter of a beleaguered planter and an enslaved woman and had been enslaved herself before becoming a slave-owner and receiving compensation. She regarded Emancipation as a sorrow for the 'poor creatures'.[111]

Elizabeth's father, Edward Barrett Moulton-Barrett, took an active interest in the Jamaica property that he had inherited along with his brother Samuel from his grandfather. The estates were very profitable and brought in an estimated income of £4,000 in 1807. Being absentees, however, raised problems and it was decided that Samuel should move to Jamaica and manage the business himself. He settled permanently at Cinnamon Hill and soon some of his nephews, Elizabeth's brothers, were coming to work with him.

By the early 1830s Elizabeth was a young woman in her late twenties and well aware of the implications of abolition for the family fortunes. Yet

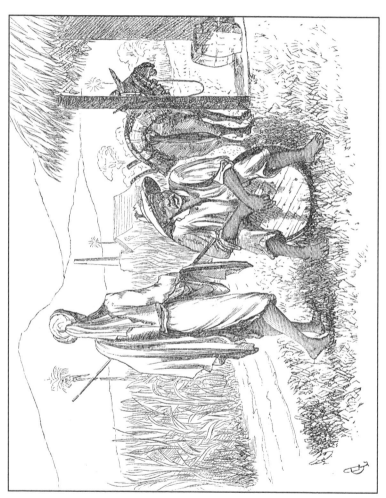

Figure 5.4 'Coolie and negro' in *At Last: A Christmas in the West Indies*, Charles Kingsley (1905).

she was also a supporter of anti-slavery. In 1832 the estate at Hope End on which they had grown up had to be sold, a casualty of the family's legal battles over inheritance, declining sugar prices, the effects of the 1831 rebellion and the expectation of abolition. Elizabeth wrote to a friend in May 1833, 'The West Indies are irreparably ruined if the bill passes.'[112] Once the bill had passed she wrote, 'Of course you know that the late bill has ruined the West Indians. That is settled. The consternation here is very great. Nevertheless, I am glad, and always shall be, that the negroes are – virtually – free.'[113] Any notion of ruin for the West Indians, however, was unduly pessimistic. Edward and Charles Moulton-Barrett received £7,734 for 397 enslaved men and women on the Oxford and Cambridge estates and Edward received a further share in £4,718 for 250 enslaved people on Retreat Pen.[114]

Concerned about the management of the property in the wake of Emancipation, Edward Moulton-Barrett sent his eldest son, known in the family as 'Bro', to Jamaica to work with his Uncle Sam. Elizabeth was convinced he 'cannot be happy there ... among the *white* savages'.[115] Her picture of Jamaica was of a benighted island dominated by slavery and capable of hopelessly polluting its white inhabitants. Bro's younger brother Sam replaced him in 1836 and lived with his uncle at Cinnamon Hill while managing the Oxford and Cambridge estates. He, however, succumbed to the vices of the plantocracy, to the great dismay of his family. In 1838 Uncle Sam died, leaving his niece Elizabeth shares in the *David Lyon*, a West India ship named after one of the original pro-prietors of the West India Dock Company. He also left her some money and this legacy from her favourite uncle made Elizabeth richer than her sisters and able to be independent from her father. She had already inherited £4,000 from her grandmother's properties in 1830. In 1840, to the deep distress of his family, Sam died of fever and was buried at Cinnamon Hill alongside his uncle. Six years later Elizabeth eloped with Robert Browning, to the fury of her father, who wanted all his children to remain unmarried. Elizabeth and Robert received significant financial help from John Kenyon, another poet and Jamaican slave-owner who had also received compensation.[116] Browning too was the descendant of slave-owners in St Kitts.

Elizabeth expressed her ambivalence about the familial connection with slavery most vividly in the poem that she began in Pisa in 1846 at the request of an American anti-slavery organisation. This was 'The Runaway Slave at Pilgrim's Point', written over a decade after abolition when it was already clear, in the eyes of many, that Emancipation was far from an unmitigated success. The poem was a melodramatic and polem-ical narrative, telling the tragic tale of an enslaved woman who fell in love with an enslaved man on the plantation. He was killed and she was then raped by her white master. But the white child that she bore 'was far too white … too white for me' so she suffocated him, to save him from the fate of a black mother who could not love him, seeing in him the face of her rapist.

> And he moaned and struggled, as well might be,
> For the white child wanted his liberty –
> Ha, ha! He wanted his master right.

She carried the body 'to and fro' and it 'lay on my heart like a stone, as chill' till she reached Pilgrim's Point and looked 'on the sea and the sky! / Where the pilgrims' ships first anchored lay'. But 'the pilgrim-ghosts' had slid away and it was the slave-hunters who came and seized her. 'I am not mad: I am black', she declared, as in the land of 'free America' they tied her and flogged her to death. She hung, 'as a gourd hangs in the sun', and cursed the slave-owners, crying out 'Up to the mountains, lift your hands, / O slaves, and end what I begun.'[117]

The poem confronted the violent nature of slavery and the fear of revenge which that engendered. Its female protagonist was a defiant heroine who was allowed to speak in the King's English. Elizabeth was proud of its anti-slavery content and thought it 'ferocious', possibly too ferocious for the Americans to publish.[118] 'I could not help making it bitter', she told her friend Mary Mitford Russell.[119] Perhaps the scale of the bitterness, as Cora Kaplan has suggested, was possible in part because she was writing about slavery in the US, not the British Caribbean, thereby distancing her own family.[120] But biographical explanations are not enough to account for the militant abolitionist sentiment in the poem. Marjorie Stone's inter-textual account of the context of its publication in the *Liberty Bell*, edited by Maria Weston Chapman and closely linked to radical abolitionists and feminists with Garrisonian sympathies, makes sense of Barrett Browning's portrayal of an enslaved black woman, both sexually and racially oppressed. She was a figure who was martyred for her race, who called on the enslaved to rebel and articulated the curse that white slave-holders bring upon themselves.[121] In a parallel reading, Kaplan suggests that the poem needs to be seen in relation to the debates about race circulating in Britain as well as the US in the 1840s. It revised earlier feminist anti-slavery writing, reworked familiar tropes and constituted a rhetorical challenge to the negative associations of blackness.[122]

Yet, like so much of the anti-slavery discourse of white male and female abolitionists, it was an ambivalent work, speaking for the enslaved woman, the adopted 'I' of the poem, a woman who had no name and who could not speak for herself. Elizabeth had had her own historic struggle, to free herself from the authority of her father, which could only be effected through her elopement. Her struggle to be an independent creative woman, which meant rejecting her father, has been justly celebrated as one of the success stories of nineteenth-century white feminists. Yet in her poem the rage of the African woman could only be expressed through the despairing act of killing her child and sacrificing herself. Barrett Browning was claiming freedom for the unfree, yet the only freedom that could be imagined was death. She hated slavery, yet she had lived much of her life on the proceeds of the plantations. Pursued with guilt, she knew her dependence on that tainted money. Her favourite uncle had died an untimely death and her beloved brother was buried at twenty-eight. Jamaica was indeed a dangerous place and 'cursed we are from generation to generation!', she reflected. She wished profoundly that she had 'some purer lineage than that of the blood of the slave'.[123]

In a letter to her friend Anna Jameson some years later, Elizabeth urged her to read *Uncle Tom's Cabin*. 'Is it possible', she asked, 'that you think a woman has no business with questions like the question of slavery?' Then, she continued,

She had better use a pen no more. She had better subside into slavery and concubinage herself, I think, as in the times of old, shut herself up with the Penelopes in the 'women's apartment', and take no rank among thinkers and speakers. Observe, I am an abolitionist, not to the fanatical degree, because I hold that compensation should be given by the North to the South, as in England.[124]

Property was property, after all. And poetry was a medium through which disturbance could be spoken.

Coda

In his autobiography, *A Sort of Life*, published in 1971, Graham Greene recounts how as he grew older he became increasingly interested in his forebears. He realised that, far from being exceptional in his sense of difference from his solidly bourgeois family, he was one of a long line of rebels. The ancestor he felt closest to was his father's father, William, who had been sent to the family estates in St Kitts aged fourteen, to assist his brother Charles in the management of the plantations after Emancipation. Two years later his brother died and William had to take on the task. Decades later, William recalled this as 'the most cheerful, careless and happy period of my life'.[125] As Greene describes it, the memories

of Mount Misery with its head buried in the clouds, of the green wastes of sugarcane, the black sands of Dieppe Bay, of the little church of Christchurch outside which his brother lay under a grey slab of stone were powerful enough to draw back the middle-aged man from the family life at Bedford with eight children and enough money to live on in reasonable comfort.[126]

Graham Greene's great-grandfather, Benjamin Greene, a Bury St Edmunds brewer, had acquired estates in St Kitts and Montserrat in the 1820s. He was an active supporter of the West India interest and through his newspaper, the *Bury and Suffolk Herald*, he engaged in acerbic polemics with Thomas Clarkson.[127] He received just over £4,000 in compensation.[128] His eldest son, Benjamin Buck Greene, was sent to St Kitts in 1829, followed by Charles in 1836 and William in 1838. The brothers managed the properties, which continued to be profitable by dint of extensive improvement, capital investment and injections of labour from England until the mid-1840s. Benjamin Buck Greene actively participated in the debates over the sugar duties but the family's business interests were moving elsewhere. He was later to become the governor of the Bank of England.

Graham Greene's identification with his grandfather was perhaps associated with his great-uncle's unsuitedness to a domesticated familial bourgeois life together with Graham's memories of the Caribbean. Greene's own powerful depictions in his fiction of the closing years of empire, disillusioned colonial officials and whisky-sodden priests may be read as one of the legacies of a long history of connection between metropolitan and colonial worlds, between slave-owners and those they enslaved. The descendants of the enslaved continue to experience across the generations a powerful connection with the traumas of their ancestors.[129] As the extent of the entanglements between black and white that Greene encountered – all those 'coloured Greenes'[130] in St Kitts – become ever more apparent, there may be space for a better understanding of the legacies of these histories into the present.

NOTES

Thanks to Cora Kaplan.
1 J. R. MacDonald, 'Scott, Michael (1789–1835), planter in Jamaica and writer', *ODNB*.
2 Michael Scott, *Tom Cringle's Log* (2 vols., Edinburgh, 1833; repr. Ithaca, 1999), pp. 126–7.
3 *Ibid.*, pp. 370–2.
4 Joseph Marryat, *Thoughts on the Abolition of the Slave Trade and Civilization of Africa* (London, 1816).
5 Florence Marryat, *Life and Letters of Captain Marryat, Vol. I* (2 vols., London, 1872), p. 82; Rachel Holmes, *The Hottentot Venus. The Life and Death of Saartji Baartman* (London, 2007).

6 Frederick Marryat, *Frank Mildmay or The Naval Officer* (London, 1829), p. 227; Frederick Marryat, *The King's Own* (London, 1830).

7 Marryat, *Life and Letters*, pp. 204–6.

8 Frederick Marryat, *Newton Forster, or the Merchant Service* (1832; repr. London, 1897), pp. 103, 117.

9 Frederick Marryat, 'The West Indian colonies in their state of transition from bad to worse', *Metropolitan Magazine* 8 (29) (1833), 88–100, at 100.

10 Archibald Alison, 'The West India question', *Blackwood's* 31 (191) (1832), 412–23, at 415, 419.

11 Michel-Rolphe Trouillot, *Silencing the Past. Power and the Production of History* (Boston, 1995).

12 Susanna Radstone and Bill Schwarz, 'Introduction: mapping memory', in Radstone and Schwarz (eds.), *Memory. Histories, Theories, Debates* (Fordham, NY, 2010), pp. 1–9.

13 See Stanley Cohen, *States of Denial. Knowing about Atrocities and Suffering* (Cambridge: 2001).

14 Michael Scott, *The Cruise of the Midge* (London, 1835), pp. 82–93.

15 T71/877 Antigua no. 35 (Mackinnon's Estate).

16 William Alexander Mackinnon, *History of Civilisation* (2 vols., London, 1846).

17 V. E. Chancellor, 'Slave-owner and anti-slaver: Henry Russell Vassall Fox, 3rd Lord Holland, 1800–1840', *Slavery & Abolition* 1 (3) (1980), 263–76. See also Catherine Hall, 'Troubling memories: nineteenth-century histories of the slave trade and slavery', *Transactions of the Royal Historical Society* 21 (2011), 147–69.

18 Abraham D. Kriegel, *The Holland House Diaries 1831–40: The Diary of Henry Richard Vassall Fox, Third Lord Holland, with Extracts from the Diary of Dr John Allen* (London, 1977), p. 269.

19 T71/871 Jamaica Westmoreland nos. 27, 30 and 31.

20 Henry Richard Vassall Lord Holland, *Memoirs of the Whig Party during My Time, Vol. II*, ed. Henry Edward Lord Holland (2 vols., London, 1854), p. 158.

21 Henry Richard Vassall Lord Holland, *Further Memoirs of the Whig Party 1807–1821 with Some Miscellaneous Reminiscences*, ed. Lord Stavordale (London, 1905), p. 195.

22 T71/892 St Vincent no. 458 (Bellevue).

23 Archibald Alison, *Some Account of my Life and Writings. An Autobiography, Vol. I* (2 vols., Edinburgh, 1883), p. 304.

24 Michael Michie, *An Enlightenment Tory in Victorian Scotland. The Career of Sir Archibald Alison* (East Lothian, 1997), p. 152.

25 Alison, *Some Account*, p. 120.

26 Benjamin Disraeli, *Coningsby, or the New Generation* (1844; repr. London, 1989), p. 151.

27 Alison, *Some Account*, p. 46.

28 Archibald Alison, *History of the French Revolution from 1789–1796, Vol. I* (10 vols., London 1833–42; repr. Paris, 1852), p. 30.

29 *Ibid.*, pp. 192–3.

30 Thomas Carlyle, *Occasional Discourse on the Negro Question* (London, 1853).

31 Archibald Alison, *History of Europe from the Fall of Napoleon in 1815 to the Accession of Louis Napoleon in 1852, Vol. V* (8 vols., Edinburgh, 1852–9), pp. 407–35.

32 Alison, *History, Vol. II*, p. 291; obituary of Alison, *Blackwood's* 102 (1867), 125–8.

33 See e.g. *The Times*, 19 August 1845, 9 November 1846, 17 November 1846. *The Times* provided employment for a significant number of West Indians and their descendants, including Mowbray Morris, the manager, who was the son of a Caribbean merchant and Thomas Chenery, also the son of a West India merchant who worked for the paper for years before succeeding Delane as editor. See p. 39 above.

34 George Webbe Dasent, *Annals of an Eventful Life, Vol. I* (3 vols., London, 1870), p. 35.

35 *Ibid.*, pp. 60–2, 74.

36 *Ibid.*, pp. 148, 191.

37 John Roche Dasent, *A West Indian Planter's Family. Its Rise and Fall* (London, 1914), p. 59.

38 T71/500 St Vincent nos. 485 (North Union) and 486 (South Union).

39 Dasent, *A West Indian Planter's Family*, p. 61.

40 *Ibid.*, p. 64.

41 John Kucich and Jenny Bourne Taylor, 'Introduction', in Kucich and Taylor (eds.), *The Nineteenth Century Novel 1820–1880* (Oxford, 2012), pp. xvii–xxx.

42 Cora Kaplan, 'Imagining empire: history, fantasy and literature', in Catherine Hall and Sonya O. Rose (eds.), *At Home with the Empire: Metropolitan Culture and the Imperial World* (Cambridge, 2006), pp. 192–211, at p. 192.

43 Fredrick Marryat, 'On novels and novel writing', *Metropolitan Magazine* 11 (42) (1834), 113–19.

44 Marryat, *Life and Letters, Vol. I*, pp. 104–5.

45 Tim Fulford, 'Romanticizing the empire: the naval heroes of Southey, Coleridge, Austen and Marryat', *Modern Language Quarterly* 60 (2) (1999), 161–96.

46 Patrick Brantlinger, *Rule of Darkness. British Literature and Imperialism 1830–1890* (Ithaca, NY, 1988). It was Brantlinger's chapter that first alerted me to Marryat. See also Louis J. Pascandarola, *'Puzzled Which to Choose'. Conflicting Socio-political Views in the Works of Captain Frederick Marryat* (New York, 1997). It is impossible to give a full account of Marryat's writing here.

47 Frederick Marryat, *Peter Simple* (1834; repr. London, 1939), p. 157.

48 Joseph Conrad, 'Tales of the sea', in *Notes on Life and Letters* (London, 1924), pp. 53–7, at p. 53.

49 T71/856 Jamaica St Mary no. 307 (Greenwood Estate); T71/880 Grenada nos. 683 (Mount Rodney Estate) and 762 (Balthazar Estate); T71/884 St Lucia nos. 329 (Mt Pleasant), 369A, 547 (Diamond), 760, 764, 775 (Anse Matriant), 800 (Vieux Fort) and 824A–E (Pointe Sable); T71/893 Trinidad nos. 643A–C and 697A & B; T71/894 Trinidad nos. 1235, 1245A (Mt Hope), 1781 (Reform), 1783 (Union Estate) and 1784 (Marabella Estate).

50 Marryat, *Life and Letters, Vol. II*, p. 157.

51 On the 'anti-slavery nation' see Richard Huzzey, *Freedom Burning. Anti-slavery and Empire in Victorian Britain* (Ithaca and London, 2012).
52 Marryat, *Peter Simple*, pp. 69–70, 420.
53 *Ibid.*, p. 261.
54 Frederick Marryat, *Mr Midshipman Easy* (1836; repr. London, 1896), p. 238.
55 *Ibid.*, p. 317.
56 Marryat, *Life and Letters, Vol. I*, p. 59.
57 Frederick Marryat, *A Diary in America, with Remarks on Its Institutions, Vol. I* (3 vols., London, 1839), p. 293.
58 Cited in Oliver Warner, *Captain Marryat. A Rediscovery* (London, 1953), p. 131.
59 Frederick Marryat, *Percival Keene* (London, 1842), pp. 130–9.
60 *Ibid.*, pp. 152, 158, 161.
61 Frederick Marryat, *Masterman Ready; or The Wreck of the Pacific* (London, 1841), p. 19.
62 *Ibid.*, pp. 174–7.
63 Cited in Warner, *Captain Marryat*, p. 141.
64 Frederick Marryat, *The Mission: or, Scenes in Africa, Vol. I* (2 vols., London, 1845), p. 51.
65 T71/853 Jamaica St Dorothy no. 2 (Lodge).
66 Theodora Elizabeth Lynch, *The Cotton-Tree: or Emily, the Little West Indian* (London, 1847), p. 1.
67 *Ibid.*, p. 14; Theodora Elizabeth Lynch, *The Family Sepulchre: A Tale of Jamaica* (London, 1848), pp. 8–9.
68 Theodora Elizabeth Lynch, *The Mountain Pastor* (London, 1852), p. 11; Lynch, *The Family Sepulchre*, p. 89.
69 Theodora Elizabeth Lynch, *Years Ago. A Tale of West Indian life in the Eighteenth Century* (London, 1865), p. 15.
70 Lynch, *The Mountain Pastor*, pp. 96, 106.
71 *Ibid*, p. 27.
72 T71/895 Barbados no. 104 (Mount Clapham).
73 Charles Kingsley, *His Letters and Memories of His Life, Vol. IV*, edited by his wife, (4 vols., London, 1901), p. 6 fn.
74 *Ibid.*, pp. 5–6.
75 James Anthony Froude, 'England's forgotten worthies', in *Essays in Literature and History* (London, 1906), pp. 34–80, at pp. 36–7.
76 *Ibid.*, pp. 47–8. On Froude see Theodore Koditschek, *Liberalism, Imperialism, and the Historical Imagination. Nineteenth-Century Visions of a Greater Britain* (Cambridge, 2011), pp. 151–205.
77 Charles Kingsley, *Westward Ho!* (1855; repr. London, 1906), p. 19. Kingsley can only be dealt with in a very brief fashion in this chapter. For a recent biography see J. M. I. Klaver, *The Apostle of the Flesh. A Critical Life of Charles Kingsley* (Leiden, 2006).
78 Simon Gikandi, *Maps of Englishness. Writing Identity in the Culture of Colonialism* (New York, 1996), pp. 97–103.
79 Kingsley, *Westward Ho!*, p. 10.
80 *Ibid.*, p. 285.

81 *Ibid.*, pp. 379, 381.

82 *Ibid.*, p. 611.

83 Kingsley, *Letters and Memories, Vol. II*, p. 265.

84 Kingsley, *Letters and Memories, Vol. III*, pp. 248–9.

85 See the 'imperial legacies' strand of the Legacies of British Slave-ownership database. For a discussion of the connections between slave-owners and the new settlers of the colonies of white settlement see Catherine Hall, 'The slave-owner and the settler', in Jane Carey and Jane Lydon (eds.), *Indigenous Networks: Mobility, Connections and Exchange* (London, 2014).

86 John Barnes, *Henry Kingsley and Colonial Fiction* (Melbourne, 1971), p. 1.

87 Henry Kingsley, *The Recollections of Geoffrey Hamlyn* (London, 1859), pp. 19, 149.

88 Jessie Mitchell, '"The galling yoke of slavery": race and separation in colonial Port Philip', *Journal of Australian Studies* 33 (2) (2009), 125–37.

89 Henry Kingsley, *The Hillyars and the Burtons. A Tale of Two Families* (London, 1865), p. 361.

90 Henry Kingsley, 'Eyre, the South-Australian explorer', *Macmillan's Magazine* (October 1865), 501–10.

91 S. M. Ellis, *Henry Kingsley 1830–1876. Towards a Vindication* (London, 1931), pp. 194–9.

92 Kingsley, 'Eyre, the South-Australian explorer'.

93 *Ibid.*

94 Cited in William H. Scheuerle, *The Neglected Brother. A Study of Henry Kingsley* (Talahassee, FL, 1971), p. 95.

95 Patrick Brantlinger, *Dark Vanishings. Discourse on the Extinction of Primitive Races, 1800–1930* (Ithaca, 2003), pp. 189–90.

96 Gikandi, *Maps of Englishness*, p. 92.

97 On Phillippo see Catherine Hall, *Civilising Subjects. Metropole and Colony in the English Imagination, 1830–1867* (Cambridge, 2002), ch. 3.

98 Theodora Elizabeth Lynch, *The Wonders of the West Indies* (London, 1856), pp. i–ii.

99 *Ibid.*, pp. 4, 12, 83, 98, 163.

100 On Trollope see Gikandi, *Maps of Englishness*, pp. 91–114; Hall, *Civilising Subjects*, pp. 209–10, 216–21.

101 Gikandi, *Maps of Englishness*, pp. 97–116.

102 Charles Kingsley, *At Last. A Christmas in the West Indies, Vol. II* (2 vols., London, 1871), pp. 37–9; Klaver, *The Apostle of the Flesh*, p. 610.

103 Kingsley, *At Last, Vol. I*, pp. 73–4.

104 *Ibid.*, p. 39.

105 *Ibid.*, p. 57.

106 Kingsley, *At Last, Vol. II*, pp. 154–5.

107 Kingsley, *Letters and Memories, Vol. IV*, p. 49.

108 Kingsley, *Letters and Memories, Vol. I*, p. 205.

109 For a longer account see Hall, 'Troubling memories'.

110 John Charlton, 'Who was John Graham-Clarke 1736–1818', unpublished paper (2010). Thanks to John Charlton.

111 On the family history see Jeanette Marks, *The Family of the Barrett: A Colonial Romance* (New York, 1938); R. A. Barrett, *The Barretts of Jamaica: The Family*

of *Elizabeth Barrett Browning* (Winfield, KS, 2000), p. 25; Mary Tripsack, T71/873 Jamaica St James nos. 258 (Cottage) and 656 (Cinnamon Hill).

112 Elizabeth Barrett Moulton Barrett (EBMB) to Julia Martin, 27 May 1833, Philip Kelly and Ronald Hudson (eds.), *The Brownings' Correspondence, Vol. III* (18 vols., Winfield, KS, 1984–2010), p. 81.

113 EBMB to Julia Martin, 7 September 1833, *ibid.*, p. 86.

114 T71/ 874 Jamaica Trelawney nos. 208 (Cambridge) and 637 (Oxford); T71/857 Jamaica St Ann no. 632 (Retreat Pen).

115 EBMB to Lady Margaret Cocks, 15 November 1833, 14 September 1834, Kelly and Hudson, *The Brownings' Correspondence, Vol. III*, pp. 101, 328.

116 T71/874 Jamaica Trelawney nos. 192 (Chester Estate) and 193 (Chester Estate).

117 Elizabeth Barrett Browning, 'The Runaway Slave at Pilgrim's Point', in *Aurora Leigh and Other Poems* (London, 1978), pp. 392–402.

118 EBMB to Hugh Stuart Boyd, 21 December 1846, Kelly and Hudson, *The Brownings' Correspondence, Vol. XIV*, p. 86.

119 EBMB to Mary Mitford Russell, 8 February 1847, *ibid.*, p. 117.

120 Cora Kaplan argues that shifting the scene to US slavery allowed Barrett Browning to use elaborate, melodramatic and violent scenarios – gang rape and child murder – that she simply could not use in a West Indian setting without implicating her family; Cora Kaplan '"I am black": aesthetics, race and politics in women's anti-slavery writing from Phyllis Wheatley to Elizabeth Barrett Browning', unpublished paper (2011).

121 Marjorie Stone, 'Elizabeth Barrett Browning and the Garrisonians: "The Runaway Slave at Pilgrim's Point", the Boston Female Anti-Slavery Society and abolitionist discourse in the *Liberty Bell*', in Alison Chapman (ed.), *Victorian Women Poets* (Cambridge, 2003), pp. 33–56.

122 Kaplan, '"I am black"'.

123 EBMB to Robert Browning, 20 December 1845, Barrett, *The Barretts of Jamaica*, p. 64.

124 Marks, *The Family of the Barrett*, p. 628.

125 Cited in Richard G. Wilson, *Greene King. A Business and Family History* (London, 1983), p. 48.

126 Graham Greene, *A Sort of Life* (Harmondsworth, 1972), p. 69.

127 For the complex business history see Wilson, *Greene King*.

128 T71/888 Montserrat no. 139, T71/879 St Kitts nos. 561 (Turtle Island) and 696 (Phillips).

129 See e.g. Saidiya Hartman, *Lose Your Mother. A Journey along the Atlantic Slave Route* (New York, 2007).

130 Greene, *A Sort of Life*, p. 71.

6 Transforming capital: slavery, family, commerce and the making of the Hibbert family

Katie Donington

Introduction

This chapter presents a case study that demonstrates the potential for the deployment of both our empirical data and integrative conceptual frameworks to explore the original accumulation and subsequent continuity of wealth and status from slavery. Using the research strands that have underpinned the overall project, this chapter examines the political, social, cultural, financial, imperial and physical legacies established by the Hibbert family following their involvement with the slavery business. The Hibbert family story charts the transgenerational transformation of capital from property in commodities to property in people and finally to investment in land, political position and cultural capital. From mercantile beginnings through to colonial plantation and finally metropolitan-land and country-house ownership, the narrative charts the movement of capital from the instability of merchant venture into investment in traditional forms of metropolitan property, thus securing for the Hibberts a lasting position – that is still maintained today – within Britain's aristocratic elite through marriage into the Holland family.

The history of the Hibbert family during the period is one in which the entanglement of metropole with colony is a central theme. Not only were the family involved in the movement of goods and people across the globe but also, more intimately, they themselves were part of a continuous ocean-borne traffic as various members supplied the personnel required for a successful colonial enterprise. The wealth generated through participation in the slavery system enabled the Hibberts to return to the imperial centre, positioning themselves within the social, political and cultural sphere of the landed classes. The sites in which they were located connect the various industries involved in making slavery work. The geographic reach of the Hibbert business network – from Manchester and Liverpool to Kingston and finally London – paralleled developments within the structure of the wider slave-economy. As they reaped the rewards of their colonial ventures and returned to England, they spread away from the metropolitan commercial centres associated with transatlantic trade into the genteel surroundings of the countryside of Cheshire, Buckinghamshire and Hertfordshire.

Using the profits accrued from the very highest levels of mercantile trading both in and with the West Indies, they began to exert their influence on their surroundings. They invested in property in both England and Jamaica and set about improving, expanding and remodelling it. They filled their houses with art, books and furniture that conformed to the dictates of fashionable taste, allowing them to participate in the culture of conspicuous consumption. As a dissenting family they were debarred from formal political power, although one of their number – George (1757–1837) – publicly adhered to the Anglican faith, enabling him to enter Parliament. As an alternative to formal political power, they adopted positions of civic power, becoming church trustees and school governors and serving on the judiciary and as high sheriffs. They used their wealth to support charities and invested in philanthropic institutions, helping to create legacies that befitted their reputation and status. The children of this generation of Hibberts would be schooled in the best institutions in England. Their marriages would seal the family transformation from merchants to gentry and even aristocracy, although for the younger Hibbert sons the commercial world continued to provide a living.

When the campaign to abolish the slave-trade and later slavery mobilised they were at the forefront of slavery's defence. Three generations of members of the Hibbert firm were involved with the Society of West India Planters and Merchants (SWIPM). They gave evidence before the select committee in 1790, presented petitions, published pamphlets, wrote to newspapers and gave speeches to Parliament. In this way they helped to constitute and disseminate anti-abolition discourse. From 1790 onwards, George (1757–1837), as the most politically powerful of the group, was an advocate of compensation. This public rhetoric belied a private acknowledgement by the 1820s that slavery would inevitably come to an end. This realisation engendered a growing interest in expanding the family's portfolio. The Hibberts championed several early railway schemes, although not all of them came to fruition. They also became involved with burgeoning areas of finance capitalism and investment in both maritime and life insurance companies. At the ending of slavery in the Caribbean, Nicholas Draper has estimated that the family were awarded £103,000 in compensation claimed either as outright owners of enslaved people or as creditors.[1]

The Hibbert family experience is not representative of all those who claimed ownership in people. As the Legacies of British Slave-ownership database demonstrates, ownership could take various forms, was of varying intensity and infiltrated a wide cross-section of metropolitan society. Instead the Hibberts are an example of the merchant–planter elite: a family who were able to exploit and profit from every stage of the processes necessary for the slave-economy to work. They were able to convert their identification as both merchants and colonial rentiers into positions of power within the metropole. This transformation was never complete; as with the younger sons of many of the landed gentry who did not inherit country houses or large sums of capital, some members continued to work for their livings. They did this through the commercial continuity offered by involvement in the family merchant house as well as expanding that interest to take advantage of new investment opportunities.

This chapter will begin by outlining the foundation of the Hibberts' commercial interests. It will break down the establishment of their colonial business empire geographically, starting in Manchester, then moving to Jamaica and finally London. It will consider the roles of family, marriage and religion in the constitution of commercial networks, giving an impression of the various interconnections that allowed the Hibberts to flourish. It will give details of the Hibberts' involvement in the campaign to secure compensation and which of them received it. It will then consider their influence on the metropole by outlining some of their activities within a series of distinct spheres: town- and country-house ownership, cultural consumption, philanthropy and charity, political and civic power, and commercial investment. It will examine the next generation of Hibberts, the marriages they made and their subsequent positions in society. The chapter will conclude with some thoughts on what kinds of legacies the Hibbert family left behind and the work that has been done to tie these legacies to the history of slave-ownership. In assembling a survey of data related to the Hibbert family, this chapter is designed to demonstrate some of the ways in which the profits and power accrued from slave-based wealth infiltrated British society in complex and varied forms, not only touching the lives of those who benefited directly from slave-ownership but also affecting those for whom slavery appeared a distant and disconnected phenomenon.

The Hibberts in Manchester

The Hibbert family formed part of a network of wealthy dissenting merchants who spread across Manchester, Liverpool, Leeds and their rural environs. Dissenting merchant communities were close knit; marriage, religion and trade were intimately entwined. Up until the repeal of the Test Acts in 1828, dissenters suffered under discriminatory legislation.

Barred from political and educational institutions that might have fostered ambitions towards power, individuals from the dissenting community found different ways of securing status. Commerce represented an alternative path to wealth and influence; using dissenting networks meant that wealth circulated within the community. Dissenters fostered these links using the twin virtues of respectability and trust to ensure the integrity of their social and economic relationships. The *Memorials of a Dissenting Chapel* tells the history of the Cross Street Chapel in Manchester. Its 'founders and worthies' were dominated by men involved in commerce and manufacturing. Many of the names to whom the author attributed 'the rise of Non-Conformity in Manchester' – the Hibberts, Touchets, Diggles, Bayleys, Philips and Robinsons – were related to one another through the interlocking ties of kinship and commerce.[2] In his discussion of Manchester's role in the slave-economy, Eric Williams named some of the individuals above, although he did not outline a specific network.[3] Marriage played a central role in forming these relations, with women acting as the conduits for commerce, bringing with them important connections. This was certainly the case for the Hibberts. For example, Sarah Hibbert married Thomas Diggles of Booth Hall in 1763. The Diggles, like the Hibberts, were involved in both the African and West Indian trades; as Eric Williams has stated, 'Robert Diggles, African slave trader of Liverpool, was the son of a Manchester linen draper and the brother of another.'[4] Robert was the uncle of Thomas, and was documented as a partner in an Africa ship that delivered cotton to Liverpool in 1716.[5] He was also a trustee of the Cross Street Chapel, as were three generations of the Hibbert men.

Manchester had a key role to play in the maintenance of the slave-economy. Finished cotton pieces were particularly in demand in the Guinea trade, as it was known. It was one of a number of desirable commodities used in the slave-trade on the coast of West Africa. Raw cotton produced by enslaved workers in both America and, more substantially, the Caribbean was then shipped back to the port at Liverpool for processing in Lancashire. Manchester's proximity to Liverpool and its port made the area into one of slavery's hinterlands. The Hibberts 'at one time supplied check and imitations of Indian goods to the African Company for the slave trade'.[6] As cotton manufacturers during the period of the traditional cottage industry of the north, the Hibberts' role involved 'organising and financing the separate stages, procuring the raw wool, linen or cotton, then delivering it to the cottagers' and finally collecting and warehousing the finished article ready for delivery to Liverpool and finally shipment to Africa.[7] The trade required a good knowledge of African tastes; specific colours and patterns were requested by ships' captains who knew the market through their experiences of trading in Africa, with bright colours and checks particularly in demand. In a letter of 1765 to the Messrs Hibbert of Manchester, the African Company asked that greens and yellows be avoided when producing cloth for the Africa trade.[8]

The Hibberts in Jamaica

In the *Memorials of a Dissenting Chapel*, the first Robert Hibbert (1684–1762) was listed as a 'linen draper'. The description of his sons – Robert (1717–84) and Thomas (1710–80) – indicated a geographic expansion of their commercial interests; 'Robert ... was a West Indian merchant, and his elder brother, Thomas, resided the greater part of his life in Jamaica, superintending estates which the family had acquired.'[9] In 1734 Thomas arrived in Jamaica and like many before him he settled in Kingston. During the eighteenth century Kingston was 'the leading metropolis of the British West Indies' and 'was inferior in population only to Havana in the Spanish Caribbean and to Philadelphia and New York in British North America'.[10] Dominated by its vast natural harbour, Kingston was by far the most important port on the island; Burnard and Morgan have estimated that, of the Guinea ships 'whose disembarkation point is known, eighty seven percent landed at Kingston'.[11] Slave factors purchased the enslaved from the ships themselves; if they were large-scale merchants they would buy in large lots, as the 'economies of scale ensured that much of the slave trade was concentrated in relatively few hands'.[12] The investors would give instruction to their ship's captains, who then agreed a bonding contract for the local factor to sell the slaves for no less than a premium price agreed beforehand. As Richard Pares has explained, 'In these cases the factor insensibly became the real purchaser of the slaves: he paid the limit demanded by the owners, resold the slaves to the planters for payment in six, nine or twelve months, and compensated himself – indeed, made his fortune – out of the difference between the cash price and the credit price.'[13]

Thomas had several commercial partners over the years. As an indication of the scale at which Thomas was trading, in partnership with Samuel Jackson, he acted as a factor for sixty-one ships over a ten-year period between 1764 and 1774, selling 16,254 enslaved people.[14] The partnership was successful enough for the firm to open 'a branch house (Barnard & Montague) at Montego Bay'.[15] Trevor Burnard has argued that the lending of money by Kingston merchants is an undervalued part of the plantation economy.[16] He has suggested that a better understanding of the internal credit system in the West Indies would add a further dimension to the discussion about the relationship between merchants and planters that both Richard Pares and more recently Simon D. Smith have explored.[17] Basing his estimate on the estate inventories left by mercantile men of a similar standing in Kingston, he has stated that debts owed to Thomas could well have reached up to £250,000. In evidence given by Hercules Ross to the parliamentary select committee in 1791, Ross spoke of 'the late Mr. Thomas Hibbert, who had for forty or fifty years before been the most eminent Guinea factor in Kingston, and a most respectable character'.[18]

Thomas compounded his economic influence with the acquisition of political and civic power, acting as an assistant judge of the Grand Court and a justice of the peace by 1751. He represented both St George and Portland before becoming Speaker of the House of Assembly in 1756.[19] Thomas' magnificent town house, built in 1755 and situated on Duke Street, was the seat of the Jamaica Assembly following the temporary move of the capital from Spanish Town to Kingston. Not content with success as a merchant, in the early 1760s Thomas invested in a large tract of land in the parish of what is now St Mary's for the purposes of developing his own sugar plantation – Aqualta Vale. In later years his nephew Robert (1750–1835) invested £14,501 in the dilapidated property adjacent to Aqualta Vale – the estate formerly owned by William Beckford Ellis Esq.[20] The Hibberts transformed the usage of the estate, replacing the coffee with a large cattle-breeding pen. The scale of the plantation is indicated by the size of the workforce, which by 1825 had reached 896 enslaved people.[21] This accumulation of economic, political and social power as well as an investment in land ownership would be repeated by the Hibberts both at home and in the colony.

With Thomas' success began a period in which the Hibberts, alongside their various partners, were a major force in Kingston's mercantile trade. His brother John (1732–69) was sent to join him in 1754, with the three eldest sons of their brother Robert (1717–84) – Thomas (1744–1819), John (1748–70) and Robert (1750–1835) – following in 1766, 1769 and 1772. Thomas (1710–80) himself never had any legitimate heirs, although he fathered three daughters with a free woman of colour, Charity Harry, whom he described euphemistically as his 'housekeeper' in his will.[22] Thomas was not alone in this practice – a number of the Hibbert men had 'outside' families. Thomas' daughter Jane Harry[23] is the best documented of these offspring; others are mentioned in wills and in the diaries kept by Thomas' nephew Robert (1750–1835).[24] John (1732–69) married Janet Gordon in 1760; she was part of a Scottish family that had become prominent within the legal profession in Jamaica with several members acting as attorney general

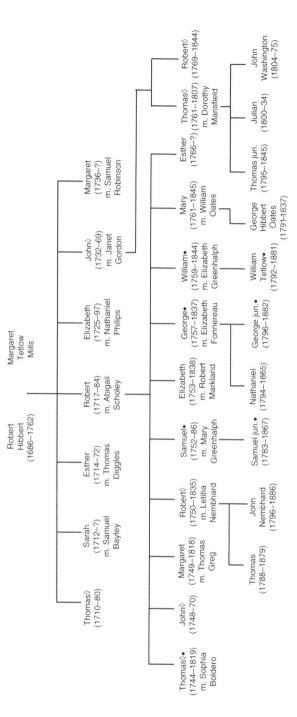

Figure 6.1 Details from the Hibbert family tree.
◊ denotes members of the Jamaica merchant house.
● denotes members of the London merchant house.

and taking seats in the House of Assembly. Their son Thomas (1761–1807), alongside his cousins from England, would go on to inherit their uncle Thomas' vast wealth, his estate and his slave-factorage business. Thomas' nephews – Thomas (1744–1819) and Robert (1750–1835) – worked within the family counting house and married into the Boldero London banking and Nembhard Jamaica planter families respectively. This consolidated their ties within both the capital's mercantile sphere and the colony's landed classes. The next generation of Hibbert men followed the pattern set by their uncle, becoming judges and members of the Chamber of Commerce and the House of Assembly. Involvement in the Assembly gave the Hibberts a voice within planter-dominated island politics, enabling them to represent both their own and the wider mercantile interest. It afforded them access to vital information regarding trade, defence, the convoy system and the mail packets, all of which were important in giving them the edge over their less-well-connected competitors. With success came expansion; having secured the Hibberts' commercial houses in Jamaica, the family looked to move into the lucrative sugar trade.

The Hibberts in London

London had always been important to the colonial slave-economy and by the third quarter of the eighteenth century it had become the centre of both finance and distribution for the sugar industry. As Richard Sheridan noted, 'Here was a large and growing market for sugar; an important source of plantation supplies; a financial, exchange and shipping centre; and the seat of imperial government.'[25] With planters consigning their sugar to the London merchant houses, the Hibberts saw an opportunity to share in the profits that were flowing into the City of London from the colonies. In 1770 Thomas (1710–80) wrote to his Jamaica correspondent and brother-in-law Nathaniel Phillips informing him of a new co-partnership between his nephew Thomas (1744–1819) and the London merchants John Purrier and Thomas Horton.[26] With Thomas (1744–1819) and his brother Robert (1750–1835) already established in Jamaica, the partnership used the relationships garnered through their uncle's commercial houses to move into plantation supply, sugar commission and finance credit. Over the years the Hibberts' partnerships went through various reconfigurations including Hibbert, Purrier & Horton (1772–81), Hibbert, Fuhr & Hibbert (1791–9), Hibbert, Fuhr & Co. (1800–2), Hibbert, Fuhr & Purrier (1802–18), Geo. Rob. Wm Hibbert (1804–5), Geo. Rob. Wm & Sam. Hibbert (1811–18), G. W. S. Hibbert & Co. (1820–38) and Hibbert & Co.(1839–63).[27] The personnel was made up of trusted business associates including John Purrier, his son John Vincent Purrier, Thomas Horton and Edward Fuhr. As with the firm in Jamaica, close family members were the cornerstone of the merchant house; brothers Thomas (1744–1819), Samuel (1752–86), George (1757–1837) and William (1759–1844), Samuel's son Samuel junior (1783–1867), George's son George junior (1796–1882) and William's son William Tetlow (1792–1881) all operated at different times within the various co-partnerships.

The London firm connected the Hibberts' interests in Manchester and Kingston, allowing bills from Jamaica to be drawn on the London house. In 1802 this connection seems to have dissipated somewhat with George (1757–1837) complaining that 'the Manchester business by their abruptly becoming merchant importers of their own account is greatly changed from what it was in my Father's day and cannot be followed up without great energies'.[28] Family also played a key role outside the co-partnership, with the Hibberts working closely with their brother-in-law Thomas Greg (1752–1832), a member of Lloyd's, to provide insurance for their correspondents. Thomas' nephew Robert Greg wrote of his uncle that

by sundry letters he appears to have started on his own account as Insurance Broker, & Underwriter in 1772. He commenced with many good connections, his Father's House of Thos & John Greg of Belfast, Robt & Nath'l Hyde of Manchester, & Philips, Hibberts & others ... The Business was first carried out in Lloyds Coffee House, then Old Bethlehem Broad St, & finally Warnford Court, Threadneedle Street.[29]

The Philips were connected to the Hibberts through marriage, the bonds of matrimony and kin providing a steady commerce between the families. The stability of the firm was one of its main strengths and undoubtedly influenced the calibre of its correspondents, who were drawn from the elite of Jamaica's plantocracy and included both Simon Taylor and John Tharp. By 1823 the scale of the Hibberts' sugar trading was vast; George (1757–1837) claimed that the family had concerns in 1,600 hogsheads brought into the Port of London that year.[30]

Merchant houses involved in transatlantic trade had to be prepared to fulfil a number of functions for their clients. They arranged for the shipping, insurance, warehousing, porterage, lighter wharfage and distribution of their goods – all of which they took a healthy commission from. Their expert knowledge of the London sugar markets was deployed to get the best value for their customers, which sometimes meant holding onto the sugar until it could achieve a better price. They acted as financiers, offering their correspondents credit, paying their debts and dispensing allowances to their family members on their accounts. They sourced plantation supplies from 'Negro clothes' to soap, candles and cooking utensils. They provided journals, ledgers and paper for book-keeping on the estates. They sourced pepper, cinnamon, mustard and cloves to flavour their correspondents' food, and wine, madeira, port and brandy to wash it down with. If their correspondents sent their children back to Britain, they sometimes acted as guardians and were involved in arranging their schooling. They were a source of information for their clients on a variety of topics from trade and politics to intimate family matters. The Hibbert counting house undertook all these activities and more.

The Hibberts eventually came to own their own ships and private quays. As well as acting as a convenient system of transatlantic transport for the Hibberts and their friends, this provided both themselves and their clients with a greater degree of control over the movement of produce and afforded a greater protection against theft when the vessels arrived in the Port of London. In evidence given to a select committee in 1823, George (1757–1837) stated that he had personally owned or held a part share in eight ships in the West India trade.[31] The Hibberts' ships were famed for the quality of their captains, a number of whom were Brethren of Trinity House. The speed of their ships was also noted – the vessel *Hibberts* broke a record in 1785 by sailing from the Downs to Port Royal in thirty-five to thirty-eight days.[32] In 1793 George became involved in the plan to build closed docks for the West India trade. The West India Docks were constructed on the Isle of Dogs and opened for business in 1802. George stated that he had invested £2,000 and acted as chairman of the West India Dock Company eight times between 1799 and 1815.[33] Two more Hibberts – Thomas and Robert – were also listed as investors. The West India Dock Act of 1799 made it compulsory for ships in the West India trade to use the new facilities. The government awarded compensation to those affected by the Act, including the Hibberts, who owned Wiggan's Quay. The Hibberts received £33,408 in compensation.[34] On top of this lump sum of capital, as both an investor in and director of the company, George was paid dividends and could exert a degree of control over the practical running of the docks; for example, he and the Court of Directors were able to set the rates for using the dock facilities.

Like the Hibberts in Jamaica, this new generation of London-based Hibberts sought to build on their economic position with political and civic representation. George (1757–1837) was the most powerful of the Hibberts in the metropole. He was the younger brother of the three Manchester Hibberts who had been sent to work for their uncle Thomas (1710–80) in Jamaica. He arrived in London in 1781 and took his place as a junior member of the firm Hibbert, Purrier and Horton. By 1782 his name had begun to appear in the minute book of the SWIPM. This organisation was the centre of the West India interest in London and was attended by the elite of planter and merchant circles. The SWIPM was effectively a lobby group; it formulated the interests' position on matters affecting trade such as freight rates, duties, the organisation of convoys, the timing of the mail packets and later in defence of the slave-trade and slavery. George was a regular attendee, as were his brothers Thomas (1744–1819), Robert (1750–1835) and William (1760–1844), and later his nephews Samuel junior (1783–1867) and William Tetlow (1792–1881), and his sons Nathaniel (1794–1865) and George junior (1796–1882).

The SWIPM was dominated by planters and merchants connected to Jamaica, and given the Hibberts' predominance there George rapidly became a useful and active member of the group.[35] By 1798 George had begun to chair the SWIPM's meetings, acting in place of the permanent chair as a trusted stand-in. George's importance to the SWIPM can be seen in his election to various committees, particularly the slave-trade sub-committee of which he became a member in 1792. The SWIPM regularly sent deputations to the government to lobby on the issues affecting the West India trade. George was routinely selected to make a representation, so much so that it was said that 'Mr Pitt was accustomed to say, that "he never got so clear a view of the objects of a Deputation, as when he saw Mr. George Hibbert at the head of it"'.[36] This gave him access to privileged information and allowed him to have an influence over important practicalities of trade such as when a convoy might leave during times of war, or the delay of the mail packet. These were not decisions he alone made but he together with the elite members of the SWIPM could ensure that their interests, and those of their correspondents, were best served. In 1806 he became MP for Seaford. From this national platform he made three speeches in defence of the slave-trade that were later published by the SWIPM, outlining the West India position and making public calls for compensation for those planters and merchants who would be affected by the loss of their source of labour.[37] Hibbert's success was crowned in 1812 when he was elected Agent for Jamaica, a position he maintained until 1830, when ill health and old age finally necessitated his retirement from public life.

The Hibberts and compensation

George (1757–1837) first made a public argument for compensation in 1790, when alongside his brother Robert (1750–1835) he was called to give evidence to the select committee looking into the slave-trade. He suggested that the £70 million invested by merchants and planters in the plantation economy would be irredeemably lost were the source of labour and therefore cultivation to be brought to halt.[38] In a speech to Parliament in 1807 he made the case for the payment of compensation using the example of the West India Dock Act, from which he himself had benefited. He argued that 'if the spirit of reform be consistent' then those whose property would be interfered with through the abolition of the slave-trade should likewise be compensated.[39] Following the abolition of the slave-trade in 1807 and the amelioration campaign, it became clear that the institution of slavery would be the abolitionists' next target. George consistently argued that both the slave-trade and slave-ownership had been sanctioned and legislated for by the British Parliament, leading to heavy investment in the plantation complex by both metropolitan merchants and colonial planters. He demanded a fair and equitable settlement to end the practice of property in people. In 1818 he wrote to Earl Bathurst, the Secretary of State for War and the Colonies, stating, 'By [British] Law Slaves are considered as Property, they are not distinguished from ordinary articles of Merchandize.'[40] He argued that people of respectable position were maintained by the system of slavery; they therefore deserved compensation for the dismantling of their economic stability. In 1827 Robert Wilmot Horton, the colonial secretary, wrote to George about the practicality of slave compensation, to which George replied, 'An Appraiser may measure a Man & ascertain his strength – but it is impossible that he could adequately estimate the importance of the Man in every relation to the Plantation.'[41] In other words, it was the incalculable value of the system of slavery and not the actual individual slave that should be taken into consideration when calculating compensation.

Given the level of involvement the Hibberts had with the West India trade, it is unsurprising they lobbied so hard for the payment of compensation. The database shows that eleven Hibberts were awarded compensation totalling £103,000: Robert (1750–1835), George (1757–1837), William (1759–1844), Robert junior (1769–1849), Samuel junior (1783–1867), Thomas (1788–1879), Thomas junior (1795–1845), William Tetlow (1792–1881), George junior (1796–1882), John Nembhard (1796–1886) and John Washington (1804–75). Robert junior, William, his son William Tetlow, George, his son George junior and George's son-in-law Samuel junior were all based in London and were involved with the merchant house. Thomas and John Nembhard were the sons of Robert Hibbert (1750–1835) and

Jamaica-born Letitia Nembhard. Thomas junior and John Washington
were the sons of Jamaica-born Thomas (1761–1807) and Dorothy
Mansfield. The Hibberts made claims as trustees, owners-in-fee, mortgagees, judgement creditors, devisees in trust and executors. Their
ownership of slaves was based both on plantation ownership and on
the complex system of credit relationships that characterised the West
India trade. George died in 1837, before the compensation process
could be completed. He did, however, recognise that he would be a
significant recipient (he received £63,000) and therefore made provisions in his will: 'My estates in Jamaica, compensation monies, stock,
leaseholds, dock, canal and other shares, and all residue of personal
est. to my Ex'ors on trust to sell.'[42] By the time compensation was
awarded, the Hibberts had already secured a place for themselves in
British society. The compensation money was no doubt of practical
use to the Hibberts but more than that it confirmed them in their
claims to respectability. It was an admission by the government that
George's arguments concerning the legitimacy of property in people
were held to be true. This allowed those who had been involved with
slavery to rebuild their tarnished reputation and reinvent themselves
ready for the dawning of a new age of Victorian imperial Britain.

The Hibbert family legacies

Over the course of three generations the Hibberts had transformed
themselves from their Manchester cotton origins through their involvement with colonial slavery. Their success can be traced in the types
of marital alliances they formed. The first generation married into the
dissenting mercantile families of the north, the second made matches
within the commercial and banking families of London and the plantocracy in Jamaica, and by the third generation the Hibbert children
were marrying into the English aristocracy and gentry. David Hancock's
detailed study of merchant men closely matches the Hibbert family's
trajectory: the amassing of a commercial fortune and its subsequent
deployment to secure social status.[43] Hancock identified key activities
that were seen as vital in the process of becoming what he termed a
gentleman improver. Among these were the acquisition of land and
an attendant interest in its improvement and cultivation, public service through political engagement, active philanthropy, the building
and renovation of country houses and gardens, and participation in
the culture of conspicuous consumption. The Hibberts enthusiastic-
ally adopted these practices, moulding themselves in the image of the
respectable metropolitan gentleman.

At home with the Hibberts: land, property and cultural capital

The Hibberts' rise can be charted through their appearance in the various London directories. Up until the 1790s they were only listed in the commercial handbooks, but by 1796 Thomas' (1744–1819) address at 38 Weymouth Street could be found in *Boyle's Court Guide: The Fashionable Court Guide or Town Visiting Directory*. Over the course of the next thirty years an increasing number of Hibberts were included in this type of publication so that by 1830 *The Royal Blue Book. Fashionable Directory for 1830; containing the Town and Country Residences of the Nobility and the Gentry* listed seven Hibberts within its pages: 'George Hibbert Esq. FRS. FSA. FLS. 38 Portland Place', 'George Hibbert Esq. Junior, 4L Albany', 'John Hibbert Esq., 47 Great Ormond Street', 'Nathaniel Hibbert Esq., 10 King's Bench Walk, Temple', 'Samuel Hibbert Esq., 78 Harley Street', 'Thomas Hibbert Esq., 16 Berkeley Street, Portman Square' and 'William T. Hibbert, 36 Upper Harley Street'. Clustered around central London, these residences allowed the Hibberts access to the social, political, cultural and economic heart of the imperial centre. The possession or rent of a fashionable London property was essential for a family like the Hibberts. Close to the City of London, Parliament and the social entertainments of the season, their residences in the capital were an important marker of status. The newly developed Marylebone area, including the Portland Estate, was popular with absentee West Indian proprietors, giving the Hibberts an instant network for social and business calling.

Interestingly, between 1796 and 1820 George Hibbert's main London residence was on Clapham Common Northside. Inhabited by the mercantile and banking classes, Clapham was also the home of the Evangelical anti-slavery sect, known afterwards as the Saints. Its residents included William Wilberforce, Zachary Macaulay, the Thorntons and James Stephens. Both the Hibberts and the Saints worshipped at Holy Trinity Church, with George paying for eleven seats for the family and their servants.[44] He was included in a list of trustees and was involved in the establishment of a Chapel of Rest located at St Paul's Clapham, where his two-year-old son George was interred after his death in 1795.

The house itself was described in detail in a sales advert of 1820.[45] The description captures vividly the lifestyle that the Hibberts had grown accustomed to. The residence is described as a 'Capacious Family House, Pleasure-Grounds, extensive Hot-Houses, PADDOCK, and LAND.' The land consisted of eleven acres and stretched back towards

Figure 6.2 'St Paul's Church, Clapham. The chest tomb in the foreground contains the remains of George's son and his brother William (1759–1844). Boys from Sierra Leone who had travelled to Zachary Macaulay's African Institution were also buried in this cemetery, although the sites of their graves are now unknown.

the Wandsworth Road. In 1795 it was recorded that 'Mr. Hibbert is allowed to fence in a piece of ground from the Common, opposite his house, and to plant trees for the ornament of the Common.'[46] The acquisition of such prime land so close to Holy Trinity Church, the worship place of the Evangelical anti-slavery Clapham sect, certainly must have caused George to make an impression on his neighbours. The interior of the house was conjured up in lavish terms by the Reverend Thomas Dibdin, who was a friend and a fellow Roxburghe Club member. In his *Bibliographical Decameron* he wrote about Hibbert using the name Honorio and stated that 'The mansion of Honorio is both capacious and richly furnished. And his *Albanos*, his *Annibal Caraccis*, *Murillos*, *Berghems*, *Bassans*, and *Cuyps*! All these – in a Palladio-proportioned room, some twenty-five feet in height – are the rich accompaniment of his stained glass book-vistos, and scattered and classically-embellished libraries.'[47]

The house was laden with cultural treasures, including George's famed library, his print and art collection and a specially painted frieze that had been executed by Henry Howard. George's garden at Clapham was considered to rival Kew in the variety of specimens that could be found growing there.[48] George was not the only Hibbert to settle in Clapham; his brother William (1759–1844) and his brother Samuel's widow Mary and their families also lived in the area. Thus it is possible to see the ways in which slave-based wealth had an impact even upon the heartland of the abolitionist movement – Clapham Common.

'The Cit's country box':[49] the Hibberts and country-house ownership

Away from the bustle of London and Manchester, the Hibberts had purchased and inherited land and estates in the surrounding countryside, allowing them to adopt a lifestyle of country gentility. The estates that were associated with the family over the course of the three generations discussed are as follows: Stockfield House, Birtles Hall and Hare Hills in Cheshire; Chalfont House in Buckinghamshire; Munden House in Hertfordshire; Bilton Grange in Warwickshire; Pains Hill in Surrey; East Hyde in Bedfordshire; and Braywick Lodge in Berkshire. Stockfield House was the original family home of the Hibberts, described by John Seed as one of several 'fine houses and small estates within the orbit of Manchester'.[50] Pains Hill, a 230-acre estate, was purchased by Robert (1750–1835); however, it only stayed in the family between 1798 and 1802. Robert sold it on to William Moffat MP, a London banker and East India Company stockholder.[51] Robert had previously offered the estate to his Jamaica-born cousin Robert (1769–1849) for the sum of £27,000, giving a rough estimate of what Moffat is likely to have paid.[52] Likewise, East Hyde in Bedfordshire did not remain in the family very long. Purchased in 1806 by Robert junior (1769–1849), the cousin to whom the offer of Pains Hill was made, it was sold in 1833 to Levi Ames, who had at one time been an alderman of Bristol. Birtles, Chalfont, East Hyde and Hare Hills were all purchased by the Hibberts during the period of slavery. Bilton Grange and Braywick Lodge were acquired shortly after the ending of slavery. Munden was inherited by George (1757–1837) through his wife Elizabeth Fonnereau, whose uncle Rogers Parker had bequeathed it to her on his death in 1829. The next section will examine three of the Hibberts' principal properties: Chalfont, Munden and Bilton Grange.

Thomas (1744–1819) acquired the estate of Chalfont in Buckinghamshire in 1794. He had made a fortune through his involvement first with his uncle's slave-factorage business and second on his own account by setting up the co-partnership Hibbert, Purrier and Horton. Thomas had been in Jamaica between 1766 and 1780 and from an extract in his brother Robert's (1750–1835) diary it seems that he did not enjoy life in the colonies; 'Take a walk in the evening with my Bro. In the back garden when he explains to me how little his present way of life agrees with his feelings and wishes.'[53] In 1780 the two brothers and their cousin Thomas (1761–1807) each inherited from their uncle Thomas a third part of his vast estate. Thomas (1744–1819) returned to England the same year and set about enjoying life as an absentee. Following his marriage to Sophia Boldero in 1784, he and his new wife lived at Upper Grosvenor Street. After purchasing Chalfont, Thomas hired John Nash to transform the house between 1799 and 1800. Chalfont was painted by Thomas Girtin and J. W. M. Turner – the Turner painting was only rediscovered in 2003 following a project by curators at the Tate to catalogue Turner's works.[54] Chalfont's owners Thomas and Sophia were captured on canvas, this time by Thomas Gainsborough. While Thomas' portrait is now in a private collection, his wife's was sold to Baron Alphonse de Rothschild of Paris for 10,000 guineas in 1885.[55] It now hangs in the Neue Pinakothek in Munich.[56]

Between 1800 and 1803 the Hibberts' counting house suffered financial instability. Thomas' brother George wrote to Simon Taylor in 1803 explaining that a 'totally misguided attack has been made upon the Credit of our House originating as I think in the failure of our next door neighbour in Mincing Lane, thank God we stand though sorely pelted'.[57] Interestingly, in the same letter he offered Chalfont as security on a loan that the Hibberts had taken out with Taylor. Chalfont then was both an

Figure 6.3 *Chalfont House, Buckinghamshire*, by Thomas Girtin, watercolour with pen in brown ink over graphite on thick, moderately textured, brown, wove mount paper, *c*. 1796.

ornamental status symbol and a practical capital investment that could be lent upon to support the Hibberts when necessary.

Thomas and his wife Sophia separated in 1796 and did not have any children. On Thomas' death in 1819 he left Chalfont to his brother Robert (1750–1835). Robert in turn bequeathed it to his younger son John Nembhard (1796–1886), his eldest son Thomas (1788–1879) having inherited Birtles Hall in Cheshire. Robert left the staggering sum of £250,000[58] in personalty as well as his 'Jamaica estates with slaves, stocks etc.'. [59] Both John Nembhard and his elder brother Thomas are listed in the slave compensation registers. John Nembhard lived at Chalfont with his wife Jane, the daughter of Sir Robert Alexander, a banker with parliamentary connections who acted as governor of the Bank of Ireland. John served in the King's Dragoon Guards as a cornet at Waterloo before retiring at the rank of major in 1848. His diary of his experiences during the Napoleonic Wars is kept in the collection of the First Queen's Dragoon Guards.[60] After John Nembhard's death in 1886, Chalfont was sold by his executors to Captain Berton, and by him in 1899 to Mr John Bathurst Akroyd, and was purchased from the latter by Mr Edward Mackay Edgar.[61]

Unlike the previous property, Munden in Hertfordshire was inherited by George (1757–1837) through his wife Elizabeth Fonnereau's uncle Rogers Parker. George, like his brothers Thomas (1744–1819) and Robert (1750–1835), was involved in the family merchant house; unlike them he never visited Jamaica. His business and political interests kept him attached to London and therefore he was content to wait for his wife to inherit the property rather than buying an estate in the mode of his brothers. The house was neither fashionable nor elegant: 'at the time of the death of Rogers Parker in 1828 Munden was merely an old fashioned farm-house'.[62] However, it held the potential, given the right balance of capital investment and taste, to become a respectable family seat. It was located at a distance from London but was not so far as to make access to the capital difficult. Relatives by marriage of the Hibberts – the Gregs and the Thellusons – already owned land in the area, allowing George to consolidate the family's presence. In 1829 Hibbert relinquished his property at Portland Place, 'retired from London, and applied himself to the improving and ornamenting his newly inherited property'.[63]

The need for extensive renovation work to be carried out on Munden necessitated George selling part of his famous and much-prized book and print collection. George was a renowned collector; his brother Robert wrote in 1801 of a 'Story of George having given £5,000 for Woodhouse's Pictures'.[64] Hibbert had major book and print sales in 1802, 1809, 1829 and 1833. Important sales of George's collection also took place after his

Figure 6.4 Munden House, Hertfordshire.

death – in 1860, 1868 and 1902.[65] The sale in 1829 was noteworthy in that it 'occupied altogether forty-two days … There were eight thousand seven hundred and ninety-four lots, representing about twenty thousand volumes; and the total amount realised was twenty-one thousand seven hundred and fifty-three pounds, nine shillings'.[66] The money enabled George to transform Munden into a resplendent Tudor Gothic mansion. The estate at Munden was passed down to George's eldest son, Nathaniel, allowing him to claim the status of country gentleman.

Following an education at Winchester, Nathaniel had been prepared for a life of genteel sociability. Unlike his father, Nathaniel went into the legal profession, although he occasionally attended the meetings of the SWIPM. In 1828 he married Emily Smith, the daughter of the renowned wit and later Canon of St Paul's, the Rev. Sydney Smith. A letter from the reverend to Lady Gray in 1827, telling her of the engagement, betrayed a degree of reticence regarding Nathaniel's association with the West Indies. As Nicholas Draper has pointed out, the letter 'characterised George Hibbert as "the Indian" rather than *West* Indian, merchant: Nathaniel he described as "Mr Hibbert of the North Circuit … a sensible high-minded young man who will eventually be well off."'[67] Inheriting Munden would distance Nathaniel from his father's roots in the increasingly unacceptable world of slave-based commerce. Nathaniel was remembered by Barbarina, the wife of Admiral Sir Francis Grey, who wrote, 'Mr. Hibbert was, I think, the most agreeable man I ever met, full of cleverness and knowledge, very original in his views, and with that rare gift of making those he talked to feel clever too.'[68] On his death Nathaniel left £9,000 in personalty. However, with Munden secured as the family seat, alongside his well-connected marriage, his daughter was well placed to make an excellent match.

Nathaniel's marriage to Emily brought with it an important social network; Emily's elder sister Saba was the second wife of Sir Henry Holland. Holland had two sons by his first wife, the eldest of whom was Henry Thurston Holland. In 1852 Nathaniel and Emily's daughter Elizabeth married Sir Henry's eldest son. Henry Thurston Holland had an illustrious political career and was eventually made Viscount Knutsford in 1895. Henry and Elizabeth had twin sons, Arthur and Sydney Holland, in 1855. Elizabeth died shortly after and Henry married again, this time to Margaret Trevelyan, the daughter of Charles Trevelyan and Hannah More Macaulay. The granddaughters of pro-slavery George Hibbert and abolitionist Zachary Macaulay were thus linked by marriage and it was Margaret who would help to raise George's great-grandchildren. Arthur entered into the Royal Navy as an acting lieutenant but retired upon inheriting Munden. There was a stipulation in his mother's will that required him to take the additional surname of Hibbert, which he assumed by royal licence in 1876. His twin brother Sydney inherited the title Viscount Knutsford from their father. Sydney pursued a successful legal career. He was also director of the English and Scottish Australian Bank, the Electric Underground Railway Company and the London and Lancashire Life Insurance Company. His philanthropic work earned him the title 'The Prince of Beggars' after he wrote thousands of letters to raise money for the London Hospital.[69] Munden remains within the Hibbert–Holland family today.

John Washington (1804–75) rented Bilton Grange in Warwickshire in 1839 and purchased it in the early 1840s. His father Thomas (1761–1807) had purchased the two-third interest held by his cousins Thomas (1744–1819) and Robert (1750–1835) in their uncle Thomas' (1710–80) plantation Aqualta Vale. Thomas' death in 1807 occurred just three years after John Washington was born. In his will he left each of his children £10,000 and a further £10,000 for each son who lived to the age of twenty-five. In 1839, aged thirty-five, John Washington married Julia Talbot née Tichborne, the third daughter of Sir Henry Joseph Tichborne. He completely remodelled Bilton Grange, employing Augustus Pugin to design both the exteriors and interiors. The work was on a grand scale: starting in 1841, it took ten years to complete and has been described as 'one of the other great domestic schemes of Pugin's mature years'. Relations between the two men were strained, with 'frequent disputes' breaking out between the architect and his client. Pugin's work has been described in detail:

Pugin greatly expanded a small eighteenth-century house, adding a new wing that completely dominated the existing structure, and creating a sequence of new rooms which included a galleried Great Hall with stained glass windows. There was a dramatic staircase with carved newel posts in the form of heraldic beasts and birds, some fine carved stone fireplaces with heraldic andirons or firedogs, a rich array of carved and painted panelling, elaborate chandeliers and decorative metalwork including some finely wrought keys, a Pugin speciality. A range of specially designed tiles and wallpapers featured the Hibbert initials and coat of arms. In its diversity, Bilton Grange represented a typically extravagant and completely coordinated Pugin interior, in his modern medieval style.[70]

Employing the Gothic architect Pugin may have been a result of Julia's connection to the Talbot family, who themselves were significant recipients of slave compensation money. Julia had previously been married to Lieutenant-Colonel Charles Talbot and their son Bertram went on to become the seventeenth Earl of Shrewsbury. John Talbot, the sixteenth Earl of Shrewsbury, had hired Pugin to remodel part of his country house, which then became known as Alton Towers. Like Talbot and Pugin, Julia was a Catholic, which may have influenced her husband's choice. The Gothic form and its later revival were strongly associated with English liberties.[71] John Washington's choice of an architectural style that was closely associated with forms of English freedom is an interesting one. Perhaps like his namesake George Washington – the slave-owning champion of American independence – he was able to reconcile slave-ownership and claims to a particular – racially bounded – notion of freedom. Or perhaps, like his namesake, he found that in relinquishing his claims to ownership he could clothe himself in the mantle of the emancipator.

In 1866 the Hibberts sold Bilton Grange and moved to London. They had transformed the house, which remains an English Heritage grade II listed building. Shortly after the Hibberts' departure, the house became a school with pupils entering under the Rev. Walter Earle in 1887. The school – Bilton Grange – still exists as an independent preparatory school.

Acquiring property and land was part of the mechanism for transforming a mercantile fortune into a more stable and respectable form of wealth. Works of improvement were part of the lexicon of gentlemanly culture; a man might talk with landed neighbours or within his club about new innovations upon his English estate in ways that he could no longer do with regard to his Caribbean holdings. Land and houses offered a sense of permanency that mercantile capital could not guarantee, although of course there was always the possibility that these acquisitions might be lost. If kept and managed well, land and property could be passed along the generations, creating a legacy of respectability and power. The Hibberts had risen from their involvement in the slavery business but they were shrewd enough to recognise that investment in land ownership in England would secure for them and their successors the position they craved within metropolitan society.

The benevolent slave-owners? Philanthropy, charity and moral capital

These estates brought with them social, political, civic and cultural power. They enabled the Hibberts to cultivate an identity in the traditional mode of paternalistic land ownership. Not only did the family exert their influence on the physicality of the estates they lived on by building, remodelling and landscaping but they also became involved in the social, moral and spiritual fabric of the area. This manifested itself through a keen concern in the local churches, hospitals and schools as well as support for the poor in the community through contributions to relief funds and the establishment of almshouses. The Hibberts were philanthropists at both a local and a national level. While some of their activities were intimately tied to their estate ownership; other projects they were involved with were designed to be of benefit to the nation. The Hibberts saw no incompatibility between their actions as philanthropists and their activities as slave-owners. A particular form of philanthropy was articulated by George (1757–1837) during the slave-trade debates of 1807. He stated that 'the rational principle of self-love ... puts first the centre in motion, and then extends itself in progressive circles of beneficence to the extremities'.[72] George believed that charity could and should be extended, but only to proper objects – the deserving of the metropole. In later years George increasingly used the discourse of benevolence to publically defend slave-ownership, as can be seen from his position in 1823 as a governor of the Society for the Conversion and Religious Instruction and Education of the Negro Slaves in the British West India Islands.

The Hibberts' philanthropic activities were in part about legacy-building. The memory of the family is closely bound up with the public reputation that they established as benevolent improvers. Charitable acts confirmed the social order of things and endowed the Hibberts with a moral authority that justified their position within society. It also provided an alternative narrative to their increasingly controversial identification with slave-ownership. Their donations were often accompanied by memorial plaques; others resulted in streets or buildings adopting the Hibbert name. These physical remnants of the Hibberts' presence remain dislocated from the history of the family's involvement in slavery, thus allowing a pamphlet to be printed in 2007 – the bicentenary of the abolition of the slave-trade – that uncritically celebrated John (1811–88) of Braywick as 'a local philanthropist' without gesturing to the origin of his wealth.[73]

Religion, almshouses and education

Religiosity was an important part of demonstrating one's respectability. The provision of religious instruction, places of worship and supporting the dissemination of the Christian faith were both an expression of one's personal devotion and a marker of social position. As wealthy landowners the Hibberts felt it their duty to ensure that adequate spiritual sustenance was available to both themselves and those who lived on or close to their properties. This was a lesson that had been learnt through the generations, with successive Hibbert men acting as trustees for the Cross Street Chapel in Manchester. In 1840 Thomas (1788–1879) of Birtles Hall built the private chapel of St Catherine's Church in Over

Alderley, Cheshire. The church is designated as a grade II listed building by English Heritage. As patron, Thomas' name was worked into the design; on the four-centred arched door case 'T. H.' was inscribed in Lombardic script in the spandrels. It became the parish church of Birtles and Over Alderley in 1890.

Saint Marie's Catholic Church in Rugby owes its existence to John Washington of Bilton Grange. John's wife Julia was a Catholic and later in life he himself converted. John Washington purchased land on Dunchurch Road and commissioned Augustus Pugin to design a church. When the congregation required an extension of the church building he and others put together the funds for Pugin's son Edward Welby Pugin to undertake the necessary work. In recognition of the part the Hibberts had played in the founding of the church, the old chancel became known as Hibbert Chapel. John Washington paid for a 200-foot tower and spire designed in the Gothic style by Bernard Wheelan, which was completed in 1872.[74] The Hibbert coat of arms can be seen entwined with that of his wife in tiling in the church. The couple were interred in the family vault beneath the Hibbert Chapel.

At Bray, John (1811–88) was responsible for the construction of St Mark's Hospital Church. Opened in 1873, the church served the inmates of Cookham Workhouse and the poor of Maidenhead. John was a Chairman of the Board of Guardians and contributed the entire £2,000 cost of erecting the church, purchasing an organ and all the necessary furnishings.[75] In memory of his father, John paid for the chancel window, underneath which was a plaque inscribed with his father's name and the date of his death. Memorial inscriptions and family vaults can be found at Aldenham churchyard in Hertfordshire, St Anne's in Manchester, Exeter Cathedral in Devon, St Peter's Chalfont in Buckinghamshire and Kingston Cathedral in Jamaica.[76]

The Hibberts did not only build churches and chapels as expressions of their religiosity; Robert junior (1769–1849) – a Unitarian – also founded the Hibbert Trust. Robert junior was born in Jamaica, the son of John (1732–69) and Janet Gordon. Despite his dissenting faith, he was a pragmatist and must have signed the Thirty Nine Articles in order to receive his BA from Cambridge. In 1791 he returned to Kingston to take his place in the family business. He was a plantation owner with one of his estates – Georgia – becoming embroiled in a newspaper controversy involving a Unitarian missionary called Rev. Thomas Cooper. Cooper had been sent to Jamaica in 1817 to assist in the process of Christianising the population but had abandoned the attempt when it became apparent he would not be allowed to educate the enslaved. Cooper published an account of his experiences in Zachary Macaulay's *Negro Slavery* in

1823.[77] Following this, George (1757–1837), Robert junior's cousin, wrote into both *John Bull* and the *Morning Chronicle* to defend his relative. Robert junior then waded in with his own tract entitled *Facts Verified on Oath*,[78] after which Cooper and his wife published a rebuff that included scandalous details about the sexual conduct of George and Robert junior's nephew George Hibbert Oates (1791–1837).[79] The correspondence between Cooper and George was published by the former in 1824 just as the debates around amelioration were set to reignite.[80]

In 1847 Robert junior executed a deed conveying to trustees $50,000 in six per cent Ohio stock, and £8,000 in railway shares. The trustees appointed alongside Robert were Mark Philips (MP for Manchester) and his brother Robert, both of whom were Robert junior's cousins. He stipulated that the income should be spent 'in such manner as they in their uncontrolled discretion shall from time to time deem most conducive to the spread of Christianity in its most intelligible form, and to the unfettered exercise of the right of private judgement in matters of religion'.[81] The Hibbert Trust, as it then became known, offered divinity scholarships. Candidates would only be considered if their degree came from an institution such as the London University, 'where degrees were granted without subscription to the articles of religion'.[82] The trust instituted an annual Hibbert Lecture, the first being delivered by Professor Max Muller in 1878, and it also published the *Hibbert Journal* between 1902 and 1968. The Hibbert Trust is still in existence today and awards grants in line with Robert junior's wishes. The Trust's website carries no biographical detail of Robert junior other than the date of his will and his status as a Unitarian. His association with slavery is dealt with – albeit sympathetically – in Jerom Murch's *Memoir of Robert Hibbert, Founder of the Hibbert Trust*.

Alongside attending to the spiritual needs of the local residents, the Hibberts made provision for their lodgings, physical health and education. In the mode of paternalistic philanthropy, the Hibberts supported the dependents of the parish through the establishment of a number almshouses. It was not just the Hibbert men who undertook this form of action; philanthropy provided an acceptable way for women to enter the public sphere as the care of the destitute was an acknowledged part of the remit of wealthy women. John Nembhard's wife Jane bequeathed £300 for the benefit of two Chalfont almshouses (which have since been demolished) through a legacy that was invested in the North British Railway Company. Robert of the Hibbert Trust purchased an estate at East Hyde in Bedfordshire in 1806. In 1819 he funded twelve cottages on Castle Street in Luton for twenty-four poor widows and also provided funds for their maintenance. These cottages were later demolished but

Figure 6.5 Hibbert Almshouse, Wandsworth Road, London.

only on the condition that new almshouses would replace them and that the street they were to be built on would be named Hibbert Street.[83] Hibbert Street still exists today, as does the Robert Hibbert Almshouse Charity, which offers housing for 'elderly persons with preference being given to those living in the ancient borough of Luton'.[84]

Robert junior's cousin William (1759–1844) lived at Crescent Grove just off Clapham Common Southside from 1810 until his death. William had been out to Jamaica in the early 1780s and as his brother George (1757–1837) explained 'was intended for a Planter, but a prize in the lottery brought him home'.[85] He was a partner in the firm Geo., Rob. & Wm. Hibbert, which first appeared in *Kent's Directory* in 1804. Despite investing in Hare Hills – a country residence in Cheshire – William died and was buried in Clapham, an indication of his attachment to the area. He died a very wealthy man, leaving upwards of £100,000 in personalty.[86] In his will of 1844 he stipulated that his two youngest daughters Sarah and Mary Anne were granted use of the house. In memory of their father the sisters erected an almshouse on Wandsworth Road.

The house remains today, and visible on the building is an inscription that reads, 'These houses for eight aged women were erected by Sarah Hibbert and Mary Ann Hibbert in grateful remembrance of their father William Hibbert Esq. long an inhabitant of Clapham anno domini 1859.' The building and the plaque have ensured that William's memory has been enshrined in the local area although it is unlikely that many people are now aware of his involvement with slavery. During 2007 historian Steve Martin conducted guided tours of Clapham that highlighted the forgotten presence of slave-owners, revealing a history that has been largely obscured by the abolitionist presence. The almshouse continues to be administered by the Hibbert Almshouse Charity.

As well as the founding and support of almshouses, the Hibberts were also involved with improving both the educational and healthcare facilities in the vicinity of their estates. John of Braywick Lodge made a significant contribution to Bray School in Maidenhead, allowing the schoolroom to be enlarged and a preparatory school to be added to the original building. He was also on the committee of management for Bray School.[87] He made contributions towards the establishment of three hospitals: Maidenhead Cottage Hospital, Windsor Hospital and Jesus Hospital. A £2,000 donation for Jesus Hospital became known as Hibbert's Gift.[88] John Washington invested in educational facilities for the local Catholic community close to Bilton Grange. He founded a boys' school, a girls' school and a convent with four Sisters of Providence to teach the female students. John Nembhard's wife Jane made contributions to a school in

Chalfont and for the establishment of the Cottage Hospital through a legacy in her will.[89]

For the benefit of a nation

While some of the Hibberts chose to concentrate their charitable efforts on improving the populace in their immediate neighbourhoods, others committed to philanthropy on a national scale. George (1757–1837) was involved in two major projects: the London Institution and the National Institution for the Preservation of Life from Shipwreck, which later became the Royal National Lifeboat Institution (RNLI). Investing in this kind of large-scale public work earned George a reputation for philanthropy that has been perpetuated over the course of centuries. The RNLI's Wikipedia entry describes George as one of the 'philanthropic members of London society' without giving any indication of the specifics of his interest in maritime ventures – his role in the shipping of slave-produced goods.[90] George had also carefully cultivated an identity as a cultural connoisseur and collector. He was involved with a variety of learned societies and kept an extensive library and print collection. The London Institution helped to fix his position among London's cultural elite, creating a legacy that was separate and distinct from that of his involvement with slave-based commerce.

The London Institution

The London Institution was founded in 1805 and paid for by subscription by members of the City's mercantile and banking elite. The enterprise involved George and his friends Sir Francis Baring and John Julius Angerstein, as well as the abolitionists Henry and John Thornton, and Zachary Macaulay, who acted as managers. An address on the founding of the London Institution decreed that, 'The metropolis of the British Empire is still destitute of a public library, upon any scale at all commensurate to the want of its inhabitants, or to the dignity of its situation as the first city in the world, the seat of the arts, of learning, and of opulence.'[91]

The Institution was intended for the diffusion of useful knowledge in the arts and sciences with an eye to increasing the productivity and efficiency of commerce and industry both at home and out in the empire. Janet Cutler has suggested that the London Institution was conceived of by its commercial founders as an alternative to the more aristocratic Royal Institution.[92] George took a leading role in its establishment and acted as both president and vice-president between 1805 and 1830. The magnificent building at Finsbury Circus was designed by William Brooks and constructed by Thomas Cubitt. Lectures took place on the subjects of chemistry, mineralogy, natural philosophy and botany. The Institution also enjoyed a well-stocked library and reading rooms. The Institution closed its doors in 1912, whereupon the library was broken up with parts of the collection going to the British Museum (later the British Library), the Guildhall Library and the University of London. The building itself was immediately afterwards occupied by the School of Oriental Studies before being demolished in 1936.

The Royal National Lifeboat Institution

Sir William Hillary was the driving force behind the establishment of the National Institution for the Preservation of Life from Shipwreck in 1824. Hillary recruited George (1757–1837) to help generate funds from his mercantile connections in the City. Hillary and George had had an uneasy relationship in the past. Hillary and his brother had an interest in the Adelphi plantation in Jamaica and had borrowed £19,607 15s 8d from the Hibberts. As George explained to his commercial correspondent Simon Taylor in 1808, 'Sir William Hillary is gone to pieces and has absconded … Hillary has scandalously treated and deceived us.'[93] Over the ensuing years the two men clearly resolved their differences, although two claims for compensation awarded for 154 and 79 enslaved persons respectively on the Adelphi estate were still being disputed by Hillary, the Hibberts, their partner John Vincent Purrier and Isaac Lascelles Winn up until the early 1840s.[94] It is clear that both George and Hillary had a vested interest in the preservation of ships, their crew and their cargo; they also doubtless had many friends among the seafaring community. The RNLI provided rescue lifeboats to retrieve the crew of foundering ships, many of whom, despite their maritime occupation, could not swim. The RNLI has continued its work up until the present day and indeed makes mention of Hibbert on their website, although he is referred to as 'Chairman of the West Indies Merchants Company' in a somewhat opaque reference to his participation in the slave-economy.[95]

Philanthropic activity secured the family's reputation in both life and death. The Hibbert name lives on through various legacies that the family endowed, in street names and carved into the very fabric of the buildings they erected. With the passing of time the family's association with the West Indies and slavery has gradually faded so that the name has become disconnected from the origins of the wealth that enabled their

Figure 6.6 The London Institution, 1819.

charitable activities. In demonstrating some of the ways in which the Hibberts invested their money in improving works, it is possible to trace the ways in which money from slavery infiltrated various geographic locations, having an impact on people and places for whom slave-ownership remained at a distance.

Political and civic power

The Hibberts' ownership of rural estates led them to seek the civic power that could be attained through the adoption of positions such as high sheriff. The post was unpaid and largely ceremonial; the holder was the sovereign's representative in the counties, serving a one-year term. Drawn from the elite of countryside landowners, the title conveyed a sense of status and social acceptance. The high sheriff represented the moral, social and legal order and as such was considered to hold a highly respectable position. The post required deep pockets owing to the expenses the high sheriff was expected to defray. This led to a Committee of the House of Commons in 1830, on the expenses that fell on the high sheriff. During a debate of the House of Lords in 1839, Lord Colborne spoke on the subject. His speech gives an indication of the type of person who might be expected to take on the role:

[T]hat the office of high sheriff was one of great importance; and yet this office of high ambition, instead of being regarded as an honour, was looked on as a burden, and every person tried to shuffle it off his shoulders ... He only knew two objections that had been started against this measure; one was, that the effect of it would be to lower the character and station of the high sheriff ... That was an objection far more specious than true ... The office of high sheriff was a very arduous task imposed on a very useful class of society – namely, the country gentlemen.[96]

The Hibberts, keen to secure their credentials as country gentlemen, felt no such fear of the office and a great number of them served as high sheriff during the period 1796–1890. For Buckinghamshire both Thomas (1744–1819) and his nephew John Nembhard of Chalfont served in 1796 and 1837 respectively. For Cheshire Robert (1750–1835), his son Thomas (1788–1879) and Thomas' son Colonel Hugh Robert Hibbert, all of Birtles, served in 1798, 1839 and 1885 respectively. For Bedfordshire Robert junior (1769–1849) of East Hyde served in 1815. John Washington's son Paul Edgar Tichbourne Hibbert of Ashby St Ledgers was high sheriff of Northamptonshire in 1889. Finally for Hertfordshire George's son Nathaniel and his grandson Arthur Henry Holland-Hibbert of Munden took the post in 1855 and 1890 respectively. That members of the family were elected across the span of nearly a hundred years is indicative of the stability and continuity in social position that involvement in the slavery business offered elite participants.

For those Hibberts who chose to remain in London, other forms of power were adopted. Both George and his son George junior became involved in the politics of the City. George entered the Clothworkers' Company by redemption in 1796. His admission to the Company had been recommended by order of the Lord Mayor and Court of Aldermen. Archivist Jessica Collins has explained:

> The few that came in by redemption were usually either wealthy and/or had ambitions for civic office. Up until the nineteenth century when reforms were made, one had to be a Freeman of the City of London to live and operate a business or shop in the City and the only means of gaining the City Freedom was to become Free of a Livery Company. One had also to be a Freeman before one could become an Alderman or Lord Mayor of the City.[97]

George went on to become Alderman for the City of London Bridge Within between 1798 and 1802. As with the office of high sheriff, 'only the richest citizens could aspire to aldermanic rank'.[98] The formidable rounds of social functions associated with participation in the City oligarchy required substantial wealth but bestowed on the holder status within the business community as well as access to, and influence within, the most powerful circles of the City. George also acted as commissioner of the Lieutenancy of London in 1825, a post that his son George junior also held in 1835. During a period in which fear of invasion and of the mob pervaded, the Lieutenancy of London was designed to maintain law and order in the City. Position within the institution allowed the postholders to present themselves as the defenders of property – respectable citizens of the metropolis.

The Hibberts also held formal political power through both the House of Commons and the House of Lords. George (1757–1837) served as an MP for the rotten borough of Seaford between 1806 and 1812, displacing fellow West Indian Charles Ellis. In a letter to their sister Mary Oates, George's brother Robert (1750–1835) commented on the family's political ambitions, writing that 'George is at Seaford electioneering. His elder Brothers are waiting for a Call to the upper House.'[99] They waited in vain; George, however, secured his parliamentary seat as the 'paying guest of John Leach'.[100] His position enabled him to lobby on issues affecting the West India trade; he made three speeches in defence of the slave-trade in 1807; and later (once the trade had been banned) he supported Brougham's motion calling for measures to put an effective end to the slave-trade, claiming he had always thought it to be against the dictates of humanitarianism.[101] As a leading member of the SWIPM he attempted to influence trade policies in Parliament; he supported the ban on grain distillation, and sought an extension to Ireland. He also supported Foster Barham's proposal to use free labour from the East Indies in the Caribbean colonies in 1811.[102]

His biographer J. H. Markland described George's political character, stating that, 'Though numbered among the Whigs in the days of Windham and Posonby, Mr. Hibbert was a temperate Reformer, and after the passing of the Reform Bill, gave his support to the Conservatives.'[103] On key reform issues George voted in favour of the release of John Gale Jones, voted for parliamentary reform and divided on the pro-Catholic side. He also supported the Middlesex petition for the release of Francis Burdett. George left Parliament to become Agent for Jamaica in 1812, a position that increased his influence on the issues that mattered most to the family – West India trade, the maintenance of slavery and the campaign for compensation. The family gained representation in the House of Lords in 1978, when Julian Holland-Hibbert, fifth Viscount Knutsford, gave his maiden speech in the upper house. He contributed again in 1983. Next to follow Julian into the Lords was Michael Holland-Hibbert, who spoke in debates in 1988, 1989 and 1999, in each case about the administration of the nation's heritage in museums.

While George was considered a temperate reformer, his cousin Thomas' (1761–1807) son Julian (1800–34) was described as a 'wealthy supporter of radical causes such as free thought'.[104] Julian's father Thomas had been a partner in his uncle Thomas' (1710–80) slave-trading firm in Kingston. He had sold his share of the business and purchased the interests of his English cousins Thomas and Robert in the family plantation Aqualta Vale. Like his younger brother John Washington, Julian had also received £20,000 in his father's will. Julian was educated at Eton and later at Trinity College, Cambridge. Julian wrote and published a number of atheist-leaning works including *Plutarchus, and Theophrastus, on Superstition; with Various Appendices, and the Life of Plutarchus*, which was printed using his personal printing press, which was kept at his home at 1 Fitzroy Place, Kentish Town in 1828.

Julian's circle included the radical activist and Chartist James Watson. When Watson was struck by illness, Julian took him into his house and cared for him. Watson wrote: 'I was attacked by cholera, which terminated in typhus and brain fever. I owe my life to the late Julian Hibbert. He took me from my lodgings to his own house at Kentish Town, nursed me, and doctored me for eight weeks, and made a man of me again.'[105]

In 1831 Julian gave his printing press to James Watson. As George William Erskine Russell noted, 'With the help of Hibbert's legacy, Watson commenced business as a printer and publisher on his own account, and for something like a quarter of a century sent forth a flood of the most advanced literature of the day.'[106] When during the early 1830s many radicals were imprisoned for publishing material deemed illegal by the government, Julian used his money to support these radicals and their families during the period of their detainment. He was the chairman and treasurer of the Victim Fund, when *The Poor Man's Guardian*, of which he was an editor, came under attack.[107]

Julian shared a close relationship with Richard Carlile, helping him financially when he was imprisoned between 1831 and 1834. Hibbert's own work was first published in Carlile's *Republican*. Carlile and Hibbert were both involved in the establishment of the National Union of the Working Classes and the transformation of the Blackfriars Rotunda into a meeting place for London's radicals. Christina Parolin has stated that the formation of the National Union of the Working Classes in 1831 'combined the talents of radical artisans William Lovett, Henry Hetherington, James Watson, John Cleave, William Carpenter, John Gast and the veteran ultra William Benbow, with Rotunda financier and radical strategist Julian Hibbert'.[108] In 1830, when Carlile took over the Blackfriars Rotunda, the building had been left in a neglected state and was in severe need of renovation. As Parolin has documented, 'With the assistance of wealthy freethinking allies, William Devonshire Small and Julian Hibbert, as well as anonymous donations to the cause of "rational debate", Carlile undertook refurbishments to make the building fit for public use at the considerable sum of £1300.'[109] By 1833 Carlile had formed a relationship with Eliza Sharples and on leaving prison she became his common-law wife. Such was the nature of the relationship between Hibbert, Carlile and Sharples that the couple named their son, born in 1835, Julian Hibbert Carlile.

Carlile's daughter Theophila Carlile Campbell wrote a history of the struggle for press freedom in which she dedicated several very flattering passages to Julian's role. Her text is revealing of the tensions between Julian's radicalism and his family's role in the slavery business. She wrote that his 'ample fortune' had 'enabled him to live in a way that sheltered him from the storms as well as the battles of life', providing the means for him 'to devote his life to study, to writing, and to acts of benevolence'.[110] Yet Julian had 'separated himself from his family at an early age, and never spoke of them or of his birth to anyone as far as known. His family affairs were a secret to his most intimate friends'. Theophila recorded that 'There was no doubt that he came of some fine family'; however, she added, 'of that or of any other part of his past, or youth, he never spoke.' Julian was so concerned to erase his past that '[a]t his death he laid the embargo of silence on all his friends as to himself, and begged them as they loved him to burn all his letters and to cease to speak of him'. Radicalism's relationship to anti-slavery was a complicated one; as Michael J. Turner has highlighted, 'radicals frequently disagreed with each other on the West Indies.'[111] Certainly men like Julian's cousin George (1757–1837) had appropriated the radical discourse of 'white slavery' during the parliamentary debates over the abolition of the slave-trade. He argued that the abolitionists were concerned with the plight of the enslaved African at the cost of improving the condition of the 'ruddy-cheeked boy' and 'blooming girl' who were immured in 'putrid haunts of vice and disease'.[112] Julian, it seems, was uncomfortable enough about his past to attempt to obscure his origins from his radical friends.

Evidence of the Hibberts' diverse political affiliations provides an interesting counterpoint to Nicholas Draper's statement that 'Slave-owning in Britain was predominantly an Anglican, Tory phenomenon'.[113] However, alongside Julian's radicalism and George's moderate Whig reformist tendencies (with the obvious exception of the issue of slavery), some of the Hibberts were more conservative in their political beliefs, particularly over issues affecting Jamaica. As Draper has emphasised, the Governor Eyre controversy during the mid-1860s polarised opinion in Britain.[114] Many former slave-owning families supported Eyre, using the rebellion as a means of vindicating their support for slavery. Julian's brother John Washington was given a prominent position on the list of individuals who had contributed to the Eyre Defence and Aid Fund and was listed as a committee member.[115] Whatever the nature of their opinions (and despite Julian's distancing of himself from his slave-owning Hibbert relatives), the Hibberts were given their entrée into the political sphere through their participation in the slavery business. It was the wealth and influence accrued from property and trade that allowed them to take part in political culture both inside and outside Parliament.

Commercial investment

While the Hibberts undoubtedly sought to establish themselves in 'circumstances independent of the hazards and anxieties of commerce', it was not possible for every member of what was an extensive family to do so.[116] This was particularly true of the younger sons. The family merchant house provided a means of supporting sons, nephews and broader kin. This was part of an inheritance that allowed elite mercantile families to maintain their wealth and position. Three of the younger Hibberts joined the merchant house under various partnerships: Samuel junior (1783–1867), George junior (1796–1882) and William Tetlow (1792–1881). Samuel was the son of Samuel (1752–86) and Mary Greenhalgh.

His father had died when he was three and the family counting house provided the living he would need to make his way in life. George junior (1796–1882) was the third son of George (1757–1837) and Elizabeth Fonnereau. He was educated at Eton and entered Trinity College, Cambridge, where he received a bachelor's degree in 1818 followed by a master's in 1823.[117] His elder brother Nathaniel had inherited the family seat at Munden and with another brother in the navy George junior joined his father in the counting house. William Tetlow was the eldest son of William (1759–1844) and Elizabeth Greenhalgh. Like their fathers before them they all led successful commercial careers.

The younger generation were attendees of the SWIPM and by 1835 George junior had become the treasurer. George and Samuel junior were involved with the West India Dock Company and acted as both the chairman and as directors.[118] In 1838 the East and West India Dock Companies merged to form the East and West India Dock Company. The company had thirty-two directors, of whom twenty were affiliated with the West India Dock company, including George junior, who remained on the board until 1877.[119] A magnificent painting of George senior, executed by society artist Sir Thomas Lawrence in 1811 and paid for by the West India Dock Company, hung on the wall of the East and West India Dock Company boardroom.[120] One of the major undertakings of improvement to the docks was the London and Blackwall Railway. The plans were underway by 1836 with George junior as the deputy chairman. In a meeting of the East and West India Dock Company to discuss the railway, the chairman, George junior, stated the benefits of the proposed plan, arguing that 'the nearer the Docks were brought to the commercial centre of the City … the greater attractions would the Docks present for steamers, and the greater facilities to the public for availing themselves for their use'.[121] The plan was a success and the London and Blackwall Railway opened in 1840, although in the end the railway failed to provide direct links to the docks, which only came in 1851, when the East and West India Docks and Birmingham Junction Railway Company's Railway Dock was opened at Poplar. In total the Hibberts contributed £26,000 in the form of various railway subscriptions, with £18,500 coming solely from John Nembhard.

While the counting house remained committed to the West Indies, the men also diversified their interests, becoming involved in finance, banking, insurance and various imperial ventures. Samuel, George and William Tetlow all moved in the direction of the lucrative insurance industry. Following the Marine Insurance Bill of 1824, the monopoly held by Lloyd's and the London Royal Exchange was finally broken and the market opened up to newcomers. George junior became a director of the Indemnity Marine Insurance Company, taking out its first ever policy on 4 August 1824.[122] This company would go on to become the insurance provider Aviva, a now familiar household name. Aviva's online heritage section mentions George junior by name; however, his association with the slave-economy is not recorded. Both Samuel and George junior became directors of the Imperial Life Insurance Company and the Imperial Fire Assurance Company, serving at various times between 1831 and 1858. Between 1851 and 1867 William Tetlow was a director of the Royal Exchange Assurance Corporation. He was a director of the Canada Company between 1826 and 1830. This was a private chartered land development company that was set up to facilitate the colonisation of Upper Canada. The Canada Company assisted emigrants by providing low-cost transport in ships, farming equipment and cheap land.[123] Hibbert Township in Ontario, Canada, was opened in 1830 and named after the family. William Tetlow was also involved in the establishment of the Colonial Bank of the West Indies. Closer to home, Samuel junior was appointed as a director of the Bank of England five times between 1820 and 1833. In 1877 George junior's personal estate was valued at £70,000, the majority of which he left to his brother Nathaniel's grandson Sydney George Holland.[124] Samuel junior prospered to an even greater degree, leaving £90,000 in personalty in his will of 1867.[125] It was William Tetlow who accrued the greatest wealth, leaving a personal estate of £165,288 1s 11d.[126]

Conclusion

The Hibberts' story is one of continuous acquisition. Spanning both metropole and colony, they accrued power in all its forms – economic, political, social and cultural – as well as expropriating the labour power of the enslaved. Their story is remarkable in that they survived in the uncertain world of global commerce during a period in which bankruptcy and financial crisis was a common feature of life. It also shares a commonality with many other successful colonial families in that it epitomises the centrality of networks of association. Beginning in the close-knit world of the dissenting north, the Hibberts used their connections to Liverpool and Jamaica before expanding into London. Once they had secured the means to, they then expanded outwards into the countryside, which (owing to the connection between land ownership and power) continued to hold status. Along the way marriage played an important part in consolidating their social position, bringing with it the solid relationships required in a system that was still deeply reliant on trust and personal reputation. Marriage also provided the means of achieving social mobility: the unions made by the third generation of Hibberts were marked by their movement into the sphere of the gentry and aristocracy. The Hibberts' narrative mirrors, in part, a traditional interpretation of the trajectory of commercial men; that 'the summit of their ambitions was to enter landed society'.[127] Certainly they set about acquiring land, building country houses and partaking in paternalistic acts of philanthropy. However, they also retained their ties to commerce; George's memorial inscription proudly proclaimed him as 'of Munden in this county, and of the City of London, Merchant'.[128] It is interesting to note that by the time of his death in 1837 the usual prefix of 'West India' had been dropped from the mercantile title. Neither his son George junior nor son-in-law Samuel junior purchased country houses, despite having wealth enough to do so. A number of the Hibberts went on to become decorated members of the British Army and Navy, serving across Europe and the empire. The family's desire for and attainment of power was a quest that spanned the generations. Over the course of that period they transformed themselves from prosperous merchants operating on the periphery of power in the north of England to a landed family with considerable economic, political and cultural influence both in the capital and the surrounding environs of their newly acquired country seats.

The historical memory of the Hibberts is both diverse and problematic. Their involvement with philanthropy secured a lasting reputation for the family as generous benefactors. This image has been perpetuated by the ongoing work of the charities and churches that benefited from their wealth. Their name is commemorated by streets named for them in Luton, Maidenhead, Battersea, Manchester and Marple. The relationship between their various activities as patrons of the arts, country-house owners and even as the devout disseminators of religion in the case of the Hibbert Trust remains dislocated from the origins of the wealth that supported them. The Hibberts were a respectable family. Their connection to slavery in no way debarred them from participation within the elite; indeed, it paved the way for their transformation from merchants to gentlefolk. However, as the abolition of slavery approached, their connection to it became increasingly controversial. Not only did the Rev. Sydney Smith attempt to elide the association of his in-laws to the slavery business but even George's biographer J. H. Markland – himself a relation of the Hibberts and a member of the West India interest – avoided all mention of the morally loaded term 'slave-owner' when he wrote his eulogising *Sketch of the Life and Character of George Hibbert* in 1837.

Figure 6.7 *George Hibbert*, by Sir Thomas Lawrence, oil on canvas, 1811.

In 2007 Britain marked the bicentenary of the abolition of the slave-trade. In the same year an exhibition opened at the Museum of London in Docklands entitled *London, Sugar, Slavery*. Situated in the old sugar warehouses of the dock complex championed by George and expanded by his son George junior and son-in-law Samuel junior, the exhibition highlights the relationship between the metropolis and the slavery business. Hanging at the centre of the exhibition is George's portrait by Sir Thomas Lawrence, the same painting that once hung in the boardroom of the East and West India Dock Company.

Removed from the context of that powerhouse of colonial commerce and repositioned in a display that explores the violent denigration of humanity in the pursuit of profit, the exhibition unflinchingly restores the connections between metropolitan enrichment and colonial exploitation. Distanced from the brutality of the plantations, the maps, the docks and the sumptuously clad figure of George Hibbert were intended to be a celebration of the achievements of commerce and empire. By placing the portrait in a narrative that begins with huge panels listing the number of enslaved people carried across the Atlantic, the exhibition asks important questions about the ways in which we think about Britain's imperial past. Michael Gove, Secretary of State for Education, has recently emphasised the need to understand 'our island story'.[129] The story of the Hibbert family, indeed the story of many of the individuals and families whose names can be found within the slave compensation records, is this island's story of the interconnection between metropole and colony. Britain's story is not bounded by its geographical borders; instead it has had a global reach. People and places far beyond its formal territories, as we now understand them, have been affected in the course of British history and those same peoples and places have had a profound influence on Britain. The imprint left by the Hibberts is also the tangible legacy of those enslaved people who generated the wealth that paid for it. It is only by acknowledging and exploring these interconnections that we can begin to understand and appreciate the global roots and routes that have paved the way to a modern British society.

NOTES

1 Nicholas Draper, *The Price of Emancipation: Slave-Ownership, Compensation and British Society at the End of Slavery* (Cambridge, 2010), p. 346.
2 Sir Thomas Baker, *Memorials of a Dissenting Chapel, Its Foundation and Worthies; Being a Sketch of the Rise of Non-Conformity in Manchester and the Erection of the Chapel in Cross Street, with Notices of its Ministers and Trustees* (Manchester, 1884).
3 Eric Williams, *Capitalism and Slavery* (1944; repr. London, 1964), p. 71.
4 *Ibid.*
5 Alfred P. Wadsworth and Julia De Lacy Mann, *The Cotton Trade and Industrial Lancashire, 1600–1780* (Manchester, 1965), p. 229.
6 Williams, *Capitalism and Slavery*, p. 71.
7 Michael James, *From Smuggling to Cotton Kings: The Greg Story* (Gloucestershire, 2010), p. 15.
8 T70/69 Letter to the Messrs Hibbert of Manchester, 15 August 1765. Quoted in Wadsworth and De Lacy Mann, *The Cotton Trade and Industrial Lancashire*, p. 231.
9 Baker, *Memorials of a Dissenting Chapel*, pp. 85, 89.
10 Trevor Burnard, '"The Grand Mart of the Island": the economic function of Kingston, Jamaica, in the mid-eighteenth century', in Kathleen E. A. Monteith and Glen Richards (eds.), *Jamaica in Slavery and Freedom: History, Heritage and Culture* (Barbados, 2001), pp. 225–41.

11 Trevor Burnard and Kenneth Morgan, 'The dynamics of the slave market and slave purchasing patterns in Jamaica', *William and Mary Quarterly* 58 (1) (2001), 205–28, at 209.

12 *Ibid.*, 212.

13 Richard Pares, 'A London West-India merchant house, 1740–1769', in Richard Pares and A. J. P. Taylor (eds.), *Essays Presented to Sir Lewis Namier* (London, 1956), pp. 75–107, at p. 103.

14 Burnard and Morgan, 'The dynamics of the slave market', 213.

15 Richard Sheridan, 'The commercial and financial organisation of the British slave trade, 1750–1807', *Economic History Review* 11 (2) (1958), 249–63, at 255.

16 Trevor Burnard, 'Credit, Kingston merchants and the Atlantic slave trade in the eighteenth century', unpublished paper for British Group in Early American History, Rethinking Africa & the Atlantic World, Stirling, 3 September 2009.

17 Richard Pares, *Merchants and Planters*, Economic History Review Supplement 4 (Cambridge, 1960); Simon D. Smith, 'Merchants and planters revisited', *Economic History Review* 55 (3) (2002), 434–65.

18 Evidence given by Hercules Ross, 1790–1, quoted in Sheridan, 'The commercial and financial organisation of the British slave trade', 255.

19 Frank Cundall, *Historic Jamaica* (London, 1915), p. 179.

20 Diary of Robert Hibbert, 6 May 1777. Transcripts of these diaries have been generously supplied by Nick Hibbert Steele, Hibbert Archive and Collection, Melbourne, Australia.

21 James Hakewill, *A Picturesque Tour of the Island of Jamaica from Drawings Made in the Years 1820 and 1821* (London, 1825).

22 Vere Langford Oliver, *Caribbeana: Being Miscellaneous Papers Relating to the History, Genealogy, Topography, and Antiquities of the British West Indies, Vol. IV* (6 vols., London, 1909–19), p. 193.

23 Judith Jennings, 'A trio of talented women: abolition, gender, and political participation', *Slavery & Abolition* 26 (1) (2005), 55–70; Judith Jennings, *Gender, Religion, and Radicalism in the Long Eighteenth Century: An 'Ingenious Quaker' and Her Connections* (Aldershot, 2006); Judith Jennings, '"By no means in a liberal style": Mary Morris Knowles versus James Boswell', in Ann Hollinshead Hurley and Chanita Goodblatt (eds.), *Women Editing / Editing Women: Early Modern Women Writers and the New Textualism* (Newcastle, 2009), pp. 227–47. See also Daniel Livesay, *Children of Uncertain Fortune: Mixed Race Migration from the West Indies to Britain, 1750–1820* (PhD thesis, University of Michigan, 2010).

24 Diary of Robert Hibbert.

25 Sheridan, 'The commercial and financial organisation of the British slave trade', 252. See also S. G. Checkland, 'Finance for the West Indies, 1780–1815', *Economic History Review* 10 (3) (1958), 461–9.

26 Thomas Hibbert to Nathaniel Phillips, London, 20 August 1770, NLA8897, Slebech Archive, National Library of Wales.

27 These are rough guides to the dates of the partnerships, which may well have predated and continued beyond the dates given. The dates are taken from listings in the London trade directories, including *New Complete Guide to*

London, Kent's Directory, London Directory, The Universal British Directory of Trade, Commerce and Manufacture, Post Office Annual Directory, Boyle's City & Commercial Companion to the Court Guide and *Holden's Triennial*. Institute of Historical Research, Senate House Library.

28 George Hibbert to Simon Taylor, 3 March 1802, M965 Reel 17/30, Simon Taylor Papers, Institute of Commonwealth Studies, Senate House Library.

29 Robert Greg, quoted in James, *From Smuggling to Cotton Kings*, p. 33.

30 Parliamentary Papers (PP) 1823 (411) IV: *Report from the Select Committee Appointed to Consider of the Means of Improving and Maintaining the Foreign Trade of the Country*, p. 142.

31 *Ibid.*, p. 145.

32 Anthony Partington, 'A memorial to Hibberts', *Mariner's Mirror* 95 (4) (2009), 441–58, at 452.

33 Evidence given by George Hibbert, PP 1823, *Report from the Select Committee into Foreign Trade*, p. 142.

34 George Hibbert to Simon Taylor, 3 May 1804, M65 Reel 17/52, Simon Taylor Papers, Institute of Commonwealth Studies, Senate House Library.

35 David Beck Ryden, *West Indian Slavery and British Abolition, 1783–1807* (Cambridge, 2009), pp. 40–82.

36 J. H. Markland, *A Sketch of the Life and Character of George Hibbert Esq., F. R. S., S. A., and L. S.* (London, 1837), p. 5.

37 George Hibbert, *Substance of Three Speeches in Parliament on the Bill for the Abolition of the Slave Trade and the Petition Respecting the State of the West India Trade in February and March 1807* (London, 1807).

38 George Hibbert, *Abridgment of the Minutes of the Evidence, Taken before a Committee of the Whole House, to Whom it was Referred to Consider of the Slave Trade, 1789[–91]*, [n.p., *c.*1792], p. 146. Available at *The Making Of The Modern World*, at http://encore.ulrls.lon.ac.uk/iii/encore/record/C__Rb3024723, accessed 1 March 2013.

39 *House of Commons Debates* (hereafter *HC Deb*), 23 February 1807, cols. 945–95.

40 George Hibbert to Earl Bathurst, April 1818, CO 137/146, National Archives, Kew.

41 George Hibbert to Robert Wilmot Horton, 2 April 1827, CO 137/166, National Archives, Kew.

42 Will of George Hibbert, 29 February 1836, in Oliver, *Caribbeana, Vol. IV*, p. 199.

43 David Hancock, *Citizens of the World: London Merchants and the Integration of the British Atlantic Community, 1735–1785* (Cambridge, 1995).

44 Trustee Minute Book of Holy Trinity Church, Clapham Common, P95 TR11–1/X077/084, London Metropolitan Archive.

45 G85/2/1/1/134 20F4, Surrey History Centre.

46 The Clapham Society Local History Series 6, at www.outlines.org.uk/clap-hamsociety/Articles/article6.html#xiv, accessed 31 July 2013. Kenneth Cozens, 'George Hibbert of Clapham – 18th century merchant and "amateur horticulturalist"', at www.merchantnetworks.com.au/periods/1775after/hibbertgeorge.htm, accessed 31 July 2013.

47 Thomas Frognall Dibdin, *Bibliographical Decameron or Ten Days Pleasant Discourse Upon Illuminated Manuscripts, and Subjects Connected with Early Engravings, Typography, and Bibliography, Vol. III* (3 vols., London, 1817), pp. 35–6.

48 Cozens, 'George Hibbert of Clapham'.

49 'The Cit's Country Box', 1757, poem by Robert Lloyd (1733–64).

50 John Seed, 'Gentlemen dissenters: the social and political meanings of rational dissent in the 1770s and 1780s', *Historical Journal* 28 (2) (1985), 299–325, at 303.

51 www.historyofparliamentonline.org/volume/1790–1820/member/moffat-william-1737–1822, accessed 31 July 2013.

52 Diary of Robert Hibbert, 18 January 1802.

53 Diary of Robert Hibbert, 2 June 1772.

54 www.georgehibbert.com, accessed 31 July 2013.

55 'Annals of T. H.' note added by Mabel Nembhard, at www.jamaicanfamilysearch.com/Members/b/bcarib28.htm, accessed 26 April 2014.

56 www.pinakothek.de/thomas-gainsborough/mrs-thomas-hibbert, accessed 31 July 2013.

57 Letter from George Hibbert to Simon Taylor, 5 September 1803, M965 Reel 17/47, Simon Taylor Papers, Institute of Commonwealth Studies, Senate House Library.

58 William D. Rubinstein, *Who Were the Rich? A Biographical Directory of British Wealth-holders, Vol. I: 1809–1839* (London, 2009), 1835/14.

59 Oliver, *Caribbeana, Vol. IV*, p. 199.

60 CARDG:1988.1764; extracts at www.qdg.org.uk/diaries.php?dy=29, accessed 31 July 2013.

61 'Parishes: Chalfont St Peter', in *A History of the County of Buckingham, Vol. III* (London, 1925), pp. 193–8, at www.british-history.ac.uk/report.aspx?compid=42545, accessed 1 October 2012.

62 'Watford: Manors', in *A History of the County of Hertford, Vol. II* (London, 1908), pp. 451–64, at www.british-history.ac.uk/report.aspx?compid=43308, accessed 16 January 2012.

63 Markland, *Sketch*, p. 18.

64 Diary of Robert Hibbert, 22 February 1801.

65 Pieces from George Hibbert's collection featured in the 'Prized Possessions' exhibition at the Fitzwilliam Museum in Cambridge, which ran from 25 May to 26 September 2010.

66 William Younger Fletcher, *English Book Collectors* (London, 1902), p. 302.

67 Sydney Smith, *Selected Letters of Sydney Smith*, ed. N. C. Smith (2nd edn., Oxford, 1981), p. 119. See also Draper, *Price of Emancipation*, p. 19.

68 Smith, *Selected Letters*, pp. 260–1.

69 John Gore, rev. Patrick Wallis, 'Holland, Sydney George, second Viscount Knutsford (1855–1931)', *ODNB*.

70 Paul Atterbury, 'Pugin and interior design', in Atterbury (ed.), *A. W. N. Pugin: Master of Gothic Revival* (New Haven and London, 1996), pp. 177–200, at p. 194.

71 Megan Aldrich, 'Gothic sensibility: the early years of the Gothic revival', in Atterbury (ed.), *A. W. N. Pugin*, p. 15.

72 *HC Deb*, 23 February 1807, cols. 945–95.

73 www.rbwm.gov.uk/public/100202_prow-greenway-leaflet_1200kb.pdf, accessed 31 July 2013.

74 www.stmaries.co.uk/history-of-st-maries.html?showall=1&limitstart=, accessed 31 July 2013.

75 'A guide to St Mark's Hospital Church, Maidenhead', www.berksfhs.org.uk/ genuki/BRK/Maidenhead/St%20Mark%27s%20Hospital%20Church,%20 Maidenhead%20Guide.pdf, accessed 31 July 2013.

76 Oliver, *Caribbeana,Vol. IV*, pp. 200–2.

77 Zachary Macaulay, *Negro Slavery; or a View of Some of the More Prominent Features of that State of Society, as It Exists in the United States of America and in the Colonies of the West Indies, Especially in Jamaica* (London, 1823).

78 Robert Hibbert junior, *Facts Verified on Oath in Contradiction of the Report of Rev. Thomas Cooper, concerning the General Condition of Slaves in Jamaica; and More Especially Relative to the Management and Treatment of the Slave upon Georgia Estate, in the Parish of Hanover, in That Island* (London, 1824).

79 Thomas Cooper, *A Letter to Robert Hibbert Jun. Esq., in Reply to his Pamphlet, Entitled, 'Facts Verified upon Oath, in Contradiction of the Report of the Reverend Thomas Cooper, Concerning the General Condition of the Slave in Jamaica'* (London, 1824).

80 Thomas Cooper, *Correspondence between George Hibbert, Esq., and the Rev. T. Cooper, Relative to the Condition of the Negro Slaves in Jamaica, Extracted from the Morning Chronicle: Also a Libel on the Character of Mr and Mrs Cooper, Published in 1823, in Several Jamaica Journals; with Notes and Remarks by Thomas Cooper* (London, 1824).

81 Jerom Murch, *Memoir of Robert Hibbert, Founder of the Hibbert Trust: With a Sketch of Its History* (Bath, 1874), pp. 32–3.

82 Murch, *Memoir*, p. 34.

83 www.seekinghyde.org.uk/13474.html, accessed 31 July 2013.

84 http://opencharities.org/charities/227358.xml, accessed 1 May 2014.

85 George Hibbert to Simon Taylor, 3 March 1802, M965 Reel 17/30, Simon Taylor Papers.

86 William D. Rubinstein, *Who Were the Rich? Vol. II*, unpublished data for 1840–59, 1844/10.

87 Charles Kerry, *The History and Antiquities of the Hundred of Bray in the County of Berks* (London, 1861), pp. 65, 67.

88 *Ibid.*, p. 77.

89 'Parishes: Chalfont St Peter'.

90 http://en.wikipedia.org/wiki/Royal_National_Lifeboat_Institution, accessed 1 November 2013.

91 Letters, printed notices and papers relating to the founding of the London Institution, 1805–1817, CLC/009MS03080, London Metropolitan Archives.

92 Janet C. Cutler, *The London Institution, 1805–1933* (PhD thesis, University of Leicester, 1976), p. 7.

93 George Hibbert to Simon Taylor, 7 July 1808, M965 Reel 17/81, Simon Taylor Papers.

94 Nick Draper, private communication, 3 February 2012; T71/873 Jamaica St James nos. 173 (Adelphi Estate) and 174 (Adelphi Estate).

95 http://rnli.org/safetyandeducation/teachersandyouthleaders/teachingpacks/ Pages/Save-lives-at-sea/Tab2/How-did-they-plan-for-success.aspx, accessed 31 July 2013.

96 *House of Lords Debates*, 27 June 1839, cols. 921–3.

97 Jessica Collins, archivist for the Clothworkers' Company, private communication, 24 August 2011.

98 Nicholas Rogers, 'Money, land and lineage: the big bourgeoisie of Hanoverian London', *Social History* 4 (3) (1979), 437–54, at 439.

99 Robert Hibbert to Mrs William Oates, Devonshire Place, 5 May 1807, D1799/C153, Blathwayth Family Collection, Gloucestershire Archive.

100 R. G. Thorne (ed.), *The House of Commons, 1790–1820, Vol. IV* (5 vols., London, 1986), pp. 193–4.

101 www.historyofparliamentonline.org/volume/1790–1820/member/hibbert-george-1757–1837, accessed 31 July 2013.

102 *Ibid.*

103 Markland, *Sketch*, p. 7.

104 Joel H. Wiener, 'Hibbert, Julian', in Joseph O. Baylen and Norbert J. Gossman (eds.), *Biographical Dictionary of Modern British Radicals, Vol. I: 1770–1830* (Hassocks, 1979), p. 221.

105 Roderick Cave, *The Private Press* (New York, 1983).

106 George William Erskine Russell, *Dr Pusey* (London, 1907), p. 16.

107 Laurel Brake and Marysa Demoor (eds.), *Dictionary of Nineteenth-Century Journalism in Great Britain and Ireland* (Gent, 2009), p. 501.

108 Christina Parolin, *Radical Spaces: Venues of Popular Politics in London, 1790–1845* (Canberra, 2010), p. 231.

109 *Ibid.*, p. 200.

110 Theophila Carlile Campbell, *The Battle of the Press as Told in the Story of the Life of Richard Carlile by His Daughter, Theophila Carlile Campbell* (London, 1899), www.gutenberg.org/files/38370/38370-h/38370-h.htm, accessed 1 November 2013.

111 Michael J. Turner, '"Setting the captive free": Thomas Perronet Thompson, British radicalism and the West Indies, 1820s–1860s', *Slavery & Abolition* 26 (1) (2005), 115–32, at 115.

112 *HC Deb*, 23 February 1807, cols. 945–95.

113 Draper, *Price of Emancipation*, p. 165.

114 *Ibid.*, p. 71.

115 *The Times*, 1 January 1867, p. 6.

116 Markland, *Sketch*, p. 18.

117 Ancestry.com, *Cambridge University Alumni, 1261–1900* (database online), accessed 21 July 2013.

118 *The Royal Kalendar and the Court and City Register for England and Scotland* (London, 1767–1890).

119 'The West India Docks: historical development', *Survey of London, Vols. XLIII and XLIV: Poplar, Blackwall and Isle of Dogs* (1994), pp. 248–68, at www.british-history.ac.uk/report.aspx?compid=46494&strquery=Hibbert, accessed 5 October 2012.

120 Margaret Baker, *Discovering London Statues and Monuments* (Buckinghamshire, 2002), p. 172.

121 *The Railway Times, Vol. II* (London, 1839), p. 367.

122 www.aviva.com/about-us/heritage/companies/indemnity-marine-assurance-company, accessed 31 July 2013.

123 Robert C. Lee, *The Canada Company and the Huron Tract, 1826–1853. Personalities, Profits and Politics* (Ontario, 2004), Appendix C.

124 *Illustrated London News*, 15 July 1882, p. 74.

125 England & Wales, National Probate Calendar (Index of Wills and Administrations), 1858–1966.

126 *Ibid.*

127 Rogers, 'Money, land and lineage', 437.

128 Markland, *Sketch*, p. 21.

129 Michael Gove, 'All pupils will learn our island story', www.conservatives.com/News/Speeches/2010/10/Michael_Gove_All_pupils_will_learn_our_island_story.aspx, accessed 31 July 2013.

Conclusion

*Catherine Hall, Nicholas Draper and
Keith McClelland*

We have argued in this volume for the reinscription of British colonial slave-ownership onto the history of modern Britain, and have presented evidence supporting that argument across the economy (especially finance and commerce), politics, culture and society. British colonial slave-ownership was only one of the interlocking components that made up the Atlantic slave-system, and at points in our work we have highlighted ways in which the effects of other components were transmitted to the metropole. In turn, the Atlantic slave-system was embedded in a global economy characterised by various forms of coerced labour. The legacies we have traced are thus only part of the wider legacies of slave-ownership.[1] In societies in which slavery was a central social institution – the US, Brazil, the Caribbean nations – the legacies of slavery are more present, more visible and perhaps more urgent than in Britain. Yet precisely because distance insulated metropolitan Britain from the physical realities of slavery at the time of slavery and has continued to shelter British history from them since, it has appeared critical to us to trace those legacies of slave-ownership in Britain, because they are so largely hidden and yet so real and so formative for Britain, just as globally slavery – comprising both slave-owners and the enslaved people – was present at the birth of the modern world.[2]

By its nature as a summary of a very large body of information, our presentation here has only deployed selected pieces of evidence. We are making *all* the evidence available in a structured form by way of the Legacies of British Slave-ownership database, and we hope that this will not only allow examination of our claims but also provide a spring-board for new work in the areas – of which there are many – in which we have not been able to pursue our investigations. It is not for us to establish priorities for the work of others, but in the areas of connoisseurship (the accumulation and transmission of cultural objects), imperial legacies and physical legacies in particular we know that opportunities exist to build on the data of the *Legacies* project. Above all, however, we believe that local and regional studies – of villages, towns, counties and cities – will continue to accumulate overwhelming evidence for the imprint of slave-ownership on the fabric of British life in the nineteenth century.

At the same time that we have demonstrated that slave-ownership must be incorporated into British history, we have remained conscious of the risk of overstating our case. In countering the elision of slave-ownership, there is a temptation to assert its absolute centrality. We do not, however, contend that slavery alone, still less slave-ownership, formed modern Britain. Slavery was embedded in a wider series of historical changes that transformed Britain and then the world in this period. As we have seen with Rubinstein's data, if 15 to 20 per cent of the British rich were directly entwined in the slave-economy, then 80 to 85 per cent were not. Within this larger number, however, feature in particular the landed gentry, hundreds of families established in rural England for generations whose wealth had no apparent links to the Caribbean; it could perhaps be argued that such families represented the forces of continuity rather than the dynamic changes that were remaking Britain and are therefore of less relevance to our thesis. Moreover, many of those not dependent on slavery for their wealth will have had family connections with those who did so depend. Nevertheless, we have sought to be scrupulous about the claims we make, to place slave-ownership when appropriate in the wider context of developments both domestically and abroad that overshadow the importance of slave-ownership in bringing about particular changes in Britain. Yet slave-ownership did permeate the British elites of the time. Because we have focused on those elites, there are very few areas of British life in which we have found *no* connections to slave-ownership. It would be a different story had we focused on agricultural workers in East Anglia, factory-workers in Leeds or crofters in the Highlands, although even here slavery, if not slave-ownership, will have touched the lives of some: those working land owned by slave-holding gentry; cotton workers; or the crofters displaced in clearances by landlords who had purchased or 'modernised' estates with money made in the slave-economy.

Among the elites we have studied, therefore, the pervasiveness and interpenetration of links right across economy and society are striking. There are, in Mark Harvey's words, 'both hybridity and fusion between slave-owner interests and almost every aspect of the British economy (and polity), post-Emancipation'.[3] But we have sought to go beyond making visible that ubiquity and to assess in addition the significance of those connections. There is no single number we – or anybody else – can provide in answer to the question 'how important was slavery to Britain's wealth?' The question has to be broken down into smaller components and then reassembled to give an overall sense from the accumulation of myriad fragments. Our great advantage in this is that we know the totality of the individual slave-owners at a given point, that of Emancipation. We are addressing our disadvantage – that we have taken no account of significant slave-owners and their families who disappeared from slave-ownership before the 1830s – as part of a new project on estate ownership since the mid-eighteenth century that will again make its data freely available.[4]

Slavery, and within slavery slave-ownership itself, did not in isolation reconfigure Britain in the nineteenth century. But it is impossible to imagine that reconfiguration taking the form it did, at the pace and direction it did, without colonial slavery and without the slave-owners who transmitted colonial slavery to the metropole. The accumulated legacies of British slave-ownership shaped the formation of modern Britain and continue to shape it today.

NOTES

1 Indrani Chatterjee and Richard M. Eaton (eds.), *Slavery and South Asian History* (Indiana, 2006).
2 C. A. Bayly, *The Birth of the Modern World 1780–1914: Global Connections and Comparisons* (Oxford, 2004).
3 Professor Mark Harvey, CRESI, University of Essex, private communication, 23 February 2013.
4 The Structure and Significance of British Caribbean Slave-ownership 1763–1833, funded jointly by the Economic and Social Research Council and the Arts and Humanities Research Council.

Appendix 1: Making history in a prosopography

Nicholas Draper and Rachel Lang

The Legacies of British Slave-ownership project seeks to analyse some large questions as to the relationship between colonial slave-ownership and the formation of Victorian Britain by drawing on data about thousands of individual slave-owners and their families captured in a prosopographical database and published online as Legacies of British Slave-ownership. This database, the foundation of the Legacies of British Slave-ownership project, contains records of all the men and women awarded a share of the compensation granted to those in legal possession of enslaved people in the British colonies as of 1 August 1834 (the record date for slave compensation under the Abolition Act of 1833). Bringing such evidence to bear on the questions in which we are interested, and justifying the uses to which we put it, raises issues concerning sources, methods and limitations that require elucidation at each step in the construction, population and deployment of the prosopography as an analytical tool. This appendix is therefore designed to provide a summary of the accumulation, organisation and structuring of the data in order that the use subsequently made of it to support the conclusions set forth elsewhere in this volume can be properly understood.

Our prosopographical database is not static but dynamic. The database will continue to be developed by contributions from other scholars, from family and local historians, and from firms and institutions. Some of our results in this volume are therefore necessarily interim in nature. However, our main conclusions will not be overturned by this process of accumulating further information. There are three potential sources of new material. First, the addition of former slave-owners newly identified as returning or travelling to Britain. Second, the addition for these newly reclassified individuals, or for slave-owners already classified as in Britain, of previously unknown legacies – that is, of activities in Britain associated with those individuals who left an imprint upon nineteenth-century society, culture, politics, business and environment. Third, the addition of new family members of slave-owners and of legacies associated with such family members. Such incremental discoveries that reveal new involvements by former slave-owners and their families would tend to strengthen our claims for the significance of slave-ownership in the formation of modern Britain. Where we have indicated in this volume that slave-ownership played only a limited or no role in specific aspects of British life – for example, the merchant banks founded by German émigrés after the end of British colonial slavery – the results are not susceptible to change in the light of such new information.

Constructing the prosopography

The cornerstone of the Legacies of British Slave-ownership prosopography is a foundational database of the awards made under the Abolition Act, constructed in 2004–5 by Nicholas Draper and compiled from the 1837–8 parliamentary return listing the awardees; this is supplemented by the Registers of Claims – maintained by the Slave Compensation Commission – for the missing claims, for estate names, for addresses attributed to some claimants, for characterisation of the capacity in which claimants were acting and for details of counterclaims.[1] The framework was thus set to include the summary details (colony, and within Jamaica parish; date of the award; claim number; name of claimant; number of enslaved people) of all known awards of slave compensation, *whether the award was made to someone in Britain, in the colonies or elsewhere in the world.* The major differences between the original database and the new one are tripartite. First, the new database is now comprehensive as to its coverage of colonies, with the addition of the awards made for Bermuda, the Bahamas, the Cape of Good Hope and Mauritius, which did not form part of the original transcription; second, the original database was organised (coded) by award (or 'claim') number while the new one was reoriented to be organised by individual; and third, the original database was synchronic (a snapshot at one moment in time) whereas the new database for the slave-owners on whom we have focused is diachronic (it moves dynamically over time). Each of these is dealt with below in turn.

Our claim that the database is a comprehensive census of the slave-owners in the British colonies covered by the Abolition Act has two dimensions. First, it includes all the awards recorded as having been made by the commissioners. Second, those awards represented virtually every slave-owner and every enslaved person registered in the most recent triennial slave registers: the commissioners dispensed 99.75 per cent of the £20 million available according to formulae driven by the populations of enslaved people in the slave registers. We have no definitive evidence of slave-owners renouncing or refusing compensation, although, in the case of the English connoisseur William Young Ottley, it has become an accepted part of his life story that he rejected slave compensation.[2] Money from slavery, however, was sticky: it adhered (as it did to Ottley) to the Quaker physician John Coakley Lettsom, who had freed the enslaved people whom he inherited in the late eighteenth century.

After his father's death Lettsom returned to the West Indies, in October 1767, to take possession of a plantation his father had bequeathed to him. He there performed a characteristically generous gesture: 'The moment I came of age', he recalled in 1791, 'I found my chief property was in slaves, and without considering of future support, I gave them freedom, and began the world without fortune, without a friend, without person, and without address.[3]

Nevertheless, 'shortly before his death a large West Indian fortune was bequeathed to him and his grandson by the widow of his son, Pickering Lettsom'.[4] In the 1830s, William Pickering Lettsom, presumably a grandson of John Coakley Lettsom, appears as an owner in the Virgin Islands.[5] By their nature, the records do not systematically record the *use* of compensation, so it is also possible that it was in some cases deployed in support of the formerly enslaved. There are two contemporary references to this discovered to date. In the case (we believe) of James Whitehorne, the anti-apprenticeship campaigners Sturge and Harvey reported that an unnamed slave-owner in Jamaica had spent his share of the compensation on the formerly enslaved people.[6] In Barbados, the will of Bezsin King Reece reportedly provided that '[h]is faithful female slaves Mary Ellen, Elizabeth and Diana to be bona fide free subjects after his executors receive compensation money from the British Government and these slaves to be paid immediately the proportion of the compensation money awarded for each'.[7]

All awards were made to individuals: no corporate or institutional ownership was recognised (for example, the award of compensation to the Society for the Propagation of the Gospel in Foreign Parts for the 410 enslaved people on its Codrington estate in Barbados was made in the name of its treasurer, James Heywood Markland[8]), although some traces of corporate forms exist, apparently in error.[9] Partnership awards were made in the names of all partners and do not differentiate among the shares in the partnership, although often the senior partner was named first.

The individuals named as awardees played various roles. *Not every awardee was a slave-owner or even a direct beneficiary of slave-ownership*, and some of the most striking names in the database (for example, the Bishops of Exeter and of Aberdeen) who appear in the compensation records were not owners but trustees or executors.[10] Awardees were those with the highest priority of legal entitlement to the 'slave-property' underpinning the compensation process, and included men and women acting as executors or executrixes of deceased owners, trustees under wills or marriage settlements, mortgagees or creditors whose debt was secured by a court judgement, or guardians of the young or infirm. The original claim form developed by the Slave Compensation Commissioners therefore offered over a dozen possible capacities in which claimants could lodge a request for compensation, to which we have added for precision, so that there are in total twenty categories under which people successfully claimed slave compensation: owner-in-fee; tenant-for-life; tenant-in-tail or remainder-man; trustee; administrator or administratix; annuitant; assignee; asignee in bankruptcy; committee; executor or executrix; guardian; heir-at-law; judgement creditor; legatee; mortgagee; mortgagee-in-possession; official assignee; receiver; residuary legatee; and sequestrator.[11] We have striven to systematically record this information as to the *capacity* in which people were awarded compensation. Owners are in the minority of the absentee awardees in Britain. Of the absentees for whom to date we have coded the capacity in which they were awarded compensation, some 40 per cent were owners-in-fee; the remainder were other types of beneficiary such as mortgagees and legatees, or agents such as trustees or executors.

These various roles beyond ownership reflect the transformation of slave-ownership into financial claims and obligations that could be transmitted across and within generations. In aggregate, they represent a nexus of material, familial and professional interests in slavery, but they also represent different *degrees of proximity* to slave-ownership. Mortgagees and mortgagees-in-possession (those who had successfully foreclosed on a delinquent mortgage) were generally merchants or bankers in Britain by the 1830s: although local circuits of credit continued to exist in the colonies, the financing of slavery had moved definitively to the metropole by the time of compensation. The surviving local credit networks tend to be reflected in the presence of judgement creditors among claimants and awardees (generally representing creditors in the colonies whose loans, typically for smaller amounts, had been secured by the judgement of a local court) and of receivers appointed by local courts (known as sequestrators in some colonial jurisdictions, notably British Guiana).

In many cases, roles such as executor or executrix, administrator, guardian, heir-at-law, committee in lunacy, legatee and residuary legatee flowed from family links with the underlying slave-owner (who was by definition deceased in awards under a number of these categories). Approximately 15 per cent of the absentee awardees of slave compensation whose capacity has to date been coded were identified as executors and executrixes. The latter were in most cases widows appointed under the wills of their husbands and were generally among the beneficiaries under such wills, but not the main beneficiary, typically receiving annuities secured on estates, which included the enslaved people upon them, while the estates themselves, the enslaved people associated with them and accumulated personalty passed to the next generation. Thus Jane Akers (née Ramsay, the daughter of the anti-slave-trade campaigner James Ramsay) was left £1,400 per annum under the will of her husband, Aretas Akers II, who died in 1816: he left £25,000 to his eldest son, Aretas Akers III (who was also the residuary legatee), £15,000 to his son James Ramsay and £10,000 to each of his two daughters.[12] The Akers, as noted in Chapter 2, became the Akers-Douglas family on succeeding to the fortune of another slave-owner, George Douglas, and took the title of Viscount Chilston in 1911.

Under the rules of the Slave Compensation Commission, guardians of minors were obliged to nominate trustees to invest the awards for the benefit of the original wards for claims over £200. Members of the Bayley family, who had claimed the compensation for the Wood Hall estate in St Dorothy, Jamaica, as tenants for life and remaindermen and as testamentary guardians of Charlotte Augusta Bayley, agreed through the Rev. William Henry Ricketts Bayley to the appointment of four London merchants as trustees after a counterclaim from an annuitant on the estate. The beneficiary, Charlotte Augusta Bayley, was the daughter of Alexander Bayley of Clifton, whose will was proved in 1832, and almost certainly the sister of the Rev. William Henry Ricketts Bayley, who in his own right was awarded the compensation for the enslaved people on Malvern estate in Barbados.[13] Guardianships could bestow temporarily at least high levels of power on the guardian. Colonel John Gordon of Cluny, a slave-owner in Tobago, was attacked by *The Times* in 1831 for his abuse, as the guardian of his nephew Sir Frederick George Johnstone, of the Pulteney/Johnstone family's electoral influence in Weymouth.[14]

Awards under the category of 'administrators' generally arose from a slave-owner dying intestate. The number of administrations overall is swollen by the fact that in Jamaica attorneys of British executors were also termed 'administrators', although their legal function was distinct. Roles as committees of lunatics, like executorships, were often filled by family members. Benjamin James Hopkinson, for example, the son of John Hopkinson and a free woman of colour named Johanna (who was herself a slave-owner), was committee of his lunatic brother John Thomas Hopkinson in England and received the compensation for enslaved people in British Guiana, as did Henry Ralph Willett of Shooters Hill, Kent, on behalf of his brother, who owned people in St Kitts (the Willett brothers were descendants of the connoisseur and collector Ralph Willett).[15] Hugh Parkin, a London solicitor, was the committee of his brother-in-law John Williams Blagrove as well as an executor and trustee of his father-in-law John Blagrove, a major slave-owner in Jamaica. Edward Eyre Williams, later knighted as a judge in Australia, was trustee for his brother Richard Burton Williams, a lunatic inmate at Kensington House; their father, Burton Williams, had moved 336 enslaved people from the Bahamas to Trinidad in the early 1820s and established four new sugar estates there.[16]

Assignees were of four basic types: those who were assigned relatively large numbers of smaller awards, whom we believe to be dealers in slave compensation claims, buying up claims from resident slave-owners and then receiving the compensation as principals; those who were assigned the compensation to settle a debt owed to them by an underlying slave-owner; those who were assignees in bankruptcy, often but not invariably appointed as such because they were themselves creditors of the bankrupt; and finally, official assignees, a new category of public official created to act in bankruptcy shortly before the compensation process in the early 1830s.[17]

Notable examples of apparent dealings in slave compensation claims include the London merchant Judah Cohen, who alone or with his partner Hymen Cohen was awarded the compensation in forty-five awards in Jamaica (twenty-nine of them in Kingston itself), of which sixteen were by assignment from Nathan Joseph, himself an assignee of the underlying slave-owner; John Bradley of St Kitts, who was the awardee of forty-one claims on the island, apparently in conjunction with the London merchants Bartrum & Pretyman; and Hester Smith, 'late of Nevis, now residing in Brunswick Place, City Road, Middlesex', who appears in eight awards as an assignee of slave-owners in Nevis.[18]

Assignees in bankruptcy were often also creditors of the bankrupt. In some cases, however, the role appears to have been a family one. Thus John Hornby of Blackburn, who counterclaimed for the compensation for the enslaved people on Rabot estate in St Lucia (still a working cocoa plantation in 2012) as the surviving assignee in bankruptcy of John Tarleton (the surviving partner of Daniel Backhouse in the major Liverpool slave-traders Backhouse & Tarleton) was a cotton manufacturer and merchant unaligned with the slave-trade but who had married the widowed daughter of Daniel Backhouse.[19] Official assignees in the City of London – such as George Gibson for Messrs Keighley & Co.,[20] George Lackington for Messrs Shipley Williams Wilson[21] and Peter Harriss Abbott – represented the beginnings of the public accountancy profession.[22]

Trustees provide the greatest challenge in deciphering the degree of proximity to slave-ownership of individuals awarded slave compensation. Trustees arose in a whole range of circumstances, from long-standing trustees under marriage settlements to those appointed specifically by the Slave Compensation Commission to collect and hold in trust awards of compensation on behalf of beneficiaries, such as tenants-in-tail and remaindermen in the case of entailed estates. Trustees were also mandated by the commissioners in awards over £200 to guardians, married women or minors, all those held to be incapable under early nineteenth-century legal principles (the existence of such trusts has given rise to the need to identify the underlying beneficiaries, as discussed below).

The trustees themselves, however, raise issues of interpretation. First, a trustee role provided very considerable degrees of control over the assets held in trust, and there is clear evidence in the slave compensation records of contestation over the trustee role itself, as well as between trustees and beneficiaries.[23] A trustee role was not therefore a neutral administrative role insulated from slave-ownership. Trustees in the period of slavery made decisions that had an impact on the lives of the enslaved people, including purchase and sale and the destruction of families.

Second, the compensation commissioners appointed trustees in London, even for slave-owners resident in the colonies, and such cases might inflate the number of recipients of slave compensation classified by us as absentees, and especially increase the number of London merchants. Nevertheless, in the majority of these cases, we believe that there were either pre-existing personal connections between the trustees and the beneficiaries or pre-existing connections with slavery on the part of merchants appointed as trustees, and sometimes both. Thus, in the first category Charles Richard Bigge, a jeweller of Ludgate Hill, and William Batly of Brompton Row were appointed by the commissioners to invest the compensation for the enslaved people on Smailfield estate in St Mary, Jamaica, according to the will of Maria Jane Pope after her widower Archdeacon Edward Pope had claimed as tenant-for-life: Edward Pope had presided over Bigge's wedding in London in 1835.[24]

The compensation process provided for counterclaims to be lodged against the original claimants. More than 4,700 claims (around 10 per cent) were contested, with more than one individual or group of individuals asserting their right to the compensation. The original claimants then had right of reply before the commissioners made a final decision, with a right of appeal to the Privy Council. A further 150 or so claims related to causes that were the subject of existing legal suits in the Court of Chancery and in these cases the commissioners paid the compensation into court to be divided up when the Court of Chancery had made its final judgement. Finally, in almost 200 more awards the compensation was paid into a colonial court to await judgement of a pre-existing suit.[25]

Counterclaims were lodged by mortgagees or judgement creditors following the non-payment of debts; by annuitants and legatees following the non-payment of annuities and legacies; and by the assignees of debts. Issues of entitlement were resolved using the legal principle of prior claim, giving preferential rights to the creditors of prior owners over the rights of creditors of later owners. In some cases, the Commission untangled disputes between competing members of the same families and business partners running over several decades and several generations. When multiple creditors of the same slave-owners lodged claims and counterclaims with equal or uncertain priority, the commissioners divided up the compensation between competing counterclaimants according to the relative size of the debts owed to each.

We believed it was important to capture not only successful claimants – the awardees – but also unsuccessful claimants, those who tried and failed to obtain compensation. Such unsuccessful claimants might occasionally have been 'nuisance' claimants, but in most cases they had what they believed to be legitimate claims to an award, arising from prior financial connections to the enslaved people for whose Emancipation the compensation was sought. In numerous cases, the unsuccessful claimants were in fact the owners of the enslaved people concerned under the claim who lost the compensation to others with claims of higher priority, usually to mortgagees and other creditors, but on occasion to prior owners, to legatees of previous owners and so on.

When compensation was awarded to trustees, executors, administrators or guardians, the *beneficiaries* of the compensation were almost invariably different people from the *awardees* of that compensation (although some executors and executrixes, for example, might also have been beneficiaries of the will under which they were appointed). In many cases, the underlying compensation records reveal the beneficiaries as well, and we have recorded these where shown in the Registers of Claims. For example, Mary Ann Eliza Peirse 'of England', the daughter of John Tharp of Chippenham Park, Cambridgeshire, claimed the compensation for Orange Grove estate in Trelawny, Jamaica, as the mother and natural guardian of Henry Stogdon Highatt, heir-at-law of John Stogdon Highatt, her late husband; the award was made to Thomas Ellis Adlington and Edward Hastings as trustees.[26] When compensation was awarded to executors, the beneficiaries can in principle be traced through the will of the deceased but we have by no means examined all the relevant wills and in the case of trusts we have not been able to identify all the beneficiaries of trusteeships.

The underlying records of the Slave Compensation Commission reveal numerous awards where counterclaimants withdrew their claims to compensation but were made the beneficiaries of these awards through a tacit understanding with the listed awardees. Draper has previously termed these agreements 'mercantile interception'.[27] The beneficiaries were usually metropolitan merchants who were owed debts by resident or absentee slave-owners. For example, Jeanne Rose Rousseau was awarded £1,588 7s 3d for the ownership of twenty-nine enslaved people in Trinidad when the Dublin-based merchants Thomas Wilson and Henry Daniel Brooke withdrew their counterclaim upon their receiving a power of attorney to enable them to receive the compensation.[28] The law that determined that compensation was awarded to named individuals rather than to commercial firms produced another category of beneficiaries – the unnamed partners in firms where other merchants were awarded compensation on the basis of their partnership roles. For example, the same Thomas Wilson and Henry Daniel Brooke lodged a joint counterclaim against P. A. Godineau as mortgagees for an award of £1,995 16s 7d for thirty-seven enslaved people in Trinidad and the award was made to Thomas Wilson alone – Henry Daniel Brooke was presumably a beneficiary of this award.[29]

We have added to the database a number of spouses of claimants where the spouse is of particular interest in the context of British life but we have only identified as beneficiaries those spouses who were themselves specified in the compensation process. For example, Samuel Boyd Barnett, a physician who appears in London for all the censuses between 1841 and 1871, was awarded compensation for the ownership of enslaved people on the Tripoli estate in St Ann, Jamaica, 'in right of wife'; therefore we have included his wife, Louisa, as a beneficiary of the award.[30]

Awards in the Parliamentary Papers are listed by claim, not by recipient, and many people – both absentee and resident – were awarded compensation for more than one claim. Other people were awardees in one claim but may have made unsuccessful counterclaims for other sums of compensation or might have been the beneficiaries of other awards. Among the awardees and beneficiaries, it therefore became necessary to identify the cases in which multiple instances of the same name referred to one specific person. We undertook this process for all absentee claimants and for all claimants who were resident in the British West Indies – we did not pursue this for claimants in Mauritius, Bermuda and the Cape of Good Hope who were resident in these colonies. By amalgamating these instances of identical names, we reduced approximately 56,000 names in the database to a *maximum* of some 47,000 distinct individuals.

In making these amalgamations, we were guided by unique identifiers provided by some names; aristocratic titles are a good example of this. So the Sir Tomkyns Hilgrove Turner who was awarded compensation for ownership of enslaved people in three different claims in St Thomas-in-the-East and Vere in Jamaica was clearly one person. The underlying records of the Compensation Commission often provide evidence to connect instances of identical names; for example, John Athill of 10 Brunswick Square, Islington, wrote to the Commission on 31 March 1836 about his claims for compensation in four different claims in Antigua, and we have identified him as the man of colour who was a merchant and administrator in Antigua and came to Britain in the 1830s as the representative of the free people of colour of his colony.[31] We were able to identify people who claimed in more than one award from a multitude of other sources, piecing together family trees where people inherited property in slaves from more than one ancestor and tracing the business activities of slaveowners and merchants through time and across different colonies.

In some cases we did not need to check the underlying records in order to consolidate individuals. When the same name was listed with identical co-claimants in a number of different claims we have assumed that this refers to a group of the same people: the Hon. William Fraser (also described as William Fraser in the records) claimed for seven awards in St Vincent plus a further award in Antigua and another in Grenada and we have identified him as a single individual as he lodged each claim in conjunction with the same co-claimants, in this case his business partners Claude Neilson, William Maxwell Alexander and Boyd Alexander.[32] In some cases, when confusion exists in identifying people with the same name, we have compared signatures on the claim forms and counterclaim forms at the National Archives in order to confirm the existence of specific individuals; in this way we were able to confirm that the same William Shand (a Liverpool merchant) was awarded compensation for thirteen separate claims in Antigua and three in British Guiana but that a different William Shand (a large-scale attorney as well as slave-owner in Jamaica who returned to Scotland, owned estates there at The Burn, Fettercairn, Aberdeenshire, and at Arnhall, Kincardineshire, and was financially distressed by 1834) was the counterparty in a Chancery suit over four estates in Clarendon and was awarded compensation for three separate smaller claims, all in Jamaica.

Given the impossibility of comparing signatures for the thousands of names of claimants who were resident in the colonies, we took three further steps in identifying multiple claims by specific people. First, we made an assumption based on the fact that claims were numbered on the basis of geographical proximity: when an identical name appeared for claims that were numbered within five of each other within the same colony (or in Jamaica within the same parish) we have assumed these identical names referred to the same person. For example, the name

Elizabeth Baird appears as an awardee in three adjacent claims, Trinidad nos. 536, 537 and 538, and so we have assumed this refers to one individual.[33] Second, when claimants had identical forenames, middle names and surnames, the award was within the same colony (or, in the case of Jamaica, the same parish) and these names were not commonplace, we have assumed they belong to the same person. For example, we have assumed that the John Clairmonte Abrams who claimed for ownership of two enslaved people in Barbados was the same John Clairmonte Abrams who made a separate claim in Barbados for ownership of a further three enslaved people.[34] Third, we made the same assumption when identically named people had the same name suffixes. For example, Judith Bernard senior who claimed for Jamaica St James no. 31 was the same person as the Judith Bernard senior who claimed for Jamaica St James no. 39.

In a very small number of cases, we have found through further investigation that applying these rules has resulted in an inaccurate elision of the records of two people with identical names. Two separate people, both called William Rhodes James, born within a year of each other in the mid-1780s and dying within three weeks of each other in 1842, provide an example of this. The underlying records show that the William Rhodes James who was awarded compensation for Haughton Tower and Westfield estates in Jamaica was a merchant who lived in London whereas the William Rhodes James who owned Newell Pen in Jamaica was resident in St Elizabeth, Jamaica. Other sources show separate marriage and death records for both of them.[35] When we have found such examples, we have corrected the record. The fact that such instances are so few and far between gives us confidence in the structure of the rules we have set.

There were many instances where we suspected a link between people of the same name but were unable to prove it. In these cases, we have not consolidated the individuals but have noted in our own material 'probable' links or 'possible' links: in the published database, we have generally highlighted these potential links only for the absentees. Here the use of abbreviations or initials and the possibility of spelling variants were also taken into account. When identical forenames and surnames were linked with an identical middle initial for claimants, we recorded a 'probable' link. For example, we judged that the James H. Carter who was awarded compensation for one claim in St Andrew, Jamaica, was probably the James Hickman Carter who was awarded compensation for another claim in St Andrew, Jamaica, but we have not been able to prove a definite connection.[36] We also assumed that an identical name with an identical role in two or more claims in the same colony indicates that the claims were probably made by the same person. Where identical forenames and surnames occurred in claims within the same colony but there was no other evidence that the names referred to the same person, including when the names involved common spelling variants, we recorded a 'possible' link.

Sometimes people appear in the compensation records with no indication of what their relationship to slave-ownership might have been. For example, William Macrae of 20 Nelson Street, Edinburgh, wrote to the Commission on 9 March 1836 enquiring into the status of a claim for Mount Edgecombe estate in Westmoreland, Jamaica, but not stating the nature of his interest and no further trace of his involvement has been found.[37] Where such people were resident in Britain and enquired about contested claims, we have usually but not always included them in the database. When enquiries were made on behalf of claimants (most commonly by their relatives or attorneys) we have usually included the enquirers in the database as well, although we have not been comprehensive in this. For example, we have included Penelope Wentworth Wickham of 5 Dean Hough, Edinburgh, who wrote to the Commission in 1842 with regard to the claim of David Moyes Macgibbon, who was married to her husband's sister.[38] We have also included the previous owners of estates when the underlying records have revealed them. When the children of awardees have contributed to our six legacy strands (commercial, political, historical, imperial, cultural and physical), we have added them to the database in their own right. By assigning roles to each person in the database – as awardees, beneficiaries, unsuccessful counterclaimants etc. – we have ensured that we can add different kinds of individuals while still being able to undertake statistical analyses for specific types of people.

Populating the database

The database is organised around biographical information about each individual (including dates of birth and death, marital status, children, occupation, addresses, education and religion); data concerning the compensation claims and awards made; and data documenting each of the six legacy strands.

A primary consideration in designing the database was the need to ensure, so far as possible, standardisation and consistency of data, such as in the classification of address information, so that robust conclusions may be drawn about, for instance, the geographical distribution of individuals or their relationship to awards and to slave-owning. Information broken into the hundreds of fields across the database is complemented by a large number of notes fields, enabling free-text entry to add additional information about, for example, a person's path to ownership or a firm or a building. Each individual is linked to specific awards in which he or she appears, either as an awardee or as an unsuccessful claimant, to other individuals where a familial or other kind of relationship is known and to the six legacy strands.

The diachronic nature of the prosopography operates along two dimensions. First, the database is intended to pick up geographic movements over time by former slave-owners between the colonies and Britain (and between different locations in Britain). In the original database, 'absentee' and 'resident' were fixed categories, assigned once depending on location at the time of slave compensation. The original definition was thus a one-time snapshot, with a small 'transatlantic' subset of those people who clearly were moving back and forward between colony and metropole in the 1830s. The new prosopography aims to capture those in the compensation process who came to Britain *after* the end of slavery, either returning or (for creoles and some continental Europeans and American citizens) settling in Britain for the first time. The major sources for identifying such people have been the censuses and the National Probate Calendar.

The second form of development over time consists of the unfolding of each of the six legacy strands: commercial, political, historical, imperial, cultural and physical. The first three of these received the most focus in terms of the accumulation of raw data and have been developed the furthest in terms of subsequent analysis. There are thus various weights in our work, a thickening of the commercial, political and historical strands by comparison with the imperial, cultural and physical, which hence offer perhaps the greatest opportunities for further work. In addition, some of the strands have different periodisations, reflecting the structure of the sources used. We have systematically cross-referenced our universe of individuals' data against some specific datasets and also deployed others less systematically. It is important that readers, and users of the database, understand the extent and limitations of the cross-referencing work we have done to date. For all absentee slave-owners, we have used the censuses and the genealogical databases held by Ancestry.com to develop basic biographical data: life dates, marriage(s), children and addresses. We have searched for *ODNB* entries and we have also cross-checked all Rubinstein's[39] entries against the database. Beyond these common sources, each of the legacy strands draws on different principal sources and poses its own challenges concerning evidence and its limitations.

Commercial legacies

All London firms identified in the slave compensation records have been traced in the trade directories held by the Institute of Historical

Research in London from 1800 to 1972, at roughly ten-year intervals for the period 1800–32, then at five-year intervals in the period of compensation and its immediate aftermath until 1850, and subsequently at approximately twenty-year intervals.[40] For Liverpool, we used the *Gore's Directories* for 1827 and 1841, and we had access to the database constructed by the Mercantile Liverpool project, which digitised trade directories from the second half of the nineteenth century.[41] For Bristol, we have used *Robson's Directory* for 1838. For Glasgow, we have used the *Post Office Directory* for 1843–4. In most cases for British firms, the development of the partnership structures has been tracked through the *London Gazette*. For earlier slave-trade involvement by mercantile firms, we have used the Trans-Atlantic Slave Trade Database, supplemented in the case of Liverpool by David Pope's work on a prosopography of the Liverpool slave-traders.[42]

There is no single prosopography of the nineteenth-century City of London. As Trebilcock noted, '[o]utside the celebrated dynasties, the Rothschilds, Barings, Sassoons, Hoares, Montefiores and the rest, few of the nineteenth century's "City men" have left historical traces; it is hardly known who they were.'[43] As a series of proxies, therefore, we used lists of the governors of the Bank of England, the directorate of the Bank of England at intervals and the directorate of the major insurers published periodically in the London trade directories noted above. We have cross-checked the railway subscription lists of 1837, 1845 and 1846 against our database to identify the certain, probable and possible matches.

Political legacies

Indispensable for tracking political legacies have been the volumes of the *History of Parliament*, produced under the aegis of the History of Parliament Trust. Each MP who appears in the compensation records has been checked against the entries in this series. In particular, those volumes covering the periods 1790–1820 and 1820–32 have been heavily used.[44] Thanks to the generous cooperation of History of Parliament Trust staff, we have also been able to consult draft entries covering the period 1832–68.[45] The new entries, it should be noted, are more systematic than previous volumes in recording where an MP had a West Indian connection, and they draw on material supplied by this project. The usefulness of the series has been greatly enhanced by the availability of the digital editions of the volumes.[46]

Also indispensable are the records of Parliament itself, especially *Hansard* for parliamentary debates. While a digital version is now available, it is not an entirely reliable record: there are numerous mistakes in transcription; sections of debates in both Houses are missing; and, at the time of writing, the ability to search has been removed.[47] It is therefore necessary to check the record against the printed volumes. Other parliamentary sources that have been consulted include many Parliamentary Papers, particularly various select committees such as PP1836 (560) XV: *Report from the Select Committee on Negro Apprenticeship in the Colonies* and PP1842 (479) XIII: *Report from the Select Committee on West India Colonies*, division lists[48] and unofficial documentation such as *Dod's Parliamentary Companions* (1832–), especially for establishing the political affiliations of members.[49] Almost as important as *Hansard* as a record of parliamentary proceedings, particularly in the early years following Emancipation, is *The Times*. It, like the growing number of provincial newspapers of the period, has also been frequently consulted for biographical information.

Historical legacies

We have worked from individuals and families in the compensation records to track relevant archival and published materials. This has not been a systematic process: rather, we have pursued such materials in cases where their existence has been readily identifiable in secondary sources or in online resources such as the *ODNB*. As a result, we will have omitted an unknown amount of material, especially in the case of family histories by less well-known individuals or about less well-known families. We are confident, however, that we have captured the output of major literary and historical figures of early and mid-Victorian Britain who had connections with slave-ownership expressed in the slave compensation records. Since we are concerned to trace the influence of representations of slavery by former slave-owners and their families, we believe that the approach of focusing on those who were major figures at the time (and in most cases continue to be seen as such) is appropriate. To the extent that we have used texts by lesser-known figures as exemplars of a wider body of unknown literature, there has been no reason to believe that our sample is skewed in any particular direction and is thus unrepresentative of the whole: our selection has been random, although not in the statistical sense.

Imperial legacies

We have systematically searched the online *Dictionary of Canadian Biography*, the online *Australian Dictionary of Biography* and the online *Dictionary of New Zealand Biography* for references to the West Indies and to specific British West Indian colonies in order to identify the imperial legacies of people in our database. Where the information has been available we have included the children and grandchildren of claimants and beneficiaries in this research. Our separate investigation of the lives of absentee awardees and beneficiaries has revealed more examples of cultural legacies that have not been recorded in dictionaries of national biography. For example, excluded from the *Australian Dictionary of Biography* is Celia King, the co-heiress of a Tobagonian slave-owner, who inherited a part share in Sherwood estate in Tobago; she moved with her husband Andrew Scott to Mount Buninyong Station, Victoria, Australia, late in 1839; it subsequently became known as Scotsburn, named after them. Andrew Scott and Celia established a cattle farm of 16,000 acres. From 1843 the family began to run sheep and the family went on to purchase property in the western district of Victoria and in New South Wales.[50]

Physical legacies

We have searched the lists of projects given for John Soane and Humphrey Repton, and earlier participated in the English Heritage search of its own properties.[51] This latter study did not cover the properties listed by English Heritage, only those owned or managed directly by the organisation. We have used, but not systematically searched, the National Trust's property lists and the database of landed estates published by the National University of Ireland in Galway.

Cultural legacies

We have recorded membership of cultural and scientific institutions such as the Royal Society and trusteeships of schools and hospitals when our biographical research has revealed these links but we have not systematically searched the membership lists of these institutions to cross-check them against the names in our database. Other sources that have been cross-checked include records of early subscribers to educational establishments such as Kings College London and University College London. There are clearly many more opportunities for cross-referencing – for example, the records of Masonic lodges – that we have not to date taken up.

We have recorded the familial connections between slave-owners for all absentees and for many residents in the database where our biographical research has revealed these connections. Usually but not always these are among multiple claimants in the same claim and occasionally involve bitter and long-running disputes over inheritances. As noted above, trusteeships were frequently formed on the basis of family connections. We cannot claim to have done full justice to recording the complex web of relationships through marriage and through more distant ties of blood, but the figures we have so far provide an indication as to the importance of family networks among slave-owners and the merchants and bankers involved in the connected economy. Because of time limitations, our large dataset is not suited to unravelling complex webs of interdependence, but individual case studies, for example of the Hibbert family in Chapter 6, reveal a fuller picture. We have focused our biographical research on absentee claimants and can expect that family connections were more intricate and prevalent among resident awardees.

In making our results widely available we have also benefited when members of the public have sent us the results of their own research. Where possible, we have verified the information we have been sent by checking against original sources and, where this has not been possible but the information appears to us to be important in allowing identification of the individual or of his or her legacies, we have included that information while clearly denoting it as unsourced. We have accepted transcribed and photocopied material and checked the sources of this where possible; where we have not been able to view the original sources we have denoted the material as sourced but not verified. We have in all cases aimed to include an acknowledgement in the public record of the people who have provided us with information.

Deploying the prosopography

We have privileged the individual slave-owner and his or her family as historical forces in transmitting slavery to Britain. As noted in Chapter 3, we are not suggesting that the slave-owner and his or her family was the only such means of transmission. Ideas, physical goods and people – including enslaved people – moved between colony and metropole from the outset of British colonial slavery in the seventeenth century.[52] The economic effects of slavery were not solely transmitted at the level of the wealth of individuals, but the individual is undoubtedly an important unit of analysis in this context. Mercantile firms were small, and investment certainly remained a personal recycling of funds, given that Victorian savings and investment were still private and decentralised, with few important intermediate organisations between savers and investors until late in the nineteenth century, when life insurance became the dominant means of stimulating middle- and working-class savings and deploying those savings for long-run investment.[53] Similarly, family ties in business continued to be fundamental. While our prosopographical study is therefore justified as one approach to the economic legacies of slavery, such an approach cannot capture the systemic effects at the level of institutional development, increased demand for manufactures, the supply of tropical commodities as raw material inputs and the multiplier effects of both of these latter activities. Our work on slave-ownership must therefore be seen as one contribution to a much wider question of the economic legacies of slavery itself.

Moving from a mass of individual and family biographies to judgements about the significance of the universe as a whole raises conceptual and practical questions. Necessarily the data held on each of the individuals and each of the families in almost every case is brief, and the capacity of that data to support wider judgements requires careful reflection. There are three ways in which the data can be used in support of such wider judgements.

The first is simply counting. We have data on thousands of individuals and their families, enabling us to express the universe of slave-owners as a percentage of other universes. Thus, we are able to quantify the proportion represented by the slave-owners of, for example, the rich in Britain, railway subscribers in specific companies or MPs. And within the universe of slave-owners we are able to count, for example, the number who attended particular schools or the number who trained as lawyers. These statistics must be used with caution as it is not always possible to distinguish between 'not known' and 'none' in fields such as education and marriage: so, for example, the fact that we have marriages recorded for a certain percentage of the absentee slave-owners does not mean that the remainder of them died unmarried. Our categories of occupation are also too blunt for comprehensive statistical analysis although they do provide indicative data.[54]

The second way of deploying the data is to contextualise case studies. There are well-known examples of slave-ownership that go back to Eric Williams and are often reproduced in secondary sources; such examples include John Gladstone, the Earls of Harewood and William Beckford senior and junior. Our material allows for the first time an analysis of how *representative* such case studies are. Thus John Gladstone was one of several dozen merchants engaged in the slave-economy who form part of a 'swing to the East' in the final years of slavery; the Lascelles (Earls of Harewood) were one of the five to ten per cent of all aristocratic families in Britain owning enslaved people at the end of slavery; William Beckford junior was one of a dozen or so absentee slave-owners in Jamaica owning more than 500 people at the end of slavery.

The third use of the data is the accumulation of 'legacies'. We conceive of three types of legacy: causal, direct and connective. 'Causal' legacies, the strongest form of claim for historians, refers to those areas of British life in which we argue that slave-owners as a distinctive group, often but not always within a wider movement, demonstrably contributed to a change of direction or of intensity of movement. An example would be the rewriting of the story of Emancipation. 'Direct' legacies constitute those areas in which we argue that slave-ownership produced the resources that made transformation possible. An example would be the physical legacies of Charles McGarel in Larne. 'Connective' legacies are those in which activities of slave-owners left a significant imprint upon Britain through networks of transmission that might screen the original slave-ownership. Examples would include the Rev. David Laing and the founding of North London Collegiate School.

The intergenerational transfer of capital and the subsequent accumulation of legacies across the generations are more difficult to assess. The intergenerational transfer of cultural capital – for example, education – is also worth capturing as a legacy of slave-ownership. For these reasons we have recorded in the database the names and dates of birth of the children of slave-owners and added notes on the next generation when its members are known to have had a substantial impact in any of the legacy strands.

Limitations

As noted in Chapter 2, race or 'colour' is absent from the compensation records as far as the slave-owners are concerned (it is certainly there for the enslaved people, who by definition are non-white: the slave registers provide further categorisation of the enslaved people as 'African' or 'creole', which was determined by attributed place of birth, sometimes supplemented by other designations of race). We have not been able to reinscribe race systematically onto the slave-owners from the compensation records, but in over a hundred cases secondary material has now provided information on race, and this number will increase as we use the slave registers (which for Barbados in 1826, for example, do include designation of owners as 'free mulattos') in the new phase of our research.

Some 40 per cent of the awardees listed in the compensation records were female, but this does not reflect the full importance of women in the compensation process. Because under English law a woman's property was transferred to the ownership of her husband upon their marriage unless protected by a marriage settlement, in many cases compensation was awarded to the husband 'in right of wife', and it is only through examination of the underlying compensation records or through researching the genealogy of the family that the roles of women can be discovered; although we have traced these records in many cases, the research is obviously incomplete. Women were also more likely to be beneficiaries where the compensation was awarded to male executors or trustees; again, this process of identification has begun but has not been exhaustively pursued. As noted above, trustees were appointed when an award of more than £200 was made to a married woman. Women tend to appear in the financial records as financial actors only if they remained single or when they became widowed.

The way we have defined and captured the legacies of slave-ownership has tended to reinforce this under-representation of women's roles. For example, physical legacies in the form of country houses are usually recorded as being owned by men when they might have been inherited through the female line or purchased with money brought by a wife to a marriage. Our emphasis on the importance of named partners in firms almost always excludes the role of women from the picture, although women were likely to be the beneficiaries of mercantile compensation and as widows sometimes inherited a share of the capital of a merchant firm. Likewise we have recorded information in separate categories about the occupations of claimants, the schools and universities they attended and their legal and military training; these categories mean we have classified more details of the lives of male claimants than of females.

The universe of slave-owners we are examining is that of men and women holding enslaved people or financial claims on enslaved people at the end of slavery. For this universe, we are advancing claims of completeness for the awardees and more limited claims for those who were beneficiaries of compensation and those who sought compensation unsuccessfully. We are by definition not capturing earlier slave-owners who severed their links with slave-ownership before Emancipation. Traces of such people certainly exist in the slave compensation records and have sometimes been identified when researching the lives of the awardees themselves, and we have recorded previous owners when we have found them. Appearing in the database, for example, is John Aitcheson senior who inherited Belmont estate in Grenada following the death of his son, also called John, c. 1770. John Aitcheson senior died at Belmont in 1780 and stipulated in his will that Belmont was to be sold and the proceeds divided between his three daughters and his nephew; the estate was subsequently bought by Robert Alexander Houston of Clerkington, Scotland. The awardee in the compensation records was Robert Houston of Clerkington, who inherited from his father Andrew Houston.[55] There are, moreover, many signs of long continuities in slave-ownership. Families such as the Drax family span the late seventeenth, eighteenth and early nineteenth centuries. But our universe does not represent the totality of those who owned enslaved people over the course of British colonial slavery. The Thellussons, for example, bankers of Huguenot extraction and successively major creditors and slave-owners in Grenada, do not appear in the slave compensation records.[56] Neither does Sir Manasseh Masseh Lopes, the notorious borough-monger of the unreformed British House of Commons whose fortune is reported to have been founded on slave-ownership.[57] How material this limitation is we do not yet know. A new project at UCL, Structure and Significance of British Caribbean Slave-ownership 1763–1833, is underway; in developing a history of estate ownership for the British Caribbean colonies and of the impact of slave-ownership in Britain in the seventy years prior to the end of slavery, it will among other results identify these 'lost' slave-owners.

Because the slave compensation data provides a snapshot of slave-ownership at a single point in time, it cuts across the colonies at different stages of development. If there were a single model for the evolution of the slave-colonies, then potential distortions might arise from taking the colonies at different stages of such a 'life cycle'. It does not appear that there is a correlation between the extent of British absentee proprietorship, for example, and the period for which the colony had been under British jurisdiction. However, the prominence and visibility of new men and new wealth among slave-owners in British Guiana and to a lesser extent in Trinidad does suggest that the 'lost' wealth of earlier periods will arise disproportionately in the older colonies, especially Jamaica.

In gathering information about individual slave-owners, the ease of finding material replicates the ways in which the archives systematically privilege particular classes of people – specifically the upper and upper-middle classes – and a particular gender: men. This is exacerbated in our use of dictionaries of national biography, for example, to trace the imperial legacies of people in our database. Our definitions of each legacy strand might preclude an assessment of the significance of smaller slave-owners in that their political power, for example, might not involve holding formal office and their economic activities might not involve holding partnerships in traceable firms. Nonetheless, an important benefit of using the compensation records to identify people with an economic interest in slave-ownership is that the records list all claims, no matter how small, and through our database we have documented hundreds of people in Britain whose involvement would otherwise have been very difficult to establish. Within this group are people for whom slavery might have been more important on an economic or a social level than it was for wealthier investors, in spite of the sums of money being much smaller.

There are of course issues in our sources other than the compensation records themselves of which users need to be aware. One of our important sources has been the work, published and unpublished, of William D. Rubinstein. Rubinstein's exhaustive and painstaking research has produced the universe of people dying in Britain between 1809 and (to date) 1874 leaving over £100,000 in personalty (i.e. non-real property such as cash, stocks, capital in partnerships). In the early years of the study, there were two or three dozen such people dying each year. By the 1870s there were 130–40 each year. This universe is the basis of the analysis in Chapter 2 of the relative significance of the wealth of individual slave-owners.

Personalty omits land in Britain, although there is a correlation with land: the profits of land ownership over time (even in the absence of mineral profits from coal) were likely to generate meaningful levels of more liquid wealth. There are certainly many people in Rubinstein's lists for whom land ownership was the prime source of wealth: almost 25 per cent in his first cohort (1809–39).[58] Personalty for slave-owners and former slave-owners, however, also omits land in the West India colonies and until 1834 the enslaved people upon it (between 1834 and 1838 the unexpired period of apprenticeship also had a value, and formerly enslaved people continued to be traded while subject to apprenticeship). The exclusion of Simon Taylor (who died in 1813) and the limitations on the apparent size of the estate of his nephew and heir Sir Simon Richard Brissett Taylor (who died in 1815) in spite of the fact that Simon Taylor was described by Governor Nugent in 1806 as 'by much the richest proprietor in the island, and in the habit of accumulating money, so as to make his nephew and heir one of the most wealthy subjects of His Majesty'[59] are discussed in Chapter 2. Personalty in Britain is thus an inherently steep test for slave-wealth relative to forms of wealth other than land in Britain. It requires slave-wealth to have been monetised before death. Manufacturing assets in Britain were not generally a material part of the value of a business, so that, even if manufacturers died before selling out their business, much of the value would be recorded as personalty. By contrast, many slave-owners retained their productive assets (not only land but also equipment and the enslaved people) after 'retirement': that is what being an absentee meant, of course. All of this wealth falls outside the value of personalty within jurisdiction of the probate records. The absolute numbers of slave-owning wealth-holders are thus almost certainly understated in the period before 1834. However, it is not possible to estimate how valuing *all* property, including land in Britain and land and enslaved people in the colonies, would affect the proportional importance of slave-related wealth: slave-owners and former slave-owners naturally feature among British landowners.

A further complication of personalty is that it was a gross figure, exclusive of claims of creditors on the estate. The estate of the London West India merchant Henry Davidson, who died in 1827 leaving £500,000, appears to have been largely consumed by creditors. Again, within a few months of the death in 1850 of William Hardin Burnley, a major slave-owner in Trinidad, the creditors of his son William Frederick Burnley, whose Glasgow mercantile partnership had failed in 1848, moved to seize William Frederick Burnley's interest in his father's estate.[60] Debt is often treated as synonymous with West Indian estates, but the systematic effect of adjusting for debt on conclusions gleaned from data on personalty is not predictable. Finally, *in vivo* giving could reduce wealth below the threshold used by Rubinstein. This was the case with John Gladstone, who gave hundreds of thousands of pounds to his children in the last years of his life and left personalty of less than £100,000 on his death in 1851.

There are therefore complexities around the use of personalty that are important to recognise even if their effects cannot be predicted. There is a further qualification as to the significance of individual wealth as such. The sources of individual wealth are not the same as the sources of national wealth. As Rubinstein pointed out, manufacturing, mining and building accounted for between 33 and 40 per cent of total national income 1831–1901, and industry and manufacturing accounted for between 43 and 49 per cent of the male labour force between 1841 and 1901; but the manufacturing sector accounted for fewer millionaires, half-millionaires and 'lesser wealthy' than commerce/finance, which employed only 1.5 per cent of the population in 1841 and less than 60 per cent in 1901, while the share of the whole trade and transport sector in the national income was around 20 per cent between 1831 and 1901.[61] Individual wealth in aggregate provides an index of power and social access, as Rubinstein argues, but does not correlate with the importance of given activities from which that individual wealth was derived to the economy as a whole.

NOTES

1 Parliamentary Papers 1837–8 (215) XLVIII: *Accounts of Slave Compensation Claims*; *Records Created and Inherited by HM Treasury: Office of Registry of Colonial Slavery and Slave Compensation Commission Records*, T71/852–914 Registers of Claims. Nicholas Draper, *The Price of Emancipation. Slave-Ownership, Compensation and British Society at the End of Slavery* (Cambridge, 2010), pp. 138–269 includes analysis based on this earlier database.

2 Nicholas Turner, 'Ottley, William Young (1771–1836), writer on art and collector', *ODNB*, which says: 'In 1833, Ottley became keeper of prints and drawings at the British Museum, a post that he accepted apparently for financial reasons, since the act abolishing slavery had reduced his income from the family's West Indian plantation.' This appears to be based on a statement by J. Allen Gere in 'William Young Ottley as a collector of drawings', *British Museum Quarterly* 18 (1953), 51–2, which went further: 'His reason [for taking the British Museum position], an economic one, is much to his credit: in 1833, the Act abolishing slavery in the British colonies was passed, and though both his father's and mother's families derived their wealth from West-Indian estates, Ottley refused, on principle, to accept any compensation for the losses caused him by the freeing of his slaves.' This claim has been repeated in, for example, the television documentary *The Mystic Nativity*, made by Fulmar and broadcast in December 2009. To date we have not identified awards that confirm or refute this. Warner Ottley, William Young Ottley's younger brother, was awarded compensation for the enslaved people on the Adventure estate on Tobago and New Adelphi on St Vincent, as well as in two other awards as trustee. It appears, however, that William Young Ottley's means derived from slavery: he received £10,000 under Richard Ottley's will, which also specified that £20,000 be invested in Tobago. William Young Ottley and Warner Ottley served as trustees of the will of Drewry Ottley late of the Island of St Vincent (PROB 11/1466/249, proved 27 August 1807).

3 J. F. Payne, rev. Roy Porter, 'Lettsom, John Coakley (1744–1815), physician and philanthropist', *ODNB*. Pickering Lettsom had been apprenticed by his father to a London lawyer, James Spearing, in 1799; Ancestry.com, *UK Articles of Clerkship 1756–1874* (database online).

4 Payne, rev. Porter, 'Lettsom'. The source appears to be Thomas Joseph Pettigrew, *Memoirs of the Life and Writings of the Late John Coakley Lettsom, Vol. I* (3 vols., London, 1817), pp. 170–1, according to which the property inherited by John Coakley Lettsom shortly before his death, 'which is supposed to amount to several thousands per annum', comprised an estate on Tortola with 'not less than 1000' enslaved people.

5 T71/883 Virgin Islands nos. 8 and 49.

6 Joseph Sturge and Thomas Harvey, *The West Indies in 1837* (London, 1838), p. 277: 'one of the Baptist missionaries who is a creole by birth, and one of a family who though they have all been brought up in contact with slavery, have cleared themselves from its contaminating connexion. His brother, now resident in England, has manumitted his apprentices and directed a considerable amount received as compensation to be expended for their benefit'; p. 261 lists all the Baptist missionaries on the island, including William Whitehorne. James Whitehorne was certainly a Non-conformist absentee owner in Britain, baptising his daughter at Dr Williams Library in 1834 and appearing as 'Editor Religious Tract Society' in the 1861 census.

7 Colonel H. M. Reece, 'The kindred of Bezsin K. Reece (1765–1838) of St Michael Barbados', in James C. Brandow, *Genealogies of Barbados Families from Caribbeana and the Journal of Barbados Museum and Historical Society* (Baltimore, 1983), pp. 495–500, at 497.

8 T71/899 Barbados no. 4215.

9 E.g. T71/856 St Mary no. 132 was recorded as an award to G. W. S. Hibbert
   & Co. as owners-in-fee.

10 For the identification of Henry Phillpotts, Bishop of Exeter, as a slave-owner,
   see Eric Williams, *Capitalism and Slavery* (1944; repr. London, 1964), p. 43; for
   his actual role as trustee under the will of the Earl of Dudley, see Draper, *Price
   of Emancipation*, p. 5. William Skinner, Bishop of Aberdeen, was an executor of
   William Lambie, who died in 1826; T71/867 St Thomas-in-the-East no. 198.

11 See Appendix 2 for a glossary of these claimant categories.

12 Vere Langford Oliver, *Caribbeana: Being Miscellaneous Papers Relating to the
   History, Genealogy, Topography, and Antiquities of the British West Indies, Vol. V*
   (6 vols., London, 1910–19), p. 313. The will included the provision 'My son
   Aretas not to be educated at public school except to a University.'

13 She married Charles Fryer Lyall at Clifton in 1845. The two are shown in the
   1871 census at 17 Henrietta Street, Bathwick, when Lyall was described as
   'Barbados proprietor'.

14 *The Times*, 5 April 1831, p. 3.

15 T71/885 British Guiana no. 616; T71/879 St Kitts nos. 747 and 748.

16 Michael Craton and Gail Saunders, *Islanders in the Stream: A History of the
   Bahamian People, Vol. I* (Athens, GA, 1999), pp. 225, 291.

17 Stat. 1 and 2 Will. IV c.56.

18 E.g. for Judah Cohen, T71/861 Kingston nos. 299, 352 and 479; for John
   Bradley and Bartrum & Pretyman, T71/879 St Kitts no. 30; for Hester Smith,
   T71/882 Nevis nos. 147, 192 and 238.

19 T71/884 St Lucia no. 624. The partnership between John Tarleton and
   Daniel Backhouse had been dissolved in 1802; *London Gazette*, 15,500, 24
   July 1802, p. 786. John Tarleton was declared bankrupt in 1816; *London
   Gazette*, 17,135, 11 May 1816 p. 890; John Porter, *History of the Fylde of
   Lancashire* (Fleetwood and Blackpool, 1876), p. 165; Michael M. Edwards,
   The Growth of the British Cotton Trade 1780–1815 (Manchester, 1967), p. 265.
   According to Edwards, Hornby left an estate worth £200,000 on his death in
   1841, although he does not appear in Rubinstein.

20 T71/867 Jamaica St Thomas-in-the-East nos. 293, 423, 433, 434, 435 and
   436; T71/871 Jamaica Westmoreland nos. 68 and 76. The commission of bankruptcy for James Inglish Keighly, Finlay Fergusson and William Armstrong
   of Keighly, Fergusson & Co. had first been issued in 1801 and then renewed
   24 March 1824; *London Gazette*, 15,390, 25 July 1801, p. 923 and *London
   Gazette*, 19,570, 19 December 1837, p. 3321.

21 T71/882 Nevis nos. 42, 100, 306 and 501. Roger Hesketh Fleetwood
   Williams and Mayson Wilson had been mercantile creditors of the Maynard
   family. A commission of bankruptcy had been issued against Roger Hesketh
   Fleetwood Williams of Liverpool, together with Mayson Wilson of Liverpool
   and Birch Harrison of the Island of Nevis trading under the firm of Williams
   and Wilson, and a commission of bankruptcy against both Liverpool men
   dated 14 December 1810 quickly followed; *London Gazette*, 16,432, 4
   December 1810, p. 1952. The bankruptcy process lasted for fifty years:
   the ninth dividend was declared in 1861 by the then official assignee Geo.
   J. Graham; *London Gazette*, 22,478, 8 February 1861, p. 543.

22 See Chapter 3 for Peter Harriss Abbott.

23 For example, the factory commissioner, banker and pro-South advocate in the American Civil War John Welsford Cowell, awarded as trustee the compensation for the enslaved people on the Llandovery and Flat Point estates in St Ann, Jamaica, was in litigation still in the 1850s to retain the trustee role, a role he appears to have inherited from his father and that dated from 1779; T71/857 Jamaica St Ann nos. 467 and 468; *London Gazette*, 22,032, 18 August 1857, p. 2837; *London Gazette*, 23,752, 4 July 1871, p. 3093. Dormant funds in this case were advertised in a supplement to the *London Gazette*, 33,919, 10 March 1933, p. 1683.

24 T71/856 St Mary no. 33. Pope served as Archdeacon of Kingston for twenty years from 1825, before returning to England and dying at Guildford in 1855. William Batly has not yet been traced.

25 Draper, *Price of Emancipation*, pp. 150–1.

26 T71/874 Jamaica Trelawney 184 (Orange Grove) (which gives her name as Pierse). John Stogdon Highatt had died off Lundy Island en route for Jamaica in 1831, although his will was not proved until 1840; will of John Stogdon Highatt of Saint Thomas Devon, PROB 11/1929/204. Mary Ann Eliza Highatt had remarried in August 1831, to Richard William Peirse; Ancestry.com, *London England Marriages and Banns, 1754–1921* (database online). Henry Stogdon Highatt moved to Australia, where he edited the *Forbes and Parkes Gazette* and apparently died there after an assault in 1885; *New South Wales Police Gazette*, 1 April 1885, p. 104.

27 Draper, *Price of Emancipation*, pp. 238–9.

28 T71/518 p. 3281 Trinidad no. 2020.

29 T71/894 Trinidad nos. 1920A & B (St Jean estate).

30 T71/857 Jamaica St Ann no. 541 (Tripoli estate).

31 T71/1593 p. 155: letter dated 31 March 1836, John Athill, 10 Brunswick Square, Islington, re. Antigua nos. 364, 462, 573 and 807.

32 E.g. T71/877 Antigua no. 1945.

33 T71/893.

34 T71/895 Barbados no. 711; T71/896 Barbados no. 1454.

35 T71/872 Jamaica Hanover no. 566 (Houghton Tower); T71/874 Jamaica Trelawney no. 107 (Westfield); T71/870 Jamaica St Elizabeth no. 753 (Newell). For the memorial inscription of William Rhodes James of St Elizabeth, husband of Eleanor James, who died 8 October 1842 age fifty-seven, see Philip Wright, *Monumental Inscriptions of Jamaica* (London, 1966), pp. 186, 287. William Rhodes James, the London merchant married to Caroline Pope, is in the 1841 census for England at Wyndham House in Suffolk with his wife Caroline and died in London aged fifty-six on 15 September 1842.

36 T71/865 Jamaica St Andrew nos. 88 and 576.

37 T71/1608 letter re. Jamaica Westmoreland no. 419.

38 Barbados no. 57, T71/1611 unnumbered batch of letters, dated 25 December 1842.

39 William D. Rubinstein, *Who Were the Rich? A Biographical Directory of British Wealth-holders, Vol. I: 1809–1839* (London, 2009). Professor Rubinstein has very generously shared his unpublished data for the years 1840–74.

40 The specific directories consulted systematically were the *Post Office Directories* for 1800, 1811, 1820, 1836, 1840, 1845, 1850, 1863, 1879, 1902, 1927, 1942, 1964 and 1972, and *Pig[g]ot's* for 1832–4.

41 We appreciate the generosity of the Mercantile Liverpool team in granting us this access.

42 www.slavevoyages.org; David Pope, 'The wealth and social aspirations of Liverpool's slave merchants of the second half of the eighteenth century', in David Richardson, Suzanne Schwarz and Anthony Tibbles (eds.), *Liverpool and Transatlantic Slavery* (Liverpool, 2007) pp. 164–226.

43 Clive Trebilcock, *Phoenix Assurance and the Development of British Insurance, Vol. I: 1782–1870* (Cambridge, 1985), p. 669.

44 R. G. Thorne (ed.), *The House of Commons, 1790–1820* (5 vols., London, 1986); D. R. Fisher (ed.), *The House of Commons 1820–1832* (7 vols., Cambridge, 2009).

45 We are particularly grateful to Philip Salmon and Kathryn Rix for sight of these.

46 www.historyofparliamentonline.org.

47 http://hansard.millbanksystems.com.

48 A number of general indexes to divisions were published in the Parliamentary Papers. For a guide to these and where to find them, see P. Ford and G. Ford, *A Guide to Parliamentary Papers* (3rd edn., Shannon, 1972), p. 20.

49 *Dod's Parliamentary Companions* underwent a number of changes of name from 1832 onwards. They are, however, readily identifiable in libraries. Michael Stenton, *Who's Who of British Members of Parliament: A Biographical Dictionary of the House of Commons Based on Annual Volumes of 'Dod's Parliamentary Companion' and Other Sources, Vol. I: 1832–1885* (Hassocks, 1976) is also useful.

50 T71/891 Tobago no. 12 (Sherwood Park).

51 Miranda Kaufmann, 'Slavery connections and new perspectives: English Heritage properties', *Conservation Bulletin* 58 (2008), 10–11. The author kindly made available to us the original report on her 2006 survey of thirty-three English Heritage properties, of which twenty-six were found to have some sort of link to the history of slavery and abolition.

52 Susan Dwyer Amussen, *Caribbean Exchanges: Slavery and the Transformation of English Society, 1640–1700* (Chapel Hill, NC, 2007).

53 Barry Supple, *The Royal Exchange Assurance: A History of British Assurance 1720–1970* (Cambridge, 1970), pp. 309–10.

54 For a discussion of the problems of occupational analysis, see Robert J. Morris, 'Occupational coding: principles and examples', *Historical Research/ Historische Sozialforschung* 15 (1) (1990), 3–29; in particular, for a discussion of the recording of women's occupations in the censuses, pp. 5–6.

55 www.belmontestate.net/grenada-history.htm, accessed 31 July 2013.

56 Susanne Seymour and Sheryllynne Haggerty, *Slavery Connections of Brodsworth Hall (1600–c. 1830): Final Report for English Heritage* (English Heritage, 2010), www.english-heritage.org.uk/publications/slavery-connections-brodsworth-hall/slavery-connections-brodsworth-hall.pdf, accessed 31 July 2013.

57 Rubinstein, *Who Were the Rich? Vol. 1*, 1831/10.
58 Landowners made up 174 out of 786 (22.1 per cent) of rich individuals dying between 1809 and 1839 with identifiable professions; Rubinstein, *Who Were the Rich? Vol. 1*, p. 14.
59 Philip Wright (ed.), *Lady Nugent's Journal of her Residence in Jamaica from 1801 to 1805* (4th edn., Kingston, Jamaica, 1966), p. 318.
60 *Edinburgh Gazette*, 5,758, 13 June 1848, p. 291; *Edinburgh Gazette*, 6,079, 6 June 1851, p. 449.
61 William D. Rubinstein, *Men of Property: The Very Wealthy in Britain since the Industrial Revolution* (1981; 2nd edn., London 2006), p. 93.

Appendix 2: Glossary of claimant categories

The roles of slave-owners can be thought of as divided into three types: owners, beneficiaries and agents. Each implies different relationships to the enslaved people in the award. The following lists each category and its description.

Owners

Owner-in-fee	The unqualified beneficial owner.
Tenant-for-life	Under the system of entail, which passed estates to the next generation but limited their right to sell those estates and nominated the successors in the following generation, a tenant-for-life was entitled to the income from the estate for his or her lifetime but could only sell the estate by obtaining a private act of Parliament to break the entail.
Tenant-in-tail or remainderman	The man or woman specified in the entail as the next beneficiary after the tenant-for-life.
Mortgagee-in-possession	A creditor who had foreclosed on a mortgage to take possession of an estate and take its income but whose tenure was subject to the right to redeem the mortgage (the 'equity of redemption') held by the original owner.

Beneficiaries

Legatee	The beneficiary of a specific lump-sum bequest secured on an estate and the enslaved people under the terms of a will.
Annuitant	The beneficiary of a specified annual income secured on an estate and the enslaved people under the terms of a will or marriage settlement. If the income was not paid in a given year, the arrears accumulated.

Residuary legatee | The beneficiary of the balance of a deceased's estate after all prior debts and specific bequests had been honoured.

Heir-at-law | The next of kin (closest blood relative) where a person had died intestate (without making a valid will).

Mortgagee | A creditor who had secured his claim on the estate and the enslaved people on it by way of a deed of mortgage entered into with the owner. A mortgagee had prior claim on the compensation money over the owner.

Judgement creditor | A creditor who had secured a debt on the estate by means of a court judgement. A judgement creditor had priority over the owner in claiming compensation.

Assignee | A person to whom a financial claim (including in some cases the compensation money) had been legally made over, perhaps to settle a debt incurred elsewhere.

Agents

Executor or executrix | A man or woman appointed under the terms of a will by the maker of the will (the testator) to carry out the terms of the will. Sometimes also a beneficiary of the will, especially if a family member such as a widow or brother or sister.

Administrator or administratrix | In Britain, the person granted control, by letters of administration from the courts, over a deceased person's estate where that person had died intestate. In Jamaica, the local agent or representative of the executors of a will made in Britain was also referred to as the administrator. In some colonial jurisdictions, an official appointee served as a 'curator' of intestate estates.

Trustee | A person appointed under the terms of a legal construction of a trust to carry out the purposes of the trust. The trust might have been established under a will, a marriage settlement or for the benefit of creditors. In addition, under the rules of the Slave Compensation Commission, trustees were appointed where the compensation monies 'belonged to or [were] vested in any married woman, infant, lunatic, or person of insane or unsound mind, or persons beyond the seas, or labouring under any other legal or material disability ... for the protection of whose interests it may be necessary to make provision'.[1] A trustee appointed under a will was sometimes referred to as a 'devisee-in-trust'.

Guardian
The person legally empowered to act on behalf of a minor (a child who had not reached the age of majority stipulated in a will or similar legal document, normally twenty-one but sometimes set by a testator's will at twenty-five or even twenty-eight).

Committee
The person legally empowered to act on behalf of another person who had been judged incapable by a commission of lunacy.

Assignee in bankruptcy
A person appointed by the creditors as a body empowered to administer the assets of a bankrupt individual or firm on behalf of creditors (6. Geo IV c. 16). This role is more recently fulfilled by a trustee in bankruptcy. The assignee might well be a creditor himself or herself.

Official assignee
An assignee by the bankruptcy court to work alongside the creditors' assignee in bankruptcy. These were permanent officials who were required to have had previous commercial experience (Stat. 1 and 2 Wil IV c. 56).

Receiver
The person responsible to the court for the protection of the assets of an estate that was subject to the proceedings of the Court of Chancery in Britain or in the colonies.

Sequestrator
The title given to the person carrying out the functions of the receiver in certain jurisdictions, notably Scotland and British Guiana.

NOTES

1 'General Rules of the Commissioners of Slave Compensation of the 10th March 1835', T71/1622.

Appendix 3: A note on the database

Keith McClelland

The data now stored in a MySQL database and that underpins the project website has its foundation in the material compiled by Nicholas Draper as a series of files in a FileMaker Pro database from the Parliamentary Papers and the Registers of Claims. The form of organisation of the data storage in a flat-file database necessarily limited what could be done with it and it was essential to move the data to exploit the possibilities of using a relational database-management system such as Microsoft Access or, eventually, the more powerful and flexible MySQL database system. The primary challenge was to enable the project to store information about individuals, claims and legacies while also tracking the relationships between these elements. This was, in part, a question of scale. We have around 47,000 unique individuals, though around 3,000 are of primary interest, and have information concerning about 46,000 claims.

A further challenge was one familiar to anyone who has tried to design a complex database, which is to anticipate what might be required even before any data for it has been collected. Moreover, the database had to be designed with a view to not only creating a means of recording the research but also, in due course, migrating it to a website and the database underpinning it. Hence, the migration from the original files complied by Draper to the current version involved two major steps. First, data had to be exported from FileMaker Pro, via Microsoft Excel, to Microsoft Access. Access was chosen for two main reasons: because it is a quite powerful and relatively user-friendly program and because it enabled each member of the research team to put in data on their own copies followed by 'replication', or the ability to synchronise copies. Second, there was a subsequent migration from Access to MySQL. At each stage it was essential that the integrity of the data be maintained, which involved a good deal of cross-checking. There were also particular issues that arose. For example, Microsoft Excel cannot handle dates before 1900 so all dates had to be converted to text and then back to dates in order to ensure accuracy and usability. There were also more taxing problems such as dealing with duplicate names (which has been discussed above).

The eventual transition from the original files to the current web-based system has involved two major transformations: first, the development of mechanisms for implementing relational data, and, second, the movement from one form of entering and presenting data to another form altogether. Each of these transformations will be discussed briefly.

If there is a single fundamental question that structures database design it is 'what do users need to be able get out of the database?' We want users to be able to find, for any individual, any engagement in any one of the legacy strands. Users also need to be able to answer aggregate questions, such as 'how many women living in London made claims on Jamaican estates?' or 'what was the number and geographical distribution of country estates connected with awardees?'

The focus of the database moved from the list of claims originally compiled in the FileMaker Pro database to the prosopographic list of individuals who were mentioned in the claims. This entailed redesigning the data to store it in eight sections – claims and awards, biographical data and each of the six legacy strands – while designing the mechanisms for showing the relationships between each of these elements.

This involved taking the original FileMaker data and breaking it into many different fields. For example, the names recorded against each claim had to be broken down into fields for first names and surnames, titles (such as 'Sir') and suffixes (such as for baronets). Names of additional claimants beyond the first named (which had been stored as lists of multiple people) had to be broken down into individuals. At the same time, individuals and claims had to be stored, in database jargon, as many-to-many relationships: that is, individuals may have made many claims while claims may have had multiple claimants.

Such operations had to be performed on most dimensions of the database. And this involved the creation of many tables – there are around eighty in the final database – and numerous fields: the number runs into hundreds.

Each strand, for example, has a considerable number of sub-sections to it so that it is possible to record in considerable detail information about a person's family, a firm, a role in imperial government and so on. Crucial to this process was the creation of 'primary' and 'foreign' keys. A *relational* database such as Access or MySQL rests on having a mechanism for establishing the relationship between data stored in one table and that stored in another. A primary key or unique identifier (which is usually a number) is stored for each record in one table and then matched to its 'foreign' counterpart in another. Thus, for example, the primary key for the individual can be stored in a table containing address information; and this can be done many times so that one person may be matched to many addresses. At the same time, each address has a unique identifier so that many people can be matched to a single address. Such procedures enable not only the joining of two tables – such as names and addresses – but also of multiple tables.

Developing the appropriate primary and foreign keys and ensuring that data on any particular aspect is stored in the right table so that we could establish the relationships we wanted to capture was central to the design of the database, as it is to any relational database. While this is not the place to document in detail the tables, fields and relationships contained in the database, if there is a single most important field in the entire database it is the unique number attached to each individual. More than any other, it makes possible the linking together of all the sections of the database in a chain of connections.

The design of the database had also to enable a clear and straightforward means for users to enter and display data and to be able to ask and answer questions of the kind indicated earlier. The migration of the data from the tables in Access to those in MySQL involved some important modifications; but the two systems are at base fundamentally compatible. What cannot be done, however, is to simply move the means of entering and searching data from one to the other. It is here that the second major transformation occurred.

On the base of a database rests the superstructure – the carapace that the user encounters when viewing data. In Access, the most important means of doing this is the form, which enables users to both enter and display data. It is relatively easy to create such forms though there may be complex elements involved. But none of the means available in Access is transferable to building a superstructure – the website – to enable both the research team to enter data and public users to explore what we have. The website interface has been built by using PHP – one of the most widely used 'scripting' languages for displaying dynamic web pages; that is, pages that can display changing information depending on what the user has asked of the database. All the means of establishing relationships between the tables and what is displayed on the screen are established through PHP scripts. There are numerous considerations that arise in creating such web pages, ranging from the need to maintain security against malicious intruders to maximising the speed with which the pages load to enabling the website to be viewed not only on conventional computers but also the new generation of devices (phones, tablet computers and so on). Here we have been very fortunate in having a website designer, Mark Hadley, who not only has the technical skills to create the pages but also understands the historical problems underpinning what we are trying to accomplish. But in the end any database or website is only as good as what users can get out of it. And that can only be answered by people who explore the Legacies of British Slave-ownership database.

Appendix 4: List of MPs 1832–80 who appear in the compensation records

Keith McClelland

An asterisk (*) in the 'Pre-1832?' column indicates those who also held seats before December 1832.

The party designations under 'Party affiliation' should be used very cautiously: although party alignments become clearer after 1832, there are cases where the affiliation is quite loose. For example, William James, classified as a 'Liberal (Radical)', was a staunch defender of West India interests over sugar while also being an advocate of radical parliamentary reform (including universal manhood suffrage, though he supported the more moderate proposals of 1831–2), free trade and abolition of the Corn Laws (which he had been in favour of since the 1820s) and economy and retrenchment in government expenditure. By contrast, Richard Godson voted for Emancipation in 1833 and was a free-trade Conservative.

Given the complexity of the compensation records, inclusion in this list has been confined to those who were directly involved in the compensation process in various capacities (including as awardees, beneficiaries, mortgagees, executors or trustees, or unsuccessful claimants). However, there were also a number of MPs who were particularly important in the 1830s–1850s and who were the immediate descendants of a claimant or beneficiary. Clearly legatees of slave-ownership by virtue of close involvement as family members with compensation claims as well as in their political activities, they include Thomas Chaplin (Conservative, Stamford, 1826–31 and 1832–8), Sir James Buller East (Conservative, Winchester, 1831–2 and 1835–64), John Neilson Gladstone (Conservative, Walsall, 1841, Ipswich 1842–7, Devizes 1852–7 and 1859–63), William Ewart Gladstone (Conservative, Newark, 1832–45, Peelite/Liberal, Oxford University, 1847–65, Liberal, Lancashire Southern, 1865–8, Greenwich, 1868–80 and Midlothian, 1880–95) and Philip William Skynner Miles (Conservative (Protectionist), Bristol, 1837–52).

There are eighty-seven MPs listed below.

Name	Party Affiliation	Constituency	Tenure	Pre-1832?
Rear Admiral Sir Charles Adam	Whig	Clackmannan and Kinross (pre-1832)	1831–2	*
		Clackmannan and Kinross (1832–)	1832–41	
Rowland Alston	Whig	Hertfordshire	1835–41	
General Sir George Anson	Whig	Lichfield	1806–41	
Sir Edmund Antrobus, second Bart.	Conservative then Liberal	Surrey Eastern	1841–7	
		Wilton	1855–77	
Hugh Duncan Baillie	Conservative	Rye	1830–1	*
		Honiton	1835–47	
James Evan Baillie	Whig	Tralee	1813–8	*
		Bristol	1830–5	
John Barham	Liberal	Stockbridge	1820–6	*
		Stockbridge	1831–2	
		Kendal	1834–7	
Alexander Baring	Whig then Conservative	Taunton	1806–26	*
		Callington	1826–31	
		Thetford	1831–2	
		Essex Northern	1832–5	
Francis Baring	Whig (1830) then Conservative (from 1832)	Thetford	1830–1	*
		Thetford	1832–41	
		Thetford	1848–57	
Thomas Baring	Conservative	Great Yarmouth	1835–7	
		Huntingdon	1844–77	
Henry Barkly	Peelite	Leominster	1845–8	
Lord William Henry Cavendish Bentinck	Whig	Nottinghamshire	1796–1803	*
		Nottinghamshire	1812–4	
		Nottinghamshire	1816–26	
		King's Lynn	1826–8	
		Glasgow	1836–9	
Hon. George Charles Grantley Fitzhardinge Berkeley	Liberal/ Independent	Gloucestershire Western	1832–52	
Ralph Bernal	Whig–Liberal	Lincoln	1818–20	*
		Rochester	1820–41	
		Weymouth and Melcombe Regis	1842–7	
		Rochester	1847–52	
Sir Thomas Bernard Birch, second Bart.	Liberal	Liverpool	1847–52	

Name	Party Affiliation	Constituency	Tenure	Pre-1832?
James Blair	Conservative	Saltash	1818–20	⋆
		Aldeburgh	1820–6	
		Minehead	1826–30	
		Wigtonshire	1837–41	
James Bradshaw	Conservative	Brackley	1825–32	⋆
John Ivatt Briscoe	Whig–Liberal	Surrey	1830–2	⋆
		Westbury	1837–41	
William Burge	Conservative	Eye	1831–52	
George Stevens Byng	Whig	Milborne Port	1831–2	⋆
		Chatham	1834–5	
		Poole	1835–7	
		Chatham	1837–52	
Marquess of Chandos	Conservative	Buckinghamshire	1818–39	
Sir Thomas John Cochrane	Conservative	Ipswich	1839–41	
Admiral Sir Edward Codrington	Liberal	Devonport	1832–9	
Henry Combe Compton	Conservative	Hampshire Southern	1835–57	
Philip Courtenay	Conservative	Bridgwater	1837–41	
Robert Westley Hall Dare	Conservative	Essex Southern	1832–6	
Sir George Henry Dashwood, fifth Bart.	Whig–Liberal Whig–Liberal	Buckinghamshire Wycombe	1832–5 1837–62	
James Colyear Dawkins	Conservative	Chippenham	1784–1806	⋆
		Chippenham	1807–12	
		Hastings	1812–26	
		Wilton	1831–7	
William Joseph Denison	Whig	Camelford	1796–1802	⋆
		Kingston-upon-Hull	1806–7	
		Surrey	1818–32	
		Surrey Western	1832–49	
Abel Rous Dottin	Conservative	Gatton	1818–20	⋆
		Southampton	1826–31	
		Southampton	1835–41	
James Douglas Stoddart Douglas	Liberal	Rochester	1841–7	
Alexander Ellice	Whig	Harwich	1837–41	
Rt. Hon. Edward Ellice	Whig–Liberal	Coventry	1818–26	⋆
		Coventry	1832–63	
John Samuel Wanley Sawbridge Erle-Drax	Conservative	Wareham	1841–7	
		Wareham	1859–65	
		Wareham	1868–80	
James Ewing	Liberal	Wareham	1830–1	⋆
		Glasgow	1832–5	

Name	Party Affiliation	Constituency	Tenure	Pre-1832?
Joseph Feilden	Conservative	Blackburn	1865–9	
William Feilden	Liberal then Conservative	Blackburn	1832–47	
George Ferguson	Conservative	Banffshire	1832–7	
James William Freshfield	Conservative (Peelite)	Penryn	1830–2	*
		Penryn and Falmouth	1835–41	
		Boston	1851–2	
		Penryn and Falmouth	1852–7	
Augustus Elliott Fuller	Conservative	Sussex Eastern	1841–57	
Sir William Payne Gallwey, second Bart.	Conservative	Thirsk	1851–80	
Thomas Steuart Gladstone	Conservative	Queenborough	1830–1	*
		Portarlington	1832–5	
		Queen's County Leicester	1835–7	
		Ipswich	1842–2	
Richard Godson	Conservative (Peelite)	St Albans	1831–2	*
		Kidderminster	1832–5	
		Kidderminster	1837–49	
Robert Gordon	Whig–Liberal	Wareham	1812–8	*
		Cricklade	1818–37	
		Windsor	1837–41	
Rt. Hon. Henry Goulburn	Conservative (Peelite)	Horsham	1808–12	*
		St Germans	1812–8	
		West Looe	1818–26	
		Armagh	1826–31	
		Cambridge University	1831–56	
Sir Alexander Cray Grant, eighth Bart.	Conservative	Tregony	1812–8	*
		Lostwithiel	1818–26	
		Aldborough	1826–30	
		Westbury	1830–1	
		Cambridge	1840–3	
James Walter Grimston, second Earl of Verulam	Conservative	St Albans	1830–1	*
		Newport	1831–2	
		Hertfordshire	1832–45	
Renn William Hampden	Conservative	Great Marlow	1842–7	
Thomson Hankey junior	Liberal	Peterborough	1853–68	
		Peterborough	1874–80	
Sir Robert Heron, second Bart.	Whig	Great Grimsby	1812–8	*
		Peterborough	1819–47	
Thomas Berry Horsfall	Conservative	Derby	1852–3	
		Liverpool	1853–68	

Name	Party Affiliation	Constituency	Tenure	Pre-1832?
John Irving the elder	Conservative	Bramber	1806–32	*
		Antrim	1837–41	
William James	Liberal (Radical)	Carlisle	1820–6	*
		Carlisle	1832–5	
		Cumberland Eastern	1836–47	
William Augustus Johnson	Whig	Boston	1820–6	*
		Oldham	1837–47	
Sir Frederick George Johnstone, seventh Bart.	Conservative	Weymouth and Melcombe Regis	1832–5	
Samuel Trehawke Kekewich	Independent	Exeter	1826–30	*
		Devon Southern	1858–73	
Thomas Barrett Lennard	Whig	Ipswich	1820–6	*
		Maldon	1826–37	
		Maldon	1847–52	
Edward Littleton, first Baron Hatherton	Whig	Staffordshire	1812–32	*
		Staffordshire Southern	1832–5	
Charles Lushington	Whig	Ashburton	1835–41	
		Westminster	1847–52	
Andrew Henry Lynch	Liberal	Galway	1832–41	
William Alexander Mackinnon	Conservative	Dunwich	1819–20	*
		Lymington	1831–2	
		Lymington	1835–52	
		Rye	1853–65	
Lachlan Maclachlan	Liberal	Galway County	1832–3	
Joseph Marryat	Whig	Sandwich	1832–5	
Philip John Miles	Conservative	Westbury	1820–6	*
		Corfe Castle	1829–32	
		Bristol	1835–7	
Charles Moore	Liberal	Tipperary	1865–9	
Alexander Murray	Whig	Kirkcudbright	1838–45	
Sir Gerard Noel Noel, second Bart.	Whig	Maidstone	1784–8	*
		Rutland	1788–1808	
		Rutland	1814–38	
Richard Alexander Oswald	Liberal	Ayrshire	1832–5	
George Palmer	Conservative	Essex Southern	1836–47	
Lord William Powlett	Liberal	Winchelsea	1812–5	*
	Conservative	Durham	1815–31	
		St Ives	1846–52	
		Ludlow	1852–7	
Edward Protheroe junior	Whig	Evesham	1826–30	*
		Bristol	1831–2	
		Halifax	1837–47	

Name	Party Affiliation	Constituency	Tenure	Pre-1832?
Sir John Rae Reid, second Bart.	Conservative	Dover	1830–1	*
		Dover	1832–47	
Abraham Wildey Robarts	Liberal	Maidstone	1832–7	
Sir George Henry Rose	Conservative	Southampton	1794–1813	*
		Christchurch	1818–32	
		Christchurch	1837–44	
James Scarlett, first Baron Abinger	Conservative	Peterborough	1819–30	*
		Malton	1830–1	
		Cockermouth	1831–2	
		Norwich	1832–4	
Abel Smith	Conservative	Malmesbury	1810–2	*
		Wendover	1812–8	
		Midhurst	1820–30	
		Wendover	1830–2	
		Hertfordshire	1835–47	
John Smith	Whig	Wendover	1802–6	*
		Nottingham	1806–18	
		Midhurst	1818–30	
		Chichester	1830–1	
		Buckinghamshire	1831–4	
Sir John Mark Frederick Smith	Conservative	Chatham	1852–3	
		Chatham	1857–65	
Humphrey St John-Mildmay	Conservative	Southampton	1842–7	
Houston Stewart	Whig-Liberal	Greenwich	1852	
John Stewart	Conservative	Lymington	1832–47	
Patrick Maxwell Stewart	Liberal (West India interest)	Lancaster	1831–7	
		Renfrewshire	1841–6	
John Tollemache	Conservative	Cheshire Southern	1841–68	
		Cheshire, West	1868–72	
Robert Charles Tudway	Conservative (Protectionist)	Wells	1852–5	
Robert Wallace	Liberal	Greenock	1832–45	
John Ashton Yates	Liberal	Carlow	1837–41	
Sir William Laurence Young, fourth Bart.	Conservative	Buckinghamshire	1835–42	

Appendix 5: MPs and their connections: an indicative list

Keith McClelland

The following list indicates some of those people where there is a direct connection to a later MP.

Charles Ashe A'Court	His daughter Mary Elizabeth (1822–1911) married Sidney Herbert, first Baron Herbert of Lea, MP for South Wiltshire 1832–61.
Sir Charles Adam	His son, William Patrick Adam (1825–81), worked for the East India Company and was Liberal MP for Clackmannan and Kinross, 1859–80.
Sir George Anson	His nephew, Major-General George Anson (1797–1857), who became commander-in-chief of the British army in India (1856) and died of cholera during the Indian Rebellion of 1857, was MP for Great Yarmouth (1818–35), Stoke-upon-Trent (1836–7) and Staffordshire South (1837–53).
Andrew Arcedeckne	His son, Andrew (1822–71), was defeated (as a Liberal) at Harwich, 1857. He was a subscriber to the Eyre Defence Committee in 1866.
Hugh Duncan Baillie	His son, Colonel Henry James Baillie (1803–85), was Conservative MP for Inverness-shire (1840–68) and under-secretary of state for India (1858–9).
Hon. George Charles Grantley Fitzhardinge Berkeley	His three brothers, Maurice, Craven and Henry, were all MPs: Maurice Berkeley (1788–1867) was Whig MP for Gloucester, 1832–3, 1835–7, 1841–57; Craven Berkeley (1805–55) was Liberal MP for Cheltenham, 1832–47, 1848, 1852–5; and Henry Fitzhardinge Berkeley (1794–1870) was an Independent Liberal MP for Bristol, 1837–70.

Henry Chaplin

Henry Chaplin (1840–1923) was the son of the Rev. Henry Chaplin, claimant on Grenada 466. Henry junior was Conservative and Protectionist MP for Lincolnshire Mid 1868–85 and Sleaford 1885–1906 and Wimbledon 1907–16. He was Chancellor of the Duchy of Lancaster 1885–6, president of the Board of Agriculture 1886–92 and president of the Board of Local Government 1895–1900 and was created first Viscount Chaplin in 1916. He inherited wealth from his uncle, Charles Chaplin, formerly MP, and was 'one of the richest commoners in the kingdom'. An important Conservative politician of the late nineteenth and early twentieth centuries, he was, among other things, a protectionist and unionist. He married Lady Florence Sutherland-Leveson-Gower, elder daughter of George Granville William Sutherland-Leveson-Gower, third Duke of Sutherland, in 1876. His elder daughter, Edith, married Lord Castlereagh, later seventh Marquess of Londonderry, in 1899.

Charles Chetwynd-Talbot, second Earl Talbot

His second son was Henry John Chetwynd-Talbot (1803–68), known as Viscount Ingestre (1826–49), the Earl Talbot (1849–58) and the eighteenth Earl of Shrewsbury and the eighteenth Earl of Waterford (1860–8). As Viscount Ingestre he was Conservative MP for Hertford 1830–1, Armagh 1831, Hertford 1832–3 and Staffordshire Southern 1837–49. Henry John's son, Charles John (1830–77), styled Viscount Ingestre (1849–68), became Conservative MP for Stafford 1857–9, Staffordshire Northern 1859–65 and Stamford 1868 until succeeding his father as the nineteenth Earl of Shrewsbury in 1868.

Sir Thomas John Cochrane

His son Alexander Cochrane-Wishart-Baillie, first Baron Lamington (1816–90), was a leading member of Disraeli's 'Young England'. Alexander was also Conservative MP for Honiton 1859–68 and for the Isle of Wight 1874–80.

Frederick White Corrance

His son Frederick Snowden Corrance (1822–1906) was Conservative MP for Suffolk Eastern 1867–74.

Isaac Currie	A banker; his son, Raikes Currie (1801–81), was Whig MP for Northampton 1837–57.
Wilbraham Egerton	His fourth son, Christopher Edward Egerton (1816–69), was Conservative MP for Macclesfield 1852–68 and East Cheshire 1868–9.
Edward Ellice	His son, also Edward, was Whig MP for St Andrews District of Burghs 1837–80.
John Samuel Wanley Sawbridge Erle-Drax	His descendant, Richard Drax (Richard Plunkett-Ernle-Erle-Drax), was elected as Conservative MP for South Dorset 2010.
Joseph Feilden	One of Feilden's sons, Randle Joseph Feilden (1824–95), army officer, businessman and politician, was Conservative MP for Lancashire Northern 1880–5 and Chorley 1885–95. He was a strong unionist in opposition to Irish home rule.
Richard Godson	His nephew Augustus Frederick Godson was Conservative MP for Kidderminster 1886–1906.
Benjamin Buck Greene	His brother Edward was Conservative MP for Bury St Edmunds 1865–85 and Stowmarket 1886–91.
Frederick Johnstone	His son Sir Frederick John William Johnstone was Conservative MP for Weymouth and Melcombe Regis 1874–85.
Samuel Trehawke Kekewich	His son (from a second marriage), Sir George Kekewich (1841–1921), was Conservative MP for Exeter 1906–10.
Henry Lascelles, second Earl of Harewood	Had numerous political and social connections.
Charles Lawrence and George Lawrence	William Frederic Lawrence, great-grandson of Charles Lawrence and great-nephew of George Lawrence, was MP for Liverpool Abercromby 1885–1906.
William Alexander Mackinnon	His son, also William, was Liberal MP for Rye 1852–3 and Lymington 1857–68.
Peter McLagan	His son Peter Maclagan of Pumpherston (c. 1823–1900) was Liberal MP for Linlithgow 1865–93.

Sir James Montgomery	His eldest son, Graham Montgomery (1823–1901), was Conservative MP for Peeblesshire 1852–68 and Selkirkshire and Peeblesshire 1868–80.
Thomas Naghten	A slave-owner and Charles McGarel's attorney in British Guiana. His son, Arthur Robert Naghten (1829–81), was Conservative MP for Winchester 1874–80.
Charles Stewart Parker	His son Charles Stuart Parker (1829–1910) was Liberal MP for Perthshire 1868–74 and for the City of Perth 1878–92 and was an important liberal intellectual and historian.
Archibald Paull	His son, Henry Paull (1822–98), was Conservative MP for St Ives 1857–68.
John Smith	Banker and MP; his sons included Martin Tucker Smith (1803–90), Conservative MP for Midhurst 1831–2 and Wycombe 1847–65.
Mary Lawrence Stevenson	Her son was almost certainly Sir William Stevenson (1804–63), governor and commander-in-chief of Mauritius 1857–63, and her grandson, Francis Seymour Stevenson (1862–1938), was Liberal MP for Eye 1885–1906.
John Tollemache	His children included Wilbraham Frederic Tollemache (1832–1904), Conservative MP for Cheshire West 1868–85. John Tollemache's nephew was Henry James Tollemache (1846–1939), Conservative MP for Cheshire Western 1881–5 and Eddisbury 1885–1906.
Maria Hawes Ware	Maria Hawes Ware's brother and executor Russell Gurney (1804–78) was one of the three commissioners appointed in December 1865 to investigate Governor Eyre's handling of the 'insurrection' on the island, and was Conservative MP for Southampton 1865–78.

Bibliography

MANUSCRIPT SOURCES

NATIONAL ARCHIVES, KEW

CO 137/146 Jamaica, Correspondence: Secretary of State. Offices and Individuals.

CO 137/161 Jamaica, Correspondence: Secretary of State. Offices and Individuals.

CO 137/166 Jamaica, Correspondence: Secretary of State. Offices and Individuals.

T71 Office of Registry of Colonial Slaves and Slave Compensation Commission: Records.

OTHER LOCATIONS

Blathwayth Family Collection. Gloucestershire Archive.

'Brundrett & Co. of 10 Kings Bench Walk, solicitors: clients' papers'. East Sussex Record Office, Additional Manuscripts, Catalogue Z AMS6417.

Codrington Papers, RP 2616/1–37. British Library microfilm.

Diary of John Nembhard, Regimental Museum, First Queen's Dragoon Guards. CARDG:1988.1764, extracts at www.qdg.org.uk/diaries.php?dy=29, accessed 31 July 2013.

Diaries of Robert Hibbert; transcripts supplied by Nick Hibbert Steele, Hibbert Archive and Collection, Melbourne, Australia.

Gordon of Cluny Papers. University of Aberdeen Special Libraries and Archives, MS 3600.

Great Western Cotton Company. Bristol Record Office, 12142/1; 12141/10a–b.

Keir of Stirling Muniments 1338–c. 1940, Glasgow City Archives, Mitchell Library, GB243/T-SK; T-SK/13/13.

Lancaster Society of Friends, Disownments. Lancashire Record Office, FRL/2/1/5/117.

Letters, printed notices and papers relating to the founding of the London Institution 1805–17. London Metropolitan Archives, CLC/009MS03080.

Simon Taylor Papers, Institute of Commonwealth Studies, Senate House Library, included in Adam Matthew publications: *Plantation Life in the Caribbean*, at www.ampltd.co.uk/collections_az/Plantation-Life-1/highlights.aspx, accessed 1 November 2013.

Slebech Archive. National Library of Wales, NLA8897.

Trustee Minute Book of Holy Trinity Church, Clapham Common. London Metropolitan Archive. P95 TR11–1/X077/084.

PRIMARY MATERIAL ACCESSED THROUGH ANCESTRY (WWW.ANCESTRY.COM)

1841 and 1851 censuses of England and Wales.
Cambridge University Alumni, 1261–1900
London England marriages and banns, 1754–1921.
National Probate Calendar.
Oxford University Alumni, 1500–1886.
UK Articles of Clerkship 1756–1874.

PRIMARY MATERIAL ACCESSED THROUGH SCOTLAND'S PEOPLE (WWW.SCOTLANDSPEOPLE.GOV.UK)

Birth, marriage and death records.
Census records.

PARLIAMENTARY PAPERS (PP) AND OFFICIAL DOCUMENTS

PP1823 (411) IV. *Report from the Select Committee Appointed to Consider of the Means of Improving and Maintaining the Foreign Trade of the Country.*

PP1831–2 (721) XX. *Report from the Select Committee on the Extinction of Slavery throughout the British Dominions.*

PP1836 (560) XV. *Report from the Select Committee on Negro Apprenticeship in the Colonies.*

PP1837 (510) VII. *Report from the Select Committee on Negro Apprenticeship in the Colonies.*

PP1837–8 (215) XLVIII. *Accounts of Slave Compensation Claims; Records Created and Inherited by HM Treasury: Office of Registry of Colonial Slavery and Slave Compensation Commission Records.*

PP1840 (151) XXXIV. *British Guiana. Copies of Correspondence between the Secretary of State for the Colonies and the Governor of British Guiana, Respecting the Immigration of Labourers into That Colony.*

PP1841 (45) XVI. *Letter from Secretary to Government of India to Committee on Exportation of Hill Coolies; Report of Committee and Evidence.*

PP1842 (479) XIII. *Report from the Select Committee on West India Colonies.*

PP1847–8 *Select Committee on Sugar and Coffee Planting.* Eight reports. Reports, paper numbers and volumes are: first (123) XXIII Pt. I; second (137) XXIII Pt. I; third (167) XXIII Pt. I; fourth (184) XXIII Pt. II; fifth (206) XXIII Pt. II; sixth (230) XXIII Pt. II; seventh (245) XXIII Pt. III; eighth (361) (361-II) XXIII Pt. III; XXIII Pt. IV.

PP1898 [C.8706] LXXXV. *Customs Tariffs of the United Kingdom, from 1800 to 1897.*

House of Commons Debates.
House of Lords Debates.

NEWSPAPERS AND PERIODICALS

The Art-Union.
Blackwood's.
Edinburgh Gazette.
Gentleman's Magazine.
Glasgow Herald.
Illustrated London News.
London Gazette.
Melbourne Argus.
The Metropolitan Magazine.
Morning Chronicle.
New South Wales Police Gazette.
The Railway Times.
The Times.

DIRECTORIES AND WORKS OF REFERENCE

Dod, Charles R., *The Peerage, Baronetage and Knightage of Great Britain and Ireland* (London, 1848).
Dod's Parliamentary Companions (1832–).
Jamaica Almanacs.
Kent's Directory, 1802.
London trade directories, including *New Complete Guide to London*; *Kent's Directory*; *London Directory*; *The Universal British Directory of Trade, Commerce and Manufacture*; *Post Office Annual Directory*; *Boyle's City & Commercial Companion to the Court Guide*; and *Holden's Triennial Directory*. All in the Institute of Historical Research, Senate House Library, London.
Oliver, Vere Langford, *Caribbeana: Being Miscellaneous Papers Relating to the History, Genealogy, Topography, and Antiquities of the British West Indies* (6 vols., London, 1909–19).
History of the Island of Antigua (3 vols., London, 1896).
Pigot's Directory (London, 1832–4).
Plummer, Thomas, Henry Davidson, Thomas Gowland, Thomas Hughan, Richard Lee, Eben[ezer] Maitland, David Mitchell, Thomas Reid, Ab[raham] W. Rutherford, Joseph Timperon and Andrew Wedderburn, *Holden's Triennial*, 1808.
Post Office Directories.
The Royal Kalendar and the Court and City Register for England and Scotland (London, 1767–1890).
'Watford: Manors', in *A History of the County of Hertford, Vol. II* (London, 1908), pp. 451–64, at www.british-history.ac.uk/report.aspx?compid=43308, accessed 16 January 2012.
White, William, *History, Gazetteer and Directory of the County of Devon including the City of Exeter* (2nd edn., London, 1878–9).

CONTEMPORARY PUBLISHED SOURCES

Alison, Archibald, *History of Europe from the Fall of Napoleon in 1815 to the Accession of Louis Napoleon in 1852* (8 vols., Edinburgh, 1852–9).

History of the French Revolution from 1789–1796 (10 vols., London, 1833–42, repr. Paris, 1852).

Some Account of My Life and Writings. An Autobiography (2 vols., Edinburgh, 1883).

'The West India question', *Blackwood's* 31 (191) (1832), 412–23.

Anon., *A Statement of the Claims of the West India Colonies to a Protecting Duty against East India Sugar, Dedicated to William Manning, Esq., MP* (London, 1823).

Baker, Sir Thomas, *Memorials of a Dissenting Chapel, Its Foundation and Worthies; Being a Sketch of the Rise of Non-Conformity in Manchester and the Erection of the Chapel in Cross Street, with Notices of its Ministers and Trustees* (Manchester, 1884).

Berkeley, The Hon. George Charles Grantley Fitzhardinge, *My Life and Recollections* (4 vols., London, 1865–6).

Two Letters Addressed to the Landed and Manufacturing Interests of Great Britain and Ireland, on the Just Maintenance of Free Trade (London, 1850).

Browning, Elizabeth Barrett, 'The Runaway Slave at Pilgrim's Point', in *Aurora Leigh and Other Poems* (London, 1978), pp. 392–402.

Campbell, Theophila Carlile, *The Battle of the Press as Told in the Story of the Life of Richard Carlile by His Daughter, Theophila Carlile Campbell* (London, 1899), at www.gutenberg.org/files/38370/38370-h/38370-h.htm, accessed 1 November 2013.

Catalogue of Anglo-Jewish Historical Exhibition 1887 Royal Albert Hall (London, 1887).

Conrad, Joseph, 'Tales of the Sea', in *Notes on Life and Letters* (London, 1924), pp. 53–7.

Cooper, Thomas, *Correspondence between George Hibbert, Esq., and the Rev. T. Cooper, Relative to the Condition of the Negro Slaves in Jamaica, Extracted from the Morning Chronicle: Also a Libel on the Character of Mr and Mrs Cooper, Published in 1823, in Several Jamaica Journals; with Notes and Remarks by Thomas Cooper* (London, 1824).

A Letter to Robert Hibbert Jun. Esq., in Reply to his Pamphlet, Entitled, 'Facts Verified upon Oath, in Contradiction of the Report of the Reverend Thomas Cooper, Concerning the General Condition of the Slave in Jamaica' (London, 1824).

Cowell, John Welsford, *La France et les États Confédérés* (Paris and London, 1865).

Lancashire's Wrongs and the Remedy (London, 1863).

Southern Secession: A Letter Addressed to Captain T. Maury Confederate States Navy, on His Letter to Admiral Fitzroy (London, 1862).

Cracroft, Bernard, 'The analysis of the House of Commons, or indirect representation', in *Essays on Reform* (London, 1867), pp. 155–90.

Dasent, George Webbe, *Annals of an Eventful Life* (3 vols., London, 1870).

Dibdin, Thomas Frognall, *Bibliographical Decameron or Ten Days Pleasant Discourse Upon Illuminated Manuscripts, and Subjects Connected with Early Engravings, Typography, and Bibliography* (3 vols., London, 1817).

Disraeli, Benjamin, *Coningsby, or the New Generation* (1844; repr. London, 1989).

Lord George Bentinck: A Political Biography (4th edn., London, 1852).

Ellison, Thomas, *The Cotton Trade of Great Britain* (London, 1886).

The Eyre Defence and Aid Fund (London, 1866).

Fletcher, William Younger, *English Book Collectors* (London, 1902).

Froude, James Anthony, 'England's forgotten worthies', in *Essays in Literature and History* (London, 1906), pp. 34–80.

Hakewill, James, *A Picturesque Tour of the Island of Jamaica from Drawings Made in the Years 1820 and 1821* (London, 1825).

Hibbert, George, *Abridgment of the Minutes of the Evidence, Taken before a Committee of the Whole House, to Whom it was Referred to Consider of the Slave Trade, 1789[–91]* (c. 1792).

Substance of Three Speeches in Parliament on the Bill for the Abolition of the Slave Trade and the Petition Respecting the State of the West India Trade in February and March 1807 (London, 1807).

Hibbert jun., Robert, *Facts Verified on Oath in Contradiction of the Report of Rev. Thomas Cooper, concerning the General Condition of Slaves in Jamaica; and More Especially Relative to the Management and Treatment of the Slave upon Georgia Estate, in the Parish of Hanover, in That Island* (London, 1824).

Hodges, Sir William, *Reports of Cases Argued and Determined in the Court of Common Pleas* (2 vols., London, 1838).

Holland, Henry Richard Vassall Lord, *Further Memoirs of the Whig Party 1807–1821 with Some Miscellaneous Reminiscences*, ed. Lord Stavordale (London, 1905).

Memoirs of the Whig Party during My Time, ed. Henry Edward Lord Holland (2 vols., London, 1854).

Kerry, Charles, *The History and Antiquities of the Hundred of Bray in the County of Berks* (London, 1861).

Kingsley, Charles, *At Last. A Christmas in the West Indies* (2 vols., London, 1871).

His Letters and Memories of His Life, edited by his wife (4 vols., London, 1901).

The Recollections of Geoffrey Hamlyn (London, 1859).

Westward Ho! (1855; repr. London, 1906).

Kingsley, Henry, 'Eyre, the South-Australian Explorer', *Macmillan's Magazine* (October 1865), 501–10.

The Hillyars and the Burtons. A Tale of Two Families (London, 1865).

The Law Journal for the Year 1833, Comprising Reports of Cases in the Courts of Equity ... Vol. XI (London, 1833).

Low, Samuel, jnr., *The Charities of London* (London, 1861).

Lynch, Theodora Elizabeth, *The Cotton-Tree: or Emily, the Little West Indian* (London, 1847).

The Family Sepulchre: A Tale of Jamaica (London, 1848).

The Mountain Pastor (London, 1852).

The Wonders of the West Indies (London, 1856).

Years Ago. A Tale of West Indian Life in the Eighteenth Century (London, 1865).

Macaulay, Zachary, *Negro Slavery; or a View of Some of the More Prominent Features of that State of Society, as It Exists in the United States of America and in the Colonies of the West Indies, Especially in Jamaica* (London, 1823).

Mackinnon William, Alexander, *History of Civilisation* (2 vols., London, 1846).

MacQueen, James, *The West India Colonies; the Calumnies and Misrepresentations Circulated against Them by the* Edinburgh Review, *Mr Clarkson, Mr Cropper, &c. &c.* (London, 1824).

Markland, J. H., *A Sketch of the Life and Character of George Hibbert Esq., F. R. S., S. A., and L. S.* (London, 1837).

Marryat, Florence, *Life and Letters of Captain Marryat* (2 vols., London, 1872).

Marryat, Frederick, *A Diary in America, with Remarks on its Institutions* (3 vols., London, 1839).

    Frank Mildmay or The Naval Officer (London, 1829).

    The King's Own (London, 1830).

    Masterman Ready; or The Wreck of the Pacific (London, 1841).

    The Mission: or, Scenes in Africa (2 vols., London, 1845).

    Mr Midshipman Easy, (1836; repr. London, 1896).

    Newton Forster, or the Merchant Service (1832; repr. London, 1897).

    'On novels and novel writing', *Metropolitan Magazine*, 11 (42) (1834), 113–19.

    Percival Keene (London, 1842).

    Peter Simple (1834; repr. London, 1939).

    'The West Indian colonies in their state of transition from bad to worse', *Metropolitan Magazine* 8 (29) (1833), 88–100.

Marryat, Joseph, *A History of Pottery and Porcelain* (London, 1850).

    A Reply to the Arguments Contained in Various Publications Recommending an Equalization of the Duties on East and West Indian Sugar (London, 1823).

    Thoughts on the Abolition of the Slave Trade and Civilization of Africa (London, 1816).

Marx, Karl, *Capital* (1867; repr. London, 1974).

Murch, Jerom, *Memoir of Robert Hibbert, Founder of the Hibbert Trust: With a Sketch of Its History* (Bath, 1874).

Peel, Sir Robert, *Tamworth Election: Speech of Sir Robert Peel, June 28, 1841* (London, 1841).

Pettigrew, Thomas Joseph, *Memoirs of the Life and Writings of the Late John Coakley Lettsom* (3 vols., London, 1817).

Pinckard, Henry, *Observations on the Management and Extraordinary Losses of the Jamaica Steam Navigation Company. By Henry Pinckard Esq., an Auditor of the Company* (London, 1838).

Porter, John, *History of the Fylde of Lancashire* (Fleetwood and Blackpool, 1876).

Proceedings before the Privy Council against Compulsory Manumission in the Colonies of Demerara and Berbice (London, 1827).

Report of the Acting Committee to the Standing Committee of West India Planters and Merchants … January 1848 (London, 1848).

Russell, George William Erskine, *Dr Pusey* (London, 1907).

Scoble, John, *Hill Coolies: A Brief Exposure of the Deplorable Condition of the Hill Coolies in British Guiana and Mauritius* (London, 1840).

Scott, Sir George Gilbert, *Personal and Professional Recollections by the late Sir George Gilbert Scott, R. A.,* ed. G. Gilbert Scott F. S. A. (London, 1879).

Scott, Michael, *The Cruise of the Midge* (London, 1835).

    Tom Cringle's Log (2 vols., Edinburgh 1833; repr. Ithaca, 1999).

Smith, John Guthrie and John Oswald Mitchell, *The Old Country Houses of the Old Glasgow Gentry* (2nd edn., Glasgow, 1878).

Smith, Sydney, *Selected Letters of Sydney Smith*, ed. N. C. Smith (2nd edn., Oxford, 1981).

Statement by the Council of the University of London, Explanatory of the Nature and Objects of the Institution (London, 1827).

Sturge, Joseph and Thomas Harvey, *The West Indies in 1837* (London, 1838).

Wright, Philip (ed.), *Lady Nugent's Journal of Her Residence in Jamaica from 1801 to 1805* (4th edn., Kingston, Jamaica, 1966).

Young, John, *A Catalogue of the Pictures at Leigh Court near Bristol, the Seat of Philip John Miles MP* (London, 1822).

PUBLISHED SECONDARY SOURCES

Aldrich, Megan, 'Gothic sensibility: the early years of the Gothic revival', in Paul Atterbury (ed.), *Pugin: Master of Gothic Revival* (New Haven and London, 1996), pp. 12–29.

Allen, R. C., 'Why the Industrial Revolution was British: commerce, induced invention and the scientific revolution', *Economic History Review* 64 (2) (2011), 357–84.

Amussen, Susan Dwyer, *Caribbean Exchanges: Slavery and the Transformation of English Society, 1640–1700* (Chapel Hill, NC, 2007).

Anderson, Clare, 'After Emancipation: empires and imperial formations', in Catherine Hall, Nicholas Draper and Keith McClelland (eds.), *Emancipation and the Remaking of the British Imperial World* (Manchester, 2014), pp. 113–27.

'Convicts and coolies: rethinking indentured labour in the nineteenth century', *Slavery & Abolition* 30 (1) (2009), 93–109.

Anderson, Perry, 'The figures of descent', in *English Questions* (London, 1992), pp. 121–92.

Anon, *Chronicles of Cannon Street, a Few Records of an Old Firm* (London, n.d., [1957]).

Athill, Diana, *Yesterday Morning* (London, 2002).

Atterbury, Paul, 'Pugin and interior design', in Atterbury (ed.), *A. W. N. Pugin: Master of Gothic Revival* (New Haven and London, 1996), pp. 177–200.

Baker, Margaret, *Discovering London Statues and Monuments* (Buckinghamshire, 2002).

Barbour, James, 'Keil through the ages', *The Kintyre Antiquarian and Natural History Society Magazine* 23 (Autumn 1988), at www.ralstongenealogy.com/number23kintmag.htm, accessed 20 August 2012.

Barnes, John, *Henry Kingsley and Colonial Fiction* (Melbourne, 1971).

Barrett, R. A., *The Barretts of Jamaica: The Family of Elizabeth Barrett Browning* (Winfield, KS, 2000).

Baylen, Joseph O. and Norbert J. Gossman (eds.), *Biographical Dictionary of Modern British Radicals, Vol. I: 1770–1830* (Hassocks, 1979).

Bayly, C. A., *The Birth of the Modern World 1780–1914: Global Connections and Comparisons* (Oxford, 2004).

Beachey, R. W., *The British West Indies Sugar Industry in the Late 19th Century* (Oxford, 1957).

Berg, Maxine, 'In pursuit of luxury: global history and British consumer goods in the eighteenth century', *Past & Present* 182 (2004), 85–142.

Luxury and Pleasure in Eighteenth-Century Britain (Oxford, 2005).

Blackburn, Robin, *The American Crucible. Slavery, Emancipation and Human Rights* (London, 2009).

The Making of New World Slavery. From the Baroque to the Modern, 1492–1800 (London, 1997).

The Overthrow of Colonial Slavery 1776–1848 (London, 1988).

Blackett, R. J. M., *Divided Hearts. Britain and the American Civil War* (Baton Rouge, 2001).

Brake, Laurel and Marysa Demoor (eds.), *Dictionary of Nineteenth-Century Journalism in Great Britain and Ireland* (Gent, 2009).

Brantlinger, Patrick, *Dark Vanishings. Discourse on the Extinction of Primitive Races, 1800–1930* (Ithaca, NY, 2003).

Rule of Darkness. British Literature and Imperialism 1830–1890 (Ithaca, NY, 1988).

Brown, Christopher Leslie, *Moral Capital: Foundations of British Abolitionism* (Chapel Hill, NC, 2006).

Burnard, Trevor, '"The Grand Mart of the Island": the economic function of Kingston, Jamaica, in the mid-eighteenth century', in Kathleen E. A. Monteith and Glen Richards (eds.), *Jamaica in Slavery and Freedom: History, Heritage and Culture* (Barbados, 2001), pp. 225–41.

Burnard, Trevor and Kenneth Morgan, 'The dynamics of the slave market and slave purchasing patterns in Jamaica', *William and Mary Quarterly* 58 (1) (2001), 205–28.

Cain, P. J. and A. G. Hopkins, *British Imperialism. Innovation and Expansion 1688–1914* (London, 1993).

Cave, Roderick, *The Private Press* (New York, 1983).

Chancellor, V. E., 'Slave-owner and anti-slaver: Henry Russell Vassall Fox, 3rd Lord Holland, 1800–1840', *Slavery & Abolition* 1 (3) (1980), 263–76.

Chapman, Stanley D., 'British-based investment groups before 1914', *Economic History Review* 38 (2) (1985), 230–51.

'British marketing enterprise: the changing roles of merchants, manufacturers and financiers, 1700–1860', *Business History Review* 53 (2) (1979), 205–34.

The Rise of Merchant Banking (London, 1984).

Charlton, John, *Hidden Chains: The Slavery Business and North East England 1600–1865* (Newcastle-upon-Tyne, 2008).

Chater, Kathy, *Untold Stories, Black People in England and Wales during the Period of the British Slave-trade c. 1660–1807* (Manchester, 2009).

Chatterjee, Indrani and Richard M. Eaton (eds.), *Slavery and South Asian History* (Indiana, 2006).

Checkland, S. G., 'Finance for the West Indies, 1780–1815', *Economic History Review* 10 (3) (1958), 461–9.

The Gladstones. A Family Biography 1764–1851 (Cambridge, 1971).

Clifford, Helen, 'Aske Hall, Yorkshire: the Dundas property empire and Nabob taste', at http://blogs.ucl.ac.uk/eicah/aske-hall-yorkshire, accessed 8 August 2013.

Cohen, Stanley, *States of Denial. Knowing about Atrocities and Suffering* (Cambridge, 2001).

Collini, Stefan, 'National lives: *The Oxford Dictionary of National Biography*', in Collini, *Common Reading: Critics, Historians, Publics* (Oxford, 2008), pp. 299–316.

Cooke, Anthony, 'An elite revisited: Glasgow West India merchants, 1783–1877', *Journal of Scottish Historical Studies* 32 (2) (2012), 127–65.

Cozens, Kenneth, 'George Hibbert of Clapham – 18th century merchant and "amateur horticulturalist"', at www.merchantnetworks.com.au/ periods/1775after/hibbertgeorge.htm, accessed 8 August 2013.

Craton, Michael, *Empire, Enslavement and Freedom in the Caribbean* (Kingston, Jamaica, 1970).

'Response to Pieter C. Emmer's "Reconsideration"', *New West Indian Guide/ Nieuwe West-Indische Gids* 69 (3/4) (1995), 291–7.

'The transition from slavery to free wage labour in the Caribbean, 1780–1890: a survey with particular reference to recent scholarship', *Slavery & Abolition* 13 (2) (1992), 37–67.

Craton, Michael and Gail Saunders, *Islanders in the Stream: A History of the Bahamian People* (Athens, GA, 1999).

Cumpston, I. M., *Indians Overseas in British Territories* (London, 1953).

Cundall, Frank, *Historic Jamaica* (London, 1915).

Curtin, Philip D., 'The British sugar duties and West Indian prosperity', *Journal of Economic History* 14 (2) (1954), 157–64.

Dasent, John Roche, *A West Indian Planter's Family. Its Rise and Fall* (London, 1914).

Daunton, M. J., '"Gentlemanly capitalism" and British industry 1820–1914', *Past & Present* 122 (1989), 119–58.

Davidoff, Leonore, *Thicker than Water. Siblings and their Relations 1780–1920* (Oxford, 2012).

Davidoff, Leonore and Catherine Hall, *Family Fortunes. Men and Women of the English Middle Class 1780–1850* (1987; 2nd edn. London, 2002).

Davis, David Brion, *The Problem of Slavery in Western Culture* (New York and Oxford, 1988).

Davis, Ralph, *The Industrial Revolution and British Overseas Trade* (Leicester, 1979).

Dawes, Margaret, *Women Who Made Money: Women Partners in British Private Banks, 1752–1906* (Bloomington, IN, 2010).

Devine, T. M., 'Did slavery make Scotia great?', *Britain and the World* 4 (1) (2011), 40–64.

'An eighteenth-century business elite: Glasgow-West India merchants *c.* 1780–1815', *Scottish Historical Review* 57 (1) (1978), 40–67.

Donald, T. F., *Centenary History of the Western Club* (Glasgow, 1925).

Draper, Nicholas, 'The City of London and slavery: evidence from the first docks companies 1785–1800', *Economic History Review* 61 (1) (2008), 432–66.

The Price of Emancipation. Slave-Ownership, Compensation and British Society at the End of Slavery (Cambridge, 2010).

'Research note: "dependent on precarious subsistences": Ireland's slave-owners at the time of Emancipation', *Britain and the World* 6 (2) (2013), 220–42.

'The rise of a new planter class? Some counter currents from British Guiana and Trinidad, 1807–1833', *Atlantic Studies* 9 (1) (2012), 65–83.

'Slave ownership and the British country house: the records of the Slave Compensation Commission as evidence', in Madge Dresser and Andrew Hann (eds.), *Slavery and the British Country House* (Swindon, 2013), pp. 1–11.

Drescher, Seymour, *Econocide: British Slavery in the Era of Abolition* (Pittsburgh, 1977).

Dresser, Madge, 'Set in stone? Statues and slavery in London', *History Workshop Journal* 64 (2007), 162–99.

Dumett, Raymond E. (ed.), *Gentlemanly Capitalism and British Imperialism* (London, 1999).

Eakin, Marshall C., *A British Enterprise in Brazil: The St John D'el Rey Mining Company and the Morro Velho Gold Mine, 1830–1960* (Durham, NC, 1989).

'Ealing and Brentford: growth of Ealing', *A History of the County of Middlesex, Vol. VII: Acton, Chiswick, Ealing and Brentford, West Twyford, Willesden* (London, 1982), pp. 105–13.

Edwards, John Richard, 'Accounting regulation and the professionalization process: an historical essay concerning the significance of P. H. Abbott', *Critical Perspectives on Accounting* 12 (6) (2001), 675–96.

Edwards, Michael M., *The Growth of the British Cotton Trade 1780–1815* (Manchester, 1967).

Ellis, S. M., *Henry Kingsley 1830–1876. Towards a Vindication* (London, 1931).

Eltis, David and Stanley L. Engerman, 'The importance of slavery and the slave trade to industrializing Britain', *Journal of Economic History* 60 (1) (2000), 123–44.

Emmer, Pieter C., 'The big disappointment. The economic consequences of the abolition of slavery in the Caribbean, 1833–1888', *History in Focus: The Guide to Historical Resources* [Institute of Historical Research], 12 (2007), at www.history.ac.uk/ihr/Focus/Slavery/articles/emmer.html, accessed 8 August 2013.

'Scholarship or solidarity? The post-Emancipation era in the Caribbean reconsidered', *New West Indian Guide/Nieuwe West-Indische Gids* 69 (3/4) (1995), 277–90.

Erickson, Amy, *Women and Property in Early Modern England* (London, 1993).

Evans, Chris, *Slave Wales: The Welsh and Atlantic Slavery 1660–1850* (Cardiff, 2010).

'Slavery and Welsh industry before and after Emancipation', in Catherine Hall, Nicholas Draper and Keith McClelland (eds.), *Emancipation and the Remaking of the British Imperial World* (Manchester, 2014), pp. 60–73.

Faber, Eli, *Jews, Slaves and the Slave Trade: Setting the Record Straight* (New York, 1998).

Fisher, D. R. (ed.), *The House of Commons 1820–1832* (7 vols., Cambridge, 2009).

Fleischman, Richard K., David Oldroyd and Thomas N. Tyson, 'Plantation accounting and management practice in the US and the British West Indies at the end of their slavery eras', *Economic History Review* 64 (3) (2011), 765–97.

Fleming, R. H., 'Phyn, Ellice and Company of Schenectady', *Contributions to Canadian Economics* 4 (1932), 7–41.

Ford, P. and G. Ford, *A Guide to Parliamentary Papers* (3rd edn., Shannon, 1972).

Franzmann, Tom L., 'Antislavery and political economy in the early Victorian House of Commons: a research note on "capitalist hegemony"', *Journal of Social History* 27 (3) (1994), 579–93.

Fulford, Tim, 'Romanticizing the empire: the naval heroes of Southey, Coleridge, Austen and Marryat', *Modern Language Quarterly* 60 (2) (1999), 161–96.

Gambles, Anna, *Protection and Politics: Conservative Economic Discourse 1815–1852* (Woodbridge, 1999).

Gauci, Perry, *Emporium of the World: The Merchants of London 1660–1800* (London and New York, 2007).

Gawthrop, Humphrey, 'George Ellis of Ellis Caymanas: a Caribbean link to Scott and the Bronte sisters', *Electronic British Library Journal* (2005), at www.bl.uk/eblj/2005articles/article3.html, accessed 8 August 2013.

Genovese, Eugene D., *The Political Economy of Slavery: Studies in the Economy and the Society of the Slave South* (New York, 1965).

The World the Slaveholders Made: Two Essays in Interpretation (New York, 1969).

Genovese, Eugene D. and Elizabeth Fox-Genovese, *Fruits of Merchant Capital: Slavery and Bourgeois Property in the Rise and Expansion of Capitalism* (New York and Oxford, 1983).

The Mind of the Master Class: History and Faith in the Southern Slaveholders' Worldview (Cambridge, 2005).

Gere, J. Allen, 'William Young Ottley as a collector of drawings', *British Museum Quarterly* 18 (1953), 51–2

Gikandi, Simon, *Maps of Englishness. Writing Identity in the Culture of Colonialism* (New York, 1996).

Slavery and the Culture of Taste (Princeton, 2011).

Girard, Charlotte S. M., 'Sir James Douglas' mother and grandmother', *BC Studies* 44 (1979–80), 25–31.

'Some further notes on the Douglas family', *BC Studies* 72 (1986–7), 3–27.

Green, William A., *British Slave Emancipation. The Sugar Colonies and the Great Experiment* (Oxford, 1976).

Greene, Graham, *A Sort of Life* (Harmondsworth, 1972).

Gross, Izhak, 'The abolition of negro slavery and British parliamentary politics 1832–3', *Historical Journal* 23 (1) (1980), 63–85.

'Parliament and the abolition of negro apprenticeship 1835–1838', *English Historical Review* 96 (1981), 560–76.

Habakkuk, John, *Marriage, Debt and the Estate System: English Landownership 1650–1950* (Oxford, 1994).

Hall, Catherine, 'Afterword: Britain 2007, problematising histories', in Cora Kaplan and John Oldfield (eds.), *Imagining Transatlantic Slavery* (Basingstoke, 2010), pp. 191–201.

Civilising Subjects. Metropole and Colony in the English Imagination, 1830–1867 (Cambridge, 2002).

Macaulay and Son. Architects of Imperial Britain (New Haven and London, 2012).

'The slave-owner and the settler', in Jane Carey and Jane Lydon (eds.), *Indigenous Networks: Mobility, Connections and Exchange* (London, 2014).

'Troubling memories: nineteenth-century histories of the slave trade and slavery', *Transactions of the Royal Historical Society* 21 (2011), 147–69.

Hall, Catherine and Sonya O. Rose, 'Introduction: being at home with the empire', in Hall and Rose (eds.), *At Home with the Empire. Metropolitan Culture and the Imperial World* (Cambridge, 2006), pp. 1–31.

Hall, Catherine, Keith McClelland and Jane Rendall, *Defining the Victorian Nation: Class, Race, Gender and the British Reform Act of 1867* (Cambridge, 2000).

Hall, Douglas, 'Absentee proprietorship in the British West Indies, to about 1850', *Journal of Caribbean History* 35 (1) (2001), 97–121.

A Brief History of the West India Committee (St Lawrence, Barbados, 1971).

Hamilton, David, *Scotland, the Caribbean and the Atlantic World, 1750–1820* (Manchester, 2005).

Hancock, David, *Citizens of the World: London Merchants and the Integration of the British Atlantic Community 1735–1785* (Cambridge, 1995).

Harling, Philip, *The Modern British State. An Historical Introduction* (Cambridge, 2001).

Hartman, Saidiya, *Lose Your Mother. A Journey along the Atlantic Slave Route* (New York, 2007).

Hay, Douglas and Paul Craven (eds.), *Masters, Servants, and Magistrates in Britain and the Empire, 1562–1955* (Chapel Hill, NC and London, 2004).

Higman, B. W., 'The West India "interest" in Parliament, 1807–1833', *Australian Historical Studies* 13 (49) (1967), 1–19.

Holmes, Rachel, *The Hottentot Venus. The Life and Death of Saartji Baartman* (London, 2007).

Holt, Thomas C., *The Problem of Freedom: Race, Labor, and Politics in Jamaica and Britain, 1832–1938* (Baltimore, 1992).

Hoppit, Julian, 'Compulsion, compensation and property rights in Britain, 1688–1833', *Past & Present* 210 (2011), 93–128.

Risk and Failure in English Business 1700–1800 (Cambridge, 1987).

Howe, Anthony, 'From "old corruption" to "new probity": the Bank of England and its directors in the age of reform', *Financial History Review* 1 (1994), 23–41.

Hudson, Pat, 'Slavery, the slave trade and economic growth: a contribution to the debate', in Catherine Hall, Nicholas Draper and Keith McClelland (eds.), *Emancipation and the Remaking of the British Imperial World* (Manchester, 2014), pp. 36–59.

Hughes, John, *Liverpool Banks & Bankers 1760–1837* (Liverpool, 1906).

Hughes, Richard, 'Who is Henry Dawes?', *The Old Johnian* (2011), www.stjohns-leatherhead.co.uk/Archives, accessed 1 November 2013.

Huzzey, Richard, 'Free trade, free labour, and slave sugar in Victorian Britain', *Historical Journal* 53 (2) (2010), 359–79.

Freedom Burning. Anti-slavery and Empire in Victorian Britain (Ithaca and London, 2012).

Hyde, Francis E., Bradbury B. Parkinson and Sheila Marriner, 'The cotton broker and the rise of the Liverpool cotton market', *Economic History Review* new series 8 (1) (1955), 75–83.

Inikori, Joseph E., *Africans and the Industrial Revolution in England: A Study in International Trade and Economic Development* (Cambridge, 2002).

Inikori, Joseph, Stephen D. Behrendt, Maxine Berg, William G. Clarence-Smith, Henkden Heijer, Pat Hudson, John Singleton, Nuala Zahedieh, 'Roundtable: reviews of Joseph Inikori's *Africans and the Industrial Revolution in England: A Study in International Trade and Economic Development* with a response by Joseph Inikori', *International Journal of Maritime History*, 15 (2) (2003), 279–361.

Institute of Commonwealth Studies, 'Archive collections – Sandbach, Tinne & Co.' (8 September 2010), at http://icommlibrary.blogspot.co.uk/2010/09/archive-collections-sandbach-tinne-co.html, accessed 11 October 2012.

James, Michael, *From Smuggling to Cotton Kings: The Greg Story* (Gloucestershire, 2010).

Jenkins, Brian, *Henry Goulburn, 1784–1856: A Political Biography* (Liverpool, 1996).

Jennings, Judith, '"By no means in a liberal style": Mary Morris Knowles versus James Boswell', in Ann Hollinshead Hurley and Chanita Goodblatt (eds.), *Women Editing / Editing Women: Early Modern Women Writers and the New Textualism* (Newcastle, 2009), pp. 227–47.

Gender, Religion, and Radicalism in the Long Eighteenth Century: An 'Ingenious Quaker' and Her Connections (Aldershot, 2006).

'A trio of talented women: abolition, gender, and political participation', *Slavery & Abolition* 26 (1) (2005), 55–70.

Jones, Geoffrey, *Merchants to Multinationals: British Trading Companies in the Nineteenth and Twentieth Centuries* (Oxford, 2000).

Judd, Gerrit P., IV, *Members of Parliament 1734–1832* (New Haven, 1955).

Kale, Madhavi, *Fragments of Empire. Capital, Slavery, and Indentured Labor Migration in the British Caribbean* (Philadelphia, 1998).

Kamm, Josephine, *How Different from Us: A Biography of Miss Buss and Miss Beale* (1958; repr. London, 2012).

Kaplan, Cora, 'Imagining empire: history, fantasy and literature', in Catherine Hall and Sonya O. Rose (eds.), *At Home with the Empire: Metropolitan Culture and the Imperial World* (Cambridge, 2006), pp. 191–211.

Karch, Cecilia, 'From the plantocracy to B. S. & T.: crisis and transformation of the Barbadian socioeconomy, 1865–1837', in Woodville Marshall (ed.), *Emancipation IV: Lectures Commemorating the 150th Anniversary of Emancipation, Delivered in February and March 1988* (Mona, Jamaica, 1993).

Karras, Alan L. *Sojourners in the Sun: Scottish Immigrants in Jamaica and the Chesapeake, 1740–1800* (Ithaca, NY, 1992).

Kaufmann, Miranda, 'Slavery connections and new perspectives: English Heritage properties', *Conservation Bulletin* 58 (2008), 10–11.

Kelly, Philip and Ronald Hudson (eds.), *The Brownings' Correspondence* (18 vols., Winfield, KS, 1984–2010).

Klaver, J. M. I., *The Apostle of the Flesh. A Critical Life of Charles Kingsley* (Leiden, 2006).

Koditschek, Theodore, *Liberalism, Imperialism, and the Historical Imagination. Nineteenth-Century Visions of a Greater Britain* (Cambridge, 2011).

Kriegel, Abraham D., *The Holland House Diaries 1831–40: The Diary of Henry Richard Vassall Fox, Third Lord Holland, with Extracts from the Diary of John Dr Allen* (London, 1977).

Kucich, John and Jenny Bourne Taylor, 'Introduction', in Kucich and Taylor (ed.), *The Nineteenth Century Novel 1820–1880* (Oxford, 2012), pp. xvii–xxx.

Kynaston, David, *The City of London, Vol. I: A World of Its Own 1815–1890* (London, 1994).

Laidlaw, Zoë, 'The Victorian state in its imperial contexts', in Martin Hewitt (ed.), *The Victorian World* (London and New York, 2012), pp. 329–45.

Lambert, David, 'The "Glasgow King of Billingsgate": James MacQueen and an Atlantic proslavery network', *Slavery & Abolition* 29 (3) (2008), 389–413.

Mastering the Niger: James MacQueen's African Geography and the Struggle over Atlantic Slavery (Chicago, 2013).

White Creole Culture, Politics and Identity during the Age of Abolition (Cambridge, 2005).

Lascelles, David, *Arbuthnot Latham, from Merchant Bank to Private Bank 1833–2013* (London, 2013).

Lee, Robert C., *The Canada Company and the Huron Tract, 1826–1853. Personalities, Profits and Politics* (Ontario, 2004).

Lester, V. Markham, *Victorian Insolvency: Bankruptcy, Imprisonment for Debt, and Company Winding-Up in Nineteenth-Century England* (Oxford, 1995).

Li, Chien-hui, 'The animal cause and its greater traditions', *History & Policy*, at www.historyandpolicy.org/papers/policy-paper-19.html, accessed 8 August 2013.

Marks, Jeanette, *The Family of the Barrett: A Colonial Romance* (New York, 1938).

Marshall, P. J., *Remaking the British Atlantic: The United States and the British Empire after American Independence* (Oxford, 2012).

Mehta, Uday Singh, *Liberalism and Empire: A Study in Nineteenth-Century British Liberal Thought* (Chicago, 1999).

Michie, Michael, *An Enlightenment Tory in Victorian Scotland. The Career of Sir Archibald Alison* (East Lothian, 1997).

Michie, Ranald C., *The London Stock Exchange: A History* (Oxford, 1999).

Mitchell, Jessie, '"The galling yoke of slavery": race and separation in colonial Port Philip', *Journal of Australian Studies* 33 (2) (2009), 125–37.

Molineux, Catherine, *Faces of Perfect Ebony: Encountering Atlantic Slavery in Imperial Britain* (Cambridge, MA, 2012).

Morgan, Kenneth, *Slavery, Atlantic Trade and the British Economy, 1660–1800* (Cambridge, 2000).

Morris, Jackie, 'The Chauncys of Little Munden', at www.mundens.net/genealogy/chauncy.htm, accessed 8 August 2013.

Morris, Robert J., *Men, Women and Property in England* (Edinburgh, 2005).

'Occupational coding: principles and examples', *Historical Research/Historische Sozialforschung* 15 (1) (1990), 3–29.

Muir, Augustus, *Blyth, Greene, Jourdain & Company Limited 1810–1960* (London, 1961).

Mullen, Stephen, 'A Glasgow-West India merchant house and the imperial dividend', *Journal of Scottish Historical Studies* 33 (2) (2013), 196–233.

Norman, Peter, *The Risk Controllers: Central Counterparty Clearing in Globalised Financial Markets* (London, 2011).

Northrup, David, *Indentured Labor in the Age of Imperialism, 1834–1922* (Cambridge, 1995).

Oliver, Vere Langford, *History of the Island of Antigua* (3 vols., London, 1896).

O'Shaughnessy, Andrew, *An Empire Divided: The American Revolution and the British Caribbean* (Philadelphia, 2000).

'The formation of a commercial lobby: the West India interest, British colonial policy and the American Revolution', *Historical Journal* 40 (1) (1997), 71–95.

Pares, Richard, 'A London West-India merchant house, 1740–1769', in Richard Pares and A. J. P. Taylor (eds.), *Essays Presented to Sir Lewis Namier* (London, 1956), pp. 75–107.

Merchants and Planters, Economic History Review Supplement 4 (Cambridge, 1960).

Parolin, Christina, *Radical Spaces: Venues of Popular Politics in London, 1790–1845* (Canberra, 2010).

Partington, Anthony, 'A memorial to Hibberts', *Mariner's Mirror* 95 (4) (2009), 441–58.

Pascandarola, Louis J., *'Puzzled Which to Choose'. Conflicting Socio-political Views in the Works of Captain Frederick Marryat* (New York, 1997).

Pearson, Robin, 'Collective diversification: Manchester cotton merchants and the insurance business in the early 19th century', *Business History Review* 65 (2) (1991), 379–414.

Insuring the Industrial Revolution: Fire Insurance in Great Britain, 1700–1850 (Aldershot, 2004).

Pedler, Frederick, *The Lion and the Unicorn in Africa, a History of the Origins of the United Africa Company 1787–1931* (London, 1974).

Penson, Lillian M., *The Colonial Agents of the British West Indies: A Study in Colonial Administration Mainly in the Eighteenth Century* (London, 1924).

Perkin, H. J., *The Origins of Modern English Society 1780–1880* (London, 1969).

Perry, Adele, '"Is your garden in England, Sir?": James Douglas's archive and the politics of home', *History Workshop Journal* 70 (1) (2010), 67–85.

'James Douglas, Canada and Guyana', *Stabroek News*, 4 April 2011, at www.stabroeknews.com/2011/features/in-the-diaspora/04/04/james-douglas-canada-and-guyana, accessed 20 April 2011.

Petley, Christer, 'Rethinking the fall of the planter class', *Atlantic Studies* 9 (1) (2012), 1–17.

Slaveholders in Jamaica: Colonial Society and Culture during the Era of Abolition (London, 2009).

Pitts, Jennifer, *A Turn to Empire: The Rise of Imperial Liberalism in Britain and France* (Princeton, 2006).

Polanyi, Karl, *The Great Transformation: The Political and Economic Origins of Our Time* (1945; repr. Boston, MA, 1957).

Pomeranz, Kenneth, *The Great Divergence. China, Europe and the Making of the Modern World Economy* (Princeton and Oxford, 2000).

Pope, David, 'The wealth and social aspirations of Liverpool's slave merchants of the second half of the eighteenth century', in David Richardson, Suzanne Schwarz and Anthony Tibbles (eds.), *Liverpool and Transatlantic Slavery* (Liverpool, 2007), pp. 164–226.

Porter, A. N., '"Gentlemanly capitalism" and empire: the British experience since 1750?', *Journal of Imperial and Commonwealth History* 18 (1990), 265–95.

Prakash, Gyan, 'Terms of servitude: the colonial discourse on slavery and bondage in India', in Martin A. Klein (ed.), *Breaking the Chains. Slavery, Bondage and Emancipation in Modern Africa and Asia* (Madison WI, 1993), pp. 131–49.

Priestley, Charles, '"France's opportunity": an Englishman's plea for French intervention', at www.acwrt.org.uk/uk-heritage_Frances-Opportunity-an-Englishmans-Plea-for-French-Intervention.asp, accessed 8 August 2013.

Radstone, Susanna and Bill Schwarz, 'Introduction: mapping memory', in Radstone and Schwarz (eds.), *Memory. Histories, Theories, Debates* (Fordham, NY, 2010), pp. 1–9.

Ragatz, Lowell J., *The Fall of the Planter Class in the British Caribbean, 1763–1833: A Study in Social and Economic History* (New York and London, 1928).

Reece, Colonel H. M., 'The kindred of Bezsin K. Reece (1765–1838) of St Michael Barbados', in James C. Brandow, *Genealogies of Barbados Families from Caribbeana and the Journal of Barbados Museum and Historical Society* (Baltimore, 1983), pp. 495–500.

Rice, C. Duncan, '"Humanity sold for sugar!" The British abolitionist response to free trade in slave-grown sugar', *Historical Journal* 13 (3) (1970), 402–18.

Rodgers, Nini, *Ireland, Slavery and Anti-slavery: 1612–1865* (Basingstoke, 2007).

Rogers, Nicholas, 'Money, land and lineage: the big bourgeoisie of Hanoverian London', *Social History* 4 (3) (1979), 437–54.

Roth, Cecil, *History of the Great Synagogue, London, 1690–1940* (1950), ch. 16, at www.jewishgen.org/jcr-uk/susser/roth/chsixteen.htm, accessed 8 August 2013.

Rubinstein, William D., 'Cutting up rich: a reply to F. M. L. Thompson', *Economic History Review* new series 45 (2) (1992), 350–61.

Elites and the Wealthy in Modern British History (London, 1987).

Men of Property: The Very Wealthy in Britain since the Industrial Revolution (1981; 2nd edn., London 2006).

'Wealth, elites and the class structure of Modern Britain', *Past & Present* 76 (1977), 69–126.

Who Were the Rich? A Biographical Directory of British Wealth-holders, Vol. I: 1809–1839 (London, 2009).

Ryden, David Beck, *West Indian Slavery and British Abolition, 1783–1807* (Cambridge, 2009).

Said, Edward W., *Culture and Imperialism* (New York, 1993).

Saville, John, *1848. The British State and the Chartist Movement* (Cambridge, 1987).

The Consolidation of the Capitalist State, 1800–1850 (London, 1994).

Scheuerle, William H., *The Neglected Brother. A Study of Henry Kingsley* (Talahassee, FL, 1971).

Seed, John, 'Gentlemen dissenters: the social and political meanings of rational dissent in the 1770s and 1780s', *Historical Journal* 28 (2) (1985), 299–325.

Seymour, Susanne and Sheryllynne Haggerty, *Slavery Connections of Brodsworth Hall (1600–c. 1830): Final Report for English Heritage* (2010), at www.english-heritage.org.uk/publications/slavery-connections-brodsworth-hall/slavery-connections-brodsworth-hall.pdf, accessed 31 July 2013.

Sheridan, Richard B., 'The commercial and financial organization of the British slave trade, 1750–1807', *Economic History Review* 11 (2) (1958), 249–63.

'Simon Taylor, sugar tycoon of Jamaica, 1740–1813', *Agricultural History* 45 (4) (1971), 285–96.

'The West India sugar crisis and the British slave Emancipation, 1830–1833', *Journal of Economic History* 21 (4) (1961), 539–51.

Sherwood, Marika, *After Abolition: Britain and the Slave Trade since 1807* (London, 2007).

Sinha, Mrinalini, *Colonial Masculinity. The 'Manly Englishman' and the 'Effeminate Bengali' in the Late Nineteenth Century* (Manchester, 1995).

'Mapping the imperial social formation: a modest proposal for feminist history' *Signs* 25 (4) (2000), 1077–82.

'Teaching imperialism as a social formation', *Radical History Review* 67 (1997), 175–86.

Slinn, Judy and Jennifer Tanburn, *The Booker Story* (London, 2003).

Smith, Simon D., 'Merchants and planters revisited', *Economic History Review* 55 (3) (2002), 434–65.

Slavery, Family and Gentry Capitalism in the British Atlantic: The World of the Lascelles, 1648–1834 (Cambridge, 2006).

Stenton, Michael, *Who's Who of British Members of Parliament: A Biographical Dictionary of the House of Commons based on Annual Volumes of 'Dod's Parliamentary Companion' and Other Sources, Vol. I: 1832–1885* (Hassocks, 1976).

Stewart, Robert, *The Foundation of the Conservative Party, 1830–1867* (London and New York, 1978).

Stoler, Ann Laura, Carole McGranahan and Peter C. Perdue (eds.), *Imperial Formations* (Oxford, 2007).

Stone, Marjorie, 'Elizabeth Barrett Browning and the Garrisonians: "The Runaway Slave at Pilgrim's Point", the Boston Female Anti-Slavery Society and abolitionist discourse in the *Liberty Bell*', in Alison Chapman (ed.), *Victorian Women Poets* (Cambridge, 2003), pp. 33–56.

Stott, Anne, *Wilberforce: Family and Friends* (Oxford, 2012).

Supple, Barry, *The Royal Exchange Assurance: A History of British Assurance 1720–1970* (Cambridge, 1970).

Taylor, Miles, 'Colonial representation at Westminster, c. 1800–65', in Julian Hoppit (ed.), *Parliaments, Nations and Identities in Britain and Ireland, 1660–1860* (Manchester, 2003), pp. 206–20.

The Decline of British Radicalism 1847–1860 (Oxford, 1995).

'Empire and the 1832 parliamentary Reform Act revisited', in Arthur Burns and Joanna Innes (eds.), *Rethinking the Age of Reform: Britain 1780–1850* (Cambridge, 2003), pp. 295–311.

Thomas, R. P. and D. N. McCloskey, 'Overseas trade and empire, 1700–1860', in R. C. Floud and D. N. McCloskey (eds.), *The Economic History of Britain since 1700, Vol. I: 1700–1860* (Cambridge, 1981), pp. 87–102.

Thompson, F. M. L., 'Life after death: how successful nineteenth-century businessmen disposed of their fortunes', *Economic History Review* new series 43 (1) (1990), 40–61.

'Stitching it together again', *Economic History Review* new series 45 (2) (1992), 362–75.

Thorne, R. G. (ed.), *The House of Commons, 1790–1820* (5 vols., London, 1986).

Tinker, Hugh, *A New System of Slavery: The Export of Indian Labour Overseas, 1830–1920* (Oxford, 1974).

Trebilcock, Clive, *Phoenix Assurance and the Development of British Insurance, Vol. I: 1782–1870* (Cambridge, 1985).

Trouillot, Michel-Rolphe, *Silencing the Past. Power and the Production of History* (Boston, 1995).

Trust, Graham, *John Moss of Otterspool (1782–1858), Railway Pioneer, Slave Owner, Banker* (Milton Keynes, 2010).

Turner, Mary, 'The British Caribbean, 1823–1838: the transition from slave to free legal status', in Douglas Hay and Paul Craven (eds.), *Masters, Servants, and Magistrates in Britain and the Empire, 1562–1955* (Chapel Hill, NC and London, 2004), pp. 303–22.

Turner, Michael J., '"Setting the captive free": Thomas Perronet Thompson, British radicalism and the West Indics, 1820s–1860s', *Slavery & Abolition* 26 (1) (2005), 115–32.

Wadsworth, Alfred P. and Julia De Lacy Mann, *The Cotton Trade and Industrial Lancashire, 1600–1780* (Manchester, 1965).

Wake, Jehanne, *Kleinwort Benson – The History of Two Families in Banking* (Oxford, 1997).

Walvin, James, 'The colonial origins of English wealth: the Harewoods of Yorkshire', *Journal of Caribbean History* 39 (1) (2005), 38–53.

Ward, J. R., 'The profitability of sugar planting in the British West Indies, 1650–1834', *Economic History Review* 31 (2) (1978), 197–213.

Warner, Oliver, *Captain Marryat. A Rediscovery* (London, 1953).

Wiener, Joel H., 'Hibbert, Julian', in Joseph O. Baylen and Norbert J. Gossman (eds.), *Biographical Dictionary of Modern British Radicals, Vol. I: 1770–1830* (Hassocks, 1979), p. 221

Williams, Eric, *Capitalism and Slavery* (1944; repr. London, 1964).

Wilson, Kathleen, 'Introduction: histories, empires, modernities', in Wilson (ed.), *A New Imperial History. Culture, Identity and Modernity in Britain and the Empire 1660–1840* (Cambridge, 2004), pp. 1–28.

'Rethinking the colonial state: family, gender, and governmentality in eighteenth-century British frontiers', *American Historical Review* 116 (5) (2011), 1294–1322.

Wilson, Richard G., *Greene King. A Business and Family History* (London, 1983).

Wood, Marcus, 'Significant silence: where was slave agency in the popular imagery of 2007?', in Cora Kaplan and John Oldfield (eds.), *Imagining Transatlantic Slavery* (Basingstoke, 2010), pp. 162–90.

Wright, Philip, *Monumental Inscriptions of Jamaica* (London, 1966).

Wullschager, Jackie, 'Turner illuminated', *Financial Times*, 16 March 2012, at www.ft.com/cms/s/2/b6616f32–6d23–11e1-b6ff-00144feab49a.html#axzz 2BSkMxRnv, accessed 6 November 2012.

Zacek, Natalie, *Settler Society in the English Leeward Islands 1670–1776* (Cambridge, 2010).

Zahedieh, Nuala, *The Capital and the Colonies: London and the Atlantic Economy 1660–1700* (Cambridge, 2010).

UNPUBLISHED SECONDARY MATERIAL: THESES

Cutler, Janet C., *The London Institution, 1805–1933* (PhD, University of Leicester, 1976).

Franklin, Alexandra, *Enterprise and Advantage: The West India Interest in Britain, 1774–1840* (PhD, University of Pennsylvania, 1992).

Livesay, Daniel, *Children of Uncertain Fortune: Mixed Race Migration from the West Indies to Britain, 1750–1820* (PhD, University of Michigan, 2010).

Lowes, Susan, *The Peculiar Class: The Formation, Collapse and Reformation of the Middle Class in Antigua, West Indies 1834–1940* (PhD, Columbia University, 1994).

Twist, Anthony, *Widening Circles in Finance, Philanthropy and the Arts: A Study of the Life of John Julius Angerstein 1735–1823* (PhD, University of Amsterdam, 2002).

Young, Hannah, *Gender, Power and Slave-ownership: The Case of Anna Eliza Elletson* (MA, University College London, 2012).

UNPUBLISHED SECONDARY MATERIAL: OTHER

Burnard, Trevor, 'Credit, Kingston merchants and the Atlantic slave trade in the eighteenth century', unpublished paper for British Group in Early American History, Rethinking Africa & the Atlantic World, Stirling, 3 September 2009.

Charlton, John, 'Who was John Graham-Clarke 1736–1818?', unpublished paper (2010).

Hoppit, Julian, 'Smith versus Keynes: the mercantile system versus mercantilism', public lecture at University College London, 19 November 2012.

Kaplan, Cora, '"I am black": aesthetics, race and politics in women's anti-slavery writing from Phyllis Wheatley to Elizabeth Barrett Browning', unpublished paper (2011).

Rubinstein, William D., *Who Were the Rich? Vol. II*, unpublished data for 1840–59.

Who Were the Rich? Vol. III, unpublished data for 1860–74.

WEBSITES

Gove, Michael, 'All pupils will learn our island story', www.conservatives.com/News/Speeches/2010/10/Michael_Gove_All_pupils_will_learn_our_island_story.aspx, accessed 31 July 2013.

'A guide to St Mark's Hospital Church, Maidenhead', at www.berksfhs.org.uk/genuki/BRK/Maidenhead/St%20Mark%27s%20Hospital%20Church,%20Maidenhead%20Guide.pdf, accessed 31 July 2013.

'Hankey & Co, London, 1685–1865', RBS Heritage Hub, at http://heritagearchives.
    rbs.com/companies/list/hankey-and-co.html, accessed 11 October 2012.
'The History of Parliament', at www.historyofparliamentonline.org.
'Jamaica Family Search', at http://jamaicanfamilysearch.com.
'The monumental inscriptions in the churchyard of St Mary's Church,
    Lewisham, noted by Leland L. Duncan, typed up by Dawn Weeks', at www.
    kentarchaeology.org.uk/Research/Libr/MIs/MIsLewisham/01.htm, accessed
    1 November 2013.
'Parishes: Chalfont St Peter', in *A History of the County of Buckingham, Vol.
    III* (London, 1925), pp. 193–8, at www.british-history.ac.uk/report.
    aspx?compid=42545, accessed 1 October 2012.
'St James's Street, west side, existing buildings', *Survey of London, Vols. XXIX
    and XXX: St James Westminster, Part 1* (1960), pp. 472–86, at www.british-
    history.ac.uk/report.aspx?compid=40623, accessed 29 March 2012.
The Trans-Atlantic Slave Trade Database, at www.slavevoyages.org/tast/index.
    faces.
'The West India Docks: historical development', *Survey of London, Vols. XLIII and
    XLIV: Poplar, Blackwall and Isle of Dogs* (1994), pp. 248–68, at www.british-
    history.ac.uk/report.aspx?compid=46494&strquery=Hibbert, accessed 5
    October 2012.

Index

A. M. Lee & Co., 85
Abbott, Peter Harriss, *On the Public Debt: With a Plan for Its Final Extinction*, 109
aboriginal people, 187–8
Accepting House Committee, 102–3
accountants, 109
Adam, Rear Admiral Sir Charles, 128
administrators, 256, 257, 260
and administratrixes, 282
Africans, representations of, 164–6, 169, 174, 177, 181, 190
Aitcheson senior, John, 272
Akers-Douglas, Aretas, 44
Akers-Douglas family, 2, 257
Alderman for the City of London Bridge Within, 235
Alexander & Co., 57, 101
Alison, Archibald, 138, 170
histories by, 172–3
'The West India Question', 168
Allen, John Carter, Admiral, 38
Allen, Stella Frances, 38
Alliance Assurance, 106
almshouses, 53, 59
women's involvement in, 228
American Civil War, 156
Ames, Henry Metcalfe, 46
Anderdon, James Hughes, 55
Anderdon, John Lavicount, 57
Anderdon, John Proctor, paintings of, 55
Anderdon, William Henry, 57
Angerstein, John Julius, 55
Anthony Gibbs & Co., 99, 103
Antigua, 43, 52, 62, 142
compensation and, 37, 55, 59, 89, 151, 171, 172
apprenticeship, 6, 139–43, 147
abolition of, 132
Arbuthnot Latham, 102
aristocracy, 14, 16, *see also* elites
Arthur's, 54

assignees, 258, 282
Atherton, Eleanora, 52, 59
Athill, Diana,
Yesterday Morning, 37
Australia, 63–4, 97
aboriginal people, 186–8
colonial administrators in, 64
representations of, 186
Australian Agricultural Company, 97
Australian Dictionary of Biography, 267
Aviva, 107

Baker, Sir Thomas, *Memorials of a Dissenting Chapel*, 206, 207
Balcarres family, 128
Bank of England, 82, 240
directors and governors of, 98–100
Bank of London, 100
Bank of Queensland, 97
bankruptcy, 82, 84
Barbados, 43, 63, 142, 177
compensation and, 56
estates in, 46, 183
Barclay, Bevan & Co., 39
Barings, 86, 99, 102
Barkly, Aeneas, 42
Barkly, Arthur Cecil Stuart, 64
Barkly, Sir Henry, 42, 64, 136
Barrett family, 192–4
Bathurst Trading Company Limited, 96
Bayley family, 257
Bayly, Charles Nathaniel, 42
Beale, Dorothea, 51
Beckford, William, 42
Bentinck, Lord George, 153
Berkeley, Grantley, 149
Bernal, Ralph, 43, 57, 130, 147
Dutch paintings of, 55
Bevan, David, 39
Bevan, Robert Cooper Lee, 2, 39
Bilton Grange, 218, 224–5
Birch, Sir Thomas, 128